The Macroeconomics of

Editor
Markus Haacker

INTERNATIONAL MONETARY FUND

Production: IMF Graphics Section
Typesetting: Choon Lee
Figures: Theodore F. Peters, Jr.
Cover design: Jorge Salazar

Cover photo: Louise Gubb/Corbis Saba.
AIDS orphans Olivia, 15, and her 2-year-old sister Sandra

Cataloging-in-Publication Data

The Macroeconomics of HIV/AIDS / editor, Markus Haacker — [Washington, D.C.] :
    International Monetary Fund, [2004]
        p. cm.

    Includes bibliographical references.
    ISBN 1-58906-360-0

   1. AIDS (Disease) — Economic aspects — Developing countries.   2. AIDS
(Disease) — Economic aspects — Developing countries — Statistics.   I. Haacker,
Markus.   II. International Monetary Fund.
RA643.8.M34 2004

Price: $28.00

Please send orders to:
International Monetary Fund, Publication Services
700 19th Street, N.W., Washington D.C. 20431, U.S.A.
Telephone: (202) 623-7430   Telefax: (202) 623-7201
E-mail: publications@imf.org
Internet: http://www.imf.org

recycled paper

Contents

Tables

Preface

I am pleased to introduce this volume on The Macroeconomics of HIV/AIDS, to be published by the IMF on World AIDS Day (December 1) 2004. This is the first IMF book to focus specifically on a public health issue. However, the HIV/AIDS epidemic is a matter of such serious concern—adversely affecting the development prospects of many of our member countries—that it calls for unprecedented actions. The effects of the epidemic touch on virtually all aspects of a country's social, economic, demographic, and political development, and thus HIV/AIDS must be a major issue of concern to the IMF. The IMF's experience in these countries increasingly reflects this reality. The studies collected in this volume are thus highly relevant to the work of the IMF.

Within its mandate, and in close cooperation with other development partners, the IMF is assisting member governments' efforts to fight the epidemic and cope with its economic and development consequences. The IMF has endorsed the call by the United Nations Secretary-General for a global campaign in the fight against HIV/AIDS, and is collaborating with the UN community to expand country-level AIDS prevention and treatment programs. In December 2003, Horst Köhler, my predecessor as the IMF's Managing Director, noted that "the IMF must do everything possible within the context of its mandate to assist the agencies that are in the front lines of the fight against HIV/AIDS."[1]

In terms of the IMF's operational work, this means that IMF country teams have tried to take account of the epidemic's adverse effects in their economic policy advice and, where applicable, in program design. More generally, concessional lending by the IMF and the World Bank, supported by Poverty Reduction Strategy Papers, and debt relief under the Heavily Indebted Poor Countries (HIPC) Initiative, have financed poverty-reducing expenditures in many countries, frequently including measures to fight HIV/AIDS and mitigate its impact. Moreover, the IMF encourages

---

[1] IMF Press Release No. 03/208.

donors to provide grants that finance enhanced service delivery as well as commit to a predictable flow of grant resources. This is particularly vital for AIDS treatment and prevention programs, because it would be highly disruptive if these programs could not make sustained financial commitments to health workers and patients alike.

There can be no doubt that the impact of HIV/AIDS, and the associated response of the international community, raises issues that go much beyond the core areas of experience of the IMF, or for that matter of any individual international organization. Close cooperation among the relevant UN agencies as well as other international organizations combating HIV/AIDS will be critical for an effective response to the epidemic. This volume exemplifies the value of such cooperation, representing a collaboration of staff members from several international organizations, government agencies, universities, and independent research institutes, including the Center for Global Development, the International Labor Organization, the International Monetary Fund, the Joint United Nations Programme on HIV/AIDS (UNAIDS), the London School of Economics, the U.S. Bureau of the Census, and the World Bank.

The publication of this volume on World AIDS Day 2004 marks an important contribution by the international community in its effort to address the consequences of this epidemic. However, as the epidemic continues, in the words of the Secretary-General, its "lethal march," there can be no reason for complacency. The fight against HIV/AIDS and its dire consequences requires our continuing best efforts to reduce the numbers of new infections, provide treatment to people living with HIV/AIDS, and assist affected individuals and countries facing severe epidemics to mitigate its adverse social and economic impact.

Rodrigo de Rato
Managing Director
International Monetary Fund

Foreword

HIV/AIDS, through its demographic effects and its social and economic consequences, has evolved into a major threat to economic development in many countries around the world. In sub-Saharan Africa, where most of the worst-affected countries are found, the Joint United Nations Program on HIV/AIDS (UNAIDS, 2004) estimates that 7.5 percent of the population aged 15–49 were infected as of the end of 2003, with HIV prevalence rates for this age group ranging from about 1 percent (in The Gambia and Senegal) to almost 40 percent (in Botswana and Swaziland). Indeed, HIV/AIDS has become one of the leading causes of death in the region. According to the World Health Organization's *World Health Report 2004,* the HIV/AIDS epidemic now accounts for about 20 percent of all deaths in sub-Saharan Africa and more than half of the deaths in some countries. Even in countries where infection rates are lower, such as Cambodia and Haiti, HIV/AIDS accounts for about one-half of the deaths of individuals aged 15–49. Low national infection rates often mask serious regional epidemics, as is the case in countries such as China and India. (India has the largest number of people living with HIV outside South Africa.)

The economic and social consequences of the increased mortality and morbidity associated with HIV/AIDS are serious and manifold. The following are only a few of them. Average life expectancy has declined by more than 20 years in some of the worst-affected countries. In addition to the trauma of losing family members, households affected by HIV/AIDS may experience a precipitous decline in living standards because of loss of income and the high cost of caring for the sick. Given that HIV/AIDS typically strikes people of childbearing and childrearing age, the number of orphans is rising. In some countries, 20 percent of the population aged 17 and under have lost one or both parents, the majority to HIV/AIDS (see UNAIDS, UNICEF, and U.S. Agency for International Development, 2004). Increasing production costs, as skilled workers succumb to AIDS-related illnesses, erode competitiveness and—together with a deteriorating economic outlook—may deter investment. Economic growth slows for many reasons, most directly because the working-age population expands more slowly or contracts, but there is considerable uncertainty regarding the size of this effect, especially in the longer run. The most visible fiscal consequences of HIV/AIDS include increased spending on prevention, care, and treatment, but the fiscal implications go far beyond this. As economic growth declines, the domestic tax base weakens and domestic revenues fall. At the same time, HIV/AIDS erodes public services as mortality rates for civil servants rise, and it drives up government spending even in areas not directly related to combating HIV/AIDS. For example, personnel costs rise as staff lost to AIDS must be replaced and new staff trained, as do social expenditures on survivors' pensions and other benefits for individuals and households affected by HIV/AIDS.

As the above sketch of the situation makes clear, policymakers and analysts simply cannot address the economic issues facing severely affected countries without taking into account the numerous social, economic, and fiscal effects of the epidemic. This, of course, is not a new insight; indeed, the impact of, and the response to, the HIV/AIDS epidemic have become central issues in economic development. Evidence of this is the fact that the contributors to *The Macroeconomics of HIV/AIDS* represent not only international organizations that are key players in the fight against HIV/AIDS (such as UNAIDS and the World Bank) but also other organizations that have added HIV/AIDS to their work agendas, primarily because of its social and economic repercussions (such as the Center for Global Development, the International Labor Organization, and the IMF). The book grew out of the authors' experience in providing economic analysis and policy advice in countries severely affected by the epidemic.

By bringing together studies by authors with diverse backgrounds and from different organizations and institutions, this book aims to provide a comprehensive resource on the social, economic, and fiscal effects of HIV/AIDS. It seeks to strengthen efforts by public policymakers to formulate and implement strategies to fight the epidemic and mitigate those effects, and to do so along two lines. First, a good understanding of the economic consequences of the epidemic can help in formulating policies and allocating scarce resources. Second, well-crafted programs designed to fight the epidemic and mitigate its impact can offset or reduce some of the serious social and economic consequences of HIV/AIDS. Thus a successful strategy will have a positive impact on the economic and fiscal outlook, which, in turn, means that more funds can be mobilized to support longer-term health strategies. In this sense, HIV/AIDS strategies are a form of economic policy. The book highlights the epidemic's fiscal consequences— direct (HIV/AIDS-related expenditures) as well as indirect (the impact of HIV/AIDS on the domestic tax base and some expenditure categories affected by the epidemic)—and links the response to HIV/AIDS to a macroeconomic framework. It also formulates a framework for assessing the various impacts of HIV/AIDS on developing economies.

The Macroeconomics of HIV/AIDS is intended to fill in the gap in the literature between studies of specific sectors—especially public health and education—and bird's-eye assessments of the broader social and economic consequences of HIV/AIDS. In contrast with most other macroeconomic studies on the subject, *The Macroeconomics of HIV/AIDS* emphasizes how HIV/AIDS affects society and the economy through its microeconomic impacts and also how the social and economic impact, combined with the increase in mortality rates, affects the welfare of individuals and households. The book has thus been written for a broad readership, which could include, for example, officials in a finance ministry assessing the impact of HIV/AIDS on the fiscal balance and outlook of their country. It could include representatives of an international financial organization and their counterparts in an AIDS-ravaged developing country, meeting to discuss the economic outlook or negotiate a policy program. The book is also likely to be of interest to members of the media and other policy observers in countries affected by HIV/AIDS, as well as to the representatives of non-governmental organizations advocating an expanded response to HIV/AIDS in their home countries or worldwide. Last but not least, as policies to fight the epidemic attain increasing macroeconomic and fiscal relevance, this book's readership could include those officials in international organizations, donor agencies, implementing agencies, and country governments who formulate and carry out such policies.

The studies that make up the book explore several separate strands of inquiry, which can be grouped under three general headings: the demographic impact, the macroeconomic consequences, and the effect on government finance and public services. Because most of the effects of HIV/AIDS arise directly from increased morbidity and mortality, the book begins, in Chapter 1, by focusing on the demographic impact, providing a basis for the analysis in the chapters that follow.

Chapters 2 through 6 discuss the macroeconomic effects of HIV/AIDS, addressing three topics in particular. The first is the relationship between the microeconomic effects of HIV/AIDS—for example, at the household or company level—and those at the macroeconomic level. This theme is taken up in Chapter 2 in a general fashion, while Chapter 3 builds its macroeconomic analysis around a household-level model. The second topic is the impact of HIV/AIDS on economic growth. Chapter 2 introduces this theme by describing the most common approaches used in accounting for growth in the context of an HIV/AIDS epidemic, while

Chapters 3 and 4 focus on the impact of HIV/AIDS on education and the accumulation of human capital. The third topic is the effect of HIV/AIDS on welfare. Because the impact of HIV/AIDS is spread unevenly across individuals and households, standard estimates of aggregate macroeconomic changes contain very little information on welfare effects. Chapter 5 therefore discusses the impact of HIV/AIDS on poverty and inequality, and Chapter 6 estimates the broader welfare effects of HIV/AIDS stemming from increased mortality rates.

Chapters 7 through 10 deal with the impact of HIV/AIDS on the public sector. First, they provide a framework for assessing the effect of HIV/AIDS on the public sector itself. Second, although most issues in the formulation of a broad HIV/AIDS strategy—particularly the choice between different interventions—are beyond the scope of this book, these chapters seek to support this work by improving the understanding of the macroeconomic and fiscal context in which such strategies will be implemented, providing policymakers and donors with tools for assessing and evaluating HIV/AIDS strategies from a broader development perspective. In this context, Chapter 7 assesses the impacts of HIV/AIDS on public services (for example, through the erosion of capacities) and on government finance. One area where HIV/AIDS can have a substantial impact is social security—pension funds in particular—and this is taken up in Chapter 8. Chapter 9 describes and assesses Botswana's National Strategic Framework on HIV/AIDS, illustrating the potential of a comprehensive national HIV/AIDS strategy to reverse the macroeconomic damage associated with the epidemic. Finally, Chapter 10 focuses on the impact of HIV/AIDS on the health sector and the challenges facing countries that set out to substantially expand access to HIV/AIDS treatment.

The book represents the efforts of many individuals from different backgrounds. The authors are drawn from a wide range of institutions, specifically (in alphabetical order), the Center for Global Development, the International Labor Organization, the International Monetary Fund, the Joint United Nations Programme on HIV/AIDS (UNAIDS), the London School of Economics, the University of California Los Angeles, the University of Heidelberg, and the World Bank. The book received material support in particular from the African, External Relations, and Fiscal Affairs Departments at the International Monetary Fund, and the AIDS Campaign Team for Africa at the World Bank. The views expressed in this book are those of the individual authors and do not necessarily reflect the opinion or policy of any of the organizations with which they are affiliated.

In addition to the authors, individuals who at some stage have contributed to or supported this effort include Tony Barnett, Abdoulaye Bio-Tchané,

Hugh Bredenkamp, Benedicte Christensen, Phil Compernolle, Patrick Connelly, Keith Hansen, Peter Heller, Alison Hickey, Robin Kibuka, Maureen Lewis, Bill McGreevey, Jeanette Morrison, Bella Nestorova, Nana Poku, Marina Primorac, Sydney Rosen, Doris Ross, John Starrels, Susan Stout, Michael Treadway, Matthias Vocke, and Alan Whiteside. On behalf of the authors, I would also like to thank Maizie Archie, Cassandra Banks, Jere Behrman, Stefano M. Bertozzi, Ramona Bruhns, Jinkie Corbin, William Easterly, Augustin Fosu, Timothy Fowler, Juan Pablo Gutierrez, Vicki Hart-Spriggs, Keith Jefferis, Benjamin Johns, Peter Johnson, Dilip Parajuli, Happy Siphambe, Rhaiza Vélez Soto, Dagmar Voelker, Staci Warden, Debrework Zewdie, the staff of the Population Studies Branch and the Eurasia Branch of the International Programs Center at the U.S. Census Bureau, and the Global HIV/AIDS Program of the World Bank.

The authors hope that their work will prove useful to all who deal with or are interested in the social, economic, and fiscal effects of HIV/AIDS, but we are also well aware that the mission—even in its analytical dimension, to say nothing of its execution—is as yet by no means accomplished. A lack of available data often means that the economic analyst, rather than providing compelling answers, can only formulate questions and hypotheses, supported by assorted observations pulled together from different countries. For various reasons, this constraint applies in particular to the impact of HIV/AIDS over time, to the macroeconomic consequences, and to the fiscal effects of HIV/AIDS, as they go far beyond specific HIV/AIDS-related expenditures. Thus, where this book cannot provide full answers, it is hoped that it may at least stimulate further research that can help us better understand the economic and fiscal consequences of the epidemic and that can complement and support efforts to fight this scourge.

Markus Haacker
Mbabane, Swaziland
November 1, 2004

Contributors

Pascal Annycke, International Labor Organization

Clive Bell, University of Heidelberg

Nancy Birdsall, Center for Global Development

Michael Cichon, International Labor Organization

Nicholas Crafts, London School of Economics

Shantayanan Devarajan, World Bank

Brynn Epstein, International Programs Center at the U.S. Bureau of the Census

Hans Gersbach, University of Heidelberg

Robert Greener, Joint United Nations Programme on HIV/AIDS

Markus Haacker, International Monetary Fund

Amar Hamoudi, University of California, Los Angeles

Iyabo Masha, International Monetary Fund

Mead Over, World Bank

Pierre Plamondon, International Labor Organization

1

The Demographic Impact of HIV/AIDS

Brynn G. Epstein

It is now 20 years since the first cases of acquired immune deficiency syndrome (AIDS) were discovered in sub-Saharan Africa. At the beginning of the third decade of the global pandemic, AIDS has reversed gains in life expectancy and improvements in child mortality in many countries; mortality among the population aged 15–49 has increased manyfold, even in countries with modest epidemics.[1] AIDS is the leading cause of mortality among adults (WHO, 2004). According to estimates by the Joint United Nations Programme on AIDS (UNAIDS), as of the end of 2003, over 20 million people had died of AIDS. Some 38 million people are estimated to be living with the human immunodeficiency virus (HIV), the virus that causes AIDS, the overwhelming majority of whom—over 90 percent—are in the developing world.

In the absence of drug therapy, survival with HIV/AIDS is estimated to be around 10 years. Because of this lag between infection and death, the deaths of those who were infected with HIV in the early 1990s are amplifying mortality rates today. In sub-Saharan Africa the increase in mortal-

This report is released to inform interested parties of research and to encourage discussion. The views expressed on statistical issues are those of the author and not necessarily those of the U.S. Census Bureau. The use of data not generated by the U.S. Census Bureau precludes performing the same statistical reviews on those data that the U.S. Census Bureau does on its own data.

[1]World Health Organization (WHO, 2004). For Thailand, a country with an estimated adult HIV prevalence rate of "only" 1.5 percent (Joint United Nations Programme on HIV/AIDS, 2004a), the WHO estimates that the "crude mortality rate for those aged 15–49 years almost doubled from 2.8 to 5.4 per thousand between 1987 and 1996" (WHO, 2004, p. 6).

ity due to AIDS is already a significant demographic event, effectively negating earlier progress made in such key human development indicators as infant mortality and life expectancy. The spread of HIV/AIDS is also affecting the attainment of almost all of the Millennium Development Goals adopted by the United Nations in 2000. In the absence of broad access to treatment, HIV/AIDS will result in radical changes in the size and structure of the population in many of the world's poorest countries.

HIV serosurveillance studies (studies based on blood tests, mainly from antenatal clinics) compiled by the U.S. Census Bureau in the HIV/AIDS Surveillance Data Base since 1987 provide some picture of the state of the epidemics in Africa, Asia, Latin America, the Caribbean, and Eastern Europe. The Census Bureau conducts further analysis of the demographic effects through estimates of AIDS mortality for countries in the developing world where the epidemics have reached a significant level. These estimates are incorporated into population projections for 56 countries to give a picture of the effect of AIDS mortality on population characteristics (see Box 1.1 for a description of this methodology). This chapter outlines the state of the various epidemics in those regions most seriously affected. It also assesses the current and future impact of HIV/AIDS on several demographic indicators for 15 countries in Africa, Asia, Latin America, and the Caribbean that are representative of the diverse global epidemics.

In addition, this chapter elaborates on certain demographic events specific to the HIV/AIDS pandemic. The mortality and morbidity associated with AIDS make it unlike most other types of sickness and disease. Whereas most diseases prey largely on the very young, the old, or the weak, the way in which HIV is contracted and spread makes young adults, and especially young women, the most vulnerable. As a result, in countries with high HIV prevalence, the socioeconomic consequences of high mortality among adults can be far-reaching, devastating households, families, and communities and eroding formal and informal mechanisms of social support.

History and State of the Pandemic

The global HIV/AIDS pandemic consists of many separate epidemics, each with its own distinct origin in terms of geography and population groups affected, and each involving different types and frequencies of risky behaviors and practices. Sub-Saharan Africa is the region of the world most severely affected by AIDS. Despite being home to just over 10 percent of the world's population, it has two-thirds of the world's HIV-positive people

Box 1.1. Methodology for Estimating AIDS Mortality

The U.S. Census Bureau compiles HIV prevalence information for developing countries in its HIV/AIDS Surveillance Data Base. This database contains over 75,000 records from various publications and surveillance reports. HIV prevalence points taken from this database are the basis for projecting HIV prevalence, estimating AIDS mortality, and estimating and projecting the impact of AIDS on the number of orphaned children.

To obtain estimates of AIDS-related mortality, a new application developed at the Census Bureau incorporates estimates of HIV prevalence from the Estimation and Projection Package (EPP), an epidemiologically realistic model developed and used by the World Health Organization (WHO) and the Joint United Nations Programme on AIDS (UNAIDS). EPP produces a national "best fit" curve of adult HIV prevalence using sentinel surveillance data pertaining to pregnant women. We use country-specific adult HIV prevalence estimates from EPP for years from the beginning of the epidemic to 2010.

The Census Bureau application applies assumptions from the WHO/UNAIDS Epidemiological Reference Group about the age and sex distribution of HIV incidence, sex ratios of new infections, the mother-to-child transmission rate, and disease progression. The model allows for competing risk of death and projects HIV incidence implied by the EPP estimates of HIV prevalence through 2010, assuming a decline in HIV incidence of 50 percent by 2050. The model can include the impact of antiretroviral therapy, but the current projections assume that no one will receive treatment.

This methodology works in conjunction with the Census Bureau's cohort component Rural-Urban Projection (RUP) program, which is used to prepare population estimates and projections. RUP is used to produce the with-AIDS and without-AIDS scenarios.

A with-AIDS series is generated, showing what has happened and what is projected to happen in a country as a result of AIDS mortality and its demographic consequences. Next, a hypothetical without-AIDS scenario shows what the Census Bureau's modeling work indicates would have happened if the country had not been affected by the HIV/AIDS epidemic. This modeling takes into account not only lower death rates but also associated changes to a country's age and sex profile and, indirectly, the combined effects of lower mortality and changing population composition on demographic indicators. The without-AIDS scenario currently assumes the same fertility rates (based on observed data) as the with-AIDS series and thus underestimates what fertility might have been in the absence of AIDS. In the with-AIDS series the number of births decreases as a result of mortality-induced reductions in the number of women of reproductive age.

Table 1.1. Key Demographic Indicators of the HIV/AIDS Epidemic by Developing Region and for Selected Countries, End-2003
(Thousands of persons except where stated otherwise)

Region and Country	People Living with HIV/AIDS — Adults[1] and children	Adults	HIV Prevalence Among Adults (percent)	AIDS Deaths Among Adults and Children in 2003
Global total	37,800	35,700	1.1	2,900
Sub-Saharan Africa	25,000	23,100	7.5	2,200
Botswana	350	330	37.3	33
Côte d'Ivoire	570	530	7.0	47
Ethiopia	1,500	1,400	4.4	120
Kenya	1,200	1,100	6.7	150
Malawi	900	810	14.2	84
Mozambique	1,300	1,200	12.2	110
Namibia	210	200	21.3	16
Nigeria	3,600	3,300	5.4	310
Rwanda	250	230	5.1	22
South Africa	5,300	5,100	21.5	370
Tanzania	1,600	1,500	8.8	160
Uganda	530	450	4.1	78
Zambia	920	830	16.5	89
Zimbabwe	1,800	1,600	24.6	170
Asia[2]	6,500	6,300	0.6	460
Cambodia	170	170	2.6	15
Thailand	570	560	1.5	58
Vietnam	220	200	0.4	9
Latin America	1,600	1,600	0.6	84
Brazil	660	650	0.7	15
Guyana	11	11	2.5	1
Caribbean	430	410	2.3	35
Haiti	280	260	5.6	24
Eastern Europe	1,300	1,300	0.6	49

Source: UNAIDS (2004a).
[1]Adults are defined as persons aged 15–49.
[2]Excluding the former Soviet Union.

(UNAIDS, 2004a). About 7.5 percent of adults (defined here as persons 15–49 years of age) in the region were HIV-positive at the end of 2003, compared with a global prevalence rate of 1.1 percent and a prevalence rate of 0.4 percent for the world excluding sub-Saharan Africa. (Table 1.1 summarizes the latest available estimates from UNAIDS of the numbers of people living with HIV/AIDS and of AIDS-related deaths in selected regions and for specific countries.) In six countries in southern Africa—Botswana, Lesotho, Namibia, South Africa, Swaziland, and Zimbabwe—it is estimated that at least one in five adults is living with HIV. Another four countries—

the Central African Republic, Malawi, Mozambique, and Zambia—have estimated adult prevalence rates above 10 percent, and another eight countries have rates exceeding 5 percent.[2]

In Asia, by contrast, estimated adult HIV prevalence exceeded 1 percent in only three countries: Cambodia, Myanmar, and Thailand. Nevertheless, the enormous size of the Asian population means that the Asia-Pacific region could account for a very substantial share of new infections in the coming years.[3] In India and China, the world's two most populous countries, prevalence rates are relatively low at present (between 0.4 and 1.3 percent in India, and about 0.1 percent in China). These country averages, however, mask concentrated epidemics in some local areas or among groups engaging in high-risk behaviors such as injecting drugs and sex work, and the experience from other countries has shown that the epidemic can spread from these groups to the general population in just a few years.

In Latin America and the Caribbean, epidemics that seem mostly driven by heterosexual transmission are found in The Bahamas, Guyana, Haiti, and Honduras, all of which are among the countries with the highest adult HIV prevalence in the region. But the nature of the epidemic varies in this region: in some countries, such as Argentina and Uruguay, HIV/AIDS is concentrated among injecting drug users, whereas in others, such as Mexico and Peru, it is concentrated among men who have sex with men.

HIV/AIDS began to spread quickly in Eastern Europe and Central Asia in the mid-1990s, fueled largely by injecting drug use. The pattern here is mainly one of locally concentrated epidemics; reported HIV prevalence rates are low among the general population, and therefore previous rounds of AIDS mortality estimates prepared by the Census Bureau do not include countries in this region. However, this may soon change, as there is evidence that the epidemic is growing through heterosexual transmission.

In all of these regions HIV-1 is the primary type of virus. This type is driving the greater part of the demographic impact. Another type, HIV-2, is found predominantly in West Africa. HIV-2 differs from HIV-1 in that the progression from HIV to AIDS and from AIDS to death is much slower.

---

[2]All estimates of adult HIV prevalence rates are from UNAIDS (2004a). In the literature, adult prevalence rates generally refer to the 15–49 age range; this chapter follows that convention.

[3]Schuettler (2003) suggests that the region could account for 40 percent of new global infections by 2010 if prevention efforts are not stepped up.

Therefore, for the purposes of assessing the demographic impact of AIDS mortality, the Census Bureau utilizes HIV-1 prevalence data for analysis in selected countries.

In taking a closer look at epidemics within regions and within countries, a good place to start is the percentage of pregnant women attending antenatal clinics (ANCs) who test HIV-positive. Several studies that have compared HIV prevalence among pregnant women with that among adult men and women from other, community-based studies have shown that antenatal clinic seroprevalence gives a reasonable estimate of HIV prevalence in the general adult population.[4] Also, for many countries antenatal clinic data are the primary source of information on prevalence trends among the population and form the basis of estimates of the demographic effects of HIV/AIDS.[5] Figure 1.1 shows trends in HIV prevalence for selected urban areas in sub-Saharan Africa, Asia, Latin America, and the Caribbean during the past two decades. Variations in trends are apparent, and the rest of this section discusses each region in greater detail.

Sub-Saharan Africa

The Census Bureau first started to incorporate estimates of AIDS mortality in its population projections in 1994. At that point a total of 14 countries had 5 percent or higher prevalence among their low-risk urban populations (the criterion then applied by the Census Bureau for explicitly including AIDS mortality in demographic estimates and projections).[6] Thirteen of these countries are located in sub-Saharan Africa, where HIV/AIDS is largely spread through heterosexual sex. In many cities of sub-Saharan Africa, HIV prevalence among sex workers approached 50 percent from the mid-1980s to the early 1990s, and in several, seroprevalence among sex workers ranged from 50 percent to over 80 percent (Way and Stanecki, 1994). During the 1990s the epidemic quickly expanded throughout the population in many countries in this region, and the cur-

---

[4]HIV prevalence among pregnant women tends to underestimate prevalence among all women but to overestimate it among men.

[5]Antenatal clinic data and HIV prevalence levels from other population groups are compiled in the U.S. Census Bureau's HIV/AIDS Surveillance Data Base, 2004 release.

[6]The 14 countries are Burkina Faso, Burundi, the Central African Republic, Congo, Côte d'Ivoire, Haiti, Kenya, Malawi, Rwanda, Tanzania, Uganda, the Democratic Republic of Congo (formerly Zaïre), Zambia, and Zimbabwe. Because previous modeling work had already been undertaken in Brazil and Thailand, those countries also had estimated AIDS mortality incorporated into their population projections.

Figure 1.1. HIV Seroprevalence in Selected Urban Areas in Africa, Asia, and Latin America and the Caribbean
(Percent)

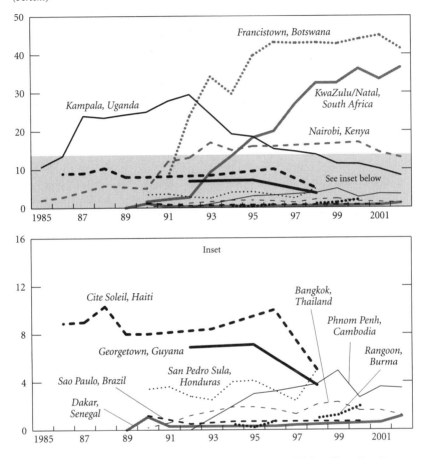

Source: U.S. Census Bureau, International Programs Center, HIV/AIDS Surveillance Data Base (2004).

rent round of population estimates and projections incorporates estimated AIDS mortality into the projections for 37 sub-Saharan African countries.

Many of the countries where HIV epidemics first erupted are located in East Africa, along the Great Rift Valley from Ethiopia to central Mozambique. From 1985 to 1992 there was a consistent and rapid increase in seroprevalence among pregnant women in the capital cities of Malawi, Uganda, and Zambia. In just five years these rates more than doubled, and in Malawi seroprevalence rose from under 5 percent to over 20 percent. In contrast, during the same period, moderate increases were documented in the Central African Republic and Kenya, with rates reaching 15 percent by 1992 (Way and Stanecki, 1994).

Many areas of Zimbabwe reported a rapid increase in HIV prevalence among pregnant women in the early 1990s. Prevalence there has since stabilized, albeit at a high rate. In 2001, in the capital city of Harare, 30 percent of pregnant women tested were HIV-positive. Zimbabwe also has high prevalence rates among such high-risk groups as sex workers and patients with other sexually transmitted infections. Both urban and rural areas appear equally affected. In the Democratic Republic of Congo, where the first cases of AIDS were discovered, prevalence rates among pregnant women attending antenatal clinics rose sharply in the early 1990s but have since declined and stabilized at a lower rate. Prevalence rates for pregnant women in Kinshasa remained below 5 percent during the last decade.

The epidemic also began in the early 1980s in Kenya and Tanzania. Prevalence tends to be higher in urban areas in Tanzania. In Kenya, however, by 1997 some rural and urban areas had prevalence rates higher than in the capital city of Nairobi. Recent data show rates stabilizing or decreasing in some urban and rural sites. In the capital cities of these two countries, prevalence rates among pregnant women remained around 15 percent in the early 1990s, and median antenatal clinic prevalence in major urban areas has stayed between 10 and 15 percent for the past 10 years. Although the apparent stabilizing of prevalence rates may seem encouraging, the reality is that HIV prevalence is a function of AIDS mortality and new infections. Because mortality among HIV-positive people is high, a prevalence rate that stabilizes at a high level can mean that a large number of new infections are replacing a roughly equal number who are dying of HIV/AIDS or related causes.

HIV prevalence among pregnant women is generally lower in western Africa. By 1994 only Burkina Faso and Côte d'Ivoire met the Census Bureau criteria for including estimated AIDS mortality in their population projections. Rates among pregnant women in several sentinel sites in Burkina Faso remained stable at or below 10 percent through the 1990s, and they remained low, at around 5 percent both in and outside major urban areas, in 2002. Côte d'Ivoire reported a rapid increase in seroprevalence in the mid-1980s but a slower increase throughout the 1990s, and current rates seem to have stabilized at around 10 percent in some urban sentinel sites.

By 1996, Cameroon and Nigeria in the west, Ethiopia in the east, and Botswana, Lesotho, and South Africa, south of the Great Rift Valley, had seen prevalence among their low-risk urban populations rise to 5 percent. And just two years later, as the epidemics continued to spread through southern Africa, Namibia and Swaziland met the criteria for including estimated AIDS mortality in population projections.

In Ethiopia estimated adult HIV prevalence remained around 4 percent from 2001 to 2003. Prevalence among pregnant women attending antenatal clinics rose sharply in the early 1990s, but levels have since declined and stabilized at a lower rate. Median antenatal clinic prevalence in major urban areas in Ethiopia declined from 20 percent in 1995 to 15 percent in 2000.

Seven countries clustered in the Southern Cone of Africa have extraordinarily high estimated adult prevalence rates. Although the HIV/AIDS epidemics in this area started later, they quickly exploded. As seen in Figure 1.1, seroprevalence among pregnant women in Francistown, Botswana, increased from 7 percent in 1991 to 44 percent in 2000. Both rural and urban areas seem to be affected to the same extent in this region. The dramatic rise in HIV prevalence among pregnant women in the mid-1990s is echoed in the neighboring countries of Namibia, where seroprevalence in this group had reached nearly 30 percent by 2002, and South Africa, where it had reached 25 percent by 2001. In Swaziland and Lesotho, two small countries surrounded by South Africa, seroprevalence among pregnant women reached nearly 40 percent in 2002 and 30 percent in 2003, respectively.

The most recent estimates, completed in 2002, include more countries in coastal West Africa and in the Sahel region, a stretch of countries lying between the Sahara to the north and the rain forest to the south, from the Atlantic Ocean in the west to the Horn of Africa in the east. Although very few data are available for these countries, UNAIDS estimates that adult prevalence levels are 2.7 percent in Eritrea and 4.8 percent in Chad. As already discussed, variations in the estimated starting dates of a generalized epidemic are a misleading indicator of its strength and severity. Many of the countries with older epidemics are now showing modest declines or stabilizing prevalence rates. On the other hand, epidemics have escalated in some of the worst-affected countries, with prevalence rising from less than 5 percent to more than 30 percent in only about 10 years. In general, there are many reasons for the variation in seroprevalence across countries. Poverty and political instability have major consequences for the spread of HIV. A large number of people migrating to specific areas to find jobs, or mass population movements such as those that followed the genocide in Rwanda and war in Angola and Mozambique, can be expected to result in an increase in prevalence rates in semiurban areas that have large numbers of migrants.

Figure 1.2. HIV Seroprevalence in Selected Cities in Uganda
(Percent)

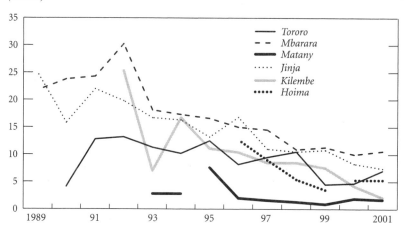

Source: U.S. Census Bureau, International Programs Center, HIV/AIDS Surveillance Data Base
(2004).

Two countries in sub-Saharan Africa, Uganda and Senegal, remain
notable success stories. In Uganda, after a dramatic rise in the early 1990s,
prevalence among pregnant women began to decline at most sentinel surveillance sites. In Kampala, the capital, HIV prevalence declined from its
peak of 30 percent in 1993 to 11 percent in 2000 (Figure 1.1). Figure 1.2
shows that, in other urban areas throughout Uganda, HIV prevalence rates
from sentinel surveillance reporting indicate a decline or leveling off of
infection levels. In Senegal, AIDS control programs are credited with
keeping HIV prevalence at very low levels, currently estimated at less than
1 percent.

Asia

HIV prevalence rates in Asia are lower, and the epidemics there started
later, first spreading during the 1990s, mostly among injecting drug users.
Today HIV transmission is occurring more through sexual contact,
although it is still concentrated among sex workers and injecting drug
users. High prevalence is also recorded among men who have sex with
men. But concentrated epidemics do not confine HIV to particular risk
groups. HIV spreads from high-risk behavior such as sharing dirty needles
and unprotected sex; those who engage in risky behavior may be a part of
more than one risk group. For example, many sex workers often use

injecting drugs, and many men who have unprotected sex with men also have sex with women. These populations serve as bridging populations and aid in the spread of HIV to the general population (MAP Network, 2001).

Thailand was one of the first countries in which the Census Bureau undertook modeling work, and estimated AIDS mortality was included for Myanmar and Cambodia by the 1998 round of Census Bureau population projections. Currently, a generalized HIV epidemic is found in just these three countries.

Cambodia has the most serious epidemic in the region. Sentinel surveillance among pregnant women in Phnom Penh show a rise in prevalence from no evidence of infection in 1992 to 5 percent by 1999. In 2002 HIV prevalence among pregnant women was 3.5 percent. Rates are similar for rural and urban areas: sentinel surveillance sites in 18 provinces reported prevalence rates ranging from 2 to 6 percent for 2002.

Located between Myanmar and Cambodia, Thailand has one of the oldest epidemics in the region but is considered a success for its ability to curtail the epidemic and keep HIV prevalence low. Throughout the latter half of the 1990s, declining or stable prevalence rates were evident among sex workers in four regions of the country (north, northeast, central, and south), ranging from 5 to 15 percent in 1990 and from 5 to 9 percent in 2002. In Bangkok rates declined from 10 percent in 1990 to 3 percent in 2002. Rates for injecting drug users have mostly remained around 40 percent in all four regions and in Bangkok since the early 1990s.

In Myanmar HIV seroprevalence rose dramatically in the 1990s among sex workers in Yangon and Mandalay, from 2 percent and 5 percent, respectively, in 1992 to 26 percent and 50 percent by 2000. In 1992 seroprevalence levels for injecting drug users was already at 50 percent or higher in both these cities and in the smaller cities of Myitkyina and Taunggyi. By 2000 the highest rates were in Mandalay (58 percent) and in two cities near the border with China, Myitkyina (90 percent) and Lashio (76 percent).

Throughout the 1990s in Myanmar, HIV prevalence among pregnant women remained stable at a low rate, and in 2000 most sentinel surveillance sites reported HIV prevalence below 3 percent in this group. However, the centrally located city of Mandalay as well as several sentinel sites within towns on or near the Chinese and Thai borders—Muse, Tachileik, Dawei, Myitkyina, and Lashio—had higher prevalence rates, ranging from 3.5 to over 5 percent.

Also, although such countries as India and China have low aggregate prevalence rates, these rates mask high prevalence rates in some populations at risk; HIV prevalence rates are also high in some regions in China where people were selling blood plasma to supplement their incomes (UNAIDS, 2004a). Given the very large populations of these two countries, a further increase in their prevalence rates could mean that most HIV-positive people in the world will be living in these countries. According to UNAIDS (2004a), India may already have the world's largest population living with HIV/AIDS,[7] and the number of people infected in China could reach 10 million by 2010.

The epidemic in India varies in scope from state to state and is concentrated among commercial sex workers and injecting drug users. HIV prevalence increased dramatically among sex workers in Mumbai, where prevalence was 1 percent in 1987, peaked at 64 percent in 1999, and then declined slightly to 52 percent in 2001. However, recent data from 2001 show 31 serosurveillance sites throughout the country reporting HIV prevalence above 1 percent among pregnant women. At four sentinel sites in Mumbai in 2001, HIV prevalence among pregnant women ranged from 2 percent to nearly 8 percent. Eight other sentinel sites in Maharashtra state reported HIV prevalence above 1 percent in pregnant women. Seven sites in Andhra Pradesh state and five sites in Tamil Nadu state also reported HIV prevalence above 1 percent.

There is recent evidence of rapidly growing epidemics in at-risk population groups in China, Indonesia, and Vietnam. In selected areas of China's Yunnan province, which borders Myanmar, Thailand, Lao PDR, and Vietnam, HIV prevalence rates among these groups ranged from 20 percent in Luxi to 70 percent in Kaiyuan in 1997. HIV prevalence rose from no evidence of infection in 1995 to 21 percent and 17 percent, respectively, for Guangdong province (where Hong Kong SAR is located) and Guangxi province in only five years. Yining, a site in Xinjiang province that borders Kazakhstan, had prevalence rates among the high-risk population of 80 percent or more from 1998 to 2000. Another group with relatively high HIV prevalence rates in this region is men who have sex with men. For example, although Indonesia records low seroprevalence among sex workers (below 1 percent), seroprevalence among transgendered persons, or *waria*, rose from no evidence of infection in 1992 to 6 percent in 1997.

---

[7]UNAIDS (2004a) provides a point estimate of 5.3 million people living with HIV/AIDS in South Africa, with a low estimate of 4.5 million and a high estimate of 6.2 million. Reflecting the lack of data, UNAIDS (2004a) does not provide a point estimate for India, but only a low and a high estimate of 2.2 million and 7.3 million, respectively.

Recent data suggest that Vietnam has an epidemic that is moving from concentrated to general. Although still at low levels, seroprevalence among sex workers steadily increased in three cities of Vietnam during the 1990s. In 1999, 6 percent of sex workers were infected in Hanoi, 5 percent in Ho Chi Minh City, and 3 percent in Haiphong, a major port and industrial city in the north of the country. Sentinel surveillance in 2002 found that more than 20 percent of injecting drug users in most provinces were HIV-positive.

Although no signs have yet emerged of a generalized epidemic in many of the countries in Asia, the conditions are ripe for a rapid spread of HIV. Serious concentrated epidemics are found in injecting drug users and sex workers in various parts of some countries. Injecting drug use is on the rise in this region (MAP Network, 2001); the spread of this behavior, coupled with low condom use rates and sharing of dirty needles, means that these epidemics could very easily spread throughout a country.

Latin America and the Caribbean

In Latin America and the Caribbean, epidemics occurred initially among men who have sex with men, but by the early 1990s there were large increases among injecting drug users and sex workers. Initially, Brazil and Haiti were the only countries to have estimated AIDS mortality explicitly included in the Census Bureau's population projections. Estimated AIDS mortality was included for Guyana in 1996, Honduras in 1998, and The Bahamas, Barbados, Belize, the Dominican Republic, Guatemala, Panama, Trinidad and Tobago, and Suriname by 2002.

UNAIDS (2004a) estimates that adult prevalence among the countries of this region ranged from less than 1 percent to nearly 6 percent. Injecting drug use and sex between men are driving the epidemic in most South American countries, whereas in Central America and in the Caribbean both sex between men and heterosexual sex are spreading HIV (UNAIDS, 2004a).

Haiti, with an estimated adult prevalence of 5.6 percent, has the most serious epidemic in this region. Seroprevalence among pregnant women in the capital, Port-au-Prince, was 10 percent in 1996 but thereafter declined to 4 percent by 1999–2000. Sentinel surveillance sites from various cities in Haiti report similar declines in rates by 1999–2000, ranging from 2 percent in Fond des Nègres to 5 percent in Jérémie.

In Rio de Janeiro, Brazil, HIV prevalence among men who have sex with men declined during the mid-1990s. In 1994, 25 percent of men in this group were HIV-positive; by 1996, only 9 percent tested positive for the virus. Seroprevalence among sex workers in various cities of Brazil during the 1990s ranged from 2 percent in 1993–94 in Fortaleza, a coastal city in Ceara state in the northeast, to 18 percent in 1998 in São Paulo, Brazil's largest city. Higher prevalences are found among injecting drug users, although there was wide variation in infection levels in various Brazilian cities during the mid-1990s. Twenty-eight percent of injecting drug users tested in Rio de Janeiro in 1995–96 were HIV-positive, and 71 percent of users in Itajai, a coastal city in Santa Catarina state in southern Brazil, tested positive in 1995–96. In a study of injecting drug users seen at the blood transfusion service at Eva Peron Teaching Hospital in the town of Granadero Baigorria, Argentina, HIV prevalence was 29 percent among male drug users and 17 percent among female users in 1995.

In 1990, 1 percent of pregnant women in São Paulo tested positive for HIV. As more sentinel sites began reporting, the median HIV prevalence rate among antenatal clinic attendees varied around 1 percent of women tested. In 1995 nearly 3 percent of pregnant women tested in Porto Alegre and Rio de Janeiro were positive for HIV, and in 1996, 5 percent of pregnant women in the port city of Santos tested positive for HIV. In 1996 federal law in Brazil mandated the free provision of antiretroviral therapy through the public health system, thus drastically reducing mortality from AIDS and extending life with HIV.

In Honduras HIV seroprevalence among sex workers in San Pedro Sula fluctuated between 12 and 21 percent during the 1990s. In 2001–02 HIV prevalence was 13 percent. Prevalence among pregnant women reached 5 percent in 1998. In Tegucigalpa, the capital, seroprevalence among pregnant women did not rise above 1 percent during the 1990s, yet the percentage of sex workers testing positive rose steadily to 13 percent in 1997; it has since declined to 8 percent. In the Dominican Republic HIV prevalence rates among sex workers in the capital, Santo Domingo, declined from a peak of 9 percent in 1993 to 5 percent in 1999. La Romana reports a similar decline, but rates from Bani fluctuated between 6 and 11 percent during the same period. Sentinel surveillance among pregnant women did not rise above 2 percent throughout the 1990s in Santo Domingo, and by 1999 rates had declined or stabilized below 2 percent for other urban areas.

Eastern Europe and Central Asia

Very few data on HIV/AIDS prevalence are available from Eastern Europe and Central Asia. UNAIDS (2004a) estimates that the total number of people living with HIV in the region is 1.3 million. In 2003, 360,000 people in the region became newly infected, and AIDS claimed 49,000 lives. The epidemics in this region are considered to be concentrated among injecting drug users, although at the same time there is evidence of a growing heterosexual epidemic. As of the most recent round of estimates, the Census Bureau will include estimated AIDS mortality in the population projections for the Russian Federation.

The worst-affected countries are the Russian Federation, Ukraine, and the Baltic states, but HIV continues to spread in Belarus, Moldova, Kazakhstan, the Kyrgyz Republic, and Uzbekistan. Injecting drug use and unsafe sex are the predominant modes of transmission in this region, especially among young people. According to the European Centre for the Epidemiological Monitoring of AIDS (2003), 41 percent of new infections in 2002 were among injecting drug users, and 10 percent were through heterosexual transmission, although the number of new infections attributed to heterosexual transmission continues to rise. In the countries first affected, the proportion of injecting drug users who were HIV-positive peaked in 1996–98, whereas cases from heterosexual contact continued to rise, accounting for 28 percent of all cases in Moldova, 29 percent in Ukraine, and 35 percent in Belarus in 2002. New infections peaked in Estonia, Latvia, and the Russian Federation in 2001, also marked by declines in injecting drug users and increases among heterosexuals.

There are more than 600,000 injecting drug users in Ukraine and up to 200,000 in Kazakhstan. Injecting drug use is on the rise—in Estonia and Latvia it is estimated that up to 1 percent of the adult population inject drugs, and in the Kyrgyz Republic it could be as many as 2 percent. The five Central Asian republics straddle major drug trafficking routes into the Russian Federation and Europe. On the whole, more than 80 percent of people who are HIV-positive in this region are not yet 30 years of age (UNAIDS, 2003).

In the Russian Federation, condom use is very low among teenagers, sex workers, and injecting drug users, making the sexual spread of HIV a more prominent feature, since most injecting drug users are young and sexually active. Four studies have revealed high prevalence levels among female sex workers who were also injecting drug users (European Centre for the Epidemiological Monitoring of AIDS, 2003).

Differences by Sex

As the global HIV pandemic is increasingly driven by heterosexual sex, women are becoming infected at faster rates. Women, and especially young women, have multiple vulnerabilities to HIV transmission: biological, cul-

Figure 1.3. Adult HIV Prevalence by Age and Sex in Three Sub-Saharan African Countries
(Percent)

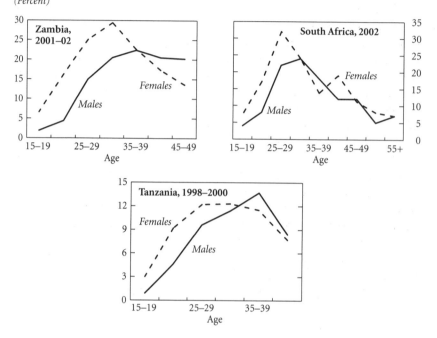

Sources: Zambia Central Statistical Office and Central Board of Health (2002); Shisana, Simbayi, and Phil (2002) for South Africa; and Urassa and others (2002) for Tanzania.

tural, social, and economic. The nature of sexual intercourse alone makes it easier for women to contract HIV, and male-to-female transmission is estimated to be twice as likely as female-to-male transmission. In addition, the immaturity of the reproductive tract in young women makes them more susceptible. Economic dependency on men, a cultural preference for high fertility, lack of power to negotiate safe sex practices, and lack of access to information and health care all combine to make it difficult and undesirable for women to be proactive in safe sex negotiation.

UNAIDS estimates that about 57 percent of adults living with HIV in sub-Saharan Africa are women and that new infections among women are increasing, especially among adolescents. Peak HIV prevalence among women occurs at younger ages and generally at a higher rate than among men, as Figure 1.3 shows for three countries in the region. This may be evidence of younger women having sexual relations with older men. Many studies from this region show that younger women from poor communities often resort to selling sex in an effort to support their family or pay their school fees.

The data in Figure 1.3 are from population-based serosurveillance. Data from this type of survey provide a clearer picture of the spread of the epidemic in the population at large. The Demographic and Health Surveys (DHS) recently incorporated an HIV surveillance module into several of their population-based surveys, and data from Zambia for 2001–02 show that prevalence among adult women is peaking at younger ages and at a higher rate than among adult men: prevalence peaks at 29 percent among 30- to 35-year-old women and at 22 percent among men 5 to 10 years older. Higher HIV prevalence among adult women is reported from both rural and urban areas: in Zambia, for example, rates of 12 percent and 9 percent, respectively, are reported for women and men from rural areas, and of 26 percent and 19 percent from urban areas (Zambia Central Statistical Office and Central Board of Health, 2002). Data from the Nelson Mandela/HSRC Study of HIV/AIDS conducted in South Africa show that HIV prevalence for 2002 peaked at 32 percent among 25- to 29-year-old women, versus 24 percent among 30- to 35-year-old men (Shisana, Simbayi, and Phil, 2002). In a rural region in Tanzania, prevalence during 1998–2000 was higher among women in each of the five-year age groups from 15 to 34 years (Urassa and others, 2002).

In other regions of the world, men still make up the majority of the HIV-positive population. In Asia, however, recent data show that seroprevalence among women is rising rapidly. In the Mekong region women are becoming infected at faster rates than men. And in Papua New Guinea infections in women 15 to 29 years old already outnumber those in men of the same age (UNAIDS, 2004b). In the Russian Federation as well, women account for an increasing share of newly diagnosed infections: 33 percent in 2002, up from 24 percent the year before (European Centre for the Epidemiological Monitoring of AIDS, 2003). One consequence of a rise in prevalence among women is a corresponding rise in the spread of HIV through mother-to-child transmission.

Mortality

The impact of AIDS mortality on demographic characteristics is detailed in Appendix Tables 1.A1 and 1.A2. Through the procedures described in Box 1.1, the Census Bureau provides estimates and projections for the analysis of how a population is affected by increased AIDS mortality. The adult crude death rate, the infant mortality rate, the under-5 mor-

Figure 1.4. Crude Death Rates With and Without AIDS in Selected Countries, 2005
(Deaths per 1,000 population)

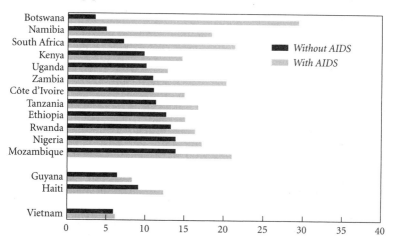

Source: U.S. Census Bureau, International Programs Center, HIV/AIDS Surveillance Data Base (2004) and unpublished tables.

tality rate, life expectancy, and the population growth rate in the presence of AIDS are compared with those in a without-AIDS scenario for the 15 focus countries of the President's Emergency Plan for AIDS Relief (for which the most current demographic estimates and projections are available at this time): Botswana, Côte d'Ivoire, Ethiopia, Guyana, Haiti, Kenya, Mozambique, Namibia, Nigeria, Rwanda, South Africa, Tanzania, Uganda, Vietnam, and Zambia. Indicators are estimated for 2005 and 2015 in Appendix Tables 1.A1 and 1.A2.

Crude Death Rates

The most direct impact of AIDS is an increase in the number of deaths in the affected populations. As seen in Figure 1.4, because of high HIV prevalence in sub-Saharan Africa, estimated crude death rates—the number of people dying per 1,000 of the population—for 2005 is already considerably higher for most countries because of AIDS. In Botswana, Kenya, Namibia, South Africa, and Haiti, crude death rates would be expected to be in the single digits without AIDS but are in double digits with AIDS. In South Africa, for example, the crude death rate in 2005 is estimated to be 21 per 1,000 with AIDS versus 7 per 1,000 without AIDS; in Botswana the

Figure 1.5. Crude Death Rates With and Without AIDS in Selected Countries, 2015
(Deaths per 1,000 population)

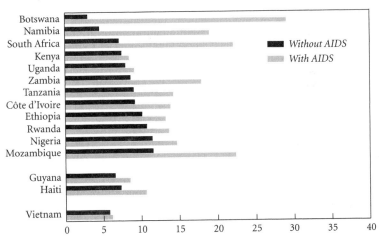

Source: U.S. Census Bureau, International Programs Center, HIV/AIDS Surveillance Data Base (2004) and unpublished tables.

crude death rate is estimated to be 29 per 1,000 with AIDS versus 3.5 per 1,000 without AIDS (Figure 1.4).

With the HIV epidemic still growing in many countries, and in light of the long time lag between infection and death, HIV-related mortality is projected to continue to increase in many countries over the coming years. This means that the adverse impact of HIV/AIDS on society and the economy is likely to worsen.

By 2015 estimated crude death rates may stabilize or decline for some countries, although they will still be higher because of AIDS than they would be otherwise. Other countries, especially those with younger epidemics, are likely to continue to experience a rise in crude death rates by 2015 even though mortality due to non-AIDS causes is projected to decline. Rates are estimated to increase by 2, 3, 5, or even 10 times as a result of AIDS in Botswana, Mozambique, Namibia, South Africa, and Zambia.

Estimated HIV prevalence is declining in Kenya and Uganda, and as a result the increase in crude death rates due to AIDS mortality will be considerably reduced in the next decade. Crude death rates are projected to decline from 15 per 1,000 to 8.5 per 1,000 for Kenya and 13 per 1,000 to 9 per 1,000 for Uganda by 2015 (Figure 1.5).

Figure 1.6. Mortality Rates With and Without AIDS by Age and Sex in Namibia, 2005
(Percent)

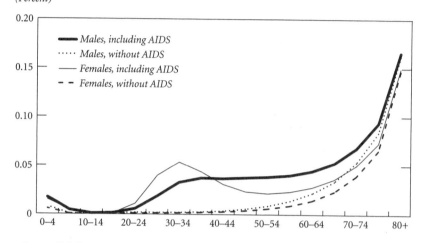

Source: U.S. Census Bureau, International Programs Center, HIV/AIDS Surveillance Data Base (2004) and unpublished tables.

Adult Mortality

Moving beyond aggregate mortality rates, one variable that is particularly relevant for the analysis of the social and economic consequences of HIV/AIDS is the mortality rate for the adult population. People between the ages of 15 and 49 years are considered to be at their most productive and reproductive age. It is this population that is involved in at least one and usually all of the following activities: working, raising a family, and taking care of the elderly population.

In a population not affected by HIV/AIDS, an expected pattern of mortality rates by age and sex under "normal" conditions takes a "J" shape. Mortality is slightly higher among infants under a year old, declines to very low levels throughout adolescence and into adulthood, and then increases steadily after middle age. However, in many countries with serious HIV/AIDS epidemics, mortality is highest at those ages when it should be the lowest, forming a hump in the middle of the J-curve. Figure 1.6 shows mortality rates by age and sex for Namibia in 2005; the increased mortality among the adult population is evident.

For 2005, with the higher AIDS mortality among adults, the estimated adult percentage of deaths already shows a measurable increase in most of the 15 countries selected for analysis. As Figure 1.7 shows, as a result of AIDS this percentage is doubled or more in many countries with high

Figure 1.7. Adult Deaths as a Share of All Deaths With and Without AIDS in Selected Countries, 2005[1]
(Percent)

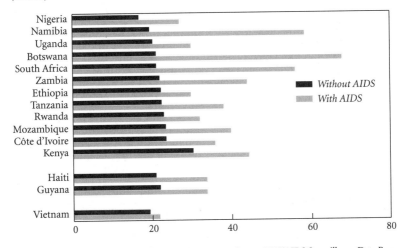

Source: U.S. Census Bureau, International Programs Center, HIV/AIDS Surveillance Data Base (2004) and unpublished tables.
[1]Adults are defined as persons aged 15–49.

estimated adult HIV prevalence. Adults are estimated to account for over half of all deaths in Botswana, Namibia, and South Africa and over 40 percent in Kenya, Mozambique, and Zambia. In countries such as Côte d'Ivoire, Ethiopia, Nigeria, Rwanda, Tanzania, Uganda, Haiti, and Guyana, with moderate or low HIV prevalence, the estimated adult percentage of deaths is still increased from one-fifth or one-fourth to a third of all deaths.

In 2005, in the 15 selected countries, AIDS is estimated to have increased deaths among adults by 1.5 million. Even countries with low estimated prevalence, where mortality due to other causes may be lower, are estimated to experience increases in deaths among the adult population. A dramatic rise will be seen among those countries with estimated adult HIV prevalence rates over 30 percent, such as Botswana, where AIDS is estimated to increase crude death rates among adults by over 30 per 1,000 (Figure 1.8).

Countries reporting stabilizations or declines in HIV seroprevalence are still likely to experience amplified adult crude death rates due to infections from 10 years previous. Zambia has an estimated adult crude death rate of 19 deaths per 1,000 adults in 2005, a tripling due to AIDS

Figure 1.8. Adult Crude Death Rates With and Without AIDS in Selected Countries, 2005
(Deaths per 1,000 adults)

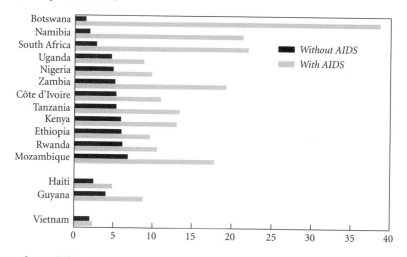

Source: U.S. Census Bureau, International Programs Center, HIV/AIDS Surveillance Data Base (2004) and unpublished tables.

mortality. Rwanda and Kenya have estimated crude death rates of 10.5 and 10 per 1,000 adults, an increase of 6 per 1,000. Even with the decline in prevalence levels in Uganda, death rates there are still inflated by 4 per 1,000 adults as a result of AIDS, to a rate of 9 deaths per 1,000 adults.

In Haiti, with an estimated adult HIV prevalence of 6 percent, the highest in Latin America and the Caribbean, the adult crude death rate is estimated at 9 per 1,000 adults, compared with 4 deaths per 1,000 without AIDS mortality. In Guyana, with an estimated adult HIV prevalence around 3 percent, estimated adult crude death rates are slightly higher with AIDS mortality. With an estimated HIV prevalence below 1 percent, the adult crude death rate for Vietnam is estimated to be only slightly increased because of AIDS. If Vietnam is able to keep its epidemic under control, rates will remain stable for the next decade.

In the absence of AIDS, by 2015 the percentage of all deaths projected to occur in adults would likely remain stable; however, with AIDS mortality an increase in the adult percentage of deaths is projected for many of the countries selected. In Côte d'Ivoire, Mozambique, South Africa, Tanzania, Zambia, and Haiti, 40 to 50 percent of all deaths are projected to occur in the adult population. In Botswana and Namibia, over 60 percent of all deaths are likely to occur among adults.

Given an assumed peak in estimated HIV prevalence by 2010, death rates are likely to remain stable or decrease by 2015, depending on the nature of the epidemic in each country. Estimated adult crude death rates will be inflated by 14 to 36 deaths per 1,000 adults in Botswana, Mozambique, Namibia, South Africa, and Zambia. Adult crude death rates are projected to remain lower for Uganda and Kenya as HIV prevalence continues to decline, at 6 and 9 deaths per 1,000 adults, respectively; these represent only slight increases over the without-AIDS scenario.

AIDS mortality patterns are driven by HIV prevalence patterns. Mortality rates among 15- to 49-year-old women are increasing dramatically as more women become infected through heterosexual transmission. As stated previously, in sub-Saharan Africa women make up more than half of all infections and are becoming infected at younger ages and in greater numbers than men. As a consequence, the impact of AIDS on mortality for women is also more pronounced: following the age pattern of HIV prevalence, mortality for women is estimated to peak among 30- to 34-year-olds, whereas the peak for men is later in life, among 35- to 44-year-olds (see Figure 1.6 for South Africa). In the absence of AIDS, deaths tend to be higher among 15- to 49-year-old men than among women of the same age, but this ratio is reversed in many countries affected by HIV/AIDS. For example, in Botswana and South Africa, countries with HIV prevalence rates over 20 percent, women accounted for over 50 percent of all deaths in the population aged 15–49 in 2005, compared with 35 percent and 33 percent, respectively, in the absence of AIDS (Appendix Table 1.A2).

Figure 1.9 further illustrates that, in the absence of AIDS, male adult crude death rates would be expected to be higher than female rates for most of the countries selected. With the addition of AIDS mortality, estimated female adult crude death rates not only jump significantly, but also are noticeably higher than those of their male counterparts in many African countries. The estimated female adult crude death rate for Botswana increases dramatically, from 1 death per 1,000 adults in the without-AIDS scenario to 40 deaths per 1,000 in the with-AIDS scenario. The latter is higher than the estimated male adult crude death rate of 37 deaths per 1,000 adults, thus decreasing the ratio of male to female adult deaths from 1.8 to 0.9 for 2005. The estimated female adult crude death rate increases by 12 deaths, to 23 deaths per 1,000 adults, for Mozambique, Namibia, Zambia, and South Africa with the addition of AIDS mortality, compared with an increase of 9 deaths, to 16 deaths per 1,000 adults, for males in the same countries.

Figure 1.9. Adult Crude Death Rates by Sex, With and Without AIDS in Selected Countries, 2005[1]
(Deaths per 1,000 adults)

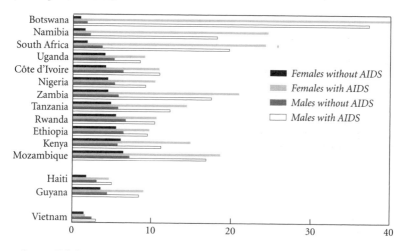

Source: U.S. Census Bureau, International Programs Center, HIV/AIDS Surveillance Data Base (2004) and unpublished tables.

[1] Adults are defined as persons aged 15–49.

Infant and Child Mortality

The fact that women are getting infected, falling ill, and dying in the midst of their reproductive years means an increase in the number of babies born HIV-positive. The relative impact of AIDS on infant mortality—the estimated number of infants per 1,000 live births who will die before their first birthday—will depend on the prevalence of HIV in the population, in addition to infant mortality from other causes. Unfortunately, because of the AIDS pandemic, much of the decrease in infant mortality seen during the 1980s and 1990s has disappeared. In sub-Saharan Africa over 30 percent of all children born to HIV-infected mothers become HIV-positive through the birth process or by breastfeeding.

It is estimated that in 2005 more infants are likely to die from AIDS than from any other cause in Botswana and Namibia (Figure 1.10). With an HIV prevalence of nearly 40 percent, Botswana has an estimated infant mortality rate of 55 infant deaths per 1,000 live births in 2005; it would be 14 per 1,000 live births in the absence of AIDS. Namibia's estimated infant mortality rate is 49 infant deaths per 1,000 live births, an increase of 26 infant

Figure 1.10. Infant Mortality With and Without AIDS in Selected Countries, 2005[1]
(Infant deaths per 1,000 live births)

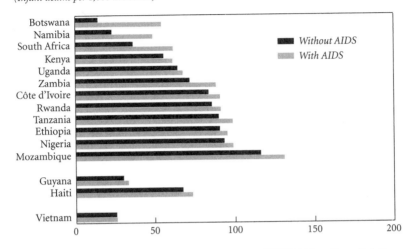

Source: U.S. Census Bureau, International Programs Center, HIV/AIDS Surveillance Data Base (2004) and unpublished tables.
[1]Deaths before the age of 1 year.

deaths per 1,000 due to AIDS. Estimated infant mortality in South Africa is increased by 40 percent as a result of AIDS. Because of more moderate HIV prevalence levels in Ethiopia, Nigeria, and Rwanda, estimated infant mortality in those countries is increased by a smaller 4 to 6 deaths per 1,000 live births.

Both Kenya and Uganda are experiencing only slightly increased estimated infant mortality rates as well, and, because of their efforts against the HIV/AIDS epidemic, infant mortality by 2015 is projected to decrease by 17 and 16 births, respectively, with increases of 1 death and 2 deaths per 1,000 live births due to AIDS. In the next decade, although infant mortality is expected to decrease, it will not decrease as dramatically as it would have in the absence of AIDS. For example, estimated infant mortality will still be inflated by 3 deaths and 6 deaths per 1,000 live births as a result of AIDS in Guyana and Haiti, respectively.

Many HIV-infected children survive past their first birthday only to die before the age of 5. AIDS deaths among children under 5 are resulting in higher mortality rates in that age group. Under-5 mortality is estimated to have more than doubled because of AIDS in Namibia; in Botswana 80 per-

Figure 1.11. Child Mortality With and Without AIDS in Selected Countries, 2005
(Deaths per 1,000 children under 5 years)

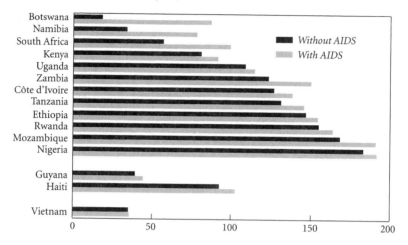

Source: U.S. Census Bureau, International Programs Center, HIV/AIDS Surveillance Data Base (2004) and unpublished tables.

cent of deaths among children under 5 are due to AIDS; and 40 percent of under-5 mortality in South Africa is due to AIDS. AIDS will also aggravate under-5 mortality rates in countries such as Côte d'Ivoire, Ethiopia, Mozambique, Nigeria, Rwanda, Tanzania, Uganda, Zambia, and Haiti, which already have high under-5 mortality rates due to other causes (Figure 1.11).

Without the prevention of mother-to-child transmission, under-5 mortality rates in 2005 are significantly higher with AIDS than without it. Even in countries with lower HIV prevalence, AIDS mortality is increasing under-5 mortality rates. By 2015 AIDS mortality is estimated to make up nearly 90 percent of deaths in this age group in Botswana, two-thirds of deaths in Namibia, and half of deaths in South Africa.

Life Expectancy

One of the most shocking markers of the demographic effect of AIDS mortality is life expectancy at birth—the estimated average number of years a person could expect to live if age-specific death rates prevail throughout his or her life. In developing countries life expectancy was chronically low mainly because of high infant mortality. Once measures were taken to alleviate the common causes of infant mortality, life expectancies began to climb. However, life expectancies in many sub-Saharan African countries are now estimated to be cut in half because of AIDS mortality among adults.

More generally, life expectancy is an important component of key indicators of welfare such as the Human Development Index (HDI) of the United Nations Development Programme, which also includes measures of educational attainment and GDP per capita. In sub-Saharan Africa most of the attainment in human development, as measured by the HDI, over the last 50 years was based on increased life expectancy; this attainment is now rapidly being eroded by the HIV epidemic. Similarly, using a method based on individual valuations of mortality risk, Crafts and Haacker (Chapter 6, this volume) estimate that the welfare impact of reduced life expectancy due to HIV/AIDS dwarfs all estimates of the impact of HIV/AIDS on GDP per capita.

Estimated average life expectancy at birth for the selected countries in Africa is 45 years in 2005—an average of 14 years of life less than it would have been without AIDS mortality. The countries with estimated adult HIV prevalence over 20 percent (Botswana, Namibia, and South Africa) are estimated to have lost 24 to 42 years of life expectancy at birth as a result of AIDS mortality (Figure 1.12). All of the selected countries in Africa would have estimated life expectancies of 50 years or more without AIDS.

Estimated crude death rates are lower in countries outside of Africa with lower HIV prevalence, but life expectancy is still affected, although to a lesser extent than in sub-Saharan Africa. With the addition of AIDS mortality, life expectancy in Haiti is 53 years instead of 61 years; in Guyana life expectancy is 65.5 years instead of 70 years.

Within less than 10 years, some countries in sub-Saharan Africa are projected to see life expectancies at birth fall to around 30 years—levels not seen since the beginning of the twentieth century. Among those selected countries that would have approached or exceeded life expectancies of 70 years by 2015 (Botswana, Namibia, and South Africa) in the absence of AIDS, life expectancy is instead projected to be 35 years in Botswana, 38.5 years in Namibia, and 44.5 years in South Africa; these figures represent losses of 45 years, 28.5 years, and 25.5 years of life, respectively.

AIDS mortality is expected to continue to result in lower life expectancies in Latin America, the Caribbean, and Asia. Life expectancies in 2015 are projected to be 5 and 8 years lower in Guyana and Haiti, respectively, than they would be without AIDS. And although estimated HIV prevalence

Figure 1.12. Life Expectancy at Birth With and Without AIDS in Selected Countries, 2005
(Years)

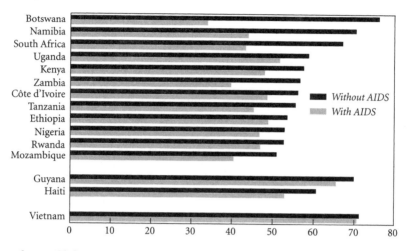

Source: U.S. Census Bureau, International Programs Center, HIV/AIDS Surveillance Data Base (2004) and unpublished tables.

is very low in Vietnam, projecting the current epidemic results in a loss of 1 year of life by 2015.

Fertility and Population Growth

Even as mortality rates are rising, fertility rates are expected to decline by 2015. HIV/AIDS affects fertility rates, as fertility tends to be lower for HIV-infected women than for uninfected women. In addition, approximately one-third of children born to HIV-positive mothers are infected and unlikely to reach childbearing age themselves. HIV/AIDS may also reduce birthrates indirectly, through its impact on sexual behavior, as women may reduce risky sexual practices by increasing abstinence and condom use and reducing the number of sexual partners they have over time. Finally, in many countries affected by the pandemic, AIDS mortality may affect population growth as the increase in deaths among reproductive-age women leads to fewer births. As Figure 1.13 illustrates, Botswana, which has a high crude death rate among adult women, is expected to experience a decline in births throughout this decade.

Figure 1.13. Births With and Without AIDS in Botswana
(Thousands)

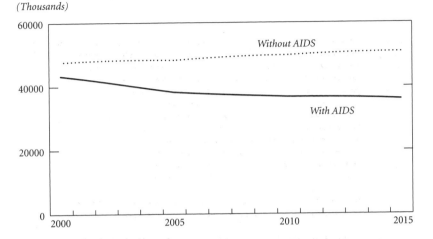

Source: U.S. Census Bureau, International Programs Center, HIV/AIDS Surveillance Data Base (2004) and unpublished tables.

Population will continue to grow in most of the selected countries, even though estimated crude death rates are high, because of high fertility and large numbers of young people. However, populations in severely affected countries are projected to decline over time, as is evident in Botswana, where the estimated 2005 growth rate is negative. In addition, population growth rates in Namibia and Zambia for 2005 are estimated to be half or less of what they would have been without AIDS.

By 2015, in addition to Botswana and South Africa, Guyana and Namibia are projected to experience negative or zero population growth rates because of AIDS mortality compounded by lower fertility and international migration. Although Uganda and Kenya are only slightly affected by AIDS mortality in 2005, estimated growth rates for these two countries will no longer be slowed by AIDS by 2015.

As a direct consequence of lower population growth rates, populations will be much smaller in the future than they would have been in the absence of HIV/AIDS in many of the affected countries. Figure 1.14 shows population projections for Botswana, where the population is projected to decline in absolute terms by 12 percent between 2000 and 2050, and where the projected 2050 population is 67 percent lower than in a scenario with no AIDS; and Uganda, where the population in 2050 is projected to be 11 percent lower than in a scenario without AIDS.

Figure 1.14. Change in Population With and Without AIDS in Botswana and Uganda
(*Thousands*)

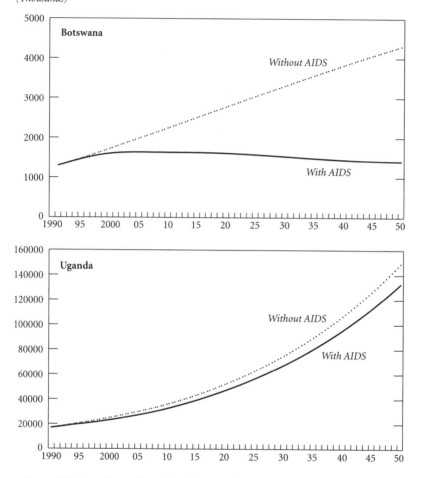

Source: U.S. Census Bureau, International Programs Center, HIV/AIDS Surveillance Data Base (2004) and unpublished tables.

Socioeconomic Aspects of Changes in the Population Structure

In countries with projected negative population growth, AIDS mortality is likely to produce population pyramids of a pattern never seen before. As mortality increases among 15- to 49-year-olds, the population structures of countries with high HIV prevalence are likely to change from the typical pyramid shape of a young and growing population to one more in the shape of a chimney. For example, in Botswana (Figure 1.15), men below the age of 20 and between the ages of 25 and 55 are likely to outnumber women in each of the 5-year age cohorts by 2025.

The socioeconomic implications of such a population chimney are not yet clear, but such a dramatic rise in adult mortality is sure to have profound and far-reaching effects. Most notable are the resulting increase in orphans and other vulnerable children, subsequent changes in household composition, a decrease in the labor force, and an increase in demand for and costs of social services.

Dependency Ratios

The estimated increase in mortality among adults may bring about a corresponding increase in the total dependency ratio, or the number of children and people of retirement age divided by the adult population available to support them. However, with infant and child mortality also increasing because of transmission from mother to child, a lower fertility rate for HIV-infected women, and a decline in the number of people reaching retirement age, this increase may not be as dramatic as one might expect.[8] Table 1.2 shows the change in the dependency ratio among the 15 countries selected for analysis. There is a small increase in the dependency ratio in the projections incorporating estimated AIDS mortality; however, there is also a decline in these ratios from 2005 to 2015.

The loss of support from an economically active adult can impose a great financial burden on the remaining members of the household, in addition to putting a strain on already weak health and social services systems. Studies conducted throughout the 1990s indicate that the death of an HIV-positive adult member of a household imposed more of a financial burden on the household than if the adult had died from another cause, that the household's consumption of basic necessities fell following the death of a member from AIDS, and that the death of an adult female had a stronger negative impact on household consumption than that of an adult male (Ainsworth, Fransen, and Over, 1998).

Parents of adults who are HIV-positive may have an unexpected financial burden to bear in addition to the physical and emotional trauma of

---

[8]Haacker (Chapter 2, this volume) attributes observed increases in dependency ratios to an increase in the ratio of the young population (ages 0–14) to the working-age population (ages 15–49) while the relative size of the old population declines, mitigating the increase in total dependency.

Figure 1.15. Population With and Without AIDS by Age and Sex in Botswana
(Thousands)

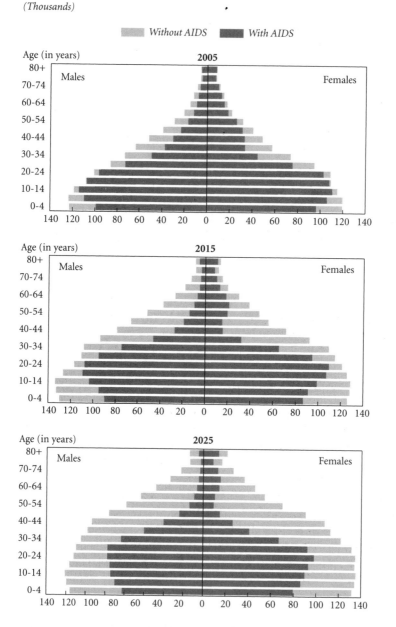

Source: U.S. Census Bureau, International Programs Center, HIV/AIDS Surveillance Data Base (2004) and unpublished tables.

Table 1.2. Projected Total Dependency Ratios for Selected Countries
(Dependent persons per 100 persons of working age)

	2005		Projected 2010	
Country	With AIDS	Without AIDS	With AIDS	Without AIDS
Botswana	74.0	66.7	62.0	54.6
Côte d'Ivoire	77.6	76.7	73.2	71.8
Ethiopia	87.4	86.9	77.2	76.4
Kenya	81.2	79.8	78.5	77.2
Mozambique	84.7	83.0	72.8	69.9
Namibia	73.3	70.6	56.7	54.6
Nigeria	83.1	82.4	82.1	81.1
Rwanda	80.2	79.6	80.5	78.9
South Africa	55.0	52.7	47.2	44.9
Tanzania	87.3	85.8	77.8	76.0
Uganda	109.7	107.8	104.2	101.2
Zambia	95.8	92.7	87.7	83.1
Guyana	46.1	45.7	45.7	44.9
Haiti	85.4	84.7	78.9	77.2
Vietnam	50.7	50.6	40.1	40.0

Sources: U.S. Census Bureau, International Programs Center, International Data Base (2004), and unpublished tables.

having to care for their ill children. They may have to assume the cost of providing material support during their offspring's illness, of paying for funerals, and of fostering grandchildren—all at an age when they would otherwise be expecting their adult children to take care of them.

Orphans and Vulnerable Children

What the dependency ratios mask is the impact of increasing numbers of children affected by AIDS. UNAIDS, the United Nations Children's Fund (UNICEF), and the U.S. Agency for International Development (USAID) estimate that, in 2003, 143 million children under the age of 18 in Africa, Asia, Latin America, and the Caribbean (8.4 percent of all children in those regions) were orphans, and that HIV/AIDS had created 15 million orphans (UNAIDS, UNICEF, and USAID, 2004).[9]

As Table 1.3 shows, these aggregates mask very substantial differences across regions and countries. Sub-Saharan Africa, the region worst affected by HIV/AIDS, has the largest share of orphans: its 43.4 million orphans in 2003 made up 12.3 percent of all children in the region; 12.3 million (28.3

---

[9]The recent estimates on orphans and vulnerable children affected by AIDS define an orphan as a child under the age of 18 who has lost at least one parent as a result of AIDS (UNAIDS, UNICEF, and USAID, 2004).

Table 1.3. Estimated Number of Orphans by Developing Region and in Selected Countries

Region/Country	2003 Orphans		2003 AIDS orphans		Orphans, Projected 2010	
	Thousands	Percent of all children	Thousands	Percent of all children	Thousands	Percent of all children
Sub-Saharan Africa	43,400	12.3	12,300	28.3	50,000[1]	12
Botswana	160	20.0	120	75.0	190	24
Côte d'Ivoire	940	13.4	310	33.0	1,000	13
Ethiopia	3,900	11.1	720	18.5	4,700	11
Kenya	1,700	11.3	650	38.2	1,900	11
Malawi	1,000	14.3	500	50.0	1,300	15
Mozambique	1,500	15.0	470	31.3	1,900	17
Namibia	120	12.0	57	47.5	180	18
Nigeria	7,000	10.1	1,800	25.7	8,200	10
Rwanda	810	16.2	160	19.8	800	14
South Africa	2,200	12.9	1,100	50.0	3,100	19
Tanzania	2,500	17.9	980	39.2	2,900	15
Uganda	2,000	11.1	940	47.0	1,900	11
Zambia	1,100	18.3	630	57.3	1,200	19
Zimbabwe	1,300	18.6	980	75.4	1,400	21
Asia[2]	87,600	7.3	...	...	80,100	7
Cambodia	670	9.6	...	...	690	9
Thailand	1,400	7.0	...	...	1,400	7
Vietnam	2,100	7.0	...	...	1,800	6
Latin America and Caribbean	12,400	6.2	...	...	12,000	6
Brazil	4,300	7.4	...	...	4,000	7
Haiti	610	15.3	...	...	560	13

Source: UNAIDS, UNICEF, and USAID (2004).
[1]Of which 36.8 percent are projected to be orphaned as a result of HIV/AIDS.
[2]Excluding the former Soviet Union.

percent) of these orphans were AIDS orphans. By 2010 the total number of orphans is projected to increase to 50 million (12.5 percent of all children), of whom 18.4 million (36.8 percent) will be AIDS orphans. In 7 of the 14 African countries in Table 1.3, half or more of all orphans are AIDS orphans. In countries with high HIV prevalence such as Botswana and Zimbabwe, three-quarters of all orphans are AIDS orphans. But a lower estimated adult HIV prevalence does not necessarily translate into less of an impact on children. Ethiopia, Kenya, Rwanda, and Uganda all have estimated adult HIV prevalence between 4 percent and 7 percent. Nearly half of all Uganda's orphans, and over a third of Kenya's orphans, are AIDS orphans, compared with one-fifth in Rwanda and Ethiopia.

Table 1.3 also reports estimates and projections of the numbers of orphans in Asia and Latin America. Countries in Asia have much lower estimated adult HIV prevalence, yet because of its large population this region has the largest number of orphans. As of 2003, although only 7.3 percent of all children in Asia were orphans, their number amounted to 87.6 million. This region also has younger epidemics, which have the potential to expand rapidly throughout the population. For example, Vietnam has an epidemic concentrated mainly among injecting drug users and sex workers; estimated adult HIV prevalence was below 1 percent in 2003 (UNAIDS, 2004a). With orphans already estimated to number over 2 million, a modest increase in HIV prevalence could increase this number dramatically.

AIDS has such a great impact on the number of orphans and vulnerable children because it so often creates double orphans—if one parent succumbs to AIDS, it is very likely that the other parent will as well. Frequently, orphans are taken care of by extended family; yet AIDS is not just killing parents, but aunts and uncles also. Often grandparents are raising their grandchildren, or orphaned children are themselves assuming the role of head of household. According to recent DHS data on household composition, one-fifth to one-quarter of households in Rwanda, Tanzania, Uganda, Zambia, and Zimbabwe are fostering children. And, in Tanzania and Zimbabwe, the percentage of children under 18 who have lost one or both parents is projected to increase over the next 10 years (UNAIDS, UNICEF, and USAID, 2004). Orphans tend to live in households with lower income per capita and may have impaired access to education: UNICEF (2003) estimates that, in sub-Saharan Africa, median dependency ratios are 20 percent higher in orphan households than in nonorphan households, and that school enrollment rates for orphans are 13 percent lower than for nonorphans.

Children under 5 who are orphaned by AIDS are at risk of dying from AIDS themselves—as noted above, without intervention approximately a third of children born to HIV-positive mothers will be infected either at birth or through breastfeeding. But many more children are vulnerable to the effects of the large number of adults dying from AIDS around them. These children will be living with and caring for one or both sick and dying parents, or living in a household that has taken in one or more orphans. Girls especially may have to cut short their education in order to support the rest of the family. Providing enough food will become an increasing problem for rural households, if there is no longer anyone to cultivate the family crops.

Labor Force

As Figure 1.3 showed, the bulk of HIV infections are occurring among young adults, those just entering the workforce. Unless they receive treat-

Table 1.4. Life Expectancy at Age 15 by Sex, With and Without AIDS, in Selected Countries
(Years)

Country	2005				Projected 2015			
	Male		Female		Male		Female	
	Without AIDS	With AIDS	Without AIDS	With AIDS	Without AIDS	With AIDS	Without AIDS	With AIDS
Botswana	60.6	23.5	64.9	23.2	63.4	24.7	67.6	24.1
Côte d'Ivoire	47.6	41.5	53.1	43.9	49.3	42.0	55.4	44.4
Ethiopia	47.5	43.3	50.5	44.9	49.1	43.8	52.7	45.3
Kenya	48.6	40.4	49.4	38.6	50.8	48.7	52.2	49.3
Mozambique	46.4	36.1	48.9	36.5	48.1	33.6	51.1	31.5
Namibia	56.3	34.8	60.0	32.4	58.0	36.2	62.2	32.6
Nigeria	49.6	44.0	52.4	44.4	50.7	45.2	54.0	46.3
Rwanda	48.1	42.8	51.0	44.1	49.6	44.5	53.0	46.1
South Africa	53.1	34.5	60.0	33.6	54.9	36.3	61.5	33.6
Tanzania	48.4	39.3	51.6	39.5	50.1	41.3	53.9	42.0
Uganda	50.9	44.7	54.0	45.7	52.5	49.4	56.1	52.1
Zambia	49.6	34.0	53.1	33.4	51.2	35.8	55.2	34.6
Guyana	54.9	51.7	61.3	56.5	56.8	53.6	63.4	58.0
Haiti	50.9	44.1	54.4	46.1	52.7	46.1	56.8	48.0
Vietnam	56.8	55.9	62.3	61.9	58.6	57.7	64.1	63.4

Source: U.S. Census Bureau, International Programs Center, International Data Base (2004) and unpublished tables.

ment, those who become infected today are expected to become ill and die within 10 years. At current estimates, life expectancy for those just reaching maturity is expected to decrease significantly in many countries struggling with an overwhelming HIV/AIDS epidemic. For several high-prevalence countries in Africa, as Table 1.4 details, in 2005 those aged 15 years are only expected to live another 25 to 35 years.

The rise in mortality among adults in their prime productive and reproductive years has implications for the labor force, and not just as a reduction in numbers, but also in terms of the structure of the working-age population. As detailed in Figure 1.15, the age pyramid will narrow as mortality, especially for the working-age population, increases and, as a consequence, fewer people live to an advanced age. This means that the pool of more experienced individuals, those who would qualify for leading positions in society and the economy, shrinks. Higher mortality causes increased attrition rates, disrupting economic processes and imposing additional costs on producers, through higher medical and death-related benefits and higher training costs associated with the replacement of staff. Long before an HIV-positive individual enters the last stage of the illness and finally dies, his or her well-being and health become impaired, and the infected person increasingly requires medical attention and home care. This rise in morbidity results in an increase in sick leave and absenteeism, as well as declining productivity on the job. At the household level, the sickness of a breadwinner reduces income and wealth, and other household members have to divert time from productive activities or education to provide care. As the expected remaining working time of the average worker declines, the expected returns on investments in training decline, with possible implications for the accumulation of human capital.

Conclusions

Twenty years ago, few would have predicted the current state of the HIV/AIDS pandemic. As the world enters a third decade with high HIV prevalence rates in many countries and the likelihood of an effective vaccine, or even widespread availability of therapeutic medication, still low, many millions more are likely to die from AIDS than have died already over the past two decades. This fact, together with increasing stress on health infrastructures and lack of institutional supports for social services, means that poor countries are likely to be under enormous strain as they attempt to cope with the consequences of AIDS morbidity and mortality—not to mention the burden future generations will likely have to bear in dealing with the pandemic.

In addition to the psychological and social strain, the increase in HIV infections and AIDS deaths among adults in their prime has implications for the public financing of services for the older population, from health care to pensions to welfare. Instead of contributing to these measures, the increase in the number of adults affected by HIV/AIDS will reduce the resources available and increase competition for these services.

Some countries in southern Africa are just beginning to experience the effects of high AIDS mortality. In many other countries the epidemic is poised to explode. Although Senegal, Thailand, and Uganda are notable success stories, that success is due to concerted efforts at all levels of society. And although HIV/AIDS prevalence in Asia has not approached that seen in some countries in Africa, the large populations of some of these countries suggest that the sheer numbers of HIV infections and of AIDS deaths could become overwhelming. Hence the current burden of disease, death, and orphanhood is likely to be a problem in many countries around the world for the foreseeable future.

Appendix: Impact of HIV/AIDS on Demographic and Mortality Indicators

Table 1.A1. Impact of HIV/AIDS on Demographic Characteristics of Selected Countries, 2005 and Projected 2015

Country and Year	Population Growth Rate (percent a year)		Crude Death Rate (deaths per 1,000 persons)		Life Expectancy at Birth (years)		Infant Mortality Rate (deaths per 1,000 live births)		Under-5 Mortality Rate (deaths per 1,000 persons)		Total Fertility Rate[1]
	With AIDS	Without AIDS	With AIDS	Without AIDS	With AIDS	Without AIDS	With AIDS	Without AIDS	With AIDS	Without AIDS	
2005											
Botswana	—	2.6	29.4	3.5	33.9	76.1	54.6	14.4	87.2	18.1	2.8
Côte d'Ivoire	2.1	2.5	14.9	11.0	48.6	56.1	90.8	83.8	138.2	126.8	4.6
Ethiopia	2.4	2.6	15.1	12.7	48.8	53.5	95.3	90.6	154.1	146.6	5.3
Kenya	2.6	3.1	14.7	9.8	48.0	57.5	61.5	55.9	91.6	81.0	5.0
Mozambique	1.5	2.2	21.0	13.9	40.3	50.9	130.8	116.0	190.9	168.1	4.7
Namibia	0.7	2.2	18.4	4.9	43.9	70.3	49.0	23.2	78.3	34.0	3.2
Nigeria	2.4	2.7	17.2	13.9	46.7	52.9	98.8	93.4	191.5	182.9	5.5
Rwanda	2.4	2.7	16.3	13.3	47.0	52.7	91.2	85.8	163.5	154.7	5.5
South Africa	−0.3	1.2	21.3	7.2	43.3	67.0	61.8	36.7	99.4	56.9	2.2
Tanzania	1.8	2.4	16.7	11.3	45.2	55.5	98.5	89.9	145.5	131.1	5.1
Uganda	3.3	3.5	12.8	10.0	51.6	58.7	67.8	64.6	114.7	108.8	6.7
Zambia	2.1	3.0	20.2	10.9	39.7	56.6	88.3	72.0	149.9	123.3	5.5
Guyana	0.3	0.5	8.3	6.4	65.5	69.9	33.3	30.3	44.5	39.4	2.1
Haiti	2.3	2.6	12.3	9.1	52.9	60.6	73.5	67.5	102.6	92.7	5.0
Vietnam	1.0	1.1	6.2	6.0	70.6	71.2	26.0	25.6	35.8	35.3	1.9
Projected 2015											
Botswana	−0.1	2.1	29.0	3.0	34.7	79.6	52.0	8.1	84.2	9.7	2.3
Côte d'Ivoire	1.7	2.1	13.9	9.2	50.7	60.1	74.0	66.2	110.1	97.1	3.8
Ethiopia	1.9	2.2	13.2	10.2	51.2	57.5	78.4	73.0	122.9	113.9	4.2
Kenya	1.8	1.8	8.5	7.5	58.8	61.4	44.6	43.6	63.2	61.3	3.3
Mozambique	0.9	2.0	22.4	11.6	38.5	54.9	111.6	94.3	162.6	134.0	3.9
Namibia	—	1.4	19.0	4.6	44.6	73.1	43.5	16.9	68.7	23.3	2.2
Nigeria	2.4	2.7	14.7	11.5	50.3	56.7	83.2	77.8	153.9	145.1	5.1
Rwanda	2.2	2.5	13.7	10.8	50.8	56.7	75.6	70.7	130.3	122.0	4.9
South Africa	−0.5	1.0	22.1	7.2	44.5	70.1	50.9	26.0	80.0	37.6	1.9
Tanzania	1.9	2.4	14.3	9.1	48.9	59.5	79.8	70.8	115.5	100.5	4.2
Uganda	3.7	3.7	9.1	8.0	58.9	62.5	53.3	51.2	85.6	82.0	6.4
Zambia	1.9	2.7	17.9	8.7	42.5	60.6	74.4	57.7	122.0	94.3	4.7
Guyana	−0.1	0.2	8.5	6.6	68.0	72.7	25.1	21.8	33.2	27.5	2.0
Haiti	2.3	2.6	10.6	7.3	56.3	64.4	56.9	50.9	78.3	68.1	4.2
Vietnam	0.9	1.0	6.2	5.8	73.2	74.0	19.0	18.5	25.2	24.5	1.8

Source: U.S. Census Bureau, International Programs Center, International Data Base (2004) and unpublished tables.

[1]The number of children a woman would have in her lifetime if she were to live to the end of her child-bearing years and bore children in accordance with current age-specific fertility rates.

Table 1.A2. Impact of HIV/AIDS on Adult Mortality Indicators in Selected Countries, 2005 and Projected 2015[1]

Country and Year	Adult Deaths (percent of all deaths)		Adult Crude Death Rate (deaths per 1,000 adults)						Ratio of Male to Female Adult Deaths	
			All adults		Males		Females			
	With AIDS	Without AIDS	With AIDS	Without AIDS	With AIDS	Without AIDS	With AIDS	Without AIDS	With AIDS	Without AIDS
2005										
Botswana	68	21	38.6	1.4	37.3	1.8	39.9	1.0	0.9	1.8
Côte d'Ivoire	36	24	11.0	5.3	11.0	6.4	11.0	4.2	1.0	1.5
Ethiopia	30	22	9.6	6.0	9.5	6.5	9.8	5.6	1.0	1.2
Kenya	44	30	13.1	6.0	11.2	5.8	14.9	6.2	0.8	0.9
Mozambique	40	23	17.8	6.9	16.9	7.3	18.7	6.5	0.9	1.1
Namibia	58	20	21.3	1.9	18.2	2.2	24.6	1.5	0.8	1.5
Nigeria	27	17	9.8	4.9	9.2	5.4	10.5	4.5	0.9	1.2
Rwanda	32	23	10.5	6.2	10.4	6.8	10.6	5.5	1.0	1.2
South Africa	56	21	22.0	2.8	19.7	3.7	24.2	1.8	0.8	2.0
Tanzania	38	22	13.4	5.3	12.4	5.8	14.4	4.9	0.9	1.2
Uganda	30	20	8.8	4.7	8.5	5.3	9.1	4.1	1.0	1.3
Zambia	44	22	19.2	5.2	17.5	5.8	20.9	4.5	0.9	1.3
Guyana	34	21	8.8	4.0	8.5	4.5	9.1	3.6	0.9	1.2
Haiti	22	19	2.3	2.0	3.0	2.5	1.7	1.5	1.8	1.7
Vietnam	34	22	4.9	2.4	5.0	3.1	4.7	1.8	1.1	1.8
Projected 2015										
Botswana	71	18	36.8	1.0	34.9	1.3	38.8	0.7	1.0	2.0
Côte d'Ivoire	42	25	11.4	4.6	11.3	5.8	11.5	3.4	1.0	1.6
Ethiopia	36	25	9.6	5.1	9.3	5.6	9.8	4.5	1.0	1.2
Kenya	37	32	6.3	4.9	6.0	4.9	6.7	4.9	0.9	1.0
Mozambique	48	25	21.1	5.8	18.6	6.3	23.6	5.3	0.8	1.2
Namibia	60	19	20.5	1.6	16.9	1.9	24.4	1.2	0.8	1.6
Nigeria	29	18	9.0	4.3	8.6	4.9	9.4	3.8	1.0	1.3
Rwanda	34	24	9.7	5.3	9.6	6.0	9.9	4.6	1.0	1.3
South Africa	54	19	21.3	2.4	17.9	3.2	24.9	1.6	0.8	2.0
Tanzania	43	25	12.1	4.5	11.3	5.1	13.0	3.9	0.9	1.3
Uganda	28	21	5.8	3.8	6.0	4.5	5.5	3.2	1.1	1.4
Zambia	50	24	18.4	4.4	16.6	5.1	20.4	3.6	0.9	1.4
Guyana	39	23	8.3	3.3	8.0	3.9	8.7	2.8	0.9	1.4
Haiti	31	18	4.8	2.2	4.8	2.8	4.8	1.5	1.1	1.9
Vietnam	20	17	2.1	1.7	2.7	2.1	1.6	1.2	1.8	1.9

Source: U.S. Census Bureau, International Programs Center, International Data Base (2004) and unpublished tables.

[1] Adults are defined as persons aged 15–49.

References

Ainsworth, Martha, Lieve Fransen, and Mead Over, eds., 1998, *Confronting AIDS: Evidence from the Developing World* (Washington: World Bank).

European Centre for the Epidemiological Monitoring of AIDS, 2003, "HIV/AIDS Surveillance in Europe, End-Year Report 2002" (Saint-Maurice, France: Institut de Veille Sanitaire).

Joint United Nations Programme on HIV/AIDS (UNAIDS), 2003, "AIDS Epidemic Update: December 2003" (Geneva).

———, 2004a, *Report on the Global AIDS Epidemic 2004* (Geneva).

———, 2004b, "Women in Mekon Region Faced With Higher Rates of HIV Infection Than Men" (Geneva).

———, United Nations Children's Fund (UNICEF), and U.S. Agency for International Development (USAID), 2004, "Children on the Brink 2004: A Joint Report of New Orphan Estimates and a Framework for Action" (Geneva, New York, and Washington).

MAP Network, 2001, "Monitoring the AIDS Pandemic: The Status and Trends of HIV/AIDS/STI Epidemics in Asia and the Pacific" (Washington: MAP Secretariat, International Programs Center, Population Division, U.S. Census Bureau).

Niambele, I., and others, 2001, "First Successful Integration of HIV Biomarkers into a National Demographic and Health Survey (DHS+) in Mali, West Africa," presented at the XIIth International Conference on AIDS and STD in Africa, Ouagadougou, Burkina Faso, December 9–13.

Schuettler, Darren, 2003, "Asia Leaders Ignore Looming AIDS Crisis—UN Envoy," Reuters, CDC HIV/STD/TB Prevention News Update 09/02/03.

Shisana, Olive, and Leickness Simbayi, 2002, *Nelson Mandela/HSRC Study of HIV/AIDS, South African National HIV Prevalence, Behavioural Risks and Mass Media: Household Survey* (Cape Town, South Africa: Human Sciences Research Council).

Urassa, M., and others, 2002, "Continuing Spread of HIV in Rural Tanzania: Prevalence and Incidence Trends in Kisesa during 1994–2000," presented at the XIV International AIDS Conference, Barcelona, Spain, July 7–12.

U.S. Census Bureau, International Programs Center, 2000, "Country Profiles." Available via the Internet: at www.census.gov/ipc/www/hivctry.html.

———, 2004, HIV/AIDS Surveillance Data Base (Washington).

———, 2004, International Data Base (Washington). Available via the Internet: www.census.gov/ipc/www/idbnew.html.

United Nations Children's Fund, 2003, "Africa's Orphaned Generations" (New York).

Way, Peter O., and Karen A. Stanecki, 1994, "The Impact of HIV/AIDS on World Population" (Washington: U.S. Census Bureau).

World Health Organization, 2004, *The World Health Report 2004—Changing History* (Geneva).

Zambia Central Statistical Office and Central Board of Health, 2002, "Zambia Demographic and Health Survey 2001–2002 Preliminary Report" (Calverton, Maryland: ORC Macro).

2

HIV/AIDS: The Impact on the Social Fabric and the Economy

Markus Haacker

In many countries, the HIV/AIDS epidemic has attained a scale at which the impact on the economy and, even more broadly, on societies, is both evident and very serious. Through its broad economic impact, HIV/AIDS thus becomes an issue for macroeconomic analysis, and policies to prevent the spread of the virus have direct implications for key economic indicators such as economic growth and income per capita,[1] and for economic development more generally. However, because the impact is very uneven across individuals or households, an analysis that captures only the main aggregate economic variables would miss many of the microeconomic effects of HIV/AIDS on living standards, which also matter for public policy and which, in turn, affect the main aggregate economic variables, for example through the accumulation of physical and human capital.

To start with the most obvious effect, increased mortality means that the economy is left with fewer workers, both in total and across different occupations and skill levels. As private employees and public servants fall ill and eventually die, the efficiency of production or administrative processes is diminished. On the consumer side, households can seldom fully compensate for the loss of a breadwinner; as a result, poverty rises and children's access to education deteriorates. In the longer run

---

[1]This point is discussed in much more detail by Masha (Chapter 9, this volume).

HIV/AIDS affects the accumulation not only of human capital but of physical capital as well. For example, as expenditure is shifted toward HIV/AIDS-related activities, aggregate saving is likely to decline, leaving fewer resources available for investment; at the same time, increased production costs and deteriorating economic prospects make investment in the affected countries less attractive. Through increased mortality and its economic repercussions, HIV/AIDS also increases economic risk, and this, too, contributes to a deterioration in welfare.

This chapter discusses the available evidence from studies on the macroeconomic impact of HIV/AIDS. The key concept that connects the various strands of analysis is this: *HIV/AIDS affects the economy and economic development through its adverse impact on the social fabric itself.* Here the term "social fabric" extends not only to the social and economic institutions already noted—households, companies, and the government—but also to more abstract concepts such as governance and social coherence. HIV/AIDS does have a serious impact on traditional economic measures such as economic growth, income per capita, and investment, but it does so by affecting very diverse areas of public, social, and economic life. To understand all the macroeconomic repercussions, the economic analyst thus needs to cast the net very widely.

This chapter will pursue three lines of inquiry. The first proceeds from the bottom up, focusing on the impact of HIV/AIDS on different social and economic institutions and highlighting its macroeconomic consequences. The second, in contrast, takes a bird's-eye perspective, addressing how HIV/AIDS, through its microeconomic impacts, affects typical macroeconomic variables, and reviewing how this is captured in various models of economic growth. The third, drawing on the first two, analyzes how HIV/AIDS, both directly and through its impact on social and economic institutions, affects poverty, inequality, individual risk, and welfare.

Impact of HIV/AIDS on Social and Economic Institutions

HIV/AIDS affects an economy primarily through increased mortality and morbidity. To capture the impact of increased mortality at all levels and across all sectors, this chapter uses the term "social and economic institutions." This term covers not only households and extended families, small and large enterprises, and local public services and the central government, but also more abstract concepts such as the strength of the legal system and of property rights.

Figure 2.1. Mortality Rates by Age and Sex in Zambia, 2004
(Percent)

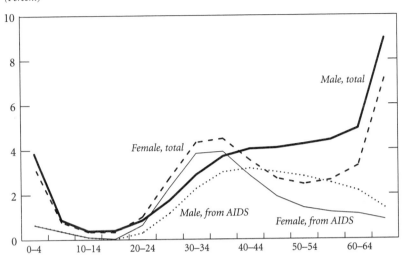

Source: International Programs Center, U.S. Census Bureau.

Increased Mortality

Figure 2.1 illustrates the impact of HIV/AIDS on mortality rates by age and sex for Zambia in 2004, where it is estimated that HIV/AIDS has raised the mortality rate for the population aged 15–49 almost fourfold, from 0.5 percent annually to 1.9 percent. For the entire population, mortality has increased from 1.0 percent to 2.1 percent, making HIV/AIDS the leading cause of death. Just as striking, Figure 2.1 shows that, in Zambia (as in the other countries in the region), AIDS-related mortality affects women to a greater extent and at an earlier age than men, because females on average begin sexual activity at an earlier age and because the risk of transmission of the virus is greater from male to female than from female to male. Among Zambian women, mortality rates from all causes peaked at 4.5 percent for the cohort aged 35–39, and 87 percent of these deaths (3.9 percent in absolute terms) were accounted for by HIV/AIDS. Among working-age men, mortality from HIV/AIDS-related causes peaks for the cohort aged 40–44 (at 3.1 percent, or 78 percent of deaths in this cohort); overall mortality for men then increases by cohort, as increasing deaths from other causes more than offset the decline in HIV/AIDS-related mortality with age.

Table 2.1. Impact of HIV/AIDS on Mortality and Life Expectancy in Selected Countries
(Percent except where stated otherwise)

Country	HIV Prevalence Rate, Ages 15–49, End-2003[1]	Mortality, All Ages, 2004		Mortality, Ages 15–49, 2004		Mortality, Ages 15–49, Projected 2010		Life Expectancy at Birth (years)	
		Total	From AIDS	Total	From AIDS	Total	From AIDS	Actual	Without AIDS
Botswana	37.3	2.9	2.5	3.8	3.7	3.6	3.5	34.2	75.7
Côte d'Ivoire	7.0	1.5	0.4	1.1	0.6	1.1	0.7	48.4	55.7
Ethiopia	4.4	1.5	0.2	1.0	0.4	1.0	0.4	48.7	53.1
Haiti	5.6	1.3	0.3	0.9	0.5	0.9	0.5	52.6	60.2
South Africa	21.5	2.9	2.5	2.3	2.0	2.1	1.9	44.1	66.7
Vietnam	0.4	0.6	0.02	0.2	0.03	0.2	0.04	70.4	70.9
Zambia	16.5	2.1	1.0	1.9	1.4	1.9	1.4	39.4	56.2

Sources: Joint United Nations Programme on HIV/AIDS (2004); U.S. Census Bureau, International Programs Center, International Data Base (2004) and unpublished tables.
[1]Data refer to the population aged 15–49.

Table 2.1 illustrates the catastrophic impact of HIV/AIDS in countries around the world where it is widely prevalent.[2] In Botswana, South Africa, and Zambia, AIDS is the leading cause of death; mortality rates for the 15–49 age group in these countries have increased dramatically. As a consequence, life expectancy at birth has declined dramatically: for some of the worst-affected countries covered in Table 2.1, it declined by 20 years or more from what it would have been in the absence of AIDS. The table also shows the severe impact of HIV/AIDS in countries with more "moderate" HIV epidemics. For example, in Ethiopia, with an estimated adult HIV prevalence rate of 4.4 percent, overall mortality has increased by 18 percent, mortality among the working-age population has risen by over 50 percent, and life expectancy at birth has declined by 4.5 years.

The demographic impact of HIV/AIDS, through increased mortality and reduced birthrates, is discussed in more detail elsewhere (see, for instance, Epstein, Chapter 1 of this volume). Some of its aspects, such as the increased numbers of orphans, changes in dependency rates, and changes in the composition of the working-age population, will be taken up below in the context of the impact of HIV/AIDS on social and economic institutions.

---

[2]The prevalence rate most frequently quoted is that for the age group 15–49. This rate is often (and somewhat imprecisely) referred to as the adult prevalence rate, or the prevalence rate for the working-age population. It is important to recognize that this rate is an average over age groups with very different prevalence rates. The proportion of the population that eventually dies of AIDS is usually closer to the prevalence rate for the worst-affected age group (which, however, does not include the members of this cohort who died earlier or will get infected later).

Households and Extended Families

HIV/AIDS has profound effects on the economic situation of those households it afflicts.[3] Income declines as breadwinners fall ill and die and as other household members are obliged to take time off from other productive activities to care for sick relatives. At the same time, households have to reallocate their spending to devote a much greater share to health care, including not only drugs and doctors' fees but also supplies for home care. The impact of HIV/AIDS also extends beyond those households directly affected, to the many other households who intervene to provide them with support. When a household affected by HIV/AIDS dissolves, members of the extended family frequently take care of the surviving children. The loss of a household member can have long-term effects on the well-being of other members, through the costs of treatment and, especially, if children have to take time off from school for financial reasons or to care for sick relatives.

Beyond this very general description of the impact of HIV/AIDS, it is important to acknowledge that the ability of a household to cope with the illness or death of a member depends on the afflicted person's status within the household. To the extent that HIV/AIDS raises mortality among very young adults (Figure 2.1), it is less likely to strike a primary income earner or head of household. The impact also depends on the household's socioeconomic characteristics. Households with low income or few assets may be in a worse position to cope with the income and expenditure shocks associated with HIV/AIDS; small farm households, because of their different economic structure and access to social support, may be affected by and respond to HIV/AIDS differently than urban households (especially those drawing their income from the formal sector). More generally, the structure of the household need not be fixed: following the death of a household member, others in the household may leave (or, in the case of orphans, be taken in by other relatives), or the household may dissolve entirely. At the same time, other people may join the household and take on the role left vacant by the deceased household member.

The aggregate demographic indicators reported in Table 2.2 provide some information on how HIV/AIDS affects households. The total dependency ratio increases, mainly because the increase in deaths among the

---

[3]For a thorough review of the literature up to 2000, see Booysen and Arntz (2001). A more current (but much shorter) discussion is included in Joint United Nations Programme on HIV/AIDS (2004, pp. 41–51).

Table 2.2. Impact of HIV/AIDS on Dependency Ratios and Orphanhood in Selected Countries
(Percent)

Country	Adult HIV Prevalence Rate, End of 2003	Dependency Ratios, 2004						Orphans as Share of Population Aged 17 and Under		
		Total[1]		Child[2]		Old-age[3]		2003		Projected, 2010 (total)
		Actual	Without AIDS	Actual	Without AIDS	Actual	Without AIDS	Total	Due to AIDS	
Botswana	37.3	95.6	88.7	76.6	69.7	19.1	19.7	20.0	15.0	24
Côte d'Ivoire	7.0	105.5	105.4	84.6	84.0	20.9	21.4	13.4	4.4	13
Ethiopia	4.4	115.3	115.0	95.1	94.6	20.3	20.4	11.1	2.1	11
Haiti	5.6	111.7	112.4	90.9	90.7	20.8	21.7	15.3	...	13
South Africa	21.5	85.4	82.9	57.3	55.2	28.1	27.7	12.9	4.5	19
Vietnam	0.4	74.3	74.2	50.2	50.1	24.1	24.1	7.0	...	7
Zambia	16.5	113.8	116.6	100.8	100.8	13.0	15.8	18.3	10.5	19

Sources: UNAIDS (2004); UNAIDS, UNICEF, and USAID (2004); and author's calculations based on data provided by the International Programs Center, U.S. Census Bureau.
[1]Sum of child and old-age dependency ratios; numbers may not sum to totals because of rounding.
[2]Ages 0–14.
[3]Ages 50 and over.

working-age population raises the relative size of the young population, as reflected in the child dependency ratio.[4] The increase in child dependency is closely related to the fact that the number of orphans increases as their parents succumb to HIV/AIDS. For Botswana and Zambia, a rough estimate is that 20 percent of the population aged 17 or younger are orphans, and the majority of these orphans (77 percent in Botswana, 60 percent in Zambia) were orphaned by HIV/AIDS. The pattern regarding old-age dependency is inconclusive at first blush, likely reflecting several effects working in different directions. In the early stages of the epidemic, old-age dependency may increase, because the disease predominantly kills young people. But as these younger cohorts decimated by HIV/AIDS themselves attain old age, this effect is reversed.

HIV/AIDS affects the income of the affected households not only through the sickness and death of household members, but also as the time previously devoted to income-generating activities by other household members must be reallocated to the care of the sick member. The impact of HIV/AIDS on the income of an affected worker depends on the

---

[4]The total dependency ratio is defined as the sum of the population aged 14 or less (P_{0-14}) and the population aged 50 or more (P_{50+}) divided by the working-age population (P_{15-49}), or $(P_{0-14} + P_{50+})/P_{15-49}$.

source of that income. If the worker is self-employed or is paid according to his or her productivity (for example, a tea picker), income declines immediately as the worker's health (and thus productivity) starts to deteriorate. If instead the worker receives a fixed salary (as is typical in the public sector and parts of the private formal sector), the income loss is not directly tied to the decline in productivity, and, as absenteeism increases, the loss is mitigated through sick leave and, possibly, a disability pension.

In assessing the impact of HIV/AIDS on income, it is useful to distinguish between time lost from work (absenteeism) and declining productivity on the job. There is substantial evidence that both time at work and productivity decline well before a worker dies or retires because of ill health. In one South African sugar mill, about 10 percent, on average, of a sick employee's working time was lost in the two years before the worker retired (Morris and Cheevers, 2000). According to Fox and others (2004), tea pickers on an estate in Kenya who retired or died from AIDS-related causes earned 16 percent less in their penultimate year at work, and 17.7 percent less in the final year. Notably, there was also a substantial increase in the number of days these employees spent on light duty.

The household's living standard also deteriorates as other household members have to reallocate time from other productive activities (not necessarily income-generating) in order to care for a sick relative. In this regard, Steinberg and others (2002), using data from a survey of 771 AIDS-affected households in different parts of South Africa, find that over two-thirds of caregivers are women. Twenty-two percent of caregivers had to take time off from work and other income-generating activities, 20 percent had to forgo school or study time, and 60 percent took time from other housework and gardening activities.

The most comprehensive study of the impact of adult mortality on rural households, that by Mather and others (2004), synthesizes studies from five countries: Kenya, Malawi, Mozambique, Rwanda, and Zambia.[5] Their findings include the following. First, HIV infection does not seem to be correlated with relative income or education.[6] Second, among women, those most severely affected by the deaths of other prime-age adults in a household are young dependents, not wives or female heads of house-

---

[5]The sample size ranges from 420 (Malawi) to 6,922 (Zambia), the data take the form of panel data (Kenya and Malawi) or cross sections with recall surveys, and the time frames of the surveys range from 4 years (1999–2002 in Mozambique and Rwanda) to 13 years (1990–2002 in Malawi).

[6]The study makes inferences on the impact of HIV/AIDS (as opposed to other causes of mortality) based on the incidence of prime-age adult mortality.

holds. Third, households affected by adult deaths do not uniformly have less available prime-age labor than nonaffected households—a finding that may reflect the ability of those households to attract new members. Fourth, the death of a male household head is associated with a larger decline in crop production and nonfarm income than the death of any other type of household member. Yamano and Jayne (2004), whose study is one of those covered by Mather and others (2004), find that the impact of adult mortality on households is related to household wealth. Splitting their sample in half based on initial asset levels, they "find negative impacts on the net value of crop production, assets, and off-farm income only in the case of male head-of-household mortality among relatively poor households." This study also finds that the death of a male household head (aged 16–59) "is associated with a 68 percent reduction in the net value of the household's crop production," and that female adult mortality is associated with an adverse effect on grain crops, whereas male adult mortality has a stronger effect on cash crops such as coffee, tea, and sugar.

HIV/AIDS results in increased demand for health-related goods and services. Because household income tends to shrink at the same time this demand is rising, the household is forced to cut other expenditures or sell some of its assets. Steinberg and others (2002) find that households affected by HIV/AIDS spend about one-third of their income on health care, compared with a national average of 4 percent. Other categories of expenditures are cut correspondingly, most notably clothing and electricity. This finding is consistent with an earlier World Bank study, which found that households affected by HIV/AIDS lowered their overall expenditures, but that the share of medical expenditure in the total rose (World Bank, 1999). One important part of HIV/AIDS-related expenditure is the cost of funerals. Steinberg and others (2002) suggest that funeral expenses are, on average, equivalent to four months' salary. Naidu (2003) reports that the average cost of a funeral for low-income households in Soweto, South Africa, was about 9,000 rand (about $1,400), or 3.5 times the average monthly household income.[7] Over 30 percent of funeral costs were paid from household savings, and 40 percent "from family and friends"; only 10 percent of the sampled households had some form of funeral insurance.

Although households directly affected by HIV/AIDS bear the brunt of the economic costs, these costs can be mitigated by various forms of formal and informal insurance provided through the private sector, the public sector, or the extended family and local community. Workers in the formal sec-

---

[7]Quoted in the *Sunday Times* (South Africa), August 31, 2003.

tor may have access to private insurance that provides medical and death-related benefits; in most countries separate insurance schemes exist for public servants. However, the coverage of such formal insurance schemes is generally quite low: in most countries in sub-Saharan Africa, for example, fewer than 10 percent of the working-age population are covered.[8] Moreover, these formal insurance schemes come under strain as HIV/AIDS becomes widespread. For the population not covered by formal insurance schemes, the public sector can provide some forms of social security. In the context of HIV/AIDS, the most important form of such implicit insurance is public health services. Other forms of social security provided through the public sector are destitution allowances and (particularly relevant here) orphan allowances (see, for example, Botswana Institute for Development Policy Analysis (BIDPA), 2000) and disability grants. One example of the potential role of grants comes from the study of the impact of HIV/AIDS on urban households in Soweto, mentioned above (Naidu, 2003). That study finds that income in households affected by HIV/AIDS was, on average, 8 percent lower than in households not affected, but that earned income was 27 percent lower; the loss of earned income was to some extent offset by higher receipts of disability grants and pensions.

Where insurance through the private or public sector is insufficient or not available, the extended family or the community can provide some form of informal insurance. As previously noted, when households affected by HIV/AIDS dissolve, other households often take in orphans who have lost one or both parents. Rugalema (1999) reports on the impact of HIV/AIDS in the Bukoba district of Tanzania; there, in addition to the 32 percent of households directly affected by HIV/AIDS, a further 29 percent experienced indirect effects, including "fostering orphans, providing labor or cash to help care for the sick person, and providing for survivors."[9] And, as noted above, friends and family covered about 40 percent of funeral expenses in Soweto, according to Naidu (2003).

The data in Table 2.2 point to a very substantial increase in the number of orphans. In Zimbabwe, for example, orphans (defined as children who have lost at least one parent) are estimated to have accounted for 18.6 percent of the young population at the end of 2003; this share is projected to increase to 21 percent by 2010. It is important to note that these shares are averages and that the share of orphaned children increases with age. For

---

[8]See Barbone and Sanchez (1999) for a broad survey of pensions and social security systems in sub-Saharan Africa, and Plamondon, Cichon, and Annycke (Chapter 8, this volume) on social security in the context of HIV/AIDS.

[9]Quoted in Whiteside (2002).

those aged 10–14 (by some accounts a group whose access to education is particularly at risk), the share of orphans is likely to be higher than the average.

The loss of one or both parents to HIV/AIDS affects the well-being of their orphaned children directly, but it also has important economic repercussions. As households affected by HIV/AIDS lose income and have to reallocate resources toward care, children are at higher risk of malnutrition. The loss of a loving parent, the increased financial hardship, and the frequent need to take time off from school to care for a sick family member cause their education and thus their economic prospects to suffer. During the parent's illness and after his or her death, members of the extended family frequently care for the children of the family. Case, Paxson, and Ableidinger (2002), using data from 19 Demographic and Health Surveys conducted in 10 countries in sub-Saharan Africa between 1992 and 2000, show that orphans tend to live in poorer households than nonorphans and that school enrollment rates for orphans tend to be lower than for nonorphans, even after controlling for household income. These findings are consistent with estimates by the United Nations Children's Fund (UNICEF, 2003), which suggest that dependency ratios (a crude proxy for income per capita) in households caring for orphans are 20 percent higher than in nonorphan households (1.8 rather than 1.5), and that enrollment rates for orphans are 13 percent (not percentage points) lower than for nonorphans. Again there is an issue regarding the aggregation over age groups: for example, Ainsworth, Beegle, and Koda (2002) provide some evidence for Tanzania that the drop in enrollment rates is larger for the 10–14 age group than for the 5–9 age group.

From a macroeconomic perspective, access to education is intimately linked to the accumulation of human capital, as the discussion below of economic growth will make clear. Also, the study by Bell, Devarajan, and Gersbach (Chapter 3, this volume) is built around the impact of increased mortality on the transfer of human capital between generations, which is disrupted through the death of one or both parents, and the incentives to invest in human capital.

Private Sector[10]

HIV/AIDS, by increasing morbidity and mortality, affects both the productivity of employees living with the disease and productivity in general,

---

[10]The section on the impact of HIV/AIDS on the private sector benefited from extensive comments by Patrick Connelly.

as the retirement or death of employees disrupts companies' operations. For most companies, however, the most important costs associated with HIV/AIDS are monetary, including medical and death-related benefits, which add to personnel expenses. HIV/AIDS also has implications for the costs of recruitment and training: employees lost to AIDS must be replaced, and their successors must be trained. These costs include not only the direct financial costs but also various indirect costs, such as managerial time devoted to hiring and training new staff, and the productivity losses incurred while the new hires are learning their job. Looking forward, increased mortality means that companies need to train more staff for each of a number of specific tasks, to ensure that a sufficient number of employees with these skills will always be available; at the same time, the financial returns to these investments in training decline, because the new hires are themselves at greater risk of dying. This section will discuss all these issues, as well as how the impact of and the response to HIV/AIDS differ between small and large companies.

Some of the costs of HIV/AIDS to companies have already been discussed in the context of the income effects on households. From studies of the effects of HIV/AIDS on worker performance, it appears that absenteeism rises and productivity declines well before the death or retirement of an employee due to AIDS. The extent to which this represents a cost to the employer depends on the context. In the case of piece workers, the infected workers themselves bear most of the costs of their lower productivity. For workers who receive a fixed salary, the company bears most of the costs.

Table 2.3, adapted from Aventin and Huard (2000), shows the breakdown of HIV/AIDS-related costs for two companies in Côte d'Ivoire: a food-processing company (company 1) and a textile company (company 2). The largest cost component is that for medical care and related costs: the sum of all health-related costs, including preventive measures, HIV screening, payments to medical workers on the payroll, and health insurance, exceeds 35 percent of all HIV/AIDS-related costs for company 1 and 25 percent for company 2. Also important are sick leave, costs related to lost productivity and reorganization, funeral costs, and (for company 1) disability pensions to staff retiring for health reasons. Funeral grants, corresponding to about one monthly salary at company 1 and almost two monthly salaries at company 2, cover a substantial proportion of the funeral costs of deceased staff.

One potential cost to companies not covered in Table 2.3 is death-related benefits (other than funeral grants) paid to surviving spouses and dependent children; these can take the form of an ongoing pension or a

Table 2.3. Costs of HIV/AIDS for Two Companies in Côte d'Ivoire
(Percent of total except where stated otherwise)

Cost Item	Company 1	Company 2
Medical care	25.2	13.0
Prevention	1.0	1.2
HIV screening	0.6	—
Wage bill for medical personnel	5.2	12.5
Increased health insurance costs	5.0	—
Disability pensions	23.7	—
Sick leave	9.3	18.2
Attendance at funerals	3.1	3.3
Dismissals and severance pay	—	1.1
Recruitment and training	—	5.2
Loss of productivity, reorganization	13.3	25.0
Funeral costs	13.5	20.5
Total HIV/AIDS-related costs[1]	100.0	100.0
Total as percent of wage bill	1.3	0.8
Memorandum:		
HIV incidence among company		
employees (percent of workforce a year)	1.9	1.1

Sources: Author's calculations based on data from Aventin and Huard (2000).
[1]Items may not sum to totals because of rounding.

lump-sum payment. It is common when discussing pensions to distinguish between defined-contribution and defined-benefit schemes. In the former, the employee or the company, or both, make contributions to a pension fund, and the invested proceeds, plus any return, are paid out at retirement or death. In a defined-benefit scheme, payments are made according to a formula, often linked to tenure, and are not directly linked to past contributions. In general, the costs of HIV/AIDS to a company with a defined-contribution pension plan are likely to be small. If instead the company has a defined-benefit scheme that provides a fixed payout in case of death, however, HIV/AIDS-related payouts can be substantial. Most death benefits reported in the literature range from two to four times annual salary; for company 1 in Table 2.3, this could amount to an additional 3.8 to 7.6 percent of the wage bill. Thus HIV/AIDS can have a marked impact on personnel costs: one much-quoted earlier study for South Africa, assuming relatively generous benefits, projected that AIDS could add up to 15 percent to the wage bill by 2010 (Moore, 1999). In the absence of successful prevention measures to contain the numbers of new infections, this could mean that the company's profits, salary levels, or benefit levels are not sustainable.

Rosen and others (2004) provide a comparative analysis of six South African companies and identify four main determinants of differences in costs per new HIV infection: the level of death and disability benefits provided, the level of medical care for lower-level employees, the status of unskilled workers (whether permanent employees or contractors), and labor productivity or the composition of the workforce. The costs are higher for skilled employees, reflecting the higher costs of absenteeism and training. In particular, for companies providing disability pensions and pensions to surviving dependents, these tend to be the largest components of total costs, followed by productivity losses and sick leave and absenteeism. Rosen and others (2004) estimate that the actual costs for the six South African companies they studied ranged from 0.4 to 6.0 percent of the wage bill, depending on the demographics and the skill level of workers, and on the types of medical or death-related benefits provided.

Companies can take various steps to contain HIV/AIDS-related costs, including measures to prevent their employees from contracting AIDS, changes in the types or amounts of benefits they offer, and screening and medical treatment for their employees. Among these, prevention stands out, since it is generally recognized as the most cost-effective class of interventions from the company's point of view. It can be even more cost-effective from a social perspective, when one takes into account that companies bear only part of the costs of a worker's illness and death. Unfortunately, many companies do not have HIV avoidance policies in place, and often companies come to recognize prevention as a priority only after HIV cost avoidance has become a necessity. For example, South Africa's Bureau for Economic Research (BER, 2004) reports that only one-fourth of about a thousand companies surveyed in that country had implemented a formal HIV/AIDS policy. Conversely, a forward-looking prevention strategy that keeps down the number of infections among the workforce can reduce the financial pressure to cut costs by reducing employee benefits. On the other hand, companies who primarily employ casual workers may have little financial incentive to invest in prevention, because they incur only modest benefit costs, if any; because training costs for such workers tend to be low; and because high turnover means that most of these workers will have left the company long before current prevention efforts result in a smaller number of AIDS cases.

Once a company faces the possibly huge financial costs of an HIV epidemic among its employees, it will presumably seek ways to reduce those costs. Because death-related benefits and pensions to surviving dependents frequently account for a large share of the direct financial costs of HIV/AIDS, they are also a primary target for cost cutting. The available evidence suggests that HIV/AIDS is already affecting retirement funds in a very substantial way. For the most common form of retirement plan in

South Africa, defined-contribution schemes, Sanlam (2004) reports that death benefit premiums have increased from 1.9 percent to 2.5 percent of the wage bill (a relative increase of over 30 percent), and disability benefit premiums have risen from 1.5 percent to 1.8 percent between 2002 and 2004. Together with declines in employer contributions and increased administrative costs, these escalating costs have contributed substantially to a decline in retirement provisions from 12.4 percent to 10.8 percent (a relative decline of 13 percent). Because defined-contribution schemes eventually pay out the accumulated contributions minus the costs of risk benefits and administrative costs, this decline would mean that payouts at retirement or upon death in service (in addition to death benefits) will eventually decline and that the increased costs of risk benefits are passed through to employees. Looking ahead, most fund managers polled (72 percent) expected a substantial further increase in the cost of risk benefits over the next two years.

As the costs of death-related, disability, and medical benefits increase, companies may respond by reducing the costs of medical benefits, for example by cutting benefit levels or shifting a larger share of the cost to employees. Reductions in benefits—medical or death-related—frequently take the form of contracting out certain tasks and replacing permanent employees (especially low-skilled workers) with fixed-term contract workers or casual labor. This is illustrated in Table 2.4, from Rosen and Simon (2003), which compares benefits for regular and casual employees; this study also provides other examples of such burden shifting. In the case of medical benefits, the erosion of private health coverage implies increased economic risk for households facing an HIV/AIDS epidemic. To the extent that households who previously relied on private health services make use of public services instead, part of the burden of the disease is absorbed by the public sector (as the demand for public health services increases) or the public at large (as a larger number of patients relying on the public sector draw on limited health resources).

The above examples have described the various costs of HIV/AIDS to companies and various approaches to reducing those costs, but expenditure on prevention and treatment can also be interpreted as a form of investment. When a company extends or expands health services benefits to its HIV-positive employees, it does incur additional costs, but these expenditures may produce savings for the company in time as the number of employees contracting the virus is reduced, as the onset of morbidity and mortality for those who do become infected is delayed. Denote, for example, the cost of a particular form of treatment as C_T, and the costs of mortality (discussed above) as C_M. The treatment delays the onset of the

Table 2.4. Compensation and Benefits Provided to Low-Skilled Employees and Contract Workers at One South African Company

Item	Permanent Employees	Fixed-Term Contract Workers
Employment term	Permanent	10-month contract, renewable annually
Average salary or wage	85 rand a day	71 rand a day
Retirement benefits[1]	Proceeds of employee's account with defined-contribution provident fund, to which company contributes 7 percent of salary	None
Disability benefits[2]	Lump-sum payment of two times annual salary	None
Death benefits	Lump-sum payment of two times annual salary	None
Funeral benefits	None	1,800 rand for coffin and transport
Health insurance (medical aid)	Company contributes 60 percent of premium[3]	None
Primary medical care	Free to worker and dependents at company clinic; referral to public hospital	Free to worker at company clinic; referral to public hospital
Paid sick leave	12 days a year, plus extensions at management discretion	12 days in each 10-month contract
Memorandum: Share of males in workforce	95 percent	97 percent

Source: Rosen and Simon (2003); the identity of the company is confidential.
[1]Payable upon normal retirement, death, or medical retirement.
[2]Payable upon medical retirement.
[3]For a family of four, the remaining 40 percent amounts to 31 percent of salary for a low-skilled employee; almost no low-skilled workers join.

symptoms of AIDS and the employee's death from time T to time T'. The net financial gain from providing this treatment is

$$Net\ financial\ gain = \sum_{i=1}^{T'} (1 + r)^{-i} C_T(i) + [(1 + r)^{-T'} - (1 + r)^{-T}]C_M, \quad (1)$$

where r is the discount rate and i indexes time. The first term on the right-hand side of equation (1) gives the present discounted value of the costs of treatment, and the second, the discounted financial gain associated with the employee's increased life expectancy. Rosen and others (2001, 2004), for example, use this approach to illustrate the cost-effectiveness of various prophylactic treatments and of HIV testing and counseling. The approach has also been used to assess the cost-effectiveness of antiretroviral treatment. Suppose, for example, that the cost of providing such treatment is $1,000 a year and that the treatment increases an employee's remaining life expectancy from two years to six years. The costs associated with the employee's death are $20,000, and the company applies a discount rate r of 10 percent. The present discounted value of the cost of treatment for six years is then $4,355, and the postponement of the employee's death lowers the present discounted value of death-related costs by $5,239.

A company following this approach would typically find that it gains financially from providing antiretroviral treatment to its higher-paid staff. An important additional consideration, however, is that employees value medical benefits as part of their compensation package. This means that the company would be able to pass on some of the cost of expanded treatment options to its employees, either through employee contributions to the company's medical plan or through lower salaries. Finally, companies that provide more extensive medical benefits packages have more to gain from effective prevention programs. The evidence available suggests that both considerations are relevant, with some examples of companies providing antiretroviral treatment to their senior staff, and others providing antiretroviral treatment to all employees and in some cases to their families as well.[11]

As companies, whether by choice or by necessity, internalize some of the costs and economic benefits of prevention measures and treatment efforts, they are frequently willing to implement or finance some HIV prevention measures among their workers. Only very large companies will find it cost-effective to develop an HIV prevention program on their own. However, some insurers have developed integrated medical and HIV prevention packages in which companies can participate, and this expands the range of companies with access to prevention programs.

HIV/AIDS also affects the availability of employees with specific qualifications. This follows from the changes in the working-age population brought about by increased mortality, but HIV/AIDS also affects the return to investment in skills. Although an employer may be able to replace a worker who has died for HIV/AIDS-related reasons, the worker's death shrinks the aggregate supply of labor. This means that wages for workers with specific skills are likely to rise, or that workers who die will be replaced with workers with less skill and less experience. At the same time, the age structure of the working-age population changes: increased mortality means that employees are, on average, younger, and that individuals

---

[11]For this latter group, examples in South Africa include AngloGold, BMW, and Sasol.

with substantial experience in their profession, normally a prerequisite for leading positions in a company, become more scarce.

Companies also invest in training, especially to enhance the skills of their employees that are job-specific. With increased mortality, the returns to such investments decline, and, as a consequence, companies are likely to reduce their investments in training. For example, suppose a company observes that its employees quit with a probability of 10 percent a year, and that the company applies a discount rate of 5 percent. In this case, if the mortality rate among its employees rises from 0.25 percent to 1 percent, returns to training employees will fall by 4.7 percent.[12] If the mortality rate rises to 3 percent, returns to training will fall by 15.3 percent. Alternatively, the company may have to maintain a constant number (say, 100) of employees with certain skills that are key to its operations. As mortality rates rise from 0.25 percent to 1 (or 3) percent, the average number of employees who need to be trained each year then rises from 10.2 to 10.9 (or 12.7), and the annual training budget would have to rise by 6.6 (or 24.2) percent. Another cost of additional training, not captured so far, is learning on the job: workers usually need time to adjust to a new work environment and become fully productive. Connelly and Rosen (2004) estimate that the time needed on the job to become fully productive ranges from 5 days for unskilled workers to 20 days for skilled workers and 60 days for managers.

The above examples of the impact of HIV/AIDS on companies derive from case studies or simulations; another important source of information is business surveys. Based on questionnaires or interviews with managers, these surveys provide qualitative assessments of the impact of HIV/AIDS, for example on employees, production costs, profits, and the economic environment. The most comprehensive survey so far is that by the BER (2004) in South Africa, which reports that 39 percent of responding companies indicated that HIV/AIDS has reduced labor productivity or increased absenteeism.[13] In the same survey 40 percent of respondents indicated that "the epidemic increased their demand for labor (e.g., via

---

[12]The returns to training are calculated as $(s + m + \delta)\int_\alpha^\omega (i - \alpha)e^{-(s+m+\delta)*(i-\alpha)}/di + (\omega - \alpha)e^{-(s+m+\delta)*(\omega-\alpha)}$, where s is the job separation rate, m is the mortality rate, δ is the discount rate, α is the employee's age, and ω is the age at which the employee retires from the labor force. In this example, α equals 15 and ω equals 60. For simplicity, it is assumed that quit rates and mortality rates do not differ across workers. The assumed quit rate of 10 percent is near the middle of the range of 6.8 to 18.3 percent (excluding workers leaving because of sickness or death) reported by the World Bank (1999).

[13]The study was commissioned by the South African Business Coalition on HIV/AIDS and is therefore frequently referred to as the SABCOHA study or survey.

work shadowing or replacement of AIDS sick workers." Although fewer than 10 percent of companies noticed an adverse impact of HIV/AIDS on sales, 30 percent expected to see an adverse impact after five years.[14] A study from Malawi focusing on micro- and small enterprises finds that the most important channel through which HIV/AIDS affects these companies is the demand for their products or services.[15]

The BER (2004) study also provides important insights into the differing impacts of HIV/AIDS on businesses of different sizes, and their responses. It reports that 25 percent of all South African businesses have an HIV/AIDS policy in place, but only 13 percent of small companies (those with fewer than 100 employees) do; in contrast, 90 percent of companies with more than 500 employees have such a policy.[16] Table 2.5 shows that, for smaller companies, productivity losses and direct costs (loss of experience, higher turnover, and recruitment and training costs) associated with the loss of employees are the principal financial repercussions of the epidemic. The survey also finds that the larger the company, the more important are the costs of higher employee benefits. Although the cost rankings are very similar for small and medium-sized companies (the only difference being the ranking of benefit costs), they are markedly different for large companies. For these companies the costs of benefits and measures to contain the adverse impact of HIV/AIDS dominate. These trends are consistent with the conjecture that there is a positive correlation between prevention efforts and benefit levels. They may also reflect a weaker capacity of small business management to implement HIV policies; from this perspective, the rankings for smaller companies reflect a more passive attitude and an emphasis on direct costs, whereas the larger companies tend to have some active policy in place. Indeed, in a survey of the major business concerns of small and medium-size enterprises (Connelly and Rosen, 2004), HIV/AIDS ranked only ninth (out of 10), although some higher-ranking concerns (including the number-one concern, worker productivity) were in some way related to HIV/AIDS. Small companies may also provide retirement benefits to workers. In

---

[14]The impact of HIV/AIDS on sales differs from sector to sector and is generally less for export-oriented businesses (such as mining companies). Companies providing health- and death-related services (such as hospitals, pharmacies, and funeral parlors) may experience a substantial increase in demand.

[15]See Ebony Consulting International and Malawi National Statistical Office (2000).

[16]Rosen (2002) and Rosen and others (2003) report a similar finding for Nigeria: firms that were part of a family of firms or an industrial group were twice as likely to take actions against HIV/AIDS (informational materials, speakers, condom distribution, training of employees as peer educators or counselors).

Table 2.5. Ranking of Importance of HIV/AIDS-Related Costs to Businesses

Importance (1 = Most Important)	Number of Employees			
	Fewer than 100	100 to 500	More than 500	All companies
1	Lower productivity and increased absenteeism	Lower productivity and increased absenteeism	Higher employee benefit costs	Lower productivity and increased absenteeism
2	Loss of experience and vital skills	Higher employee benefit costs	Voluntary counseling and testing or HIV/AIDS awareness program	Higher employee benefit costs
3	Higher labor turnover rates	Loss of experience and vital skills	Lower productivity and increased absenteeism	Loss of experience and vital skills
4	Higher employee benefit costs	Higher labor turnover rates	HIV/AIDS treatment[1]	Higher labor turnover rates
5	Higher recruitment and training costs	Higher recruitment and training costs	Research into the impact of HIV/AIDS	Higher recruitment and training costs

Source: Bureau for Economic Research (2004).
[1]Including provision of antiretroviral therapy.

most cases these would be provided through a provident fund that manages benefit programs for many companies. Because the contribution rates to such a retirement fund would not reflect AIDS mortality in the workforce of any individual small company, there is no direct link between HIV/AIDS (at the company level) and the costs of benefits, and managers have less of a financial incentive to take action.[17]

The discussion above has already highlighted some of the differences between small and large businesses in the impact of and the response to HIV/AIDS. The role of small businesses is discussed in more detail below, in an effort to bridge the gap between the chapters on households and the discussion of larger private businesses. Because smaller businesses are more likely to be part of the informal sector, much of what follows can also be interpreted in terms of differences between the formal and the informal economy.[18]

---

[17]Of course, there is an externality involved here. On risk benefits in small companies, see Connelly and Rosen (2004).

[18]This concept of "small businesses" is similar to the one used in Ebony Consulting International and Malawi National Statistical Office (2000), who "visited a stratified sample of over 22,000 households and small businesses to identify active business activities of all kinds employing fewer than 50 employees. This study also enumerated on-farm agricultural activities, as long as 50 percent of the production was sold. . . ."

Apart from issues related to data availability, much of the focus of the literature has been on larger companies, because these include some of the major contributors to GDP, and because the government's tax base is largely associated with the formal economy. However, in many countries with severe AIDS epidemics, the majority of the population works in the informal sector. Also, incomes are generally lower in the informal economy, and many of the instruments available in the formal sector to mitigate the impact of HIV/AIDS on households (such as medical and death-related benefits) do not exist there. In assessing the welfare effects of HIV/AIDS, it is therefore important to give appropriate weight to small businesses.

Small companies are less likely to adopt prevention and awareness measures, because there is a fixed cost involved in developing an HIV/AIDS policy or contracting HIV/AIDS-related services, and they may find it harder than large enterprises to replace key staff. The impact of HIV/AIDS on a small business is also less predictable.

Phororo (2003) discusses in some detail the response of small Namibian businesses to HIV/AIDS among their workers. In light of the resource and time constraints hindering an active response of small businesses to HIV/AIDS, most of the policy measures she discusses rely on collaboration to hold down the costs of HIV policies to small companies (for example, by building a national business coalition on HIV/AIDS) or on including small businesses in programs implemented by other companies. Connelly and Rosen (2004) emphasize that the costs per employee of HIV/AIDS-related services are much higher for small companies, largely because of fixed costs incurred by providers and the additional costs of marketing and delivering services. One of the costs of developing a response to HIV/AIDS is that of obtaining information. Public awareness measures can therefore facilitate the adoption of HIV prevention strategies by small companies. Rosen (2002), drawing on earlier work (published as Rosen and others, 2003), observes that "receiving information from an outside source" is a "good predictor of company action."

When key employees fall ill or die from HIV/AIDS, small companies can find themselves at a disadvantage with respect to large companies in covering for and eventually replacing those individuals. Large enterprises can cope temporarily with the loss of an employee by reallocating work to co-workers with similar experience and skills. This is especially relevant if the position requires specialized training or some experience within the company, as in the case of the branch manager of a bank, a software specialist, or an accountant. The ability to reallocate work within the company also makes it easier to find a permanent replacement for workers retiring or dying from HIV/AIDS. Small businesses are much less likely to be able to replace key employees from within the company, raising the cost of replacement; in extreme cases, the loss of a key member can result in the dissolution of the business.[19] However, small companies, especially those in the informal sector, rely more on casual employees for their unskilled labor.[20] The company does not have to cover any medical or death-related benefits for these employees and can easily replace them if they are no longer able to fulfill their tasks.

Size—and the law of large numbers—also makes the impact of HIV/AIDS more predictable for large companies. Large employers can expect the HIV prevalence rate among their employees to be close to the relevant population average; small companies, in contrast, will see greater dispersion, with some lucky ones barely affected, while others experience prevalence rates well above the average. This greater predictability also allows large companies to mitigate the impact of HIV/AIDS through forward-looking resource management. For example, a large company that employs 100 accountants might simply decide to hire two more in order to self-insure against a likely increase in absenteeism and HIV/AIDS-related attrition. In contrast, a small company would likely not find it cost-effective to employ even one more accountant to insure against the loss of the one already on the payroll. At the extreme, a very small single proprietorship may well cease to exist if the owner dies or retires.

Finally, HIV/AIDS complicates small businesses' access to credit. Large businesses tend to be incorporated, and therefore HIV/AIDS does not change their default risk other than through its impact on company profits. The owner of a small business, in contrast, is likely to have to borrow in his or her own name. In this case a substantial increase in mortality owing to HIV/AIDS increases default risk, reducing the business's access to or cost of credit.

Public Sector

The implications of HIV/AIDS for the government are fundamentally different from those discussed above for other social and economic institutions, because of the government's public mandate and its key role in

---

[19]One implication of this for researchers is that surveys of the impact of HIV/AIDS on small businesses tend to underestimate the effects, because many of the worst-affected firms no longer exist and are therefore missed by the survey. This measurement problem also arises in the context of the dissolution of HIV/AIDS-affected households.

[20]See Coetzee (2003) for an illustration.

formulating and implementing the country's response to HIV/AIDS. The impact of HIV/AIDS on the public service and government finance is discussed in some detail in Haacker (Chapter 7, this volume); therefore the discussion that follows highlights only a few issues that are particularly relevant for the impact of HIV/AIDS on the economy in general and on welfare. These issues include the impact on the delivery of public services, the government's personnel costs, the demand for certain government services, and the role of international assistance in supporting and, in particular, financing the response to HIV/AIDS in low-income countries.

HIV/AIDS causes disruptions to government services in ways similar to those discussed above for the private sector. As public servants fall ill and die, the efficiency of government agencies declines because of falling productivity and disruptions related to increasing attrition rates. These disruptions can be particularly severe if employees are allowed extended sick leave, or if long lags intervene between the advertising of a position and the hiring of a replacement. Disruptions can be particularly severe for decentralized government services, such as local education and health services.[21] Because a given small community receives these services from only one or a few public servants, illness or death among them can cause a prolonged local disruption in these services.

HIV/AIDS also erodes the government's financial resources, from both the revenue and the expenditure side. Countries afflicted by the epidemic see their tax base and thus their domestic revenue grow more slowly or even shrink, even as demand for government expenditure, including for personnel, increases. Although countries can often obtain external finance for specific HIV/AIDS-related interventions (according to Table 2.6, almost 80 percent of public spending on HIV/AIDS in low-income countries was financed by external grants), such funding is typically not available to cover the *indirect* costs of HIV/AIDS, such as the impact on the government payroll or certain categories of social expenditure.

The impact of HIV/AIDS on the government's personnel costs, through increased medical and death-related benefits and increased training and recruitment costs, can be severe. These effects are similar to those discussed above in the context of the private sector and need not be further discussed here. However, the financial costs of benefits are likely to be higher for the public sector, because benefits are typically more compre-

---

[21]See Topouzis (2003) for a discussion of the impact of HIV/AIDS on agricultural extension services.

**Table 2.6. Estimated Funding for HIV/AIDS Spending in
Low-Income Countries, 2003**
(Millions of dollars)

Source of Funding	Amount Spent
Bilateral, United States	852
Bilateral, other governments	1,163
Global Fund	547
UN agencies	350
World Bank[1]	120
Foundations and other NGOs	200
Governments of affected countries	1,000
Total	4,232

Source: Summers and Kates (2003).
[1]Grant component of concessional loans.

hensive than in the private sector. Public servants are more likely to be permanently employed (a condition associated with higher benefit levels),
and governments may refrain, for political economy reasons, from cutting
benefit levels as a way of containing costs. Thus personnel costs are likely
to increase in all areas of the public service.[22]

The sector most directly affected by HIV/AIDS is the health sector.[23]
The demands on the public health service rise sharply with the spread of
the epidemic; at same time, health personnel, too, are affected by
HIV/AIDS. Initially, with antiretroviral treatment in low-income countries out of reach for all but a few (who could afford it or who benefited
from a pilot program), public health services could provide little more
than palliative care and treatment of opportunistic infections. Even so,
reported occupancy rates of hospital beds by HIV patients—ranging
between 30 and 70 percent—indicate that HIV/AIDS absorbed much of
the existing capacities of health services at that stage. With the dramatic
fall in the price of antiretroviral treatments in recent years, however, more
and more countries have started to make these treatments available
through the public health service. At the same time, the international
community is working diligently to provide financing and other support
to expand access to treatment in low-income countries. Even with such
support, however, expanding health services sufficiently to meet the

---

[22]Some of the costs may not appear directly in the government's budget, for example if the
public sector pension fund is not part of the general budget, or if some forms of benefits are
covered from discretionary funds at the ministerial level.

[23]For a thorough discussion of the impact of HIV/AIDS on the health sector, see Over
(Chapter 10, this volume).

potential demand for treatment remains a serious challenge in many countries.

International donors play a critical role in the financing of HIV/AIDS-related expenditure in sub-Saharan Africa and (to a somewhat lesser extent) of health expenditure generally. Table 2.6 reports estimates of the sources of funding of HIV/AIDS-related expenditures in low-income countries for 2003. More than three-fourths of public health expenditure was financed through external grants. The data do not distinguish clearly which agencies would provide the services: some grants would finance government activities included in the budget, whereas others would go to international nongovernmental organizations (NGOs) providing services directly in the affected countries. But the data do show that governments that offer a convincing and comprehensive HIV/AIDS program can raise a substantial proportion of the necessary funds from external grants. On the other hand, managing the aid flows, catering to the specific needs of different donors, and coordinating the activities of numerous agencies and NGOs, some of which are directly financed from abroad, can be a challenge for a government whose human resources are already stretched thin by the epidemic.

In the longer run, the impact of HIV/AIDS in a given country does depend on the government's policies and its actions to fight the epidemic and mitigate its impact. A policy that brings down the incidence of new infections and improves the health status of people living with HIV, through prevention campaigns and improved access to treatment, will reduce the adverse macroeconomic effects. As the domestic revenue base improves (or at least deteriorates less rapidly) and outlays related to HIV/AIDS fall, some of the costs of a comprehensive HIV/AIDS framework will be offset by these indirect fiscal gains arising from reduced HIV prevalence and improved health.

Impact of HIV/AIDS on the Economy and Society

HIV/AIDS, through its impact on mortality and morbidity and the resulting demographic changes, affects all levels of an economy and society, from individuals and households to small and large businesses to the different levels and activities of government. Most of these changes can be described in terms of frictions that affect the efficiency of some entity or process, demographic changes (especially losses in human capital), and changes in the composition of domestic demand. These frictions relate to entities that are in some way tangible. But HIV/AIDS can also affect the less tangible social and economic institutions of a country, such as its civil society, its democratic processes, the acceptance of government by the public, the quality of governance, and social cohesion, which in turn have very direct consequences for economic development.

This chapter has already described (drawing on Chapter 7 of this volume, by Haacker) how HIV/AIDS erodes government's capacities and disrupts public services. Although the emphasis there was on the delivery of services, HIV/AIDS also affects legislative bodies and policymakers. Political processes are adversely affected, especially because this is an area in which experience is particularly important. For all these various reasons, the efficiency of government at all levels is likely to suffer. One possible consequence is increased political instability, spurred by dissatisfaction with the government in place or with the political process in general. More broadly, an essential complement to democratic institutions is a strong civil society, and this, too, is eroded by increased mortality and by many of the social and economic impacts of HIV/AIDS discussed elsewhere in this chapter.[24]

HIV/AIDS, through the economic repercussions of increased mortality and weakened social institutions and government capacities, also contributes to deteriorating security at the individual, community, and national level, and does so both in economic terms and in a more fundamental way.[25] Some of the economic dimensions of increased risk are discussed elsewhere in this chapter, for example in the context of the impact on households (above) and in the discussion on risk and welfare (below). In particular, domestic security deteriorates when the government's capacities are eroded,[26] and weakened governments and deteriorating economic prospects are associated with increased crime and instability.[27]

In an already fragile society, HIV/AIDS can contribute to the outbreak of civil war or prolong its duration. According to a recent World Bank Policy Research Report (Collier and others, 2003), "if a country is in economic decline, is dependent on primary commodity exports, and has a low per

---

[24]For a more thorough discussion of the impact of HIV/AIDS on democracy, governance, and security and vice versa, see Nelufule (2004).

[25]A report by the International Crisis Group (ICG, 2001) on "HIV/AIDS as a Security Issue" provides a thorough analysis of the multidimensional impact of HIV/AIDS on security.

[26]ICG (2001) lists some examples of how HIV/AIDS has affected policing in Kenya, Namibia, and South Africa.

[27]Various authors have also addressed the economic and security implications of the dramatically increasing number of orphans, currently estimated at about 20 percent of the young population in some of the countries worst affected by HIV/AIDS. See Nelufule (2004) for a recent discussion.

capita income and that income is unequally distributed, it is at high risk of civil war." This description applies to many countries affected by HIV/AIDS (sometimes even before the escalation of the epidemic), and, through its economic impact, the epidemic thus exacerbates a country's vulnerability to civil war. The discussion of democracy and political processes is also relevant: according to Collier and others (2003), "in such conditions the state is likely to be weak, nondemocratic, and incompetent, offering little impediment to the escalation of rebel violence, and maybe even inadvertently provoking it." This observation echoes the discussion above of the effects of HIV/AIDS on government capacities.

What this discussion shows is that the impact of HIV/AIDS on an economy and society goes far beyond disruptions of more or less tangible economic or administrative processes within households, businesses, or government agencies. To the extent that a stable and efficient government, a strong civil society, and economic and social stability contribute to economic development, these broader effects tend to reinforce the other adverse effects of HIV/AIDS on the economy. The discussion later in this chapter of the impacts of HIV/AIDS on economic growth focuses on a narrower set of economic effects. Thus it is important to stress here that the increases in mortality, the declines in birthrates, and the resulting demographic changes may so transform an economy and society as to give rise to economic effects that these models do not capture—or the models may not be structurally stable in such a dramatically altered setting.

Economic Growth and Income per Capita

Drawing on the evidence discussed above on the impact of HIV/AIDS on social and economic institutions, many studies have attempted to assess the epidemic's impact on economic growth and income per capita. Projections of the induced changes in economic growth are useful in several regards. For example, such changes are closely associated with changes in the domestic tax base and thus can be used in forecasting the resources that will be available for general government operations, including the policy response to HIV/AIDS. Changes in income per capita have implications for living standards, although here it is important to take into account the composition of spending (see Arndt and Lewis, 2001) and the distribution of income (as discussed below and in Greener, Chapter 5 of this volume).

Most studies of the impact of HIV/AIDS on economic growth and income per capita utilize some form of the neoclassical growth model, incorporating assumptions regarding the impact of HIV/AIDS on productivity and labor efficiency, on saving and investment behavior, and on demographics. HIV/AIDS has an immediate macroeconomic impact owing to the productivity losses it imposes on the private sector, as discussed above; macroeconomic studies generally include some assumptions about aggregate productivity changes inspired by this microeconomic evidence. The assumption of changes in the saving rate is in most cases motivated by the increase in medical expenditure observed to accompany increased HIV/AIDS prevalence and its impact on households' ability to save. Finally, demographic changes have three kinds of effects in these models: a smaller labor supply translates into lower output; a lower growth rate of the labor supply is associated with a higher capital-output ratio (mitigating the otherwise adverse effects of HIV/AIDS on output per capita); and higher mortality, by eroding human capital (as measured by tenure or experience), lowers the average efficiency of labor. The principal differences between studies following this approach concern the level of disaggregation of the labor force by skill (studies typically distinguish in some way between skilled and unskilled labor) and by sector (distinguishing, for example, between a formal and an informal sector). This chapter will also explore the potential impact of HIV/AIDS on investment, in an open-economy model in which investment responds to changes in the rate of return to capital.

However, HIV/AIDS has a much more direct and severe effect on the accumulation of human capital: it destroys it in those it kills. Taking a longer view, investment in human capital is also likely to be affected. First, by increasing mortality, HIV/AIDS has a strongly adverse effect on the returns to investment in human capital (schooling and training), which may discourage individuals or companies from undertaking such investment.[28] Second, because so many of its victims are adults of parenting age, HIV/AIDS is associated with an increase in orphans—as noted above, orphans now make up around 20 percent of the under-18 population in some of the worst-affected countries—and there is empirical evidence that orphans have poorer access to education than nonorphans. More generally, HIV/AIDS, through increased uncertainty and the deteriorating economic outlook, will further discourage any form of investment, whether in human, physical, or social capital, and some authors, mirroring the above

---

[28]For this to be true, individuals and companies must do an adequate job of projecting mortality rates; in a setting where these rates are rapidly rising, this may not be a realistic assumption.

discussion of the impact of HIV/AIDS on the social fabric, suggest that this will magnify the impact on economic growth.

Turning to the empirical studies, one can distinguish between two types of models. Some studies try to estimate the impact of HIV/AIDS on economic growth by means of some form of growth regression. Others use larger macroeconometric models originally developed for macroeconomic and fiscal analysis and policy advice. The relationships between the major macroeconomic variables in these models are based on an econometric analysis (rather than calibration), and they also capture short-term demand side effects. However, on the production side, and thus in the long run, these models have similar features to the simpler and more aggregated growth models. The prime example of a model of this type is that presented in BER (2001).

Productivity Effects

When the death or illness of a worker disrupts a company's production, or when that of a family member disrupts household production, aggregate productivity declines. This is illustrated in the following equation:

$$c = \alpha d_W + \beta s_W + \gamma d_p + \varepsilon s_p, \tag{2}$$

where c stands for the direct costs of HIV/AIDS (in percent of GDP), d_W and s_W stand for mortality and morbidity among the working-age population (in percent), and d_p and s_p are the corresponding variables for the total population.

The productivity losses associated with HIV/AIDS are represented by the first two terms on the right-hand side of equation (2), where α stands for the disruptions to production associated with AIDS mortality (replacement of workers, funeral attendance), as a percentage of GDP per capita, and β stands for the productivity losses associated with morbidity.[29] Other costs associated with HIV/AIDS are funeral and other death-related expenses (γ) and the costs of care and treatment (ε); these costs are expressed in terms of the *use* of output rather than as direct output costs, and for an analysis of the impact of HIV/AIDS on living standards it makes sense to add them.[30] Although this type of analysis of the direct costs of HIV/AIDS provides some useful insights, in the longer run HIV/AIDS also affects output through changes in the accumulation of

---

[29]In practice this relationship is often simplified, linking estimates of total costs during the course of the illness to estimates of HIV/AIDS-related mortality.

[30]This point is made by Arndt and Lewis (2001).

capital (including through an increase in HIV/AIDS-related expenditure, as represented by parameters γ and ε), or in the composition of the supply of labor. Looking beyond the very short run, it is therefore necessary to adopt a more general framework.

Studies Using the Neoclassical Growth Model

The earliest studies of the macroeconomic impact of HIV/AIDS used the neoclassical growth model, to explore different channels through which the epidemic affects the economy. These studies included those by Over (1992) and Cuddington (1993a, 1993b). This model still is frequently used, both as a framework for synthesizing estimates of the impact of HIV/AIDS on various macroeconomic aggregates, and to draw inferences about how the impact will evolve over time.[31]

Many of the insights from these studies can be summarized using a one-sector growth model, in which output (Y) is a function of the levels of capital (K) and labor (L), with the latter disaggregated into highly skilled and unskilled labor:

$$Y = AK^{\alpha}(e_H p_H L)^{\beta}(e_U p_U L)^{\gamma}, \tag{3}$$

where $\alpha + \beta + \gamma = 1$; p_H stands for the proportion of highly skilled individuals in the working population; and $p_U = 1 - p_H$ for the proportion of unskilled individuals. A denotes total factor productivity, and e_H and e_U represent the efficiency of highly skilled individuals and unskilled individuals, respectively.

The capital stock evolves according to

$$\dot{K} = sY - \delta K, \tag{4}$$

where $\dot{K}$ denotes the rate of growth of the capital stock over time. Studies following this approach usually assume that gross investment equals domestic saving (sY) and that net investment therefore is equal to saving minus the depreciation of capital. The supply of labor (and of its skilled and unskilled components) grows at rate n. Transforming the model into per capita terms (with $k = K/L$ and $y = Y/L$), the capital-labor ratio evolves according to

$$\dot{k} = sy - (\delta + n)k, \tag{5}$$

---

[31]Haacker (2002b) provides a more detailed and technical discussion of the issues covered in this section.

and the economy moves toward an equilibrium in which $sy - (\delta + n)k$ and the capital-labor ratio, and therefore output per capita, are constant. Solving for the steady-state capital-labor ratio (k^*) and output level (y^*) yields

$$k^* = \left(\frac{sA}{\delta + n}\right)^{1/(\beta+\gamma)}(e_H p_H)^{\beta/(\beta+\gamma)}(e_U p_U)^{\gamma/(\beta+\gamma)} \tag{6}$$

and

$$y^* = A(k^*)^\alpha (e_H p_H)^\beta (e_U p_U)^\gamma; \tag{7}$$

that is,

$$y^* = A^{1/(\beta+\gamma)}\left(\frac{s}{\delta + n}\right)^{\alpha/(\beta+\gamma)}(e_H p_H)^{\beta/(\beta+\gamma)}(e_U p_U)^{\gamma/(\beta+\gamma)} \tag{8}$$

Equations (6), (7), and (8) provide a framework for the assessment of the economic impact of HIV/AIDS, at least in the longer run, described by the steady state. In particular, the various channels through which HIV/AIDS can affect GDP per capita are as follows.

- Changes in total factor productivity (A) or in the efficiency of skilled or unskilled labor (e_H and e_U). Usually, changes in A are taken to reflect the disruptions caused by increased mortality, whereas changes in e_H and e_U capture losses in human capital associated with the loss of experienced workers. Estimates of the change in A are based on studies of the impacts of HIV/AIDS on productivity or on production costs (although, from a macroeconomic perspective, the latter partly reflect transfers). In line with the microeconomic studies cited above, most studies would assume that an increase in AIDS incidence of 1 percent is associated a decline in total factor productivity of 0.5 to 1 percent.
- Changes in the composition of the workforce (p_H and p_U). If HIV prevalence is higher among the unskilled, the workforce share of the skilled (p_H) will rise, and output per capita will rise. There is no clear pattern across countries regarding the skill bias of HIV/AIDS. Studies from South Africa (such as BER, 2001) and Botswana (BIDPA, 2000) typically suggest that HIV prevalence is higher among workers with low skills, but these results are not robust across countries and may change during the course of an epidemic.
- Changes in the saving rate. The assumptions adopted in the literature regarding changes in aggregate saving are inspired by studies of the impact of HIV/AIDS on individual households. If, for example, households affected by HIV do not save because they must meet the costs of treatment and care, this translates into a decline in aggregate saving, which can be related to observed HIV prevalence rates. As dis-

Figure 2.2. Estimated Impact of HIV/AIDS on Economic Growth Rates in Selected Countries
(Percentage points of GDP)

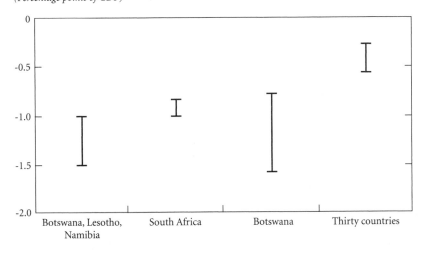

Source: UNAIDS (2004).

cussed below, however, studies addressing the optimal saving behavior of households who face a substantially increased risk of mortality predict a much larger decline in saving rates.

- *Changes in the rate of population growth.* HIV/AIDS is associated with a decline in population growth, initially owing to increased mortality but later also reflecting lower birthrates. A decline in the growth rate of the working-age population is associated with an increase in the capital-labor ratio (and thus of income per capita), as the existing capital stock is spread across fewer incoming workers.

Studies projecting the impact of HIV/AIDS on economic growth using an approach similar to that outlined above typically predict declines of 1.0 to 1.5 percentage points for the worst-affected economies, defined as those with HIV prevalence rates for the working-age population over 20 percent (in Botswana and Swaziland, the rate exceeds 35 percent).[32] This is illustrated in Figure 2.2, adapted from Joint United Nations Programme on HIV/AIDS (UNAIDS, 2004). As the rate of population growth also slows, the estimated impact on GDP per capita becomes even smaller. Box 2.1,

---

[32]The studies represented in Figure 2.2 may have a more elaborate sectoral structure; this issue is discussed further below.

Box 2.1. Impact of HIV/AIDS on Output and Income per Capita

The table below summarizes the impact of HIV/AIDS in a growth model as described in equations (3) through (9), both for a closed and for an open economy. For the open economy, the table differentiates between the impacts on output and on income, as capital outflows result in investment income accruing to domestic residents (or, vice versa, lower inward investment is associated with lower interest payments to foreign residents).

Consider an economy with an HIV prevalence rate of 10 percent. The growth rate of the working population falls by 1 percentage point, from 3 percent to 2 percent a year. Skilled workers account for 20 percent of the working population. Factor shares are 37 percent for capital, 28 percent for

Impact of HIV/AIDS on Output and Income per Capita
(Percent)

Type of economy and output or income	Total	TFP[1]	Saving	Population growth	Labor efficiency Skilled	Unskilled
Closed economy						
Output per capita	−0.5	−2.4	−1.2	4.5	−0.9	−0.6
Income per capita	−0.5	−2.4	−1.2	4.5	−0.9	−0.6
Open economy with perfect capital mobility						
Output per capita	−3.8	−2.4	0.0	0.0	−0.9	−0.6
Income per capita	−1.7	−2.4	−0.7	2.8	−0.9	−0.6

Source: Haacker (2002b).
[1]Total factor productivity.

which draws on Haacker (2002b), provides an example of the impact of HIV/AIDS on steady-state GDP per capita.

In one important regard there is a disconnect between the framework described above and the concerns in the business and political communities regarding the impact of HIV/AIDS on domestic and foreign direct investment. Whereas the latter fear that an uncertain and deteriorating economic outlook could deter investment, and thus worsen the economic impact of HIV/AIDS, the above closed-economy framework assumes that investment changes only in line with domestic saving, and that an increase in the capital-labor ratio offsets much of the adverse impact of HIV/AIDS. At the same time, the rate of return to capital declines (as the capital-labor ratio increases); the assumption that investment responds passively to changes in saving is therefore implausible.

skilled labor, and 35 percent for unskilled labor. The rate of depreciation is 10 percent a year. In the open-economy model, the economy starts out with a net investment position of zero. As a result of increasing mortality rates, average labor productivity falls by 2 percent for skilled workers and by 1 percent for unskilled workers. The aggregate saving rate (for both the formal and the informal sector) falls from 15 percent to 14.7 percent—that is, by 2 percent (0.3 percentage point)—and total factor productivity declines by 1.5 percent.

As a result of these changes, output per capita declines by 0.5 percent in the closed-economy model, owing to declines in total factor productivity and the efficiency of labor, which together account for a decline in output per capita of 3.8 percent. Although the saving rate decreases (accounting for a further decline of output per capita of 1.2 percent), most of the adverse effect on output per capita from all these sources is offset by slower population growth (which, other things equal, would raise output per capita by 4.5 percent), so that the overall effect on output per capita is relatively small.

If investment is sensitive to changes in the rate of return to capital, as in the open economy described by equation (9), the impact of HIV/AIDS on output per capita is much stronger, because changes in the population growth rate (and in the saving rate) no longer have an impact on output per capita. Since in this case the country's net investment position changes (as residents accumulate foreign assets or the level of foreign-owned assets in the domestic economy declines), it is important to take into account the associated interest income streams. In this example, output per capita declines by 3.8 percent, whereas income per capita falls by only 1.7 percent.

A simple model that does take these considerations into account is the open-economy version of the neoclassical growth model.[33] In this model the rate of return to capital is tied to the world interest rate, possibly adjusted for country risk.[34] In the present context this means that

$$\frac{\partial Y}{\partial Y} = r^* + risk\ premium. \tag{9}$$

---

[33]For a general discussion of this model, see Barro, Mankiw, and Sala-i-Martin (1995) or Haacker (2002b).

[34]One possibility not explored here is that an HIV/AIDS epidemic may itself increase a country's risk premium, reflecting the country's deteriorating and more uncertain economic outlook. Instead the risk premium is assumed to be constant.

As the rate of return to capital falls—for example, because of the costs and productivity losses associated with an HIV/AIDS epidemic—domestic and multinational investors in this model reduce their investment in the affected economy and instead invest abroad. This means that the capital-labor ratio declines, and the adverse impact of HIV/AIDS is exacerbated rather than mitigated as above. Box 2.1 provides a numerical example for this type of model, drawing on Haacker (2002b).[35]

One of the issues frequently raised regarding the impact of HIV/AIDS on GDP is whether and to what extent the impact can be mitigated or income per capita can rise through shifts of workers from the informal to the formal sector. When an employee of a high-productivity company in the formal sector retires or dies and is replaced by a hitherto less gainfully employed worker from the informal sector, income per capita rises. This argument, however, is at best misleading and, in many situations, wrong, because it rests on the assumption that the demand for labor in the formal sector is a given. First, it is important to understand that the formal sector relies to a larger extent on employees with particular qualifications, whereas people moving from the informal to the formal sector (and those in the formal sector they replace) typically have fewer professional skills. Second, HIV/AIDS also affects professionals with formal skills, and in the aggregate this is likely to have an adverse effect on the demand for unskilled labor.

Indeed, for the most common forms of the neoclassical growth model, it can be shown that an equiproportionate change in the number of skilled and unskilled workers will eventually leave the shares of skilled and unskilled workers working in the two sectors (and thus GDP per capita) unchanged. In this case changes in GDP per capita would need to come from changes in the composition of the labor supply or in the accumulation of capital, along lines similar to those discussed above.[36]

Several studies have addressed the impact of HIV/AIDS using more complex, computable general equilibrium models.[37] Although these models typically feature a much larger number of sectors, the dynamic structure is similar to that of the neoclassical growth model. One of the distinct advantages of this approach is that it allows a more realistic sectoral disag-

---

[35]Although they do not make it explicit, Drouhin, Touzé, and Ventelou (2003) also use this framework regarding the accumulation of physical capital.

[36]For a thorough discussion for the impact of HIV/AIDS in a dual economy, see Haacker (2002b).

[37]Examples include Kambou, Devarajan, and Over (1992) for Cameroon, Arndt and Lewis (2001) for South Africa, and Arndt (2003) for Mozambique.

gregation of GDP. However, the insights from these models resemble those of the dual-economy model discussed above: those sectors that use factors that are more affected by a shock will contract. An analysis of this family of models is beyond the scope of the present study, but the studies referenced also discuss some of the more general issues regarding computable general equilibrium models.

Saving and the Accumulation of Human Capital

The studies discussed above make rather simple assumptions about the link between HIV/AIDS and saving, typically relating changes in saving to the cost of treatment. There are good reasons to believe, however, that HIV/AIDS has a much more extensive and complex impact on saving. The increased risk of mortality means that individuals have less of an incentive to save, both for themselves and for their offspring. This approach also extends to the accumulation of human capital. The models discussed above interpret HIV/AIDS as a disruption to production processes, which reduces productivity, but the impact on productivity can be much larger in the longer run as individuals invest less in their own or their children's education, or as companies reduce their investment in employee training.

Freire (2002) addresses the impact of HIV/AIDS on saving using a model with intertemporally optimizing consumers; her paper also includes an application to South Africa. Linking the optimal consumption paths to a representative individual's mortality, she estimates that saving as a proportion of GDP will be about 14 percent (not percentage points) lower by 2010, a much larger number than would be obtained using the more common approach, whereby some of the direct costs of HIV/AIDS are financed from savings. Several other studies focus on the impact of HIV/AIDS on the accumulation of human capital. Ferreira and Pessoa (2003) adopt a model in which individuals allocate their lifetime between education and work in order to maximize the present discounted value of lifetime income. Equilibrium is characterized by some optimal level of schooling, a steady-state capital-labor ratio, and an allocation of agents to the goods and education sectors. Although the calibrations of the model yield projections of the impact of HIV/AIDS that are on the high side (for Zambia, for example, the estimate is of a decline in education time by half, and a drop in income per capita by one-third), the authors very thoroughly discuss their findings in the context of the earlier literature.

The most ambitious attempt so far to assess the impact of HIV/AIDS on economic growth is that by Bell, Devarajan, and Gersbach (2003 and

Chapter 3, this volume). The unit of analysis is the individual household. HIV/AIDS may result in the death of one or both parents in a household, which affects the accumulation of human capital in several ways. It affects their children's ability to accumulate human capital, and it reduces the family's income. Looking ahead, the increased risk of mortality reduces the returns to investment in the children's education. This is an effect similar to those described above, and it applies to all households. In light of the large numbers of orphans in countries with severe epidemics, these authors' emphasis on the asymmetric effects on orphans is highly relevant: not only do orphans attain lower levels of human capital in this analysis, but, because a child's level of human capital depends on that of the child's parents, their own offspring will be affected as well.

Birdsall and Hamoudi (Chapter 4, this volume) assess the impact of HIV/AIDS on the accumulation and utilization of human capital. The key to their argument is that lower life expectancy reduces the returns to accumulating human capital, thus reducing the demand for education, and they present evidence that increased life expectancy has indeed been associated with increased duration of schooling and higher primary school enrollment rates. The impact of HIV/AIDS on GDP will be exacerbated if, because of HIV/AIDS, the economy falls back below a critical mass of human capital. Finally, the authors point out that, as HIV reduces the accumulation of physical capital, this would in turn reduce the returns to human capital.

Incorporating the Impact of HIV/AIDS into a Large-Scale Macroeconomic Model

Several studies have analyzed the impact of HIV/AIDS in South Africa using more complex macroeconomic models. A study commissioned by ING Barings South African Research (2000) emphasizes the impact of HIV/AIDS on the labor force (distinguishing among four skill levels), on productivity (through absenteeism and illness), on production costs, and on the demand for health services. They predict that the labor supply (weighted by skill level) will decline by 12.8 percent by 2010 and that real GDP will decline by 3.1 percent compared with a scenario without AIDS, implying a substantial increase in per capita income.[38] Arndt and Lewis (2001), using a 15-sector computable general equilibrium model, draw on

---

[38]This substantial increase in income per capita appears to stem from a decline in unemployment and an increase in aggregate demand (in per capita terms).

the same demographic projections used in the ING Barings study. They project that GDP per capita will decline by 8 percent by 2010, relative to a no-AIDS scenario, and that domestic absorption, excluding food, medical services, and HIV/AIDS-related government expenditure, will fall by 13 percent. BER (2001) focuses on the epidemic's effects on the overall population and the labor force, the direct and indirect costs to private businesses, and government and household expenditure. The study projects that GDP growth will decline by between 1.4 and 1.8 percentage points between 2002 and 2015, and that GDP growth per capita will increase by 0.7 to 1.0 percentage points over the same period.

Empirical Studies

Several studies have attempted to evaluate the impact of HIV/AIDS on economic growth empirically, with mixed results. An early study by Bloom and Mahal (1997), using data through 1992, finds an insignificant link between growth of GDP per capita and cumulative AIDS cases for a cross section of 51 countries. Bonnel (2000) finds that HIV/AIDS may affect growth of GDP per capita both directly and through its impact on policy institutions. He reports that, in the 1990–97 period, increased HIV prevalence was associated with a decline in growth of GDP per capita. For a country with an HIV prevalence rate of 15 percent, for example, he postulates a decline in growth of GDP per capita of 1 percent. Using panel data from 41 African countries between 1960 and 1998, Dixon, McDonald, and Roberts (2001) find a significant effect of HIV/AIDS on "health capital" (as measured by life expectancy), but no significant impact of health capital on growth.

In interpreting these empirical studies, it is important to bear in mind two principal shortcomings. First, it is generally not possible at this stage of the epidemic to distinguish whether the observed changes in the growth rate of GDP per capita (if any) reflect long-term changes or changes in the level of steady-state GDP per capita associated with a temporary change in GDP growth as the economy adjusts to the new equilibrium. For example, it is not possible to extrapolate the findings of Bonnel (2000) beyond the 1990–97 period he considers. Second, the empirical analysis of the impact of HIV/AIDS on economic growth is beset with serious problems arising from errors in variables, affecting both the dependent variable (economic growth) and the HIV-related variables (mortality, prevalence, and so forth). Regarding GDP growth, the national accounts framework in many countries with high HIV prevalence rates is weak, and the data on GDP growth are unreliable. Data on HIV prevalence and mortality, in turn, are usually derived from relatively few observations, usually seroprevalence data from blood tests at antenatal clinics, which are incorporated into an epidemiological and demographic model to obtain aggregate estimates at the national level, with a large margin of error.

Balance of Payments

The two components of the balance of payments are the capital account (also called the financial account, which captures investment flows) and the current account (which comprises payments for goods and services, and transfers, including external grants). One of the concerns regarding the macroeconomic impact of HIV/AIDS, alluded to above, is that the deteriorating and uncertain economic outlook and higher production costs in afflicted countries are likely to deter investment. Domestic investors would shift funds abroad, and international investors would refrain from investing in the affected economy; as a consequence, the balance on the capital account would decline. At the same time, the grant flows associated with an expanded response to HIV/AIDS can be substantial, amounting to several percent of GDP in some countries. One of the possible adverse macroeconomic effects of such increased aid flows is Dutch disease: an inflow of external grants can cause the domestic currency to appreciate, reducing the competitiveness of domestic industry.

To understand the potential implications of capital outflows, consider the discussion above of the impact of HIV/AIDS on the growth of output and income per capita in an open economy. In the most commonly used closed-economy models, increased mortality and lower birthrates result in an increase in the capital-labor ratio, which mitigates the impact on output per capita. A higher capital-labor ratio, however, is associated with a decline in the rate of return to capital. In the open-economy model, investment responds to a decline in the rate of return to capital, by rising until this rate is back in line with the rate of return of some comparator asset. What are the quantitative implications for the capital account? In the numerical example in Box 2.1, based on Haacker (2002b), capital outflows cause output per capita in the open economy to decline by an additional 3.3 percent. Given an elasticity of output with respect to capital of 37 percent (see Box 2.1) and a capital-output ratio of 2 (a not-uncommon ratio for many developing countries), the accumulated change in the capital account (through larger capital outflows or a decline in foreign direct investment) could eventually amount to 19 percent of

GDP.[39] Even under the assumed conditions of perfect capital mobility, this accumulated change would materialize only as the demographic and economic impacts of the epidemic unfold over time. On an annual basis, the changes in the balance of payments are therefore much smaller than the eventual accumulated change. A second issue for the balance of payments is the increased grant inflows associated with an expanded response to HIV/AIDS. Most of these funds would initially finance prevention-related activities such as voluntary counseling and testing (which are projected to account for 9.5 percent of the total costs of scaling up HIV/AIDS activities in low- and middle-income countries in 2005; see UNAIDS, 2004), programs for populations at risk (19.3 percent), condom marketing and provision (8.7 percent), and management of sexually transmitted diseases (5.7 percent), or social expenditures such as community and orphan support (9.3 percent). Treatment and care—presumably with a somewhat higher import content—are projected to account for only about one-third of the costs of scaling up HIV/AIDS-related programs in 2005 and 2007. Thus most of the grant financing would finance locally provided services with a rather low import content, or transfers and social expenditure.

This raises the question of whether these grant inflows would create some imbalance in the balance of payments, causing currencies to appreciate in the recipient countries—a phenomenon commonly referred to as "Dutch disease." The empirical literature on the link between aid and Dutch disease is inconclusive.[40] In the case where grant inflows finance HIV/AIDS-related spending, it is also important to distinguish between changes in the nominal exchange rate and changes in productivity and competitiveness. From a macroeconomic perspective, HIV/AIDS-related expenditures are productive expenditures, enhancing the productive capacity of the economy both immediately (through treatment) and in the longer run (through enhanced prevention and orphan support). This would enhance productivity and competitiveness and facilitate the sterilization of foreign currency inflows.

Finally, although this discussion has treated the current and capital accounts as separate issues, one should not simply add up the effects of HIV/AIDS on the two, because the effects are interdependent. A comprehensive response to HIV/AIDS, financed through external grants, would mitigate many of the effects on demographics, productivity, and produc-

---

[39]This is calculated as (capital/GDP) × (percentage change in output)/(elasticity of output with respect to capital).

[40]For a more thorough discussion of the macroeconomic effects of external aid, see Nkusu (2004).

tion costs that give rise to capital outflows, and it would give rise to new investment opportunities, especially in the health sector. Thus a reduction in capital outflows (or an increase in foreign direct investment) would be part of a successful scenario financed by external grants.

Poverty and Inequality

HIV/AIDS affects most of the common indicators of living standards, such as income, health standards, and access to education. Success in combating HIV/AIDS, malaria, and other diseases is therefore itself one of the Millennium Development Goals (MDGs) defined by the United Nations, and it will have a direct effect on at least five other MDGs: eradicating extreme (income) poverty and hunger, achieving universal primary education, promoting gender equality and empowering women, reducing child mortality, and improving maternal health.[41] At the same time, poverty affects people's vulnerability to HIV/AIDS, both by increasing the risk of contracting the virus oneself (for example, through lack of education or sexual choice) and by reducing one's ability to deal with the economic and social consequences of AIDS: poor households are in a worse position than others to cope with the illness and death of a household member.

The primary objective of this and the following section is to show how HIV/AIDS, through its demographic and economic impacts, affects living standards at the individual and the household levels. Although it echoes the discussion of the microeconomic effects of HIV/AIDS, especially at the household level, the discussion also draws on the analysis of the impact of HIV/AIDS on economic growth. The key hypothesis guiding the discussion is that, in light of the uneven impact of HIV/AIDS across individuals and households, the distributional aspects of the impact of HIV/AIDS are as much a part of the picture for the economic or fiscal analysis of HIV/AIDS as the impacts on economic growth or income per capita. Without prejudice to the other dimensions of the impact of AIDS on poverty, the analysis here focuses on that impact in terms of household and individual income, since this most directly relates to the contents of this chapter. The discussion in this section is also complemented by the more extensive analysis by Greener (Chapter 5 of this volume).[42]

---

[41]The MDGs less directly affected are ensuring environmental sustainability and developing a global partnership for development.

[42]For broader discussions of the impact of HIV/AIDS on poverty, see also Loewenson and Whiteside (2001), van Donk (2002), and Whiteside (2002).

HIV/AIDS can affect poverty and the distribution of income in several ways. As wages and salaries (and other factor income) change, reflecting changes in factor markets, the income distribution changes. The most visible effects are on those households with an HIV-positive member. Through the loss of an income earner, or as other household members need to divert time from work to the care of one who is sick, the household's income declines. At the same time, the household's needs increase because of higher medical expenses.

Before discussing the link between HIV/AIDS and poverty, it is worth taking one step back to discuss the meaning of poverty in this context.[43] In most cases poverty is defined in terms of income, either in absolute terms such as dollars per capita or per household, or in relative terms, for example as a percentage of average household income in the economy. Households or individuals whose income is below some critical value, or poverty line, are classified as poor. A more comprehensive definition of poverty is needs based; here the poverty line is defined as the price of a consumption bundle, whose content is based on an assessment of critical needs, which may differ according to household characteristics. Because HIV/AIDS is associated with an increased need for health-related spending in those households affected, the critical income level will be higher for those households.

Not only can HIV/AIDS cause poverty, but poor households, in turn, are also more vulnerable to HIV/AIDS, in that they are less able than other households to maintain a given level of consumption when faced with some new adversity. Although health expenditure as a share of household income is frequently similar across households with different incomes, higher expenditure, of course, buys better health care. Moreover, higher-income households have better access to credit and insurance markets (for example, through employment-based health and social insurance), mitigating the impact of illness on living standards. Especially in the absence of well-functioning credit and insurance markets, a household's wealth is also relevant. A household that derives a larger share of its income from assets that it owns is in a better position to smooth consumption in response to changes in its income.

The discussion above of the macroeconomic effects of HIV/AIDS already has some implications for the distribution of income (and, to a much lesser extent, the incidence of poverty), primarily through changes

---

[43]The applicable definitions of poverty are discussed in more detail in Greener (Chapter 5, this volume).

Table 2.7. Income and Expenditure of Households Affected by Illness in South Africa
(Percent of income or expenditure in unaffected households)

Item	Any Illness	HIV/AIDS
Household income		
Total	84	71
Per person	74	61
Per adult equivalent	78	65
Household expenditure		
Total	81	78
Per person	70	68
Per adult equivalent	74	72

Source: Bachmann and Booysen (2003).

in wage rates. Typically, studies of the effects of HIV/AIDS on GDP per capita, inspired by the neoclassical growth model, distinguish between different types of labor (skilled and unskilled, for example) and between sectors (formal and informal; agriculture, manufacturing, and services; and so forth). Wage rates reflect the scarcity of each type of labor. If the macroeconomic model predicts that the incomes of skilled workers will increase, this points toward an increase in inequality, because skilled workers already typically draw higher salaries than unskilled workers. The principal limitation of this type of model in analyzing poverty and inequality, however, is that it focuses on the aggregate supply of labor rather than the well-being of households. Thus, in such an analysis, a worker dying of AIDS simply disappears from the labor force, whereas in fact the death of an income earner has obvious implications for the income and welfare of the affected household.

The most direct information on the impact of HIV/AIDS on households comes from case studies comparing households affected with those not affected by the disease (or by illness in general). For example, Bachmann and Booysen (2003), using a sample of 404 households from South Africa, find that income and expenditure for households affected by HIV/AIDS or other illness is substantially lower than for households not affected (Table 2.7). The impact of HIV/AIDS on income seems to be more severe than for other illnesses, and this is consistent with a higher incidence of hospital visits for people living with HIV.

The principal shortcoming of detailed case studies of the impact of HIV/AIDS is the limited sample size. An alternative approach, taken by Greener (Chapter 5, this volume) and the earlier study from Botswana that this chapter draws on, by Greener, Jefferis, and Siphambe (2000), combines a macroeconomic framework with detailed data on household income and household composition from a Household Income and Expenditure Survey and a definition of poverty based on the costs of a basket of basic goods. Unlike Bachmann and Booysen (2003), this study focuses on the impact of HIV/AIDS owing to increased mortality only, modeled as a one-time shock, and thus does not capture the adverse impact on the households of people living with HIV.

The primary effect of HIV/AIDS on poverty and inequality in Greener (Chapter 5, this volume) derives from its impact on household incomes. The study finds that, for a given wage rate, HIV/AIDS results in an increase in the poverty rate, and that poor households are disproportionately affected. The household poverty count increases from 37.7 percent to 43.7 percent. At the same time, however, inequality as measured by the Gini coefficient barely changes. Adding the changes in the macroeconomic environment to the analysis mitigates the impact on the household poverty count by 1 percentage point, as household income in this case rises. Thus the study confirms that income per capita is not a meaningful indicator of the impact of HIV/AIDS on poverty: although income per capita rises on average, poverty rates increase.

The studies just discussed cover a relatively short time horizon. In fact, the impact of HIV/AIDS on poverty is likely to evolve over a longer period, as more households become affected; on the other hand, the fortunes of a household affected by HIV/AIDS today may improve in the future. In the absence of empirical studies thus far, a hypothetical example will illustrate this point. Consider an economy in which all households are either "rich" or "poor." The evolution of the income distribution over time can be characterized by a transition matrix, which shows the probability that a household will remain rich or poor in the next year or move up or down this simplistic income distribution. Formally,

$$\begin{bmatrix} s_{r,t}+1 \\ s_{r,t}+1 \end{bmatrix} = \begin{bmatrix} \alpha_{rr} & \alpha_{rp} \\ \alpha_{rr} & \alpha_{rp} \end{bmatrix} \begin{bmatrix} s_{r,t} \\ s_{r,t} \end{bmatrix}, \tag{10}$$

where $s_{r,t}$ and $s_{p,t}$ represent the shares of the rich and the poor in the population at time t, respectively, and α_{rp} denotes the probability that a poor household will belong to the rich group in the next period. Assume that, in a given year, 2 percent of rich households experience an adverse shock and become poor ($\alpha_{pr} = 0.02$, and therefore $\alpha_{rr} = 0.98$), and 4 percent of poor households become rich ($\alpha_{rp} = 0.04$). Over time the economy will then converge to a steady state in which 67 percent of households are rich and 33 percent are poor. Now assume that, because of HIV/AIDS, 2 percent of households each year will lose an income earner. As a consequence, half of the rich households affected will become poor (and α_{pr} rises by about 1 percentage point, to 0.0298), and none of the poor households affected will become rich (α_{rp} falls to 0.0392). This would mean that, over time, with more rich households becoming poor and fewer poor households becoming rich, the poverty rate rises from 33 percent to 43 percent in the new steady state. Although this example is only illustrative, it suggests that even a relatively low incidence of HIV/AIDS can have a substantial impact on poverty rates as this impact accumulates over time.[44]

Booysen (2003) uses this type of approach over a relatively short time horizon and shows that HIV/AIDS is associated with a decline in the income ranking of the affected households. He uses a relatively small sample (325 households, with three semiannual observations for each), which he sorts into five income quintiles.[45] His findings suggest that households affected by HIV/AIDS are more likely to move down the income distribution and less likely to move up. The principal difference between this analysis and the example above is that Booysen focuses on the income distribution (and movements of households affected by HIV/AIDS within the distribution) rather than movements relative to some poverty line.

One study concerned with the impact of HIV/AIDS on poverty in the long run is that by Bell, Devarajan, and Gersbach (Chapter 3, this volume), already discussed above in the context of economic growth. In that chapter HIV/AIDS has an immediate impact on household income; in terms of the above transition matrix, α_{pr}, the probability of a rich household turning poor, increases. Additionally, there are some factors at play that affect the future prospects of household members, including a disruption of the transfer of human capital between parents and children and a disadvantage in access to formal education. Thus for those households α_{rp}, the probability of becoming rich, may decline.

Two primary conclusions can be drawn from this analysis of the impact of HIV/AIDS on poverty (as measured here in terms of household or individual income). First, because the economic impact of HIV/AIDS is very uneven across households (depending, in the first place, on whether a household member has become infected or dies), aggregate measures of the economic impact of HIV/AIDS provide very little information regarding the impact on poverty. Second, the impact of HIV/AIDS may accumulate over time, because an increased risk of becoming poor at some point during a given period of time—measured in terms of the coefficients in a

---

[44]In this numerical example, it takes 10 years to complete half of the adjustment toward the new steady state.

[45]The sample appears to be the same as in Bachmann and Booysen (2003), apart from attrition between the second and third wave of the exercise.

transition matrix as in equation (10)—translates into larger changes in the steady-state income distribution. Similarly, but looking at a longer time frame, the impact of HIV/AIDS may be cumulative because its adverse effects are passed on to the next generation, for example in terms of children's education as in the study by Bell, Devarajan, and Gersbach.

Risk and Welfare

The presence of HIV/AIDS increases individual risk—to health and life, but also in terms of material living standards—and most measures of welfare are in some way affected by such changes. This section discusses first some of the direct economic effects of the increased risk to individuals due to HIV/AIDS. However, the fact that economic and social institutions must adjust to cope with the impact of increased mortality often has implications of its own for individual risk. Against this background, this section will discuss several measures of welfare and provide examples of the impact of HIV/AIDS on welfare in several countries.

Economic Repercussions of Increased Risk

Through its impact on morbidity and mortality and its many economic repercussions, an increased prevalence of HIV/AIDS is associated with an increase in economic risk. This increased risk derives most directly from the decrease in life expectancy, but also from increased uncertainty about future living standards, business prospects, and the general economic outlook. Increased risk, in turn, affects the behavior of those subject to it and, consequently, the whole economy. The broad economic repercussions, in turn, generally result in a further increase in individual risk. Figure 2.3 illustrates the macroeconomic effects of increased economic risk and how the impact of HIV/AIDS on the economy indirectly increases individual risk.

Through its impact on mortality and life expectancy, HIV/AIDS reduces the expected returns to investments in human capital, both directly for the individuals concerned and—in the context of an overlapping-generations model—for their children. This insight is at the core of the theoretical analysis in Bell, Devarajan, and Gersbach (2003, and Chapter 3, this volume); Birdsall and Hamoudi (Chapter 4, this volume) provide some empirical evidence for this relationship. Increased mortality risk also affects the expected returns from other forms of savings. When individuals perceive that their mortality risk has increased, they will discount

Figure 2.3. HIV/AIDS, Individual Risk, and the Economy

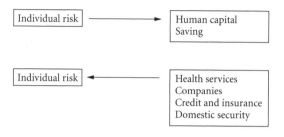

future earnings at a higher rate. Thus the incentive to save income or invest in assets declines.[46] Moreover, domestic private savings decline if additional health expenditures are partly financed from savings. On the other hand, the economic risk associated with HIV infection could encourage precautionary saving.

Through its macroeconomic impacts, HIV/AIDS also has more indirect effects on the economic risk faced by households and individuals. The most important of these are the impact on public health services, on companies (especially their willingness and ability to provide employment-based risk benefits), and on credit and insurance markets. In most countries facing severe epidemics, health insurance coverage is very limited, but public health expenditure implicitly provides some degree of insurance. The available evidence suggests that, so far, existing health services can barely cope with the increased demand, and they respond by rationing services. Thus, in the absence of greatly increased resources, public health services can no longer fulfill their role of providing some degree of health insurance to those not covered by formal health insurance schemes.

As discussed in more detail above, employees in the formal sector are frequently covered by a corporate health insurance policy and receive certain death-related benefits. In response to the rising cost of these benefits, many companies have reduced the coverage of their health insurance plans and have shifted their pension plans from defined-benefit schemes to defined-contribution schemes. Such a change in pension arrangements typically means that employees dying from AIDS will receive less, because they are likely to die at a relatively young age.

Additionally, HIV/AIDS affects the functioning of credit and insurance markets, as increased mortality raises individual default risk for personal

---

[46]Freire (2002) analyzes this aspect in the context of South Africa.

loans and increases the cost of life insurance.[47] Regarding loans, it is useful to distinguish between personal loans and mortgages. For personal loans the primary effect of increased mortality-related default risk is an increase in the cost of lending. To the extent that prevalence rates differ across population groups, borrowers in high-prevalence groups are likely to see their access to credit deteriorate. For people known to be HIV-positive, Jurisich, Liber, and Elkounovitch (2002) report that "some 30 percent of non-mortgage lenders would decline a loan, [and the other lenders indicated that] a solution might be found using a combination of a shorter loan term, other security methods . . . [or] ensuring that there is existing insurance in place." For mortgages, which tend to involve larger sums and longer repayment periods, banks tend to be more concerned about mortality-related default and may ask that the borrower take out life insurance as a condition for lending. In that case, if HIV-positive borrowers cannot obtain life insurance, they are excluded from obtaining or refinancing a mortgage.

Finally, and echoing the earlier discussion of social and economic institutions, HIV/AIDS increases individual risk to the extent that it adversely affects domestic security. Most directly, widespread prevalence of HIV/AIDS impairs the capacities of government institutions to fulfill their tasks, including the enforcement of domestic security. At the same time, poverty rates may increase and access to education may decline, both of which could eventually increase the incidence of crime. More generally, the World Bank's recent report on civil war and development policy (Collier and others, 2003, discussed above) makes the case that the incidence of civil war is much higher in low-income countries whose economies are stagnant or declining. Thus, in politically unstable countries, an HIV/AIDS epidemic, by hindering or reversing economic development, contributes to a political and economic setting that makes domestic conflict more likely.

Welfare

Changes in income per capita fail to capture the full impact of HIV/AIDS on living standards, primarily because increased mortality means that lives become more uncertain and, on average, shorter, but also

---

[47]Jurisich, Liber, and Elkounovitch (2002), in a study from South Africa, report that death-related defaults accounted for 28 percent of defaults on loans and 20 percent of defaults on mortgages. Because mortality is expected to rise over the next several years, these shares (and overall default risk) are likely to increase.

Table 2.8. Human Development Indices for Selected Countries, 1950–2001

Country	1950	1975	2001 Actual	2001 In absence of AIDS
Botswana	0.25	0.50	0.57	0.77
Malawi	0.27	n.a.	0.48	0.52
Mozambique	0.16	0.32	0.39	0.48
Haiti	0.18	n.a.	0.32	0.36
South Africa	0.48	0.65	0.68	0.77
Swaziland	0.24	0.51	0.58	0.74
Thailand	0.39	0.60	0.78	0.79

Sources: Crafts (2001); and author's calculations based on data from United Nations Development Programme (2003) and the U.S. Census Bureau.

because of the manifold economic repercussions of HIV/AIDS discussed above. Having already addressed the impact of HIV/AIDS on many of the specific aspects of economic development (such as access to education, health standards, and poverty rates), this chapter will instead focus in this section on two summary measures of the impact of HIV/AIDS on welfare. The first of these is the Human Development Index (HDI) developed by the United Nations Development Programme (2003), and the second (used, for example, in Crafts and Haacker, Chapter 6 of this volume) is a measure based on individuals' valuations of increased mortality risk.

The HDI attaches equal weights to educational attainment, income per capita, and life expectancy at birth, all three of which are likely to be affected by HIV/AIDS. The largest impact, however, comes from declining life expectancy; changes in the other two factors are more uncertain and dependent on the policy response and as such are not included in the present analysis. Table 2.8 illustrates the changes in the HDI brought about by the lowering of life expectancy due to HIV/AIDS and establishes a historical perspective. It demonstrates how the reduced life expectancy at birth due to HIV/AIDS slows an economy's development as measured by the HDI and offsets any gains in educational attainment and GDP per capita. For example, whereas countries like Botswana, South Africa, and Swaziland—had they not been affected by severe HIV/AIDS epidemics—might have attained living standards (as measured by the HDI) comparable to those in Brazil or Russia, their HDIs are now more comparable to those in countries like Bolivia (for South Africa), or India and Cambodia (for Botswana and Swaziland).

The second approach involves imputing the costs of increasing mortality from individuals' valuations of increased mortality risk. This approach has an explicit foundation in the microeconomic theory of the consumer:

Table 2.9. Aggregate Welfare Effect of Increased Mortality, 2004

Country	Change: In mortality (percentage points)	Change: In life expectancy (percent)	Change: In welfare (percent)
Botswana	3.1	−59.1	−88.9
Côte d'Ivoire	0.4	−13.3	−37.3
Ethiopia	0.2	−8.5	−25.3
Haiti	0.3	−12.7	−33.9
South Africa	1.1	−32.3	−69.6
Thailand	0.02	−0.8	−2.3
Zambia	1.1	−32.3	−68.8

expected lifetime utility declines if mortality rises (and, consequently, life expectancy falls). One can measure the welfare loss associated with increased mortality by determining the loss in income that, for a given individual, would yield the same loss in lifetime utility as the observed loss in life expectancy. In general, risk aversion implies that the welfare loss thus defined will exceed the loss in expected income owing to reduced life expectancy. This means that an increase in risk, as measured by increased mortality owing to HIV/AIDS or through its economic repercussions, can have strong implications for welfare.

Estimating the welfare loss associated with increased mortality requires estimating the trade-off between income and mortality or life expectancy. In the literature, such estimates of the "value of statistical life" are typically obtained from wage differentials between jobs with different mortality risks; data on these differentials are often available from past assessments of environmental or health interventions. Table 2.9 summarizes estimates of the welfare loss due to HIV/AIDS from Crafts and Haacker (Chapter 6, this volume), which also describes this approach in more detail.

The estimates reported in Table 2.9 suggest that the welfare effects of increased mortality are huge, dwarfing even the most pessimistic estimates of the economic impact in terms of GDP per capita. Among the countries covered here, welfare losses range from 2.3 percent of GDP in Thailand, where life expectancy declines by 0.8 percent, to 89 percent of GDP for Botswana, with life expectancy declining by 59 percent.[48] Whatever the significance of these point estimates, they clearly show that the impact of

---

[48]The fact that the estimated welfare loss is larger than the decline in life expectancy can be linked to individuals' preferences; the estimates imply that these preferences exhibit some degree of risk aversion, which is a standard assumption in the microeconomic literature. See Crafts and Haacker (Chapter 6, this volume) for a more detailed discussion.

HIV/AIDS on economic growth and income per capita, although a useful measure in many respects, is not a meaningful indicator of the full economic costs of the epidemic.

Conclusions and Outlook

The primary effect of HIV/AIDS is an increase in mortality and a deterioration in health. The epidemic affects primarily young adults, who are integrated into all areas of economic and social life, and this chapter has highlighted its effects at the household level, for businesses, and for government services. With mortality rates for the working-age population increasing manyfold in countries with severe epidemics, the economic impact is grave: indeed, HIV/AIDS is clearly the most serious impediment to economic growth and development in these countries. Therefore an understanding of the economic consequences of HIV/AIDS is essential for economic analysts and policymakers working in countries with severe epidemics.

However, the channels through which HIV/AIDS affects economic growth are not well understood. Most of the earlier studies focused on disruptions to the production process associated with increased mortality and morbidity and on the impact of increased health expenditure on domestic saving. This chapter's analysis of the microeconomic effects of HIV/AIDS, for example on households and the private sector, and of the impact on social and economic institutions in general, suggests that these effects are very serious and that many are not captured in macroeconomic assessments. Studies that have attempted to capture some of these effects (such as Bell, Devarajan, and Gersbach, Chapter 3, this volume, for households, and Haacker, 2002b, for investment) find substantial downside risks to economic growth, related, for example, to the accumulation of human capital and its transfer between generations at the household level, and to capital outflows or declines in foreign direct investment.

Although the impact of HIV/AIDS on economic growth is important for a variety of reasons, it is necessary to keep in mind that this impact is spread very unevenly across the population. It is obviously most profound for people living with HIV/AIDS, and their households, especially when the afflicted member is an income earner. On the other hand, many households are affected only through the macroeconomic repercussions of HIV/AIDS, and some may even benefit, for example when a worker is promoted to replace someone who has died, or when a business competitor closes down. Thus, even if the estimated impact of HIV/AIDS on average income per capita is small, poverty rates can increase.[49] More generally, it is questionable whether GDP and GDP per capita are meaningful measures of the economic impact of HIV/AIDS. If, for example, the probability for a 20-year-old to survive until age 60 declines from over 70 percent to less than 30 percent, this has a serious impact on living standards beyond any changes in consumption.[50] Several studies have attempted to assess the impact of increased mortality on welfare directly,[51] and they find that it dwarfs any estimated effects on economic growth. Even for countries with only moderate HIV epidemics, such as Vietnam (Table 2.9), the welfare losses can be significant; for some of the worst-affected countries, such as South Africa and Botswana, they can exceed three-fourths of GDP.

HIV/AIDS, through its numerous impacts on households and individuals, on the productive capacity of the economy, and on government finances, is a serious constraint on economic development. In many countries with severe epidemics, it is the single most serious challenge today to maintaining and, where possible, improving living standards. However, getting the response right, in terms of preventing new infections and mitigating the impact of those that do occur, represents a huge challenge to governments and their development partners, especially where the human capacities of the public services are themselves eroded by the epidemic. The international community has responded by developing programs, such as the WHO's "3 by 5" initiative, designed to increase access to treatment quickly and substantially. The analysis in this chapter shows that these international efforts are warranted, indeed imperative, when measured against the economic development objectives of the international community.

References

Ainsworth, Martha, Kathleen Beegle, and Godlike Koda, 2002, "The Impact of Adult Mortality on Primary School Enrollment in Northwestern Tanzania," Africa Region Human Development Working Paper (Washington: World Bank).

Arndt, Channing, 2003, "HIV/AIDS, Human Capital, and Economic Growth Prospects for Mozambique," Africa Region Working Paper No. 48 (Washington: World Bank).

---

[49]See Greener (Chapter 5, this volume)

[50]The numerical example of survival rates by age is based on Table 7.1 in Haacker (Chapter 7, this volume) and applies to Zambia in 2004.

[51]See, for example, Crafts and Haacker (Chapter 6, this volume) and Jamison, Sachs, and Wang (2001).

————, and Jeffrey D. Lewis, 2001, "The HIV/AIDS Pandemic in South Africa: Sectoral Impacts and Unemployment," *Journal of International Development*, Vol. 13, No. 4, pp. 427–49.

Aventin, Laurent, and Pierre Huard, 2000, "The Cost of AIDS to Three Manufacturing Firms in Côte d'Ivoire," *Journal of African Economics*, Vol. 9, No. 2, pp. 161–88.

Bachmann, Max O., and Frederick le Roux Booysen, 2003, "Health and Economic Impact of HIV/AIDS on South African Households: A Cohort Study," *BMC Public Health*, Vol. 3, No. 1.

Barbone, Luca, and Luis-Alvaro Sanchez B., 1999, "Pensions and Social Security in Sub-Saharan Africa: Issues and Options," World Bank Africa Region Working Paper No. 4 (Washington: World Bank).

Barro, Robert J., N. Gregory Mankiw, and Xavier Sala-i-Martin, 1995, "Capital Mobility in Neoclassical Models of Growth," *American Economic Review*, Vol. 85, No. 1, pp. 103–15.

Bell, Clive, Shantayanan Devarajan, and Hans Gersbach, 2003, "The Long-Run Economic Costs of AIDS: Theory and an Application to South Africa," Policy Research Working Paper No. 3152 (Washington: World Bank).

Bloom, David E., and Ajay S. Mahal, 1997, "Does the AIDS Epidemic Threaten Economic Growth?" *Journal of Econometrics*, Vol. 77, No. 1, pp. 105–24.

Bonnel, René, 2000, "HIV/AIDS and Economic Growth: A Global Perspective," *South African Journal of Economics*, Vol. 68, No. 5, pp. 820–855.

Booysen, Frederick le Roux, 2003, "Poverty Dynamics and HIV/AIDS-Related Morbidity and Mortality in South Africa," paper presented at an international conference on "Empirical Evidence for the Demographic and Socio-Economic Impact of AIDS," Health Economics and HIV/AIDS Research Division (HEARD), University of KwaZulu-Natal, South Africa, March 26–28.

————, and Tanya Arntz, 2001, "The Socio-Economic Impact of HIV/AIDS on Households: A Review of the Literature" (Blomfontein, South Africa: Centre for Development Support and Joint Centre for Political and Economic Studies).

Botswana Institute for Development Policy Analysis (BIDPA), 2000, "Macroeconomic Impacts of the HIV/AIDS Epidemic in Botswana" (Gaborone, Botswana).

Bureau for Economic Research (BER), 2001, "The Macro-Economic Impact of HIV/AIDS in South Africa," Economic Research Note No. 10 (University of Stellenbosch, South Africa).

————, 2004, "The Impact of HIV/AIDS on Business in South Africa" (University of Stellenbosch, South Africa).

Case, Anne, Christina Paxson, and Joseph Ableidinger, 2002, "Orphans in Africa," Working Paper No. 9213 (Cambridge, Massachusetts: National Bureau of Economic Research).

Coetzee, Celeste, 2003, "Hiring Patterns, Firm Level Dynamics and HIV/AIDS: A Case Study of Small Firms on the Cape Flats," Centre for Social Science Research (CSSR), Working Paper No. 52 (Rondebosch, South Africa: University of Cape Town).

Collier, Paul, and others, 2003, *Breaking the Conflict Trap. Civil War and Development Policy* (New York: World Bank and Oxford University Press).

Connelly, Patrick, and Sydney Rosen, 2004, "Will Small and Medium Enterprises Provide HIV/AIDS Services to Employees? An Analysis of Market Demand" (unpublished; Boston: Center for International Health and Development, Boston University School of Public Health).

Crafts, Nicholas, 2001, "The Contribution of Increased Life Expectancy to Growth of Living Standards in the UK," 1870–1998" (unpublished; London School of Economics).

Cuddington, John T., 1993a, "Modeling the Macroeconomic Effects of AIDS, with an Application to Tanzania," *World Bank Economic Review,* Vol. 7, No. 2, pp. 173–89.

———, 1993b, "Further Results on the Macroeconomic Effects of AIDS: The Dualistic, Labour-Surplus Economy," *World Bank Economic Review,* Vol. 7, No. 3, pp. 403–17.

Dixon, Simon, Scott McDonald, and Jennifer Roberts, "HIV/AIDS and Development in Africa," *Journal of International Development,* Vol. 13 (May), pp. 381–521.

Drouhin, Nicholas, Vincent Touzé, and Bruno Ventelou, 2003, "AIDS and Economic Growth in Africa: A Critical Assessment of the 'Base-Case Scenario' Approach," in *Economics of AIDS and Access to HIV/AIDS Care in Developing Countries: Issues and Challenges,* ed. by Jean-Paul Moatti and others (Paris: Agence Nationale de Recherches sur le SIDA).

Ebony Consulting International and Malawi National Statistical Office, 2000, "Malawi National Gemini MSE Baseline Survey" (Lilongwe, Malawi).

Ferreira, Pedro Cavalcanti, and Samual Pessoa, 2003, "The Long-Run Economic Impact of AIDS" (Rio de Janeiro: Graduate School of Economics, Fundação Getulio Vargas).

Fox, Matthew P., and others, 2004, "The Impact of HIV/AIDS on Labour Productivity in Kenya," *Tropical Medicine and International Health,* Vol. 9, No. 3, pp. 318–24.

Freire, Sandra, 2002, "Impact of HIV/AIDS on Saving Behaviour in South Africa," paper presented at the IAEN Symposium on the Economics of HIV/AIDS in Developing Countries, Barcelona, July 6–7.

Greener, Robert, Keith Jefferis, and Happy Siphambe, 2000, "The Impact of HIV/AIDS on Poverty and Inequality in Botswana," *South African Journal of Economics,* Vol. 68, No. 5, p. 888–915.

Haacker, Markus, 2002a, "The Economic Consequences of HIV/AIDS in Southern Africa," IMF Working Paper 02/38 (Washington: International Monetary Fund).

———, 2002b, "Modeling the Macroeconomic Impact of HIV/AIDS," IMF Working Paper 02/195 (Washington: International Monetary Fund).

ING Barings South African Research, 2000, "Economic Impact of AIDS in South Africa: A Dark Cloud on the Horizon" (Johannesburg, South Africa: ING Barings South Africa).

International Crisis Group (ICG), 2001, "HIV/AIDS as a Security Issue" (Washington and Brussels).

Jamison, Dean, Jeffrey D. Sachs, and Jia Wang, 2001, "The Effect of the AIDS Epidemic on Economic Welfare in Sub-Saharan Africa," CMH Working Paper No. WG1:13 (Geneva: Commission on Macroeconomics and Health, World Health Organization).

Joint United Nations Programme on HIV/AIDS (UNAIDS), 2004, *2004 Report on the Global AIDS Epidemic* (Geneva).

————, United Nations Children's Fund (UNICEF), and U.S. Agency for International Development (USAID), 2004, "Children on the Brink 2004: A Joint Report of New Orphan Estimates and a Framework for Action" (Geneva, New York, and Washington).

Jurisich, Stephen, Dominic Liber, and Ron Elkounovitch, 2002, "The Calm Before the Storm (1): Perceptions of, and Responses to, the Risk of HIV/AIDS in the Low-Income Housing Finance Sector," Occasional Paper No. 6 (Johannesburg, South Africa: Housing Finance Resource Programme).

Kambou, Gérard, Shantayanan Devarajan, and Mead Over, 1992, "The Economic Impact of AIDS in an African Country: Simulations with a Computable General Equilibrium Model of Cameroon," *Journal of African Economies*, Vol. 1 No. 1, pp. 109–30.

Loewenson, Rene, and Alan Whiteside, 2001, "HIV/AIDS: Implications for Poverty Reduction," background paper for the UN General Assembly on HIV/AIDS, June 25–27, United Nations Development Programme.

Mather, David, and others, 2004, "A Cross-Country Analysis of Household Response to Adult Mortality in Rural Sub-Saharan Africa: Implications for HIV/AIDS Mitigation and Rural Development Policies," International Development Working Paper No. 82 (East Lansing, Michigan: Michigan State University).

Moore, Deane, 1999, "The AIDS Threat and the Private Sector," *AIDS Analysis Africa*, Vol. 9, No. 6, pp. 1–2.

Morris, Chester N., and Edward J. Cheevers, 2000, "The Direct Costs of HIV/AIDS in a South African Sugar Mill," *AIDS Analysis Africa*, Vol. 10, No. 5, pp. 7–8.

Naidu, Veni, 2003, "Economic Impact of HIV/AIDS on Urban Households—A Pilot Study in Soweto." Available via the Internet: www.jeapp.org.za/attachment.php?attachmentid=14.

Nelufule, Maanda David, 2004, "AIDS and Democracy: What Do We Know?" (Durban, South Africa: Health Economics and HIV/AIDS Research Division, University of KwaZulu-Natal).

Nkusu, Mwanza, 2004, "Aid and the Dutch Disease in Low-Income Countries: Informed Diagnoses for Prudent Prognoses," IMF Working Paper No. 4/49 (Washington: International Monetary Fund).

Over, Mead, 1992, "The Macroeconomic Impact of HIV/AIDS in Sub-Saharan Africa," Africa Technical Working Paper No. 3 (Washington: Population Health and Nutrition Division, Africa Technical Department, World Bank).

Phororo, Hopolang, 2003, "HIV/AIDS and the Private Sector in Namibia: Getting the Small Businesses on Board," Occasional Paper No. 3/2003 (Windhoek, Namibia: Hanns Seidel Foundation Namibia).

Rosen, Sydney, 2002, "What Makes Nigerian Manufacturing Firms Take Action on HIV/AIDS?" Findings Report No. 199 (Washington: Africa Region, World Bank).

———, and Jonathan L. Simon, 2003, "Shifting the Burden: The Private Sector's Response to the AIDS Epidemic in Africa," *Bulletin of the World Health Organization*, Vol. 81, No. 2, pp. 131–37.

Rosen, Sydney, and others, 2001, "Investing in the Epidemic: The Impact of HIV/AIDS on Businesses in Southern Africa," presentation at the Center for International Health, Boston University School of Public Health.

———, 2003, "Why Do Nigerian Manufacturing Firms Take Action on AIDS?" Health and Development Discussion Paper No. 3 (Boston: Center for International Health and Development, Boston University School of Public Health).

———, 2004, "The Cost of HIV/AIDS to Businesses in Southern Africa," *AIDS*, Vol. 18, No. 2, pp. 317–24.

Rugalema, Gabriel, with Silke Weigang and James Mbwika, 1999, "HIV/AIDS and the Commercial Agricultural Sector of Kenya—Impact, Vulnerability, Susceptibility, and Coping Strategies" (Rome: Food and Agriculture Organization of the United Nations).

Sanlam, 2004, "The 2004 Sanlam Survey on Retirement Benefits" (Bellville, South Africa).

Steinberg, Malcolm, and others, 2002, "Hitting Home: How Households Cope with the Impact of the HIV/AIDS Epidemic," Publication No. 6059 (Washington: Kaiser Family Foundation).

Summers, Todd, and Jennifer Kates, 2003, "Global Funding for HIV/AIDS in Resource Poor Settings" (Washington: Kaiser Family Foundation).

Topouzis, Daphne, 2003, "Addressing the Impact of HIV/AIDS on Ministries of Agriculture: Focus on Eastern and Southern Africa" (Rome: Food and Agriculture Organization and Joint United Nations Programme on HIV/AIDS).

United Nations Children's Fund, 2003, *Africa's Orphaned Generations* (New York).

United Nations Development Programme, 2003, *Human Development Report* (New York).

van Donk, Mirjam, 2002, "Conceptual Shifts for Sound Planning: Towards an Integrated Approach on HIV/AIDS and Poverty," Concept Paper No. 1 (Pretoria, South Africa: UNDP Regional Project on HIV and Development).

———, 2003, "Understanding the Link Between Development Planning and HIV/AIDS in Sub-Saharan Africa," Concept Paper No. 2 (Pretoria, South Africa: UNDP Regional Project on HIV and Development).

Whiteside, Alan, 2002, "Poverty and HIV/AIDS in Africa," *Third World Quarterly*, Vol. 23, No. 2, pp. 313–32.

World Bank, 1999, *Confronting AIDS: Public Priorities in a Global Epidemic* (New York: Oxford University Press, rev. ed.).

World Health Organization, 2004, *The World Health Report 2004—Changing History* (Geneva).

Yamano, Takashi, and T.S. Jayne, 2004, "Measuring the Impacts of Working Age Adult Death on Rural Households in Kenya," *World Development*, Vol. 32, No. 1, pp. 91–119.

3

Thinking About the Long-Run Economic Costs of AIDS

Clive Bell, Shantayanan Devarajan, and Hans Gersbach

In his book *Plagues and Peoples*, McNeill (1976) views history as the interplay between an array of parasites and their human hosts—a struggle in which communicable diseases and human responses to them have profound social, economic, and cultural effects. Following the outbreak of the AIDS epidemic in the 1980s, humanity must now contend with a new great plague, the scale and character of which will surely put McNeill's thesis to the test. One vital lesson to be drawn from his account is that any attempt to understand the effects of the AIDS epidemic must take a long-term perspective. That is a salient feature of the approach we adopt here: we will argue that, from modest beginnings, the economic damage caused by AIDS can assume catastrophic proportions over the long run, and thereby threaten the social fabric itself.

The disease is selective, and its individual course is both lengthy and, until the end stages, largely free of symptoms. Yet when they do sicken, its victims are still overwhelmingly young adults or those in the prime of life, the great majority of them with children to raise and care for. The nature of the long-term threat to social well-being now becomes clear. If parents sicken and die while their children are still young, then the means available with which to raise their children so that they can become productive and capable citizens will be greatly reduced. The affected families' lifetime income will shrink, and with it the means to finance their children's education, whether in the form of school fees or taxes. When a parent dies, moreover, the children lose the love, knowledge, and guidance that complement formal education. AIDS does much more, therefore, than destroy the existing abilities and capacities—the human capital—embodied in its victims; it also weakens the mechanism through which human capital is formed in the next generation and beyond. These ramifications will take decades to make themselves fully felt: like the course of the disease in individuals, they are long drawn out and insidious. To this it should be added that the incessant reminders of the likelihood of an untimely death can seize both individuals and society with a pessimism that hinders provision for the future.

AIDS, like all causes of premature adult mortality, is also a potentially powerful generator of poverty and inequality. Some children will grow up enjoying the care and resources provided by two parents, others will have to make do with only one, and still others will suffer the loss of both. In societies based on nuclear families, special arrangements are required to support one-parent families, and full orphans must hope for adoption into a loving family as the alternative to an orphanage—or to life on the streets. Determined and compassionate policies can provide material security and education, but hardly love and affection. The ideal extended family, in which all children, natural and adopted alike, are valued and treated identically by the surviving adults, solves both problems of insurance. When premature adult mortality is rising, however, both systems come under increasing strain, as the burden on surviving adults grows. AIDS therefore poses a threat not only to the support of needy nuclear families, but also to the traditional extended family as an institution.

The above account assigns central roles, first, to the formation of human capital through a process in which childrearing and formal education combine to produce the wellspring of long-term economic growth, and, second, to premature adult mortality as the primary threat to that process. The setting is one in which the decision-making unit is the household, nuclear or extended, and premature adult mortality can result in inequality among households. These features are in sharp contrast to much of the existing literature on the long-run macroeconomic effects of AIDS, in which a "beneficial" lower rate of population growth vies in an aggregate world with the diversion of savings away from the formation of physical capital, with a heavy emphasis on steady-state analysis. The natural choice of framework for our purposes is therefore the overlapping-generations (OLG) model, rather than the usual Solow (1956) model.

The plan of the chapter is as follows. We first motivate our approach by identifying the main economic consequences of AIDS and describing the sheer scale of the wave of premature adult mortality that now threatens to engulf many countries in eastern and southern Africa. A detailed treatment of the OLG model, which incorporates a wide array of these effects, is set out in the next section, followed by an analysis of the outbreak of the epidemic and its effects. We then examine the policy problem, namely, how to find the right combination of interventions to preserve economic growth in the face of the epidemic. In the penultimate section we discuss some of the economic effects of the epidemic that the earlier sections mostly neglected and show how they, too, can be incorporated into that framework. We draw together our conclusions in the final section.

The Approach and Its Motivation

We begin by listing what are arguably the primary effects of morbidity and mortality in the age groups that AIDS typically strikes, namely, young and prime-aged adults. It is useful to order such effects, whether due to AIDS or to other causes, in the following way:

(a) Morbidity reduces productivity on the job or results in outright absenteeism. If the worker dies, his or her skills and experience are destroyed.

(b) Firms and the government lose trained workers on both counts and must replace them. In particular, many teachers die prematurely of AIDS.

(c) Substantial expenditure, public and private alike, may be required to treat and care for those who become sick. (This is certainly so in the case of AIDS.)

(d) Savings are also diverted out of net investment in physical and human capital into the treatment and replacement of workers who fall sick and die.

(e) Lifetime family income is greatly reduced, and with it the family's means to invest.

(f) Children lose the love, care, guidance, and knowledge of one or both parents, which plausibly weakens the transmission of knowledge and capacity from generation to generation.

(g) The tax base shrinks.

(h) Collateralization in credit markets becomes more difficult, and as a consequence credit markets function less well.

(i) Social cohesion and social capital decline.

Most of the earlier work on the macroeconomic effects of AIDS focused on the first two effects, which are concerned with disruptions to the production process. These contributions have been based on variants of the Solow (1956) model, in which the level of productivity in the long run depends on thrift and the rate of population growth. In this framework a general increase in mortality, with unchanged fertility and thrift, will reduce the pressure of population on existing land and physical capital, and so increase productivity in both the short and the long run. When applied empirically to countries heavily afflicted by AIDS, the model yields predictable results, namely, that the epidemic tends to reduce the aggregate rate of growth—the estimates range from –0.3 to –1.5 percentage points a year—but to *increase* the rate of growth of GDP per capita.[1] The latter finding has driven some authors to tinker with other elements of the model, commonly in the form of diverting savings from the formation of physical capital into expenditure on health—effects (c) and (d) above—and of lowering the productivity of infected individuals in an attempt to overturn it; but these exertions often bring about only modest "corrections."

This chapter will argue that a different sort of framework, with a wholly different emphasis, is needed. The center stage is given over to the formation of human capital as the main wellspring of economic growth, in which the transmission of capacities and knowledge across generations within nuclear or extended family structures plays a vital role. Effects (e) through (g) weaken the mechanism through which human capital is accumulated, by depriving the victims' children of parental upbringing and, very likely, of as much education as they would otherwise have enjoyed. Expectations concerning the future level of premature adult mortality come into play here, because it affects the expected returns on investment in human capital. To the extent that the education both of children in general and of needy children in particular is supported by public expenditure, and that medical treatment and survivors' pensions are publicly provided, a reduction in tax revenue aggravates the problem. Completing the list, poorly functioning capital markets also hinder economic growth, as does a lack of social cohesion and social capital understood in the broad sense, for both form part of the larger structure within which transactions are made. Effects (h) and (i) therefore intensify those of (e) through (g).

The magnitudes of all the effects listed above clearly depend heavily on the levels of morbidity and premature adult mortality. The first step in any attempt to assess the economic effects of AIDS, therefore, is to establish the scale of such mortality before and after the outbreak of the epidemic. Mortality was already high among all age groups in sub-Saharan Africa in the 1950s and 1960s. It then began to fall, especially among infants and young

---

[1]See for example, Cuddington (1993) and Over (1992). Multisector models of this genre are to be found in Kambou, Devarajan, and Over (1992) and Arndt and Lewis (2000).

children, so that by the middle of the 1980s great improvements in life expectancy at birth and substantial improvements at prime ages had been achieved. In most countries, however, premature adult mortality was still significant when the AIDS epidemic began to take its toll. Its impact on the profile of mortality is reduced by what some demographers call the substitution effect: some of those who contract AIDS would have died prematurely of other causes. The higher the level of preexisting mortality, the larger this effect will be. By studying countries such as South Africa and Zimbabwe, where premature adult mortality was comparatively low in the 1980s but is now very high, we should therefore be able to get a good idea of the disease's net effect on such mortality, and hence of the gravity of the threat it poses to economic progress.

It is common practice among demographers who deal with AIDS to define premature adult mortality as the probability of dying before the age of 60, conditional on surviving to the age of 15 (Feeney, 2001); this probability is denoted by $_{45}q_{15}$, that is, the probability of dying within 45 years, starting at age 15. This is evidently unsuitable for purposes of studying the effects of mortality on childrearing; more natural choices are $_{20}q_{20}$ and $_{30}q_{20}$. The former better fits the cycle of childrearing, because new parents are typically between the ages of 20 and 40; the latter captures the substantial mortality due to AIDS among those, especially men, in their forties, when adults are still very much in their productive years. Yet whatever the measure adopted, premature adult mortality has risen dramatically in both South Africa and Zimbabwe following the full-scale outbreak of the epidemic (Table 3.1). The levels for 2010 forecast by Dorrington and others (2001) are grim; those of the U.S. Census Bureau, as reported by Dorrington and others, are grimmer still.

It should be emphasized that these measures refer to steady states, in the sense that the q for each year is calculated on the basis of the continuation of that mortality profile. Note, however, that the HIV/AIDS prevalence rate among adults in the age group 15–49 in South Africa rose from about 1 percent in 1990 to about 20 percent in 2000. In the latter year the rate in Zimbabwe had reached 25 percent. According to Dorrington and others (2001), the rate in South Africa will peak in about 2006. In light of the long lags between infection and death, the above estimates of q for 2010 are therefore close to the values that would prevail if the disease established itself in the population at that level for good. The observed values for 1990 (1986 for Zimbabwe) correspond to the counterfactual case in which there is no epidemic at all.

That this developing wave of morbidity and mortality will considerably slow or even reverse the growth in the numbers of those of working age in

Table 3.1. Adult Mortality by Sex in South Africa and Zimbabwe

Country	Year	$_{45}q_{15}$[1]		$_{20}q_{20}$[2]		$_{30}q_{20}$[3]	
		Male	Female	Male	Female	Male	Female
South Africa	1990	0.265	0.265	0.106	0.040	0.182	0.098
	2000	0.419	0.419	. . .	. . .	. . .	. . .
	2010	0.790	0.790	0.359	0.541	0.616	0.707
Zimbabwe	1986	0.310	0.195	. . .	. . .	0.169	0.107
	1997	0.553	0.417	. . .	. . .	0.414	0.331

Sources: Dorrington and others (2001); Feeney (2001, Table 1); and authors' calculations.

[1] $_x q_y$ denotes the probability of living y more years having reached age x. Data for $_{45}q_{15}$ for South Africa are from Dorrington and others (2001), who report only the average over both sexes.

[2] Calculated by the authors using data from Dorrington and others (2001).

[3] Data for Zimbabwe are from Feeney (2001), who reports $_{35}q_{15}$ instead of $_{30}q_{20}$.

the decades to come is clear. Yet this effect on the labor force fails by a wide margin to convey the force of the prospective effects on families with children, and hence on the formation of human capital through the mechanism discussed above. It is one thing when 11 percent of 20-year-old males, and 4 percent of 20-year-old females, will fail to see their fortieth birthday (the case in South Africa in 1990); it is a problem of an altogether different kind when those proportions are 36 and 54 percent, yet this is the appalling prospect confronting South Africa in the coming two decades. Seen in this light, the loss of workers in their most productive years signals only the beginning of the damage the epidemic will eventually wreak upon the economy and society.

Overlapping-Generations Framework

The structure that follows draws upon and in some ways extends that in Bell, Devarajan, and Gersbach (2003). For simplicity we confine the exposition to the case of two overlapping generations, each going through two periods of life, which we call childhood and adulthood.[2] Rather than provide an exhaustive technical description of the model, here we seek to provide an accessible discussion of the factors listed in the previous section

---

[2] An extensive literature analyzes the main differences and equivalences between models populated by immortal representative agents and those by mortal overlapping generations in terms of determinacy, Pareto optimality, and existence and dynamics in general, which is relevant for the type of model in this paper; see Aiyagari (1987, 1992), Huo (1987), Woodford (1986), and Lovo (2000).

and how they relate to one another. Even so, a precise account demands a certain degree of formality. Since some readers may find the flavor of the main exposition unduly formal, we begin with a narrative sketch of the main idea.

The basic economic unit is the family, nuclear or extended, in which the adult members decide how current resources available to the family are to be allocated between consumption and the children's education. The level of those resources is heavily determined by the parents' human capital and their survival rate through their offspring's early childhood and school years, but the children themselves can also contribute labor instead of attending school. How much of childhood, if any, is spent at school depends not only on the family's available resources, but also on three other factors. The first is the strength of the parents' altruism, which expresses itself in their willingness to forgo some current consumption in favor of investment in their children's schooling, and hence in favor of the children's human capital when they attain adulthood in the next period. Second is the efficiency with which schooling is transformed into human capital, and this arguably depends on the quality both of the school system and of childrearing within the family; the latter is expected to improve with the parents' own human capital (if indeed they survive this phase of life). Third, the returns to the investment in any child will be effectively destroyed if that child dies prematurely in adulthood. This implies that the *expected* returns to education depend on parents' (subjective) assessment of the probability that their children will meet an untimely death. At the end of each generation, or "period" in the model, the surviving adults die in old age, and the story continues as the children become adults in their turn.

Dynamic elements are at work in this story through several channels. The levels of human capital and premature adult mortality in the present generation play a key role in determining the level of human capital attained by the next generation, as do present expectations concerning premature adult mortality in the future. Dynamic systems of this kind can exhibit multiple equilibria and regimes of behavior. If current levels of human capital are low, families may be so poor that parents are not prepared to make the investments in schooling that would raise their children out of poverty upon reaching adulthood. In this case poverty can perpetuate itself. At much higher levels of human capital, in contrast, affluence will yield a fine upbringing and education, and so beget still more affluence. High levels of premature adult mortality can give rise to a poverty trap, with an increasing share of the population mired in poverty and facing little or no prospect of upward mobility, and may dampen the accumulation of human capital even under conditions of affluence. The outbreak of an epidemic may even pitch what was a growing system into the widening jaws of a poverty trap.

Basic Model

The place to start is with the formation of families and of human capital. For the present, let the family structure be nuclear. At the beginning of each period (generation) t, every young adult chooses a partner with the same level of human capital—that is to say, there is assortative mating. Each cohort begins with equal numbers of young men and women, and all find a partner. All couples have their children soon afterward. With AIDS very much in mind, premature adult mortality is assumed to occur about a decade into full adulthood, this being the median time from infection to death in the absence of treatment with antiretroviral drugs. Thus, when the children have just started school, some parents sicken and then die, leaving their children as half or full orphans. At this stage, therefore, the family will find itself in one of the following four states:

- both parents survive into old age ($s_t = 1$),
- the father has died ($s_t = 2$),
- the mother has died ($s_t = 3$),
- both parents have died ($s_t = 4$).

Let $\Lambda_t(s_t)$ denote the surviving adults' total human capital when the family is in state s_t, so that

$$\Lambda_t(1) = 2\lambda_t, \Lambda_t(2) = \Lambda_t(3) = \lambda_t, \Lambda_t(4) = 0,$$

where λ_t denotes the level of human capital possessed by each parent. Let the probability that a family formed at the beginning of period t winds up in state s_t be denoted by $\pi(s_t)$. Given the assumption that each cohort begins adulthood with equal numbers of males and females, the proportion of adults surviving into old age is given by

$$\kappa_t = [2\pi(1) + \pi(2) + \pi(3)]/2 = [1 + \pi(1) - \pi(4)]/2. \quad (1)$$

The relationship among between $\pi(s_t)$, κ_t, and the mortality statistic q is deferred to a later section.

Apart from innate ability, the two main factors that influence the level of human capital a young adult attains are the quality of childrearing and formal education. The former involves not only care and a loving upbringing, but also the transfer of knowledge. As a rule, it is surely both increasing with the parents' human capital and complementary with formal education. Let the latter be represented by the fraction of childhood, $e_t \in [0, 1]$, spent in school, where this phase of childhood may be thought of as spanning the period from 6 to 18 years of age. Then the process whereby these factors yield human capital in adulthood in period $t + 1$ for a child born in period t can be represented by

$$\lambda_{t+1} = z(s_t)g(e_t) \Lambda_t(s_t) + 1, \text{ with } s_t = 1, 2, 3, 4. \tag{2}$$

The term $z(s_t)$ may be thought of as a transmission factor, in the sense that its magnitude expresses the strength with which the parents' human capital creates in their children a potential capacity to acquire human capital themselves. If, as is plausible, fathers and mothers are not perfect substitutes for one another, then having both parents will be better than having only one: formally, $z(1) > \max[z(2)/2, z(3)/2]$. It is plausible, too, that z depends on the number of children within the family, but we defer discussion of this point for the moment. The function $g(e_t)$ represents the educational technology, where g is increasing in e_t. That $g(e_t)$ and $\Lambda_t(s_t)$ enter into equation (2) multiplicatively expresses the complementarity between the quality of childrearing and formal education: the stronger the transmission factor and the greater the parents' human capital, the more productive of human capital is any given level of the child's schooling. Now suppose further that some formal education is needed if a child is to realize at least some of the potential $z(s_t)\Lambda_t(s_t)$ created by childrearing: formally, $g(0) = 0$. It then follows that any child deprived of all formal schooling will attain $\lambda = 1$ as an adult, whatever the parents' level of human capital, whereby the value $\lambda = 1$ is simply a convenient normalization.

As it stands, the difference equation (2) is a purely "technical" relationship, in the sense that it yields the resulting formation of human capital for any given level of education but says nothing about how that level is chosen. This difference equation is also a stochastic one, in that the child of a union formed in period t with human capital $2\lambda_t$ can attain any of four arguably different levels of human capital as an adult one generation later, depending on the incidence of premature mortality among the child's parents in period t. Given the state s_t, and hence $\Lambda_t(s_t)$, the choice of e_t determines the outcome for the child, in the form of the level of λ_{t+1}.

How, then, is e_t chosen? One possibility is that school attendance is rigorously enforced by the authorities, and that full orphans are taken into first-rate care. Remedial measures might also be needed to offset the disadvantages suffered by half orphans. Such a policy would ensure the continued formation of human capital in society at large, while holding inequality within tolerable bounds. Yet the chances of actually implementing it in most poor countries are remote, to say nothing of the financial demands on the national treasury. In view of these difficulties, it seems much more compelling to treat e_t as the parents' decision, which they make in light of the resources available to them and the expected returns to education.

We start with output and income. As in the Solow model, there is an aggregate consumption good, which is taken to be the numéraire, and there are constant returns to scale in its production, but the only input is labor, which is measured in efficiency units. In this setting it is natural to define an adult's endowment of labor so measured as λ_t, which he or she supplies completely inelastically. Children will be less productive workers than their parents, and, given the reasoning underlying equation (2), it seems plausible to assume that a child could supply at most γ (< 1) efficiency units of labor to production. A family with N_t children then has the following level of full income, measured in units of the aggregate consumption good, in state s_t:

$$\Omega_t(\Lambda_t, N_t, s_t) \equiv \alpha[\Lambda_t(s_t) + N_t \gamma], \text{ with } s_t = 1, 2, 3, 4, \tag{3}$$

where the positive scalar α denotes the productivity of human capital, measured in units of the numéraire, and the expression in brackets is the total labor, measured in efficiency units, that the household can supply. It is seen at once that we are employing what is known in the literature on economic growth as an AK model. The sole means of production is human capital, which is itself produced through a process involving childrearing and formal education, and each unit of input of human capital in the production process yields α units of output.

The allocation of full income among competing uses lies in the parents' hands, so long as at least one of them survives into old age. We rule out bequests at death, so that full income is spent on the consumption good and the children's education. For simplicity, let the adults behave as equal partners, and let each child receive the fraction $\beta \in (0, 1)$ of a surviving adult's consumption. Since children of school age can also work, let this be the alternative to attending school, and let all siblings be treated in the same way. For the present, let the only costs of schooling be the opportunity cost of the children's time. Then, in the absence of taxes or subsidies, the household's budget line in the "goods" $c_t(s_t)$ and $e_t(s_t)$ may be written as

$$[(3 - s_t) + \beta N_t] c_t(s_t) + \alpha \gamma N_t e_t(s_t) = \Omega_t(s_t), \text{ with } s_t = 1, 2, \tag{4}$$

where $c_t(s_t)$ denotes the level of each adult's consumption. The assumption of assortative mating implies that states 2 and 3 are identical in this regard, so that equation (4) implicitly covers state 3. Observe that, given λ_t and N_t, single-parent families have less full income and face a higher relative price of education than do two-parent families. Full orphans ($s_t = 4$) are left to fend for themselves: they do not attend school and they consume whatever income they earn as child laborers.

To complete this account of the family's decision problem, we must specify its preferences. Let mothers and fathers have identical preferences over their consumption of the aggregate good and their children's welfare as adults, the level of which they can influence by choosing the level of schooling $e_t(s_t)$.[3] It is clear from equation (4) that they will maximize their own consumption by using the children as full-time workers, so that one can say that their altruism toward their children is operative only when they choose $e_t(s_t) > 0$. When both parents survive, let there be no "joint" aspect of the bundle $[c_t(1), e_t(1)]$: each adult enjoys $c_t(1)$ as a private good, whereas the children's resulting level of human capital as adults, λ_{t+1}, as given by equation (2), is a public good within the marriage. Since all their children will attain that value of λ_{t+1}, the only uncertainty that arises concerns the number of children who will die prematurely as adults in period $t + 1$, each such death being regarded as a "wasted" investment. To be exact, we assume that parents in period t form expectations about the premature mortality that will afflict their children as adults in period $t + 1$ and that they take the average number of survivors in weighting the payoff to schooling in the form of λ_{t+1}.

The appendix sets out a formal statement of the household's decision problem. Let $[(c_t^0(s_t), e_t^0(s_t)]$ denote the household's optimum bundle of current consumption and schooling. It can be shown that, under weak assumptions, $e_t^0(s_t)$ is increasing in λ_t whenever $0 < e_t^0(s_t) < 1$. For any given value of λ_t, (a) children in two-parent families receive at least as much schooling as those in single-parent families, and, strictly, more if the latter choose some, but not full, schooling; (b) children in two-parent families attain, as adults, at least as much human capital as those in one-parent families, and, strictly, more if fathers and mothers are not perfect substitutes in childrearing; and (c) an increase in expected premature mortality in period $t + 1$ will reduce schooling in period t if $0 < e_t^0(s_t) < 1$, and may do so if $e_t^0(s_t) = 1$ ($s_t = 1, 2, 3$). All these results accord with elementary intuition. To complete matters, we introduce a further, plausible assumption, namely, that uneducated couples ($\Lambda_t = 2$) are so poor that, in the

---

[3]This implicitly assumes that adults are concerned directly only with their own consumption and the size of their children's budget sets, whereby the grandchildren's opportunities appear in the latter, and so on. Thus all generations are effectively connected. For further discussion of this formulation in the context of this OLG structure, see Bell and Gersbach (2003).

absence of compulsory education, they choose not to educate their children; that is, $e_t^0(s_t) = 0$, even if neither dies prematurely.

Dynamics

The next step is to investigate the system's dynamic behavior. By replacing the nonspecific e_t in equation (2) with $e_t^0(s_t)$, we obtain the system's equation of motion, as governed by the rational, forward-looking behavior of individual households in the technical and mortality environment in which they find themselves:

$$\lambda_{t+1} = z(s_t)g\{e_t^0[\Lambda_t(s_t), s_t, \kappa_{t+1}]\}\Lambda_t(s_t) + 1, \text{ with } s_t = 1, 2, 3, 4, \tag{5}$$

where κ_{t+1} is a measure of the children's survival chances after they have reached adulthood in period $t + 1$, as assessed by their parents in period t. Like equation (2), equation (5) is a stochastic difference equation, a full treatment of which would go well beyond the scope of this chapter. Note that there are 16 possible cases: a child in any of the four family states in period t may wind up, as an adult, in any of the same four states in period $t + 1$. What follows, therefore, is an intuitive sketch of the main idea.

Full orphans ($s_t = 4$) can be dealt with at once. In the absence of support, they do not attend school, and each will marry another uneducated individual. In the absence of support or compulsion, the offspring of these unions will also go uneducated, and so on. Observe that any premature adult mortality will produce a new crop of orphaned children in each period and that these lineages will fall into poverty and illiteracy, even if they were not in that condition before. Hence, as time progresses, a steadily increasing proportion of the whole population finds itself in poverty. Caring for orphans is not, of course, a new problem for humankind, and societies have devised various ways of dealing with it. Whether these arrangements can withstand the burden of an epidemic like AIDS, however, remains to be seen. We return to this question below.

At the other extreme, consider children who have the good fortune not only to see both parents survive into old age, but also to experience the same outcome themselves in adulthood (this is the case where $s_t = s_{t+1} = 1$). If premature adult mortality is not too high, this is the typical case, the essentials of which are captured in the phase diagram in Figure 3.1. Let $\Lambda^d(1)$ be the parents' endowment of human capital such that, for all larger values, their children will receive some schooling, but otherwise none. As the individual level of human capital (λ) cannot fall below one, the parents' combined level of human capital (Λ) cannot fall below two. Observe that $\Lambda^d(1)$ is determined by the parents' altruism, family income, and

Figure 3.1. Human Capital of Succeeding Generations in the Absence of Premature Adult Mortality

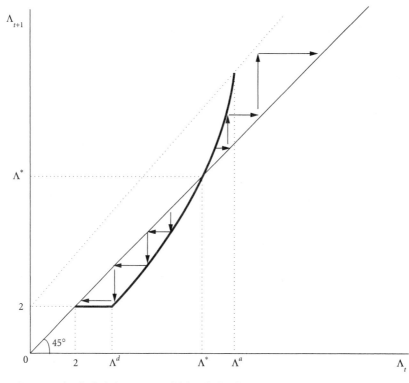

Source: Authors' calculations using model described in the text.

the expected level of premature adult mortality in the next generation. Similarly, let $\Lambda^a(1)$ $(= 2\lambda^a)$ be the smallest value of the parents' human capital such that their children will receive complete schooling. As the value of $\Lambda_t(1)$ rises from 2 to $\Lambda^d(1)$, the children will remain wholly uneducated. As it rises further, from $\Lambda^d(1)$ to $\Lambda^a(1)$, increasing affluence will cause $e_t^0(1)$ to rise from zero to unity, so that, from equation (5), λ_{t+1} will increase from unity to $[z(1)g(1)\Lambda^a(1) + 1]$. Suppose further that $[z(1)g(1)\Lambda^a(1) + 1] > \Lambda^a(1)/2$, that is, that every child of couples with $\Lambda^a(1)$ attains a level higher than $\Lambda^a(1)/2$, the human capital of each such parent. Now consider the graph of $\Lambda_{t+1}(1)$ $(= 2\lambda_{t+1})$ and $\Lambda_t(1)$. For all $\Lambda_t(1) \in [2, \Lambda^d(1)]$, the children will not attend school, with the outcome $\Lambda_{t+1}(1) = 2$. For all $\Lambda_t(1) \in [\Lambda^d(1), \Lambda^a(1)]$, $\Lambda_{t+1}(1)$ is increasing in $\Lambda_t(1)$, and its graph cuts the 45-degree line through the origin at least once, by virtue of the assumption that $[z(1)g(1)\Lambda^a(1) + 1] > \Lambda^a(1)/2$. Suppose it does so just once, at $\Lambda_t(1) = \Lambda^*(1)$.[4] Then the system possesses two stationary equilibria: $\Lambda_t(1) = 2$ and $\Lambda_t(1) = \Lambda^*(1)$. It is clear from Figure 3.1 that the former is stable, that the latter is unstable, and that the system exhibits a poverty trap. We show in the appendix that when the transmission factor and educational technology combine to ensure that the condition $2z(1)g(1) > 1$ holds, long-term growth is, in principle at least, possible. In what follows we assume that this condition indeed holds, and Figure 3.1 is drawn accordingly.

Children in single-parent families ($s_t = 2, 3$) face a less favorable situation. All of $\Lambda^d(s_t)$, $\Lambda^a(s_t)$, and $\Lambda^*(s_t)$ will be larger than their counterparts $\Lambda^d(1)$, $\Lambda^a(1)$, and $\Lambda^*(1)$, respectively; in other words, the size of the trapdoor into poverty will be correspondingly larger. The long-term rate of growth will also be lower if fathers and mothers are not perfect substitutes in childrearing, for if they are not, then $2z(1) > \max[z(2), z(3)]$. Indeed, unbounded growth may not be possible at all for one or both of these subgroups, even when it is so for two-parent groups. Summing up, premature adult mortality in a nuclear family setting is a powerful force for inequality in the future as well as in the present.

Social Response to Premature Adult Mortality

The death of parents while their children are still young poses such grave problems in strictly nuclear families that societies have been driven to find solutions to them. In Africa the widespread practice of fostering and adoption within the circle of kinship is such a response. In effect, this is a collective, or pooling, arrangement to deal with the individual risks of premature adult mortality as they affect the rearing of children and hence the future well-being of the group or society. Since any such pooling arrangement also needs rules, one can suppose that one such rule is that all children must be treated alike. We now analyze such an arrangement in a starkly simplified form.

Let there be complete pooling, in the sense that all the surviving adults take on responsibility for all children. This family structure, or "state," will be denoted by $s_t = 0$. The rule that all children be treated the same then ensures that there will be no inequality within each generation. The proportion of all adults surviving into old age in period t is denoted by κ_t. For

---

[4] A sufficient condition for this to hold is that the graph be convex over the specified interval. For a full discussion see Bell and Gersbach (2003).

simplicity, let premature mortality afflict men and women equally, so that each surviving "couple" will raise, not N_t children, but

$$N_t(0) = N_t/\kappa_t. \tag{6}$$

The couple's budget constraint is

$$[2 + \beta N_t/\kappa_t]c_t(0) + \alpha\gamma(N_t/\kappa_t)e_t(0) = \alpha[2\lambda_t + (N_t/\kappa_t)\gamma] \equiv \Omega_t(0). \tag{7}$$

A comparison of equation (7) with equation (4) reveals that, relative to an otherwise identical two-parent nuclear family, the burden of pooling implies, first, a lower relative price of current consumption and, second, a lower level of full income, measured in units of an adult's consumption, provided $\beta > \gamma$. Both effects work in the direction of reducing schooling relative to what would occur in the two-parent nuclear family.

Turning to preferences, let the couple go beyond the requirements of the social rule of equal treatment and regard all the children in their care, natural and adopted alike, with the same degree of altruism. Altruism in this degree therefore furthers investment in education by increasing the weight attached to the payoff in the form λ_{t+1}, since $N_t(0) > N_t$. Whether altruism or even equal treatment prevails in practice will be taken up later in the chapter.

Given the burden of rearing $N_t(0)$ as opposed to N_t children, it is natural to ask whether the transmission factor will not be correspondingly weakened. To allow for this possibility, we write the latter as $z(0, \kappa_t)$, where it is plausible that $z(0, \kappa_t)$ is increasing in κ_t. Note also that, in the absence of premature adult mortality, pooling will be superfluous and all children will be raised by their natural parents, so that $z(0, 1) = z(1)$. The fundamental difference equation now takes the form

$$\lambda_{t+1}(0) = z(0, \kappa_t)g\{e_t^0[\Lambda_t(0), 0, \kappa_t, \kappa_{t+1}]\}\Lambda_t(0) + 1, \tag{8}$$

where it should be noted that the current level of premature adult mortality influences both investment in schooling and the transmission factor.

The dynamics are comparatively simple, in the sense that there is only one family state in all periods—so long as the institution of pooling can bear the weight of mortality among young adults. For any given κ_t, there is effectively a two-parent family with $N_t(0)$ children and transmission factor $z(0, \kappa_t)$, and Figure 3.1 may be used once more. Whether the trapdoor into poverty is larger than its counterpart in the corresponding nuclear family setting depends on whether the effects of pooling on the family's budget line and the transmission factor outweigh those of altruism. In any event the long-term rate of growth will be lower, since $z(0, \kappa_t) < z(1)$ whenever $\kappa_t < 1$. When all the single-parent households and full orphans are brought into the reckoning, however, the average growth rate of a society of nuclear families may well be smaller than the growth rate under pooling, namely, $[2z(0, \kappa_t)g(1) - 1]$.[5]

Calibration

In order to apply the model, certain qualitative choices must be made and a whole variety of parameters estimated. How all this is to be done depends, naturally enough, on the data and resources available. One thing, however, is immediately clear: the system is almost certainly heavily underidentified, so that a resort to calibration is unavoidable. That is, the functional forms are chosen exogenously, and the values of the parameters are then derived by solving the system in an exactly identified form so that it reproduces some set of past configurations. There is no cookbook recipe for this procedure. What follows is a brief description of how we accomplished this task for South Africa, with the aim of conveying the nature of the difficulties we encountered and how we attempted to overcome them.[6]

The phenomena of interest are inherently of a time-series nature, the available data for which are overwhelmingly of the aggregate kind: GDP, labor force, average years of schooling completed, total fertility rate, and so forth. This simple fact makes an approach based on a representative unit virtually unavoidable, so that the choice of institutional arrangement falls on what we have called pooling, with all the advantages of simplification it brings. It must be conceded that, especially in light of South Africa's history of apartheid, the assumption of pooling is also nothing short of heroic. Indeed, the calibration is based on the period 1960–90, at whose close apartheid was about to collapse and the epidemic was in its very early stages.

With this much decided, we can work with various aggregates. At any point in time, total output (GDP) is defined as the product of the unknown parameter α and the total input of labor, measured in efficiency units. If we ignore open unemployment and child labor, the total input of

---

[5]Note that, with a representative family unit of this kind, the OLG model is equivalent to a Solow model in which output is proportional to inputs of efficiency units of labor. The difference is that whereas the OLG model provides the structure that yields the evolution of human capital, the latter must be supplied exogenously to the Solow equivalent, which is then, in effect, the fifth wheel of the coach.

[6]Readers interested in the detailed derivations are directed to Bell, Devarajan, and Gersbach (2003).

efficiency units of labor is the product of the labor force, which we can observe, and the average value of λ_t, which we need to estimate. Since a (quinquennial) series for average years of schooling completed among the adult population is available for 1960–90 (Barro and Lee, 1996), the next step is to employ the difference equation (2) with $s_t = 0$ as a purely technical relationship. To save on degrees of freedom, two further assumptions are now needed: first, that the function $z(0, \kappa_t)$ is a constant throughout this period, and second, that the educational technology, as defined by the function $g(e_t)$, takes the very simple form $g(e_t) = e_t$. Repeated application of equation (2), with appropriate rescaling to allow for the fact that, when but two overlap, a single generation spans 30 years and that some of the data are annual and others quinquennial, permits us, at length, to coax out the following estimates: $\alpha = 3{,}419$, $z = 0.818$, and $\lambda_{1960} = 2.62$.

These estimates yield the following implications. First, a wholly uneducated adult, who by definition possesses 1 efficiency unit of labor ($\lambda = 1$), will produce \$3,419 a year (in 1995 dollars). Second, the starting value of human capital (λ_{1960}) is not only much larger than this reference value, but also placed South Africa well out of reach of the poverty trap that existed at the levels of premature adult mortality prevailing at that time. Third, the value of z is such that, when all children receive a full education, output per capita will eventually grow at the rate of $(2 \times 0.818) - 1 = 0.636$ per generation, or about 1.64 percent annually. Although this rate is hardly in the East Asian league, it does promise considerable prosperity within two to three generations.

The remaining steps involve treating the Barro and Lee series for average years of schooling as the outcome of rational decisions made by an extended family, as set out above and in the appendix. That is to say, a representative couple in 1960 chose e_{1960} such that individuals born between 1935 and 1965 attained, on average, the Barro-Lee estimate of five years of schooling for adults aged 25 years and older in 1990. The couple's preferences over current consumption and the level of human capital attained by each of their children in adulthood are assumed to be additively separable in logarithms—a formulation in keeping with common practice throughout the macroeconomics literature. The parameters β and γ are set exogenously, the former at around one-half, the latter at one-fifth of the value of α. The total fertility rate N_t is taken from the *World Development Indicators* (World Bank, 2002), and values for κ_t are derived from a procedure that we describe in the next section in connection with the outbreak of the epidemic. With the "taste" and mortality parameters thus determined, the family's choice $e_t^0(\Lambda_t(0), 0, \kappa_t, \kappa_{t+1})$ can be derived in every given situation.

Outbreak of an Epidemic

What happens when the outbreak of a hitherto unknown disease brings about a dramatic rise in premature adult mortality, albeit with a lag of a decade or so? At first, very little, because those infected show no symptoms. As time wears on, however, they begin to sicken and die, and the survivors begin to revise their assessments of the chances that their children will die prematurely on reaching adulthood. The first wave of deaths leaves behind orphans on a scale not seen in earlier generations.

A careful distinction between nuclear and collective family structures is needed. Given the nature of AIDS, infection of one partner in a marriage is likely to be followed by infection of the other, so that the proportion of full orphans in the child population will rise dramatically as well. Yet the effects of the adverse shift in the proportions of nuclear families falling into the four states will make themselves fully felt only in the next generation and beyond, in the form of lower levels of human capital averaged over the population as a whole. Under pooling, the fall in κ_t has both an immediate, adverse effect on the common budget set, by increasing $N_t(0)$, and a damaging long-term effect on the accumulation of human capital.

If the disease persists—or, rather, if the adults expect it to do so—there will be a further effect in the present, certainly adverse and perhaps devastating. If families are nuclear, a fall in the expected level of κ_{t+1} will cause $\Lambda^d(s_t)$, $\Lambda^a(s_t)$, and $\Lambda^*(s_t)$ to increase for two-parent and single-parent families alike, for it will reduce the expected returns to education. In other words, it will make the trapdoor larger, so that groups that were enjoying sustained growth before the outbreak could slide into poverty. Again, this effect will make itself felt only with a long lag, but if the (expected) increase in mortality is large enough, the whole system could switch regimes from one generation to the next. Under pooling, the sharing of resources and responsibilities will stave off such a collapse if neither κ_t nor the expected level of κ_{t+1} falls too far, even though a permanent fall in κ will tend to reduce the long-run rate of growth by weakening the transmission factor. Otherwise the entire group will slide into poverty together, a disaster that may well undermine the institution's rules and even the institution itself.

We now use the model, as calibrated to South Africa, to investigate the epidemic's effects on human capital formation and economic growth. Although a mere glance at Table 3.1 reveals that the situation is already grave and threatens to become worse, what we actually need in order to apply the OLG model are the probabilities of each of the four family states, that is, the $\pi(s_t)$, which, through equation (1), also yield the survival statistic κ needed in the pooling case. In order to derive the $\pi(s_t)$ from the mortality measures q, an assumption has to be made about the occurrence of mortality within marital unions. In the absence of AIDS, one could perhaps make a case for treating the premature deaths of spouses as independent events, at least as a working approximation for the population as a whole. Given the nature of the disease, however, it is tempting to assume that the infection of one partner outside the relationship will soon be followed by the infection of the other within it. Viewed in a time frame of 20 or 30 years, single-parent households would become rather rare.

In fact, the probability of transmission within a union appears to be on the order of 10 percent a year under the conditions now prevailing in East Africa (Marseille, Hoffman, and Kahn, 2002). Cumulated over the median course of the disease from infection to death, namely, about a decade, this implies that the probability that both partners will become infected, conditional on one of them getting infected outside the relationship, is about 0.65; this is high, but still far removed from infection being perfectly correlated within a union. Since it would take anywhere from one to two decades for both to die, the chances that all their children will lose both parents before reaching the end of adolescence are correspondingly reduced. This has a strong bearing on deriving the state probabilities using $_{20}q_{20}$, which is the natural measure in connection with analyzing the effects of premature adult mortality on the distribution of family types. To err on the side of caution where the numbers of full orphans are concerned, let us therefore assume that infection is indeed an independent event within a union. This yields the state probabilities corresponding to any choice of q as follows:

$$\pi(1) = [1 - q(M)] \cdot [1 - q(F)]$$

$$\pi(2) = q(M) \cdot [1 - q(F)]$$

$$\pi(3) = [1 - q(M)] \cdot q(F)$$

$$\pi(4) = q(M) \cdot q(F).$$

Various constellations, together with the corresponding values of κ_t, are set out in Table 3.2.

The effects of the AIDS epidemic on families are appalling to contemplate. In its absence, about 86 percent of South African children in nuclear families would have grown up in the happy circumstances of having both parents to care for them, and fewer than 1 percent would have been completely orphaned. In the mature phase of the epidemic, as described by the steady state corresponding to 2010, these proportions will lie close

Table 3.2. Family State Probabilities and Survival Rates in South Africa and Zimbabwe

Country	Year	Both Parents Surviving $\pi(1)$	Father Only Surviving $\pi(2)$	Mother Only Surviving $\pi(3)$	Neither Parent Surviving $\pi(4)$	Survival Rate[1] κ
South Africa	1990	0.855	0.101	0.039	0.005	0.925
	2010	0.294	0.168	0.347	0.194	0.550
Zimbabwe	1986	0.742	0.151	0.089	0.018	0.862
	1997	0.392	0.277	0.194	0.137	0.628

Source: Authors' calculations, based on $_{20}q_{20}$ for South Africa and $_{35}q_{15}$ for Zimbabwe (Table 3.1).
[1]Proportion of adults surviving into old age.

together, at 29 and 19 percent, respectively, and just over half of all children will be raised by a single parent. The fraction of adults surviving beyond the age of 40 would have been 93 percent; instead, only about 55 percent will do so, which speaks eloquently of the burden already beginning to fall on survivors under pooling arrangements. In Zimbabwe, where the epidemic broke out earlier, the observed shift over the period 1986–97 is scarcely less dramatic, and the epidemic still had not peaked at the end of that period. One should not, of course, make too much of a few percentage points here or there, but the broad qualitative nature of the results is surely robust to any reasonable amendments to the underlying mortality profiles. Viewed in the light of how human capital is formed, these drastic shifts in family state probabilities and adult survival rates contain the very real threat of an economic collapse if the epidemic continues unabated on its present course.

To pursue this possibility, the model is run from 1960 onward in three variants. The first is the counterfactual, in which the AIDS epidemic never occurs and the mortality profile in 1990 continues on into the indefinite future. In this happy event, the South African economy would have enjoyed modest economic growth, with almost universal and complete primary education (of 10 years) attained in one generation, that is, by 2020. Income per family, $y(0)$, which includes the contribution of child labor, if any, would have quadrupled over its 1990 level in three generations (Table 3.3).

With the outbreak of the AIDS epidemic, and with no interventions to stem it, this salutary path will be interrupted. In the second variant not only do the surviving parents have to cope with a very heavy burden of child dependency from 1990 onward, but they also immediately revise their expectations about future mortality: they correctly forecast current mortality in their generation, as described by the steady-state value of κ in

Table 3.3. Three Growth Paths for the South African Economy

| | No AIDS | | | With AIDS | | | | | |
| | | | | $E_{1990}(\kappa_{2020}) = \kappa_{1990}$ | | | $E_{2020}(\kappa_{2050}) = \kappa_{1990}$ | | |
Year	Human capital λ	Schooling e	Family income $y(0)^1$	Human capital λ	Schooling e	Family income $y(0)^1$	Human capital λ	Schooling e	Family income $y(0)^1$
1960	2.62	0.50	19,500	2.62	0.50	19,500	2.62	0.50	19,500
1990	3.14	0.64	22,340	3.14	0.20	26,370	3.14	0.68	23,400
2020	4.32	0.97	29,590	2.01	—	17,770	4.52	0.39	34,690
2050	7.86	1.0	53,720	1.0	—	12,900	3.80	0.29	30,280
2080	13.85	1.0	94,720	1.0	—	12,900	2.78	0.14	24,250

Source: Bell, Devarajan, and Gersbach (2003). All results are based on $_{30}q_{20}$.

[1]In rand. From 1990 onward a representative "family" comprises two surviving adults and 3.49 children in the absence of AIDS, and two surviving adults and 8.87 children in its presence.

2010 and denoted formally by κ_{1990}, and they expect that level to rule in the next generation, too: formally, $E_{1990}(\kappa_{2020}) = \kappa_{1990}$. With current resources much reduced and the outlook grim, primary education levels begin to decline, and if this scale of mortality continues, the society will be full of uneducated adults in two generations. Economic performance declines accordingly, and income per family, instead of quadrupling by 2080, declines to about half its 1990 value.

It might be argued that the second variant constitutes too harsh an estimate of the conditions prevailing in 1990–2020, and that, in particular, the revision of expectations will take time. Suppose, therefore, that this revision does not occur until the very start of the next generation, when the childhood experience of death among their parents will be vivid in the minds of the next cohort of young adults: their firm expectations are $E_{2020}(\kappa_{2050}) = \kappa_{1990}$. Suppose, further, that these expectations are realized and that this scale of mortality persists into the future. The happy, but false, expectations about future mortality in 1990, coupled with what is assumed to be the rich altruism of full pooling, induce adults to invest heavily in the children's education, despite the heavy reductions in resources caused by the outbreak of the epidemic. Yet although the generation of adults starting out in 2020 are every bit as well endowed with human capital as they would have been in the absence of the epidemic, their expectations concerning their children's future are so bleak as to induce them to roll back investment in schooling to levels not seen since the middle of the twentieth century, and the result is to send the entire system into a progressive decline. Income per capita peaks in the period starting in 2020, and two generations later the fresh cohort of adults will be scarcely more productive than their forebears in 1960. Only a revival of optimism about the future—and the resumption of low levels of premature adult mortality to confirm it—will stave off a complete collapse.[7]

Policy

The real possibility that the economy can have two strikingly different equilibria—a poverty trap and steady growth—means that there is a job for the government to do, namely, to bring about the latter state by ensuring the reproduction of human capital and its accumulation. Yet although the need for intervention to secure such an outcome is clear enough, the rationale for it must be sharpened if the government is to intervene in the right way. The first reason is paternalistic, for the failure to attain, or maintain, growth may stem from parents' weak altruism. In the formulation of private preferences chosen by Bell, Devarajan, and Gersbach (2003), weak altruism expresses itself in the form of parents assigning a low value to their children's level of human capital in adulthood, which effectively competes with their own current consumption. A closely related consideration is that although parents are not necessarily myopic, inasmuch as they recognize that their children will, in turn, care about their own children, and so on, they may not *directly* value any generation's welfare beyond their children's. All else being equal, the fewer the number of future generations whose well-being today's parents directly value, the weaker are the incentives to invest in education today. Although it is hard to distinguish between these aspects of altruism in a practical calibration, the distinction is still important.

The second reason for intervention is that AIDS, as a communicable disease, involves an externality whose full ramifications can be enormously damaging. The third reason has to do with information: the course of the disease is long and insidious, and in many communities knowledge of how it is transmitted and how to prevent it is often sketchy and sometimes woefully wanting and distorted. A fourth reason is that there is—or should be—a social aversion to inequality, a condition that premature adult mortality does much to promote.

In formulating policies it will be useful to begin by drawing a distinction between preventive and remedial measures, with a firm emphasis on

---

[7]The fact that false expectations can be helpful in overcoming shocks raises some delicate questions concerning the value of transparency in public policy in the present context. We shun them religiously here.

their economic and social consequences. A second, more conventional distinction is among the socioeconomic sectors in which intervention is undertaken: education, health, and support of the needy. We take them up in that order. Once formulated, the spending programs must be financed, and raising the additional revenue will itself have an effect on the accumulation of human capital through the channels identified above. The framework laid out above enables us to treat interventions in a way that reveals their full ramifications in a long-run setting.

Premature adult mortality in the present and expectations concerning its level in the future emerged above as key factors influencing long-term economic performance. The outbreak of a disease like AIDS calls for containment on both scores. The first *economic* preventive measure is, almost tautologically, the vigorous pursuit of public health measures to stem the spread of the epidemic, ideally in the very early stages. (AIDS is, after all, very much a preventable disease.) The second such measure, however, involves medical treatment of the infected, to maintain their productivity and prolong their lives, and so enable them to provide more of the vital things their children need to become productive members of society. Although there is yet no cure for AIDS, treating opportunistic infections and providing antiretroviral therapies still enter into the reckoning, at least potentially. The second class of measures is unquestionably much more expensive than the first, but both directly further the formation of human capital and equality in the next generation.

Premature adult mortality cannot be eliminated, however, and therefore remedial action in the form of supporting the survivors, adults and children alike, is also essential. In a nuclear family setting this will involve making payments to single-parent and foster families, as well as establishing orphanages for those children who would otherwise lack a home. In extended family settings the aim must be to support the institution itself, while seeing to it that all children enjoy equal treatment. Note that all these measures are also preventive, to the extent that they further investment in the children's education and so help them to become productive adults.

It is here that social and educational policy overlap. The case for the government to intervene rests heavily on market failures that result in socially suboptimal levels of schooling, especially when the family structure is nuclear. Received theory tells us that distortions of this kind should be attacked as close to their source as possible, which suggests that the right form of intervention is a subsidy payable to the family contingent on each child's attendance at school. In poor societies this intervention is generally desirable even in the absence of premature adult mortality (Bell and

Gersbach, 2003; Siemers, 2002); in the face of the AIDS epidemic, such a sharp instrument is surely of great importance. It is quite possible, of course, that the government is unable to implement such a policy, in which case it might have to fall back on unconditional transfers to all needy households. But this is an administratively troublesome policy, too.

What, then, is the right balance between preventive and remedial measures? This is a complicated question to which there is no ready, general answer. The need to finance any bundle of policies selected from the above menu also enters into the reckoning, and, as in all questions involving public economics, the means available will exert an influence on the right choice. Foreign aid, in the form of outright grants, will relieve the burden, but no society can expect help on a scale that will make increases in domestic taxation unnecessary. For clarity of exposition, therefore, we go to the other extreme of self-reliance. We treat pooling first, since this is relatively straightforward, and then outline the additional considerations that arise when families are nuclear. The framework presented earlier will enable us to formulate the problem in such a way as to gain qualitative insights. We then follow this discussion with a sketch of how to estimate the relationship between public spending and premature adult mortality for purposes of incorporating it into the framework, and then we offer a brief account of the quantitative results obtained for South Africa.

Optimal Policy Under Pooling

There is neither scope nor need for redistribution among families under pooling, and therefore the government can impose poll taxes to finance its expenditure. Let each "couple" pay the amount τ_t in period t. For the moment let us rule out school attendance subsidies, so that τ_t will be used solely for "economic" preventive measures, that is, effectively to increase the survival statistic κ_t. To emphasize the connections, we write $\kappa_t = \kappa_t(\tau_t)$, and hence $z(0) = z[0, \kappa_t(\tau_t)]$, both of which are increasing in τ_t. These are two of the factors yielding benefits, whereby diminishing returns will set in at some point. The drawback is the reduction in full income in the amount τ_t. The budget constraint in equation (7) becomes

$$\left[2 + \beta \frac{N_t}{\kappa_t(\tau_t)}\right] c_t(0) + \frac{\alpha \gamma N_t}{\kappa_t(\tau_t)} e_t(0) = \alpha\left[2\lambda_t + \frac{\gamma N_t}{\kappa_t(\tau_t)}\right] - \tau_t \equiv \Omega_t(0, \tau_t). \quad (9)$$

Thus parents must form expectations not only about the general mortality environment in the next period, but also about the level of the government's expenditure (equals tax revenue) on mitigating it. Hopes of a less dangerous future will induce more schooling; pessimism will reduce it. A failure to act swiftly and publicly can therefore do enormous damage through this channel alone.

Armed with this pair of instruments, the government has the task of choosing a sequence of taxes, or "plan," over some time horizon starting in period 0, $\{\tau_t\}_{t=0}^T$, with the aim of maximizing social welfare. This is a difficult problem, for not only are all the periods connected through the formation of parents' (rational) expectations about the course of future policy, but in addition there may be problems of credibility if the government is unable to commit itself to a certain future course of action. This is not the place to go into the details. A sketchy account is given in the appendix, and the interested reader is referred to Bell, Devarajan, and Gersbach (2003).

To complete the formulation of the government's decision problem, we must define social welfare. Since there is no inequality within each generation, but the threat of a collapse is ever present, it is intuitively appealing to put a heavy emphasis on accumulating human capital rapidly. Bell, Devarajan, and Gersbach (2003) argue that the following claim is valid when each generation covers a sufficiently long period.

The pooling case: If, in each and every period, the government chooses the level of the tax in that period so as to maximize the level of human capital attained by a child on reaching adulthood in the next, the resulting plan will be "good," in the sense of not departing very far from the optimum.

That is to say, it is enough for the government to look just one generation ahead in order to attain a "good" result, given the expenditure instruments at its disposal. The government's problem is set out formally in the appendix.

We now introduce school attendance subsidies, which, if available, will yield a further improvement. Let the amount paid per child in period t be σ_t for each unit of time the child spends in school. The fact that the government must allocate its revenue between combating mortality and subsidizing schooling directly calls for a little additional notation. Denote total spending on the former by η_t, where this expenditure should be thought of as producing a public good within the family, so that $\kappa_t(\eta_t)$ replaces $\kappa_t(\tau_t)$. The family's budget constraint then reads

$$\left[2 + \beta \frac{N_t}{\kappa_t(\eta_t)}\right] c_t(0) + (\alpha\gamma - \sigma_t) \frac{N_t}{\kappa_t(\eta_t)} e_t(0)$$

$$(10)$$

$$= \alpha\left[2\lambda_t + \frac{N_t}{\kappa_t(\eta_t)}\,\gamma\right] - \tau_t \equiv \Omega_t(0,\eta_t,\tau_t).$$

a comparison of which with equation (9) reveals that the subsidy works by reducing the opportunity cost of the child's time, and so encourages investment in schooling directly. The government's budget constraint will always bind at the optimum, so that the ministries of health and education will be competing for funds.

The trade-off is subtle and complex. For any level of taxation, additional spending on reducing mortality will increase not only current full income, but also positive expectations about future mortality. Both work to increase schooling and so offset the reduction in schooling brought about by the correspondingly smaller subsidy on school attendance. Finding the right balance between them involves solving problem (A9) in the appendix; but it is intuitively clear that, when a society is threatened by very high mortality, the best policy will always involve a fairly substantial effort to combat it if the available measures are even moderately effective.

Optimal Policies with Nuclear Families

In societies with strictly nuclear family structures, premature adult mortality brings about inequality within each generation unless there is countervailing action by communities or government. In this respect, therefore, the government's task is more complicated than under pooling. Indeed, avoiding such inequality may not be possible, depending on the instruments available and the pressures exerted by the need to ensure long-term growth. Yet most of the elements that make up the policy program are clear. Suppose, for simplicity, that the authorities are able to observe each family's status. The tax base is normally provided by two-parent households, for only under conditions of some affluence will single-parent households have any taxable capacity when their children attend school full-time. The society's needy, therefore, are the members of single-parent households and full orphans, who must be cared for in special institutions. The budget constraints for households with adults can be expressed as before, taking into account whatever taxes and subsidies are payable. Suitable standards must be drawn up for orphanages, whose staffing must suffice to provide decent care for their charges, and whose staff must be paid their opportunity cost in the production of the aggregate consumption good. At the very least, the children should receive the package of consumption and education enjoyed by their counterparts in single-parent households. The government's budget constraint is written out accordingly.

The absence of pooling as a form of insurance and as an instrument to ensure equality within each generation requires a reformulation of the policy program. Bell, Devarajan, and Gersbach (2003) argue that one way of arriving at a "good" program is as follows.

> **The nuclear family case:** In each and every period, choose a tax and expenditure plan so as to maximize the society's expected taxable capacity in the next period.

Observe the switch from the future attainment of the representative child under pooling to future *aggregate* taxable capacity. The intuition here is that, given the need sooner or later to undertake redistribution within a generation, it is this capacity that ultimately determines whether the whole society can eventually escape from want and illiteracy. In dire circumstances, however, it may happen in some periods that it is not optimal to grant support to all those in need. The full problem is written out formally in Bell, Devarajan, and Gersbach (2003) and will not be repeated here. Suffice it to say that the tension between providing direct support to families (whether conditional on school attendance or otherwise) and combating mortality necessarily arises once more, with the further twist that avoiding premature mortality in period t has an immediate effect both on the tax base and on the numbers and types of the needy, through its influence on the distribution of family types in period t.

Estimating the Costs and Effects of Policies

We introduced above public spending on combating premature adult mortality from all sources as an instrument to improve economic performance and well-being. What especially concerns us in this chapter, of course, is spending on combating AIDS, and here we know much less than we would like about the effects of the disease on the level of mortality. This obstacle notwithstanding, we need to estimate the function $q(\eta)$ if we are to reach defensible conclusions about the right policies to be pursued. There follow a discussion of the elements of the approach and a short summary of the results it yields when applied to South Africa.

We begin with two useful reference cases. The first is the counterfactual, in which the human AIDS virus never came into existence; we denote this disease environment by $D = 0$. This, as we argued above, can be taken as corresponding to the mortality profile that prevails in the very early stages of the epidemic, as exemplified by Zimbabwe in 1986 and South Africa in 1990. The second step involves the second reference case, which arises when the epidemic simply runs its course, unhindered by public action of any kind. Specifying this alternative poses various problems, for even here the course of the epidemic depends on individual behavior, which may, in its own turn, respond to the experience of the epidemic, and on whether the virus adapts to its human hosts by becoming less virulent over the longer run. There is, unfortunately, not a single historical example of this particular epidemic simply running its full course in some society to offer any guidance on this matter. In neither South Africa nor Zimbabwe had the epidemic reached maturity by the end of the 1990s, grim though the situation had already become in both countries. Describing this second case is therefore a task more for epidemiologists and virologists than for social scientists. For South Africa the forecast by Dorrington and others (2001) for 2010 reflects such considerations, and it seems to be a good working approximation of what is needed, with the reservation that palliative care of the sick and the treatment of opportunistic infections are already absorbing resources on a substantial scale.

The next step is to connect these two reference cases through the plausible assertion that very heavy spending on combating the disease would restore the status quo ante profile of mortality. If this much is granted, then the probability of premature mortality, viewed as a function of spending on combating the disease, namely, $q(\eta; D = 1)$, will be anchored at both ends of the spending range. To supply the shape of the curve in between, it is natural, for economists at least, to appeal to diminishing returns; thus $q(\eta; D = 1)$ would be downward sloping and convex, steep when η is small and flat when it is large. It is also tempting to associate these endpoints of the spending range with preventive measures and antiretroviral treatments, respectively.

One intervention that commends itself in connection with the control of all sexually transmitted diseases is to target sex workers and their clients; in this context the use of condoms is also strongly promoted. Marseille, Hoffman, and Kahn (2002) give the corresponding cost of averting a single case of AIDS in Kenya, for example, as $8 to $12. This is cheap indeed, but given the nature of the disease and of people, it must be inferred that this is an expenditure that will recur annually. They also present evidence that other preventive measures, such as ensuring a safe blood supply and treating mothers at birth with nevirapine, are less cost-effective by a factor of 10 or more. Choosing a bundle of diverse preventive measures, they estimate the resulting cost per disability-adjusted life-year (DALY) so saved at $12.50.

At the other end of the range, the overwhelming bulk of expenditure is devoted to treating those with the disease. Such treatment covers not only opportunistic infections, especially in the later stages of the disease, but also antiretroviral therapies. These measures keep infected individuals healthier and can extend their lives for a few years, thereby raising lifetime family income and improving parental care. It seems perfectly defensible, therefore, to interpret these gains as equivalent to a reduction in q within the OLG framework. Marseille, Hoffman, and Kahn (2002) put the cost of saving one DALY by these means at $395, on the very conservative assumption that the drugs take the form of low-cost generics and that the costs of the technical and human infrastructure needed to support an effective HAART (highly active antiretroviral therapy) regimen of this kind can be wholly neglected.

At this point the reader may be forgiven for wondering how much a comprehensive HAART program might cost. The elements of an estimate for Burkina Faso, a poor West African country in which the AIDS prevalence rate is about 8 percent, are set out in World Bank (2003). If generic antiretroviral drugs can be purchased from Indian firms, the annual cost of treating each individual would be about $810; under the next-best, negotiated alternative, it would more than double, to $1,730. At the prevailing prevalence rate, the lower of the two estimates translates into an aggregate outlay roughly equivalent to 80 percent of the health ministry's current budget, or about 1.8 percent of GDP. In Kenya, where the prevalence rate is about 15 percent and GDP per capita is similar, the aggregate outlay would be roughly twice as large. These are sobering numbers, but broadly in line with the values of $\{\eta_t\}$ that emerge from the "good" programs derived in Bell, Devarajan, and Gersbach (2003) for South Africa, which we now summarize.

In the pooling case without school attendance subsidies, the sequential procedure described earlier yields a "good" plan $\{\eta_t\}$ in which total expenditure per family or subfamily is $960 in 1990 and $1,030 in 2020 and thereafter, which correspond to about 4.5 and 3.6 percent of GDP, respectively. This represents a very considerable fiscal effort, over and above that already implicitly contained in the calibration for the period 1960–90, which must also continue into the future to maintain the validity of the parameter values so derived. If this effort is politically possible, not only would it stave off a collapse and virtually restore the status quo ante with respect to premature adult mortality, but it would also leave λ in 2080 only about 12 percent lower than that in the counterfactual case without AIDS.

Such satisfactory results where long-run growth is concerned are not attainable under a nuclear family system, if inequality in individual levels of human capital is to be avoided in each and every generation. The two-parent families that form the tax base must finance spending programs not only to combat the epidemic, but also to support one-parent families and full orphans. Recall that, since there is no extended family to ensure equality within each generation, formulating a "good" plan under these circumstances involves maximizing a different objective function, namely, aggregate taxable capacity in the next period. The corresponding sequential procedure described there yields expenditure on combating the epidemic that is about 15 percent higher than under pooling; in addition, each one-parent family receives a (lump-sum) subsidy that is about twice as large as η_t. To finance all this, each two-parent family pays about twice the amount of the subsidy as a lump-sum tax. The higher levels of spending to combat the disease in each period are warranted because they lead to fewer needy families and orphans in that period, and hence to less inequality among adults in the next generation. Put slightly differently, these results confirm the importance of keeping premature mortality among adults low, so that parents can provide and care for their children. This clutch of ambitious interventions does stave off collapse and the emergence of inequality, but at the cost of much slower growth. Full education for all is reached only in 2080, and λ in 2080 is less than half its level in the counterfactual case without AIDS. These findings point to the macroeconomic significance of informal social insurance through extended family structures in the face of increasing adult mortality.

Other Economic Losses

Certain of the primary effects of morbidity and mortality among young adults listed at the outset have received rather short shrift thus far. Here, therefore, we show how they can be given a home in the framework developed above.

An adult who dies prematurely will, all else being equal, produce less over the life cycle than one who does not. This loss of output and all its consequences are fully taken into account in the OLG framework, and there is no real need to estimate it independently in its own right. Much is sometimes made of the loss of trained workers in particular. Here, too, to the extent that productivity in adulthood depends only on the quality of child-drearing and formal education, this loss of human capital is captured in full in the above framework. To the extent that workers acquire specific skills through training on the job, however, premature mortality among them will indeed entail losses for which that framework does not allow, and so the results derived from it will be on the optimistic side. Assuming that firms are rational in their investment in workers through such training, the costs of training replacements places a lower bound on such losses.

Some idea of the order of magnitude of these losses in the case of financial services companies in South Africa can be gained from estimates by Schneider and Kelly (2003). Their analysis covers the following items: main risks costs (for example, the costs of death-related and disability benefits), defined pension benefits, replacement and retraining, sick leave, economic costs of absences, maternity benefits, and ancillary insured benefits. In the absence of AIDS the combined costs of these items to a hypothetical company in the financial services sector are estimated to account for 24.8 percent of the firm's outlay on basic payroll. (The contribution of replacement and retraining is a very modest 1.1 percent.) In the current phase of the epidemic, this combined total is estimated to have risen by 2.8, 2.9, and 2.3 percent of basic payroll in Gauteng, KwaZulu-Natal, and Western Cape provinces, respectively. Of these increases, only 0.1, 0.2, and 0.1 percentage point, respectively, arise from additional replacement and retraining costs (Schneider and Kelly, 2003, pp. 9–10). For a hypothetical manufacturing company in Gauteng province, the contribution of replacement and retraining costs is not only larger in the absence of AIDS (1.4 percent of basic payroll) but also more sensitive to the epidemic, which induces an increase of 0.9 percentage point (Schneider and Kelly, 2003, p. 75). None of these estimates is strikingly large, but they are costs all the same.

What we have called the transmission factor $z(s_t)$, $s_t = 0, 1, 2, 3, 4$, and the educational technology $g(.)$ play a vital role in determining the dynamic behavior of the system, especially where its long-run rate of growth, $2zg(1) - 1$, is concerned. Our direct empirical knowledge of these elements, so formulated, is limited, but something can be said about the direction of the epidemic's effects. For strictly nuclear families, the value of $z(s_t)$ is given, and changes in mortality work their effects by changing the state probabilities $\pi_t(s_t)$. If, however, surviving couples take in orphans— pooling arrangements provide an extreme "ideal"—then the sheer burden of caring for more children will at some point surely reduce the quality of childrearing they can provide, although the magnitude of the effect remains a matter for speculation. Given the related financial stress, it is only to be expected that these parents might favor their natural children over their adopted or foster ones, not only in matters of nutrition, education, and health but also in that vital intangible, loving care and attention. Some recent empirical work supports the view that these adverse effects are indeed at work. A study of Indonesian children, for example, yields the finding that orphans are less healthy, less likely to go to school, and overall less prepared for life (Gertler, Levine, and Martinez, 2003). Case, Paxson, and Ableidinger (2002) find, in a group of African countries, that the schooling of orphans depends heavily on how closely related they are to the head of the adopting household. In another recent study of 28 countries, 22 of them African, Ainsworth and Filmer (2002) arrive at a more cautious conclusion.

Although enrollment rates in the majority of the countries studied are lower among orphans than among children with two living parents, the differences are frequently modest in comparison with those between children from rich and poor households, so that targeting on the basis of orphan status is not always obviously the right option. As Ainsworth and Filmer emphasize, moreover, the ultimate aim is not enrollment in itself, important though that is, but rather learning; yet we know little about how orphans perform compared with children with two living parents. As the numbers of orphans swell with the wave of adult mortality now beginning to sweep through sub-Saharan Africa, gaining such knowledge has become a pressing need.

Turning to the educational technology or, more broadly, the supply side of education, much has been made of the very high mortality among teachers, of its grave consequences if replacements are not trained or found, and of the costs of those replacements. None of these considerations appears in this chapter's analysis thus far, but they are readily introduced into the OLG framework. The essentials are fully captured by looking at pooling arrangements, which have evident expositional advantages. Since a teacher's time in the classroom is spread over the children present, it bears a relation to the average value of e_t in generation t. For simplicity, let it be a fixed fraction r thereof for each child. Teachers in period t, like all other adults, are endowed with human capital λ_t and are correspondingly paid $\alpha\lambda_t$. Equation (7), the extended family's budget constraint when normalized to a single "couple," becomes

$$\left[2 + \beta\,\frac{N_t}{\kappa_t(\tau_t)}\right]c_t(0) + \alpha(\gamma + r\lambda_t)\,\frac{N_t}{\kappa_t(\tau_t)}\,e_t(0)$$

$$= \alpha\left[2\lambda_t + \frac{N_t}{\kappa_t(\tau_t)}\,\gamma\right] - \tau_t \equiv \Omega_t(0,\tau_t), \qquad (11)$$

from which it is seen that the need for teachers to bring about learning expresses itself as the component $r\alpha\lambda_t(N_t/\kappa_t(\tau_t))$ of the total "price" of education. This component is increasing in the current levels of both productivity and premature mortality among adults. Thus, even if mortality among teachers is no different from that in the rest of the population, it still discourages investment in education. If, further, teachers require special training, then the costs discussed above compound the problem by imposing an additional burden on the national treasury, and hence on families through taxation.

It was argued above that parents effectively choose the level of schooling, so that e_t is influenced by the whole range of factors discussed above, including premature adult mortality. Disentangling them empirically is a very tall order indeed, but one can still attempt to establish whether there is an association between such mortality and schooling, and thereby provide indirect support for the approach chosen here. This has been undertaken by Hamoudi and Birdsall (Chapter 4, this volume), using data from Demographic and Health Surveys conducted in 23 sub-Saharan African countries. Employing two specifications, they settle on the estimate that a reduction in life expectancy at birth of 10 years is associated with a fall of 0.6 year in the average schooling attained by that cohort. Given that life expectancy at birth in most countries in southern and East Africa fell by 10 years or more from 1985 to 2000 (Dorrington and Schneider, 2002), and that average schooling among the population aged 25–49 was in the modest range of three to six years, this is a disturbing finding. In the light of the OLG framework, it would be useful to know whether the general magnitude of this effect also holds good for the more pertinent indicators $_{20}q_{20}$ and $_{30}q_{20}$, but no such results appear to be available.

Conclusion

Like the Black Death of the 1300s (Cohn, 2003), AIDS has the potential to transform the societies in which its victims live. But unlike that great plague, AIDS can have this effect largely by undermining the transfer of human capital from one generation to the next—arguably the core mechanism by which societies grow and flourish. The reason is that, in contrast with other epidemics, AIDS is overwhelmingly a fatal disease of young adults. Not only does AIDS cause unspeakable human suffering, but it also makes it difficult for these young men and women to provide for the education of their children, not to mention offer them the love and care they need to complement their formal schooling. The result is possibly a whole generation of undereducated and hence underproductive youth, who in adulthood will find it difficult to provide for *their* children's education, and so on. In this way an otherwise growing economy could, when hit with an enduring and sufficiently severe AIDS epidemic, spiral downward into a low-level subsistence economy in three or four generations.

This threat of a progressive collapse of the economy is particularly insidious because the effects will not be felt immediately. Thus estimates of the economic impact of AIDS that look only at the short- to medium-term effects of reductions in labor supply are dangerously misleading. They risk lulling policymakers, especially those concerned with short-term economic fluctuations, into a sense of complacency. As this chapter has shown, it is possible to avert the downward spiral, but only with an aggressive set of policies aimed at shoring up the faltering mechanisms of human capital transmission between generations—policies that prevent AIDS, prolong the lives of its victims, and support the education of their children. These policies are expensive, but, when viewed against the specter of a collapse of the economy and possibly of society itself, they seem like a bargain.

Appendix: Some Technical Notes

The Household's Decision Problem

Let preferences be separable in c_t and λ_{t+1}, with representation in terms of the (expected) utility function

$$EU_t(s_t) = (3 - s_t)\{u[c_t(s_t)] + E_t A_{t+1} v(\lambda_{t+1})\}, \text{ with } s_t = 1, 2, \qquad (A1)$$

where the random variable $A_{t+1} \in \{0, 1, \ldots, N_t\}$ is the number of the N_t children born in period t who survive into old age in period $t + 1$, and E_t is the expectations operator. To put it somewhat differently, parents in period t form expectations about the premature mortality that will afflict their children as adults in period $t + 1$, and they consider the average number of survivors in weighting the payoff $v(\lambda_{t+1})$.

We are now in a position to write out the household's problem formally. As a preliminary, we substitute for λ_{t+1} in equation (A1) using equation (2), which yields

$$EU_t(s_t) = (3 - s_t)\{u[c_t(s_t)] + E_t A_{t+1} v[z(s_t)g(e_t)\lambda_{t+1}]\}, \text{ with } s_t = 1, 2. \quad (A2)$$

A family in state s_t (=1, 2, 3) chooses the bundle $(c_t(s_t), e_t(s_t))$ so as to maximize EU_t, subject to equation (4),

$$c_t(s_t) \geq 0, \text{ and } e_t(s_t) \in [0, 1]. \qquad (A3)$$

A full analysis of problem (A3) is provided in Bell, Devarajan, and Gersbach (2003).

Dynamics

To establish whether unbounded growth is possible, consider the interval $[\Lambda^a(1), \infty)$, in which $e_t^0(1) = 1$. The growth rate of human capital in period t in those families such that $s_t = s_{t+1} = 1$ is

$$\frac{\Lambda_{t+1}(1)}{\Lambda_t(1)} - 1 = [2z(1)g(1) - 1] + \frac{2}{\Lambda_t(1)}.$$

Hence, for all families in the group such that $s_t = s_{t+1} = 1$ for all t and $\Lambda_t(1) > \Lambda^*(1)$ at some point in time, human capital per capita will indeed grow without bound if and only if $2z(1)g(1) \geq 1$, the asymptotic growth rate being $2z(1)g(1) - 1$.

Preferences Under Pooling

Given the assumptions about altruism in the text, the "couple's" preferences are represented as

$$EU_t(0) = 2\{u[c_t(0)] + E_t A_{t+1}(0)v(\lambda_{t+1})\}, \tag{A4}$$

where the random variable $A_{t+1}(0) \in \{0, 1, \ldots, N_t(0)\}$ is the number of the $N_t(0)$ children born in period t who survive into old age in period $t + 1$. The term $E_t A_{t+1}$ depends on the parents' expectations in period t about premature adult mortality among their children in period $t + 1$. In the presence of the poll tax τ_t, the variable $N_t(0)$ must be rewritten accordingly: the random variable $A_{t+1}(0) \in \{0, 1, \ldots, N_t[0, \kappa_t(\tau_t)]\}$ and

$$E_t A_{t+1} = [E_t \kappa_{t+1}(\tau_{t+1})] \cdot N_t / \kappa_t(\tau_t). \tag{A5}$$

Thus the parents must form expectations about not only the mortality environment in the next period, but also the level of the government's expenditure (equals taxation) on mitigating it. If these expectations are stationary, that is, that the future will be like the present, then equation (A5) will specialize to the simple form

$$E_t A_{t+1} = N_t. \tag{A6}$$

Optimum Policy

Where expectations are concerned, Bell, Devarajan, and Gersbach (2003) argue that a good approximation to a full optimum can be achieved as follows. Suppose there are stationary expectations, so that equation (A6) holds and the forward connection among periods is cut. Then, starting from period t, the sequence $\{\tau_t\}_{t=0}^T$ can be constructed as a series of taxes, each element of which is derived independently of all future values as the optimum for the period in question. There is, however, an important connection with the immediately preceding period: the condition $\tau_{t-1} \leq \tau_t$ must not be violated, for otherwise the extended family will have chosen the level of education in period $t - 1$ on the basis of falsely optimistic expectations about mortality in period 1. Observe that if the sequence settles down into a stationary one, it will also involve a rational expectations equilibrium.

Formally stated, the government's problem is as follows. Starting in period 0,

$$\max_{\tau_t} \{2z[0, \kappa(\tau_t)]g[e_t^0(\Omega_t(0, \tau_t), 0, \kappa(\tau_t)]\lambda_t + 1\}, \tag{A7}$$
$$\text{subject to } \tau_t \geq 0 \text{ and } \tau_t \geq \tau_{t-1} \, \forall t.$$

Observe that the potential problem of credibility is implicitly assumed away: when the family forms its (stationary) expectations in period t, the government has found some way to commit itself to $\tau_{t+1} = \tau_t$.

Following the introduction of school attendance subsidies as an additional instrument, the government's own budget constraint reads

$$\eta_t + \sigma_t[N_t/\kappa_t(\eta_t)]e_t^0[\Omega_t(0, \eta_t, \tau_t), 0, \sigma_t, \kappa_t(\eta_t)] \leq \tau_t. \tag{A8}$$

Problem (A7) becomes

$$\max_{\eta_t, \sigma_t, \tau_t} \{2z[0, \kappa(\eta_t)]g[e_t^0(\Omega_t(0, \eta_t, \tau_t), 0, \sigma_t, \kappa_t(\eta_t))]\lambda_t + 1\}, \tag{A9}$$
$$\text{subject to } \tau_t \geq 0, \tau_t \geq \tau_{t-1} \text{ and (A8) } \forall t.$$

References

Ainsworth, Martha, and Deon Filmer, 2002, "Poverty, AIDS and Children's Schooling: A Targeting Dilemma," Policy Research Working Paper No. 2885 (Washington: World Bank).

Aiyagari, S. Rao, 1987, "Optimality and Monetary Equilibria in Stationary Overlapping Generations Models with Long-Lived Agents: Growth Versus Discounting," *Journal of Economic Theory*, No. 43, pp. 292–313.

———, 1992, "Co-existence of a Representative Agent Type Equilibrium with a Non-representative Agent Type Equilibrium," *Journal of Economic Theory*, No. 57, pp. 230–38.

Arndt, Channing, and Jeffrey D. Lewis, 2000, "The Macro Implications of HIV/AIDS in South Africa: A Preliminary Assessment," *South African Journal of Economics*, Vol. 68, No. 5, pp. 856–87.

Barro, Robert J., and Jong Wha Lee, 1996. "International Measures of Schooling Years and Schooling Quality," *American Economic Review, Papers and Proceedings*, Vol. 86 (May), pp. 218–23.

Bell, Clive, and Hans Gersbach, 2003, "Child Labor and the Education of a Society," IZA Discussion Paper No. 338 (Heidelberg, Germany: Alfred Weber Institute, Heidelberg University).

Bell, Clive, Shantayanan Devarajan, and Hans Gersbach, 2003, "The Long-Run Economic Costs of AIDS: Theory and an Application to South Africa," Policy Research Working Paper No. 3152 (Washington: World Bank).

Case, Anne, Christina H. Paxson, and Joseph D. Ableidinger, 2002, "Orphans in Africa," Working Paper No. 9213 (Cambridge, Massachusetts: National Bureau of Economic Research).

Cohn, Samuel K., 2003, *The Black Death Transformed: Disease and Culture in Early Renaissance Europe* (London: Arnold).

Cuddington, John T., 1993, "Modeling the Macroeconomic Effects of AIDS, with an Application to Tanzania," *World Bank Economic Review*, Vol. 7, No. 2, pp. 173–89.

Dorrington, Rob, and others, 2001, "The Impact of HIV/AIDS on Adult Mortality in South Africa," Technical Report, Burden of Disease Research Unit (Tygerburg, South Africa: Medical Research Council of South Africa).

Dorrington, Rob, and David Schneider, 2002, "Fitting the ASSA2000 Urban-Rural AIDS and Demographic Model to 10 Sub-Saharan African Countries" (unpublished; Rondebosch, South Africa: Centre for Actuarial Research, University of Cape Town).

Feeney, Griffith, 2001, "The Impact of HIV/AIDS on Adult Mortality in Zimbabwe," *Population and Development Review*, Vol. 27, No. 4, pp. 771–80.

Gertler, Paul J., David Levine, and Sebastian Martinez, 2003, "The Presence and Presents of Parents: Do Parents Matter for More Than Their Money?" (Berkeley, California: University of California at Berkeley).

Hamoudi, Amar, and Nancy Birdsall, 2002, "HIV/AIDS and the Accumulation and Utilization of Human Capital in Africa," Working Paper No. 2 (Washington: Center for Global Development).

Huo, Teh-Ming, 1987, "Observational Equivalence of the Overlapping Generations and the Cash-in-Advance Economies," *Economics Letters*, Vol. 25, pp. 9–13.

Kambou, Gerard, Shantayanan Devarajan, and Mead Over, 1992, "The Economic Impact of AIDS in an African Country: Simulations with a Computable General Equilibrium Model of Cameroon," *Journal of African Economies*, Vol. 1, No. 1, pp. 109–30.

Lovo, Stefano, 2000, "Infinitely Lived Representative Agent Exchange Economy with Myopia," Discussion Paper (Toulouse, France: IDEI, Université de Sciences Sociales de Toulouse).

Marseille, E., P.B. Hoffman, and J.G. Kahn, 2002, "HIV Prevention before HAART in Sub-Saharan Africa," *The Lancet*, Vol. 359, No. 9320, pp. 1851–56.

McNeill, William H., 1976, *Plagues and Peoples* (Chicago: Anchor Press).

Over, Mead, 1992, "The Macroeconomic Effect of AIDS in Sub-Saharan Africa," AFTN Technical Working Paper No. 3 (Washington: Population, Health and Nutrition Division, Africa Technical Department, World Bank).

Schneider, D.H., and N.J. Kelly, 2003, *AIDS Impact Assessment: Financial Services Companies in South Africa* (Gaborone, Botswana: Actuarial Solutions).

Siemers, Lars, 2002, "Human Capital Transfers: Conditional and Unconditional Subsidies" (Heidelberg, Germany: Alfred Weber Institute, University of Heidelberg).

Solow, Robert M., 1956, "A Contribution to the Theory of Economic Growth," *Quarterly Journal of Economics*, Vol. 70, No. 1, pp. 65–94.

World Bank, 2002, *World Development Indicators 2002* (Washington: World Bank).

———, 2003, "A Technical Guide to the Contemporary Context and Procurement of HIV/AIDS Medicines and Related Supplies Under Bank-Funded Programs" (Washington).

Woodford, M., 1986, "Stationary Sunspot Equilibria in a Finance-Constrained Economy," *Journal of Economic Theory*, Vol. 40, pp. 128–37.

4

AIDS and the Accumulation and Utilization of Human Capital in Africa

NANCY BIRDSALL AND AMAR HAMOUDI

Among the great challenges of development, education continues to take pride of place. In this chapter we highlight some of the channels by which the AIDS pandemic in Africa may affect the continent's ability to produce education and to use it effectively for growth and poverty reduction. Our assessment is preliminary; we hope here to sketch a larger research agenda rather than to dispose of it.

The effect of the pandemic on the supply of and demand for adequate public education matters because education is both *constitutive of* and *instrumental in* the process of development (Sen, 1999). Education is an end in itself, a vital part of individuals' capacity to lead lives that they value. Furthermore, it is an important instrument with which people can improve their lives in other ways. For example, more education, particularly of women, is associated with better family health and improved capacity to plan and time births. Education also enhances the capacity of poor people to participate in the political process, and thus to organize for other social and political rights and to demand governments that are more representative and accountable.

The effect of the pandemic on African economies' ability to use education to enhance growth matters because faster growth is important to sustain poverty reduction and human development. Education contributes to higher individual productivity and income, and thus to sustainable economic growth, although education alone is not sufficient for faster growth. High measured levels of education and human capital did not generate healthy growth in the Soviet Union, nor have rapid increases in average education done so in Egypt, Latin America, and much of sub-Saharan Africa in the last three decades. But microeconomic analyses demonstrate repeatedly the contribution of education to productivity at the individual, household, and farm and firm level.[1] Where the relationship between "more" education and faster growth has failed to materialize—both within countries and between countries (see, for example, Pritchett, 1999)—one or more of several difficulties may be responsible. First, "more" education is often assessed in terms of increasing public spending on education; but, if education systems are weak, more public spending may not translate into true increases in the human capital stock. Second, even where the human capital stock is increasing, problems in other policy spheres (including, for example, macroeconomic instability, civil unrest, or market distortions) may prevent these gains from being translated into economic growth.[2] Third, it may be that as long as the existing stock of human capital remains below some threshold, modest increases are relatively ineffective in producing growth; indeed, the deficit between the existing stock and this threshold, combined with an adverse economic structure and low organizational and institutional capacity, could perpetuate a poverty trap (an issue to which we will return). The contribution of education to high and relatively equitable growth in much of East Asia over the last five decades, where educational systems were relatively high in quality and where market and other distortions were limited, provides the best counterexample on all these scores (Birdsall, Ross, and Sabot, 1995).

In addition to its effect on growth, education also affects the *distribution* of incomes; universal education is essential to creating the pattern of growth that is most likely to reduce poverty. For the poor, the human capital acquired through formal education is a critical economic asset that, once acquired, cannot be appropriated by others. At the societal level, edu-

---

[1]Schultz (1961) first made this point; Schultz (1989) reviews the now-large microeconomic literature.

[2]In fact, various market distortions in developing countries typically keep the marginal private return, if not the average private return, high compared with that in industrial countries. In Egypt, for example, a policy of guaranteeing a public sector job to all secondary and university graduates ensured high marginal private returns, especially to higher education, but these returns were independent of the quality of education; of the actual productivity of people attributable to some combination of their human capital, their motivation, and complementary inputs on the job; and, of course, of whether or not a real demand existed for their skills in the public sector. The policy probably also reduced the demand for and the pressure on the educational system to achieve real gains in learning and skills as opposed to simply certifying graduates (Birdsall and O'Connell, 1999).

Figure 4.1. Life Expectancy at Birth in Five Sub-Saharan African Countries
(Years)

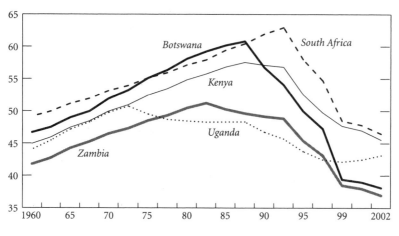

Source: Data from World Bank (2004).

cation that is broadly shared contributes to a more equitable distribution of total wealth (including human capital wealth; Birdsall, 1999; Birdsall and Londoño, 1997) and thus ultimately to a more equitable distribution of opportunities and of income.

Prospects for accumulation and effective economic deployment of education in Africa have to be assessed against the backdrop of the ongoing HIV/AIDS epidemic. According to estimates by the Joint United Nations Programme on HIV/AIDS (UNAIDS), AIDS claimed the lives of about 2 million to 2.5 million adults and children in sub-Saharan Africa in 2003. Over the same period, an estimated 3 million Africans were newly infected with HIV; barring very dramatic increases in treatment coverage, almost all of these individuals will die over the next decade (UNAIDS, 2004). As the death toll from the epidemic has mounted, life expectancies across the continent have plummeted. In Zambia, for example, life expectancy at birth increased from 43 years to 51 years between 1962 and 1982, only to decline again from 50 years to 38 years between 1985 and 1999—a loss of over 20 years' progress in less than a decade (World Bank, 2001). Figure 4.1 shows some of the more dramatic declines in life expectancy among African countries over the past four decades. Economists and others have begun to focus attention on the likely effects of the epidemic on overall social welfare and material well-being. However, its more specific effects

Figure 4.2. Mean Years of Schooling by World Region
(Years)[1]

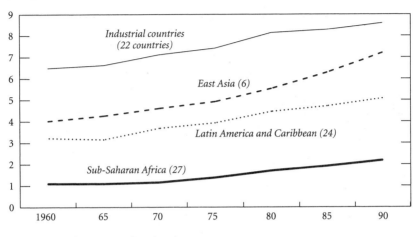

Source: Data from Barro and Lee (1996).
[1]Regional data are unweighted country averages for the population aged over 24 years.

on the supply of, demand for, and productive use of education have not been explicitly explored.

To be sure, the problem of Africa's small human capital stock predates the arrival of the epidemic. Figure 4.2 shows the evolution of one (very crude) measure of the region's human capital stock: average years of schooling attained among the general population aged 25 years and older. Although the rate of growth in human capital by this measure in sub-Saharan Africa picked up briefly in the late 1970s, the continent continues to lag behind other developing regions.

This chapter explores some of the ways in which the AIDS epidemic is likely to affect the rate of new human capital formation on both the supply and the demand sides, and the productivity of the existing human capital stock in Africa. We focus on four specific channels:

- The loss of millions of adults—among them tens of thousands of teachers—affects the rate at which education systems in Africa are able to train the next generation for any given cost and with any given quality.
- The foreshortening of time horizons attendant on these premature deaths reduces the expected lifetime private return to schooling and therefore may reduce demand for education. In addition, increasing household dependency ratios, as the children of AIDS victims are

transferred to the care of foster parents, may reduce the likelihood that children are enrolled in school.[3]

- The loss of so many already-educated people could reduce the social returns to skill among the educated people who survive, to the extent that there are positive externalities associated with a larger total stock of human capital. This could result in a smaller contribution of education to aggregate growth. In addition, if general human capital acquired through education does not substitute perfectly for job-specific human capital acquired through experience, the loss of experienced workers could slow growth.
- As higher production costs result in lower investment by businesses, the consequent decline in physical capital assets would likely reduce the ability of educated people to contribute to economic production, to the extent that physical capital and human capital are complementary inputs.

The last two of these channels could also affect the long-run private demand for education, insofar as average, if not marginal, private returns to education remain low in low-productivity settings. This is the case even though marginal private returns to education, especially above the primary level, could well remain high because of the relative scarcity of well-educated workers (including managers and administrators).[4]

Of course, there are other ways in which AIDS is likely to affect education and human capital in Africa. For example, increasing fears, especially for girls, about exposure to HIV in schools may reduce demand for secondary schooling. In this chapter we abstract from such social or psychological effects, to focus on the primarily economic channels, direct and indirect.

HIV/AIDS and the Supply of Schooling in Sub-Saharan Africa

Of the 25 million people in sub-Saharan Africa estimated by UNAIDS (2004) to be living with HIV infection, about 90 percent are adults and youths over the age of 15 years. Partly as a result of the epidemic, adult

---

[3]We do not use the phrase "AIDS orphans" here, only because many children may be fostered out to new homes before their ill parents actually die.

[4]Psacharopoulos (1994) reports that, on average, marginal private returns to education, especially higher education, are higher in developing countries than elsewhere. This does not mean, of course, that the average returns reflected in wage or salary levels are higher, but only that the additional return over and above that realized by less educated workers is greater.

mortality rates in Africa are over three times the world average. During 1999, an African between the ages of 15 and 60 stood, on average, a 1.4 percent chance of dying; the world average that same year was 0.4 percent (World Bank, 2001). According to UNAIDS, UNICEF, and USAID (2004), by the end of 2003 about 12 million African children had lost either their mother or both parents to AIDS, and, in some of the worst-affected countries, close to 20 percent of all children under age 17 had lost at least one parent, the majority to HIV/AIDS. Furthermore, empirical evidence suggests that among those adults who were infected early in the epidemic, and who are falling ill and dying now, a disproportionate number are relatively well educated, urban, white-collar workers (Ainsworth and Semali, 1998; Filmer, 1998; Deheneffe, Caraël, and Noumbissi, 1998). It is not surprising, therefore, that educators are one of the hardest-hit professions in many AIDS-ravaged African countries. In Zambia, for example, the World Bank estimates that mortality rates among teachers are 70 percent higher than among the general adult population (World Bank, 2001). The United Nations Children's Fund (UNICEF, 2000) estimates that, in 1999 alone, 860,000 African schoolchildren lost their teachers to AIDS (out of a total population of some 70 million pupils), on a continent that in 1997 had only one teacher for every 59 students (World Bank, 2001).

Demographic projections, using specialized software packages, have been employed to speculate on some of the likely effects of the loss of teachers to AIDS in specific African contexts (Malaney, 2000). One general way to assess these effects is to consider a simple two-equation model. Divide the population in the education system into two mutually exclusive groups, teachers and students, and divide each person's lifetime into two periods, childhood and adulthood. Assume that all students are children, added to the system at some constant net rate determined by the difference between enrollment and attrition. Teachers are assumed to be adults, added to the system by training some proportion of the previous period's students, and lost to the system by death, retirement, and other sources of teacher attrition.

With these assumptions, the number of teachers and students in any given period can be expressed as

$$S_t = [1 + n] \, S_{t-1}$$
$$T_t = [1 + d_t] \, T_{t-1} + rS_{t-1}.$$

In these equations n is the rate at which students are added to the education system (net of the rate at which they graduate or drop out), r is the proportion of the last period's students who complete school and then are retained within the system as teachers, and d is the rate of teacher attrition. Using these two equations, one can determine the teacher-student ratio in each period as a function of n, r, d, and the teacher-student ratio in the previous period:

$$\frac{T_t}{S_t} = \frac{r}{1+n} + (1-d_t)\left(\frac{T_{t-1}}{S_{t-1}}\right).$$

Using plausible parameter estimates, we can apply this model to a real-world case in order to speculate on the scale of the effects of future increases in teacher mortality.

According to the World Bank, the current student-teacher ratio in one of the hardest-hit countries in Africa, Botswana, is about 28. (Rather than teacher-student ratios, the World Bank reports the inverse; the ratio for Botswana is less than half the continent-wide average of 59.) According to the World Bank, the population under 14 years in Botswana is projected to grow over the next 15 years at an average annual rate of –0.4 percent.[5] Abstracting from any changes in the proportion of this population that is of primary school enrollment age, and from any changes in enrollment rates, the net rate of increase in the student population (n), therefore, would be –0.004. Data indicating the rate at which students are trained to become teachers in Botswana are not readily available. However, neighboring Namibia trains about 1,000 teachers each year, or some 0.2 percent of the student body (Malaney, 2000). Assuming that Botswana's education system retains this same proportion of its student body to become teachers, we can set $r = 0.002$. Finally, we assume that the "background" rate of teacher attrition—that is, the rate of teacher attrition due to retirement and other traditional sources—is about 5 percent a year, and that the teacher mortality rate in Botswana is about 3 percent a year (the current adult mortality rate in the country).

Given these assumptions, Figure 4.3 shows the evolution of the student-teacher ratio over the next 20 years under three scenarios. The

---

[5]This projected decline reflects the expected decline in fertility and the effects of forecasts of adult mortality as much as or more than any increase in mortality at young ages. Declines in fertility are occurring elsewhere in Africa, as the education of mothers and access to health care, including modern family planning services, have been increasing, the latter especially in urban areas. As noted below, our simulation results are highly robust to variations within plausible ranges of this parameter, but obviously a faster growth rate of the school-aged population would exacerbate the problem we illustrate.

Figure 4.3. Projected Student-Teacher Ratios in Botswana Under Alternative Assumptions[1]
(Students per teacher)

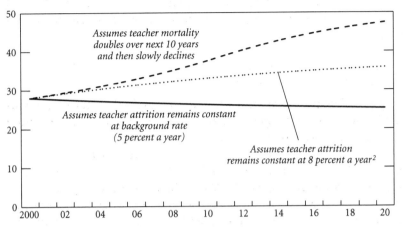

Source: Authors' calculations using the model described in the text.
[1]Assumptions underlying all scenarios are that there are 28 students per teacher in 2000, that the student population (net) grows at a rate of –0.4 percent a year, that 0.2 percent of each year's students are trained to become teachers the following year, and that teacher attrition is 5 percent a year plus the rate of teacher mortality, which equals the rate of adult mortality.
[2]Background rate (5 percent a year) plus adult mortality of 3 percent a year.

first scenario holds teacher attrition constant at the background rate. The second holds teacher attrition at 8 percent—of which the background rate accounts for 5 percentage points and the current adult mortality rate in Botswana for the remainder. The last scenario assumes—in keeping with projections by the United Nations Development Programme (2000)—that adult mortality (and hence, by assumption, teacher mortality) will double over the next 10 years and decline very gradually thereafter.

These projections are highly robust to changes in the assumptions about the rate of growth in the student population—which, after all, is likely to be affected by the epidemic as well, although almost certainly not as dramatically as the rate of growth in the teacher population. The World Bank (2001) has projected, for example, that the primary-school-aged population in Zimbabwe is likely to contract by about 0.8 percent a year over the next decade. Adjusting our assumptions to examine the effects if the school-aged population in Botswana suffered the same decline, however, does not significantly change the projections shown in Figure 4.3 over the time horizon of the simulation.

By contrast, the projections are more sensitive to assumptions about the rate of retention of students to become teachers.[6] For example, the increase in student-teacher ratios shown in the most pessimistic scenario in Figure 4.3 can be entirely averted if the rate at which students are trained to become teachers is increased from 0.2 percent a year to about 0.35 percent a year. Figure 4.4 plots the retention ratio necessary to maintain a constant student-teacher ratio for various rates of teacher attrition; at points above each line, the student-teacher ratio is improving (that is, declining), whereas at points below, it is worsening.

The focus here on student-teacher ratios is not meant to imply that this is the sole measure—or even a good measure—of school quality or efficiency. However, these ratios do reflect clearly one of the most direct effects of the HIV epidemic on the supply of schooling in sub-Saharan Africa, namely, the loss of enormous numbers of teachers over the medium term. For example, from Figure 4.4 it is straightforward to discern that, in order to maintain its current ratio in the face of excess annual adult mortality, a country like Botswana must plow nearly 150 percent more of its students back into the education system to become teachers. Therefore, in order to continue to supply schooling services at current enrollment rates, African education systems will either have to tolerate a dramatic increase in class sizes, or find ways to retain significantly more of the country's precious human capital within the education system, or both. And this must happen at a time when other sectors of the economy are also desperate to replace their own educated workers who are being lost to the epidemic (African Development Forum, 2000). The implication is that, even with increases in class size, public education systems will need to increase the salaries of teachers to attract a larger proportion of graduates into the field. Yet salaries of teachers in sub-Saharan Africa are already higher, relative to average wages in the economy, than in other regions of the world, probably reflecting the relative scarcity of postsecondary graduates.[7] These results imply an increase in an already high fiscal burden of teacher salaries relative to other regions, or the need to reduce the educational requirements for teachers. The latter adjustment is likely to be necessary, especially in rural

---

[6]This, of course, is not surprising, given the structure of the model, in which an increase in the size of today's student body has two effects that work in opposite directions. First, it increases the student-teacher ratio in the present, but, second, it provides a larger pool of new potential teachers in the future. The effects of a decrease in the rate of teacher training, however, are not mitigated in any analogous way.

[7]On this point, World Bank (2000) cites Alain Mingat.

Figure 4.4. New Teachers Required to Be Trained to Maintain a Constant Student-Teacher Ratio in Botswana
(Percent of preceding year's student population)

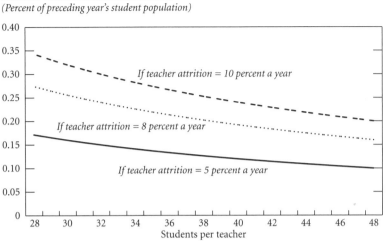

Source: Authors' model described in the text.

areas, and is likely to be even more costly in terms of quality than any increase in class size.[8]

Furthermore, focusing as these results do on nationwide averages implicitly assumes that the government is able to deploy teachers relatively easily throughout the country, in order to ensure that the effects of teacher shortages are evenly felt. The reality, of course, is decidedly more complicated. Student-teacher ratios are generally much higher in rural areas, for example, than in urban areas, and the increase in teacher morbidity and mortality may be worsening this disparity by increasing demand for posts in urban areas closer to health facilities (UNICEF, 2000). The effects of the epidemic in some rural schools, especially the smaller ones with only one or two teachers teaching multiple grades, may be far more dramatic than these model results suggest. In the Democratic Republic of the Congo, for example, some schools have reportedly been forced to close entirely for lack of teachers (African Development Forum, 2000).

---

[8]Behrman and Birdsall (1983) use differences in teacher education as a proxy for differences in the quality of schools across U.S. states. The resulting differences in the quality of schooling across individuals have a strong and highly robust effect on the private returns to schooling (and presumably the social returns).

HIV/AIDS and Demand for Schooling in Sub-Saharan Africa

The previous section framed an approach to assessing the possible supply-side effects of the AIDS epidemic on education. Since the basic findings—that student-teacher ratios are likely to rise unless retention increases as a proportion of the total population leaving school—are fairly robust to assumptions about demand-side changes, we were able to abstract from these. However, two of the major channels through which the epidemic is likely to affect demand for education include time horizon effects and liquidity effects. We will discuss the latter briefly, and then the former at greater length.

Liquidity Effects

For many reasons (including the fact that individuals cannot be dispossessed of their own human capital), adults cannot formally borrow on behalf of their children in order to finance their education. As a result, any private investments in children's education must be financed out of parents' or caregivers' wealth. If parents and caregivers face liquidity constraints as a result of increasing household dependency ratios, they may find that financing more difficult. Furthermore, Case, Paxson, and Ableidinger (2004), Deininger, Garcia, and Subbacao (2003), and Bishai and others (2003) all find descriptive evidence suggesting that parents may favor their own biological children over foster children. If, in fact, a causal relationship exists between biological relatedness and parental "altruism," the displacement of millions of orphans to the care of nonbiological parents may adversely affect their educational opportunities.

Time Horizon Effects

Recent theoretical and empirical work has explored the relationships between life expectancy and investment in human capital. The reasoning is that, when individuals and households anticipate a longer time horizon over which to reap returns, they are likely to be more willing to incur the up-front costs of investment in schooling. Kalemli-Ozcan, Ryder, and Weil (2000) develop a model in which individuals facing a constant probability of death weigh the earnings forgone during the time spent in school against the anticipated returns to schooling in deciding when to leave school and enter the labor force. Calibrating their model using reasonable parameters based on real-world data, these authors speculate that changes in life expectancy over the past 150 years can explain a significant fraction of the observed increases in schooling rates in the most developed countries.[9]

Such a model would also capture stylized facts from developing countries over the more recent past. In an empirical treatment of this question, Behrman, Duryea, and Székely (1999) relate the educational attainment of birth cohorts—using data from household surveys conducted in Latin America—to fixed-country effects, secular trend effects, and several year- and country-specific variables, including life expectancy, that reflect the broader economic and institutional setting.[10] Their results suggest that changes in life expectancy were associated with quantitatively and statistically significant changes in educational attainment. On average, they found a 10-year increase in life expectancy to be associated with a 0.3- to 0.4-year increase in schooling completed.

Here we use a similar "quasi-panel" technique to try to describe this relationship in African contexts over the past generation. We use data from the Demographic and Health Surveys (DHSs), in which nationally representative samples of 15- to 49-year-old women are interviewed on such topics as reproduction, household assets, children's health, employment status, and educational attainment. We emphasize that the main lesson to be drawn from our results is descriptive, not directly causal, and more qualitative than the econometric results could be taken to imply. Our findings, like those of Behrman, Duryea, and Székely, point to a decline in demand for education accompanying a decline in life expectancy; this is as far as we intend to interpret the results presented below. One of many causal interpretations of this descriptive finding includes the sort of time horizon effects that Kalemli-Ozcan, Ryder, and Weil outline in their theoretical model. Empirical analysis to identify such a causal effect is an important direction for future research.

The DHS data demonstrate steady improvements in the educational attainment of birth cohorts across the continent over time. (Figure 4.5 shows attainment profiles for five-year birth cohorts that reached ages

---

[9]Of course, it is not clear that increasing life expectancy per se has had a direct causal effect on these increases in schooling; life expectancy is usually closely associated with other changes, including increasing average income, technological shifts, and improving institutions, all of which would raise the returns to and the demand for education. These factors are guaranteed to confound any empirical investigation of the effects of life expectancy on demand for education, including the one we undertake here. Given the impossibility of conducting controlled experiments, any empirical analysis—including this one—will necessarily be more suggestive of the direction of such effects than conclusive regarding their magnitude.

[10]As with life expectancy, these other variables have mostly statistically significant effects in the expected direction on differences and changes in average education.

Figure 4.5. Educational Attainment Profiles of Selected Birth Cohorts in Uganda, Zambia, and Zimbabwe[1]
(Percent of cohort population)

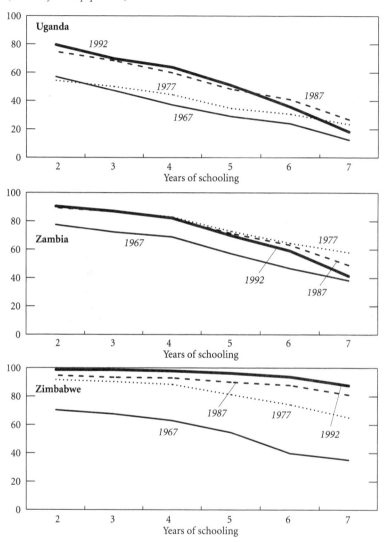

Source: Authors' calculations using data from Demographic and Health Surveys for Uganda (1995), Zambia (1996), and Zimbabwe (1999).

[1]Profiles are constructed by stratifying survey responses according to the respondent's year of birth and tracking the proportion of respondents who reported having completed each year of school. Responses are weighted by sampling weights.

[2]Years are those in which the indicated cohort reached age 12–17.

12–17 in 1967, 1977, 1987, and 1992 in Uganda, Zambia, and Zimbabwe.) The older cohorts in almost all countries reported lower attainment. In each of the 23 countries for which surveys were available, the same general trend may be observed.[11] It is important to be careful in interpreting these observations, however. The observations are not truly longitudinal, since they are derived from cross-sectional surveys. The time component comes from subdividing the cross-sectional responses to the survey questions according to the year of birth of each respondent. We discuss this at greater length later in this section.

However, it is worth observing a few country experiences over time. Figure 4.6 shows differences in average years of schooling between birth cohorts and changes in life expectancy at birth in the three countries shown in Figure 4.5. In Uganda and Zambia, for example, each five-year birth cohort appears to have been more educated than the one before it until 1977. Those reaching ages 12–17 in 1982 and after, however, began to see shorter and shorter life expectancies and had the same or fewer years of schooling as the cohorts before them.

With this approach we seek to explore the extent to which changes in educational attainment among individuals and cohorts can be correlated with differences in life expectancy in the years when the individuals and cohorts are making decisions about whether to remain in school. To this end we compiled comparable data from 37 DHSs conducted in 23 sub-Saharan African countries over 12 years, resulting in individual data on some 192,000 respondents. We collapsed these respondents into 214 five-year birth cohorts and related average years of schooling within these cohorts to household and national characteristics. The oldest of the cohorts was born during 1935–39, and the youngest during 1980–84. The choice of functional form is similar to that employed by Behrman, Duryea, and Székely, with household and country characteristics relating to schooling attainment in a linear fashion.[12] Table 4.1 shows the results of ordinary-least-squares (OLS) regressions of average years of schooling in each five-

---

[11]The attainment profiles for the other 20 countries are not shown but are available on request from the authors.

[12]Although the objective here is description, this linear functional form refers back to a specific structural model, namely, the standard Mincerian (Mincer, 1974) model in which individuals seek to maximize their expected income, weighing forgone time in the labor force against the wage premium attributable to schooling. In such a model, individuals would be expected to remain in school until the present value of their expected lifetime returns to an additional year of school equals potential earnings from a year in the labor force. These expected returns are of course linearly related to life expectancy, with each additional year of life in the labor force bringing one additional year of returns.

Figure 4.6. Educational Attainment and Life Expectancy for Selected Birth Cohorts in Uganda, Zambia, and Zimbabwe[1]

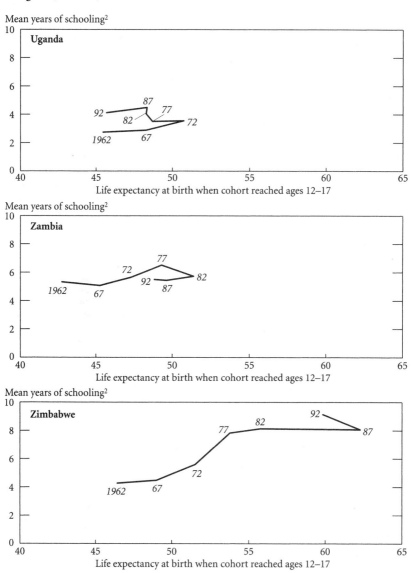

Mean years of schooling[2]

(Uganda)

Mean years of schooling[2]

(Zambia)

Mean years of schooling[2]

(Zimbabwe)

Life expectancy at birth when cohort reached ages 12–17

Source: Authors' calculations using data from Demographic and Health Surveys for Uganda (1995), Zambia (1996), and Zimbabwe (1999) and World Bank (2001).

[1]Each point represents the five-year birth cohort that reached ages 12–17 in that year.

[2]Calculated by collapsing DHS respondents into cohorts based on birth year and averaging the years of education reported by respondents in each group, weighted by survey sampling weights.

Table 4.1. Ordinary-Least-Squares Regressions of Educational Attainment on Life Expectancy and Other Variables

Independent Variable	Regression[1]					
	(1)[2]	(2)[2]	(3)	(4)	(5)[2,3]	(6)[2,3]
Life expectancy at birth (in years)	0.175	0.064	0.170	0.086	0.070	0.062
	(0.053)	(0.045)	(0.085)	(0.075)	(0.051)	(0.050)
Real GDP per capita (in 1987 international dollars)[4]			0.002	0.001		
			(0.001)	(0.001)		
Year[5]	.0069	0.494	−0.068	0.513	0.055	0.404
	(0.027)	(0.069)	(0.052)	(0.159)	(0.023)	(0.180)
Year squared		−0.003		−0.004		−0.002
		(0.000)		(0.001)		(0.001)
Number of observations	144	144	107	107	105	105
R^2	0.97	0.98	0.96	0.97	0.95	0.96

Source: Authors' regressions using data from Demographic and Health Surveys (DHS) and World Bank (2001).

[1]The dependent variable is average years of schooling; data are calculated from the DHS for cohorts reaching ages 12–17 in 1962, 1967, 1972, 1977, 1982, 1987, and 1992 in 23 sub-Saharan African countries. Cohort averages are taken by collapsing individual respondents into five-year cohorts defined by the year of their birth and taking an average of responses (weighted by survey sampling weights). Some cohorts were omitted from the regressions for lack of data. For robustness to heteroskedasticity, standard errors of coefficient estimates (in parentheses) are calculated using the Huber-White estimator of the variance-covariance matrix. All regressions include country-specific intercepts and country-specific time trends except where noted otherwise.

[2]Regressions include indicators of household asset wealth (percent of cohort with electricity, radio, bicycle, motorcycle, car).

[3]Only those cohorts that reached the ages of 12–17 before 1987 are included. Country-specific time trends are not included.

[4]Dollars adjusted for differences in purchasing power across countries.

[5]Variable defined as year minus 1900.

year birth cohort on national average life expectancy at birth when the cohort was aged 12–17. (Sample sizes in some of the regressions are reduced because of lack of data on many of the DHS wealth variables or on GDP per capita adjusted for purchasing power parity.[13]) Control variables for each cohort in each country include indicators of household asset wealth or average income per person, the proportion of each cohort living in urban

---

[13]Because of incomplete data, our regressions do not include all 214 birth cohorts. No aggregate data were available for those birth cohorts that reached ages 12–17 before 1962, leaving 161 cohorts. For some of these, data on household wealth and GDP per capita were not available. However, we used a probit regression to test for systematic differences between those observations for which GDP and household wealth data were available and those for which they were not; the two groups were not statistically different in terms of the other regressors or the dependent variable.

areas, a separate time trend for each country, and country dummy variables to capture fixed effects on demand for schooling within countries.

As already noted, this "quasi-panel" technique is not truly longitudinal, since the time-varying component in the data comes from sorting individual respondents into groups based on the five-year period in which they were born. One difficulty that arises from this procedure relates to the question of selection bias due to mortality rates possibly being correlated with education level. Say, for example, that the more educated individuals in each birth cohort are likely to live longer than their less educated peers. Then, even in the absence of any true secular trend, older birth cohorts would appear relatively more educated than younger ones at any moment in time, since the less educated among the older cohorts will be more likely to have been removed (by death) from the sample of potential respondents.[14] To correct for this effect, we include a linear time trend in the regressions relating schooling attainment to life expectancy, which implicitly assumes that the effect of education on an individual's mortality risk is constant across birth cohorts.[15] This assumption may fail, however, because of the nature of the AIDS epidemic: as noted above, the epidemic (at least in its first wave) appears to have greatly increased the risk of mortality among younger, more educated people *relative to* younger, less educated people. As a result, the younger birth cohorts may have been purged by the time of the surveys of the more educated among them, whereas the older birth cohorts would have been purged of the less educated. Even in the absence of any true time trend, this would create an apparent concave relationship between time and average schooling. We know (see Figure 4.1) that the same sort of relationship holds between life expectancy and time, because of the epidemic. Therefore some of the *apparent* relationship between life expectancy and schooling may simply be an artifact of this "differential mortality" problem. One way to try to separate out this effect from the "true" relationship between schooling and life expectancy is to include the square of the year in the regressions, as we do in columns (2) and (4) of Table 4.1. The difficulty with this approach, however, relates to multicollinearity in the data: life expectancy among the 138 "quasi-cohorts" in columns (1) and (3) is almost perfectly quadratic in time, after

---

[14]Of course, selection bias may result from dynamics other than just mortality risk. For example, if educated people are more likely at any time to emigrate, the same problem would result. The reasoning is essentially the same, regardless of the selection factor.

[15]Of course, this is not the *only* reason we include a time trend. Including a year trend also captures institutional and technological changes and other developments, so long as these things occur monotonically (and in fact linearly) over time.

controlling for the other factors.[16] It is difficult, therefore, to determine from the existing data how much of the apparent relationship between schooling and life expectancy is simply an artifact of selection bias.

Another way to deal with this is to restrict the period of analysis to the time before the epidemic, as we do in columns (5) and (6) of Table 4.1. After all, it is likely that any effect of education on the relative risk of mortality would be constant across time during this period, so that including time linearly in this regression would control for the possibly differential effect of education on mortality.[17] But, again, before 1987 improvements in life expectancy were almost perfectly linear with time across Africa, after controlling for household wealth and country-specific factors.[18] Therefore this approach does not entirely solve the problem.

Nonetheless, it is worth underlining that we account for time-invariant country-specific differences (such as differences in economic and social policy and institutions) by including a country-level fixed effect, and for any country-specific effects that change linearly with time by including country-year interaction terms.[19] These results suggest that, in cohorts whose life expectancy was 10 years longer, schooling attainment was some 0.6 to 0.9 year higher.

Table 4.2 reports results of the same regression, but with each individual entered into the regression as a single observation, rather than with individuals aggregated into birth cohorts. Because schooling attainment for individuals is truncated at zero years (one cannot spend a negative number of years in school), we use a tobit specification.[20] The results sug-

---

[16]A regression of life expectancy at birth against the other regressors in column (2) of Table 4.1 produces an R^2 of 0.99.

[17]The coefficient on year squared in column (6) is not statistically significantly different from zero at the 5 percent confidence level.

[18]A regression of life expectancy at birth against the other regressors in column (5) of Table 4.1 produces an R^2 of 0.96, with each additional calendar year bringing an additional 0.39 year of life expectancy (with a standard error of 0.02).

[19]Analysis of the country dummies and country-specific year trends (not shown) indicates that among the large positive outliers are Ghana and Uganda, and among the large negative outliers are war-torn Ethiopia as well as Nigeria and Niger; these findings are consistent with our intuition about at least institutional variation across countries in the region.

[20]The tobit functional specification assumes that the schooling attainment data are truncated, not censored by some independent set of dynamics that determines whether individuals go to school separately from those that determine how long they remain in school, once enrolled. To test whether this assumption is appropriate, we estimated the probability that a respondent will have obtained any schooling at all—regardless of how much—and compared the coefficient estimates from this regression with those of the tobit regression in Table 4.2. If the assumption underlying the tobit specification holds, we should expect the coefficient estimates (scaled by the standard error of the estimate) to be equal. The estimates were indeed quite close.

Table 4.2. Tobit Regressions of Educational Attainment on Life Expectancy and Other Variables

Independent Variable	Regression[1]			
	(1)	(2)	(3)[2]	(4)[2]
Life expectancy at birth (in years)	0.058	0.029	0.107	0.060
	(0.019)	(0.019)	(0.020)	(0.022)
Year	0.097	0.947	0.156	0.677
	(0.017)	(0.058)	(0.007)	(0.118)
Year squared		−0.005		−0.003
		(0.000)		(0.001)
Dummy variable for urban residence	3.135	3.126	3.475	3.475
	(0.058)	(0.058)	(0.078)	(0.078)
Number of observations	54,830	54,830	37,650	37,650
Left-censored observations (zero years of school)	24,985	24,985	18,577	18,577

Sources: Authors' regressions using data from Demographic and Health Surveys (DHS) and World Bank (2001).

[1]The dependent variable is average years of schooling; regressions are as in Table 4.1 except that each individual respondent is entered as a separate observation rather than included in a five-year birth cohort. Only those individuals who reached age 12 in 1962, 1967, 1970, 1972, 1977, 1980, 1982, 1985, 1987, 1990, and 1992 are included in the regressions. All regressions include country-specific intercepts, country-specific time trends (except where noted otherwise), and indicators of household asset wealth (whether the respondent's household has electricity, radio, bicycle, motorcycle, car).

[2]Regression includes only those individuals who reached age 12 before 1987 and does not include country-specific time trends.

gest that individuals facing 10 years greater life expectancy attained some 0.3 to 0.6 year more schooling—somewhat less than the 0.6 to 0.9 year obtained using the "quasi-cohort" data.

Another way to attack the problem empirically—one that is less subject to the differential mortality problem—is to examine the relationship between gross primary enrollment ratios at the national level and life expectancy at birth. In generating internationally comparable estimates of schooling attainment, Barro and Lee (1996) employ a "perpetual inventory" method to translate gross enrollment ratios and demographic structure into stocks and flows of population at various levels of educational attainment (no schooling, incomplete primary, complete primary, and so on).[21] They estimate, for example, that the population over age 15 who has completed at least some primary education in any five-year period is equal to the primary-educated population from the previous period that has

---

[21]They have subsequently used "adjusted gross enrollment ratios" in order to avoid double-counting individuals who repeat grades (Barro and Lee, 2000).

survived, plus the population that turned 15–19 over the previous five years and attended any primary school. The latter population is estimated by multiplying the total population of each five-year birth cohort by the gross primary enrollment ratio in the period when that cohort was aged 10–14.

The assumption, therefore, is that the gross primary enrollment ratio when a five-year birth cohort is aged 10–14 indicates the proportion of 15- to 19-year-olds who have at least some primary education. Employing this assumption, we regress gross national primary enrollment ratios across countries and over time against period- and country-specific life expectancy at birth, income per person, and time trends. This approach is useful for comparison with our previous results, since it is not subject to the differential mortality problem. As Table 4.3 shows, the results suggest that, in environments where life expectancy at birth was 10 years longer, primary enrollment ratios were about 0.2 to 0.3 (or about 20 to 30 per-centage points) higher.[22]

Of course, more than one causal model can be constructed to account for these descriptive results. However, the most obvious causal stories—specifically, those involving factors that are time invariant, or secular trends within countries—can be ruled out, since the relationship observed is net of such effects. Such effects might include, for example, differences among countries in the quality of social services or the rate of improve-ment of these services. Furthermore, Table 4.4 shows the results of first-difference regressions, in which the *change* in gross primary enrollment ratios in each country from one five-year period to the next is related to the proportional change in GDP and life expectancy over the same period. Consistent with the results in Table 4.3, these results suggest that countries in which life expectancy increased by 10 years between one five-year period and the next also saw improvements in school enrollment ratios of about 0.2 (or 20 percentage points) over the same interval. This is also compatible with our descriptive findings using the DHS data.[23]

---

[22]Since gross primary enrollment ratios are not bounded from above at one as net enroll-ment ratios are, and since there were no country-period observations where gross enroll-ment ratios were at the lower bound of zero, a functional form that is linear, rather than tobit or cumulative normal or logistic, is not inappropriate.

[23]In translating enrollment rates into average schooling attainment, Barro and Lee multi-ply the proportion of the population enrolled at each educational level by the number of years in that level, and then by the probability of completion. The Barro-Lee data suggest that about 25 percent of those in Africa who enroll in primary school complete it. Therefore, assuming six years in primary school, an increase in enrollment of 0.2 would translate into an increase of $(0.2) \times (0.25) \times 6 = 0.3$ year in attainment.

Table 4.3. Regressions of Primary Enrollment Ratios on Life Expectancy and Other Variables

Independent Variable	Regression[1]			
	Africa only (1)[2]	World (2)[2]	World (3)	World (4)[2]
Life expectancy at birth (in years)[3]	0.023 (0.013)	0.021 (0.002)	0.016 (0.002)	0.016 (0.002)
Life expectancy × Africa dummy			0.012 (0.006)	0.014 (0.002)
Real GDP per capita (in 1987 dollars)[4]	0.000 (0.000)	0.000 (0.000)	0.000 (0.000)	0.000 (0.000)
Year				0.020 (0.008)
Year squared				0.000 (0.000)
Constant				−0.921 (0.296)
Country- and region-specific intercepts	39 countries[5]	8 regions[6]	8 regions[6]	None
Number of observations	224	743	743	743
R^2	0.93	0.45	0.46	0.32

Sources: Authors' regressions using data from World Bank (2001).

[1]The dependent variable is the ratio of gross primary enrollment to the number of children of primary-school age; data are from 122 countries (including 39 African countries, listed below) at five-year intervals beginning in 1965. Some observations were omitted from the regressions for lack of data. Standard errors of coefficient estimates (in parentheses) are robust to heteroskedasticity and are calculated using the Huber-White estimator, adjusting for clustering by country. All regressions include country-specific time trends except where noted otherwise.

[2]Regression includes fixed country effects and does not include time trends.

[3]In latest year of the preceding five-year period for which data were available.

[4]Not adjusted for purchasing power parity because of lack of data before 1980.

[5]Algeria, Angola, Benin, Botswana, Burundi, Cameroon, Cape Verde, Central African Republic, Chad, Côte d'Ivoire, Comoros, Democratic Republic of Congo, Republic of Congo, Ethiopia, Gabon, The Gambia, Ghana, Guinea, Guinea-Bissau, Kenya, Lesotho, Madagascar, Malawi, Mali, Mauritania, Mauritius, Mozambique, Niger, Nigeria, Rwanda, Senegal, Sierra Leone, South Africa, Swaziland, Tanzania, Togo, Uganda, Zambia, and Zimbabwe.

[6]Sub-Saharan Africa; East Asia; Eastern Europe; Latin America and Caribbean; Mediterranean, Middle East, and North Africa; South Asia; South Pacific and Southeast Asia; and industrialized countries of North America and Europe and Japan.

Of course, any causal conclusions that one might draw from these cross-country regressions are subject to the usual caveats. Among other things, it may be that decisions about whether and how much to invest in education are too complex to be captured in linear cross-country or cross-household regressions. This is essentially similar to the criticism leveled by many against cross-country regressions to explain economic growth.

Table 4.4. Regressions of Changes in Primary Enrollment Ratios on Changes in Life Expectancy and Other Variables

Independent Variable	Regression[1]		
	(1)	(2)	(3)
Change in life expectancy at birth over previous five years (in years)	0.015	0.025	0.020
	(0.005)	(0.015)	(0.010)
Change in real GDP per capita over previous five years (in 1987 dollars)	0.000	0.000	0.000
	(0.000)	(0.000)	(0.000)
Constant			0.003
			(0.021)
Country- and region-specific intercepts	8 regions	39 countries	None
Number of observations	613	181	181
R^2	0.05	0.25	0.04

Sources: Authors' regressions using data from World Bank (2001).

[1]The dependent variable is the change in the gross primary enrollment ratio (see Table 4.3) over the preceding five years; data are from 122 countries (including 39 African countries, listed in the notes to Table 4.3) at five-year intervals beginning in 1970 (change from 1965) and ending in 1995. Some observations were omitted from the regressions for lack of data. See Table 4.3 for other details of the regression.

Direct causal analysis is also hampered by the lack of truly longitudinal data in Africa. In its absence, more detailed and qualitative "case study" approaches, which examine changes in educational attainment, attitudes toward investment in human capital, and health status in specific communities or countries over time, could serve well. As these data become available in sufficient detail in African contexts, this line of inquiry deserves a high priority.

Furthermore, even if life expectancy has had an effect on demand for schooling similar to the effects we estimate here, that effect may be dramatically different depending on the *direction* in which life expectancy is changing. That is to say, even if 10 additional years of life expectancy really did increase demand for schooling by some number of years, this by no means necessarily implies that a *loss* of 10 years of life expectancy would *reduce* demand for schooling by the same number of years. In an epidemic, after all, past trends are not always replicated in the future.

This is particularly the case if life expectancy in the past reflected a range of institutional and policy factors that would remain relatively constant (or could even improve) in countries hit by the epidemic. On the other hand, we cannot be sure that the future relationship will not be tighter (and thus worse where life expectancy declines), since the effect of demand for education could be exacerbated by the disproportionate number of adults affected, compared with the past when increased life expectancy resulted heavily from improvements in infant mortality. In short, although our results are only illustrative and certainly not definitive in terms of causality, they do at least provide a point from which to begin thinking about the effects of declining life expectancy on the demand for education.

HIV/AIDS and the Productivity of Africa's Human Capital

AIDS is unlike many other diseases in that it disproportionately affects adults of working age. Furthermore, at least for the first decade of the epidemic, HIV was much more likely to infect the relatively well educated. The epidemic will therefore carry off an unprecedented proportion of Africa's existing human capital stock. Beyond the incalculable human tragedy visited upon those who die prematurely and their loved ones, we can expect these deaths to have effects on the productivity of those who survive.

An agglomeration of skilled workers is much more productive than an equal number of skilled workers acting alone. One of the most dramatic illustrations of this principle of increasing marginal returns to human capital is the stylized fact of the "brain drain." Skilled workers in many industries tend to migrate from places where they are relatively scarce to those where they are relatively abundant, in order to increase their income. Indian engineers, for example, can quadruple their income by moving from Kerala to Silicon Valley. Similarly, African professionals in many fields are likely to be concentrated in urban rather than rural areas, wherever they may have been born. Another indication of this phenomenon is in the formation of universities, which, after all, exist because they offer individuals with particularly specialized skills the opportunity to be in a community with others of similar or complementary skills.

Becker, Murphy, and Tamura (1990) use the idea of increasing returns to human capital to generate a model of multiple equilibria in the size, overall schooling, and welfare of households. Their reasoning is that, in the more desirable equilibrium, each household has fewer children but invests more heavily in the "quality" of each child. This increases aggregate human capital in the succeeding generation, which increases the opportunity cost of the grown children's time and the future returns to their skills, thereby inducing them, as parents themselves, also to have fewer children while increasing the attractiveness of investment in the "quality" of those children. This in turn increases their productivity, leading to the long-run persistence of a highly skilled and productive workforce. In contrast, in the less desirable equilibrium, where skills are relatively scarce, returns to

Figure 4.7. Distribution of Countries Worldwide by Real GDP per Capita, 2002

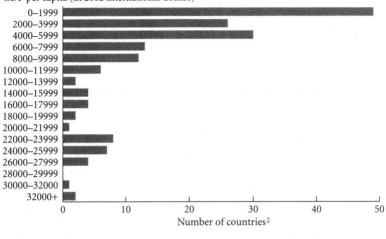

GDP per capita (in 2002 international dollars)[1]

Number of countries[2]

Source: Data from World Bank (2004).
[1]Real GDP per person in 2002, corrected for purchasing power parity.
[2]Data were available for 148 countries, including 39 in sub-Saharan Africa.

investment in schooling are smaller and the opportunity cost of parents'
time is relatively low. Parents are therefore inclined to invest time and
resources in a larger number of children, who obtain less schooling,
thereby perpetuating the scarcity of skills.[24]

The real world does indeed seem to bear out these sorts of stories based
on multiple equilibria. For example, as Figure 4.7 demonstrates, the distribution of average income per capita across the countries of the world is
highly bimodal, with a large cluster of very poor countries (with GDP per
capita, adjusted for purchasing power parity, of up to $2,000), another
cluster of very rich ones (with GDP per capita at or around $22,000 to
$28,000), and a smattering of countries in between. In the case of sub-
Saharan Africa, only 7 of the 39 countries included in Figure 4.7 have GDP
per capita (adjusted for purchasing power parity) at or above $4,000.

This highly bimodal distribution of countries is consistent with any
number of stories about the nature of economic growth. However, it also

---

[24]Empirical evidence offered in studies by Psacharopoulos that private and social rates of
return to education are fairly constant across countries might appear to militate against such
a hypothesis. However, these studies do not capture the true social returns to education
(Birdsall, 1996).

rules out many traditional ones. For example, it is much easier to reconcile this stylized fact with the notion of a poverty trap—whereby very poor economies remain very poor until some positive external shock breaks the vicious cycle—than with some stagewise model of development. Therefore, although of course the stylized fact of bimodal income distribution does not by itself imply the existence of poverty traps, it is quite consistent with such a hypothesis.

A sufficiently large increase in life expectancy could jump-start an economy (Bloom and Canning, 2000), as could a large decline in fertility, since the latter subsequently produces a greatly increased ratio of workers to children (Kelley and Schmidt, 1996, 1999; Williamson, 1998). In these and other cases, the story is generally applied to various of the so-called miracle economies of East Asia, where large gains in life expectancy, declines in fertility, and subsequent huge increases in the number of workers relative to children (and the elderly) occurred throughout much of the high-growth decades of the 1970s and 1980s.[25] In a case study in Uganda, Bigsten and Kayizzi-Mugerwa (1999) suggest that the structural constraints typical of a poverty trap (although they do not use that expression) make it difficult to capture the benefits of globalization in the short run, even with a substantially improved policy environment.

Similarly, the accumulation of human capital beyond some critical mass is likely to be one such shock in itself. Lau and others (1996), analyzing cross-sectional evidence from Brazilian states, find that the impact of education on total economic output becomes particularly dramatic only after the average level of education of the workforce reaches a certain threshold; in Brazil this threshold was reached when average educational attainment reached about three to four years. Most African nations, especially in the southern part of the continent, have made progress in building their own critical mass of skills. In Botswana gross secondary school enrollment increased from 19 percent of the school-aged population at the beginning of the 1980s to 56 percent in the mid-1990s. Over the same period this rate increased from 8 percent to 47 percent in Zimbabwe, and from 3 percent to 98 percent in Malawi. Between the early 1970s and the mid-1990s, South Africa's gross secondary school enrollment ratio increased from 20 percent to 84 percent (World Bank, 2001). The AIDS epidemic, however, has hit

---

[25]Similarly, Bloom, Canning, and Malaney (1999) describe for East Asia a world of "cumulative causation," in which low incomes and adverse demographic and health conditions in East Asia formed a web of cause and effect until the early 1960s. These authors attribute the escape from the vicious cycle to rapid improvements in health, which reoriented the causal cycle, resulting in extremely rapid economic growth.

these nations hardest: the six countries worst affected by HIV/AIDS are located in Southern Africa, with adult HIV prevalence ratios exceeding 20 percent in 6 countries, including Botswana and Swaziland where they approach 40 percent (UNAIDS, 2004). By skimming off the most skilled workers in the economy (at least in the first wave), HIV/AIDS threatens to forestall the emergence of a critical mass of these workers.

These effects are difficult to quantify at the microeconomic level, since they follow a dynamic in which the number of already-educated people increases the social (that is, external to individuals) return to education, but not necessarily the private return. The measured private return may actually decline, as noted above, as more people are educated and skilled workers become relatively more plentiful. This is what explains Psacharopoulos's finding that private returns, especially to higher education, tend to diminish as country GDP per capita rises.[26] (Implicitly, the model presented by Becker, Murphy, and Tamura assumes that, other things equal, some of the positive externalities associated with a larger total stock of human capital are reflected at least in the form of higher absolute private returns.) At the aggregate level, however, it is individuals' decisions about these investments that determine the number of educated people. Increasingly sophisticated empirical techniques have been employed to quantify effects in the context of these sorts of causal cycles. In the meantime, however, it is sufficient to understand the qualitative implications of the loss of the positive externalities generated by Africa's stock of skilled and educated workers. The first of these is an increase in the rate of brain drain, as skilled workers move to take advantage of these externalities elsewhere. The second is a decrease in the average productivity of those workers (unskilled as well as skilled) who do survive. The third is a decline in the demand for schooling among workers in the future, attendant on a decline in the absolute, if not the marginal, private returns to education.

HIV/AIDS, Physical Capital, and Human Capital

Human capital and physical capital are complementary. For example, Birdsall, Pinckney, and Sabot (1997) posit that, where credit markets are incomplete or imperfect, poor households must finance their investments

---

[26]Psacharopoulos (1994) also reports diminishing social returns to education with higher GDP per capita, but this is because he measures the "social" return at the country level as simply the private return minus the country-specific cost of schooling at different levels.

entirely out of their own savings. These credit-constrained households, therefore, save not only to buffer against stochastic income shocks, but also to finance investment. Because they will invest only when the expected return exceeds the (relatively high) discount rate, investments available to the poor are likely to have higher returns than those available to the rich, who are unable to take advantage of these investment opportunities because of imperfections in the credit market.

This situation holds particularly true for investments in human capital, which yield extremely high private returns relative to most other investments, but are nontransferable and hence extremely difficult to guarantee. For example, once trained, an individual has no reason to fear expropriation of his or her newly acquired skill, and so, in the absence of sophisticated credit monitoring mechanisms, that individual may choose not to make good on any commitment to repay the training costs. The rich, therefore, supplement investments in their own human capital with investments in third-party instruments, including, for example, equity markets and other traditional instruments. These are easier to guarantee, but they are also likely to be less productive than the investments of the poor (in their farms and businesses as well as in their human capital).[27] In such contexts, if the poor are forced to forgo investments in their own education for lack of savings, the potential benefits are lost to the economy.

One of the most salient clinical characteristics of HIV/AIDS is the long period of illness before the infected person finally succumbs. Evidence from a recent cohort study in rural Uganda suggests that the median time from infection to death in that setting is about 10 years, during which the illness becomes more and more debilitating, with the last 10 months usually spent in a state of complete incapacity (Morgan and others, 2002). Since those infected are likely to be adults of working age, this protracted illness hits household saving and investment twice: first by depriving the household of a wage earner, and then by requiring an outlay of household resources to care for the infected person. Although some of these outlays are financed by diverting present consumption or through interhousehold transfers, evidence suggests that most of it is financed by reductions in saving and the selling off of physical assets (Menon and others, 1998; Béchu, 1998). Poorer households, when forced to make these adjustments, are obviously more likely to have to forgo investment in the human capital of their children. Amplifying this effect is the fact that the loss of adults in a household often increases the opportunity cost of the children's time,

---

[27]See also Acemoglu (1997) and Acemoglu and Pischke (1999).

because their work becomes more vital to the ongoing operation of the household (Mutangadura, 2000).

Furthermore, using year- and country-specific data from Latin America, Behrman, Birdsall, and Székely (2001) find evidence that, when and where the financial markets in the region have been more open to international capital flows, the skill premium in wages has been higher; that is, the returns to secondary and higher education are greater relative to the returns to primary schooling. They infer that skilled labor is complementary to capital, so that new investments in physical capital generate increased demand for skills. Intuitively, the idea that physical capital and human capital are complementary is appealing—specialized skills are required, for example, in the operation and maintenance of most machines. The AIDS epidemic is likely to have a dramatic effect not only on domestic saving (through the foreshortening of time horizons and the increased demand for present consumption to finance medical care), but also on the attractiveness of foreign investment. These effects together are likely to erode the physical capital stock in many of the hardest-hit countries. Insofar as this in turn reduces the skill premium, it will reduce incentives for households to invest resources and time in the education of their children beyond the basic, primary level.

Conclusion

This chapter has explored four channels by which the epidemic of HIV/AIDS in Africa may affect the size, rate of growth, and productivity of the continent's human capital stock. It would make for a compelling presentation, no doubt, if we could add up the effects of these four channels both on the future expected stock of total human capital and on economic growth itself through any change in the economy-wide return to the adjusted stock. We have not developed the complex model that might guide us in doing that, and we believe in any event that the results of any such simulation would be highly sensitive to some basic assumptions about the dynamics of the process. Such models must take into account the likelihood of multiple equilibria, the interactions between general and local characteristics, and other complicating factors about which we still have very little information. This is true both in terms of the expected total stock and certainly in terms of the expected economic effects.

However, we do believe that the evidence for the channels described adds up to the qualitative conclusion that, absent offsetting policies and programs, the AIDS epidemic is likely to worsen Africa's dearth of human capital. The epidemic could have this effect not only from the supply side, by reducing the capacity of the educational system to train the next generation, but also from the demand side, by foreshortening time horizons and increasing the opportunity cost of children's time, thus making investment in schooling less attractive. These effects will slow the rate of Africa's *accumulation* of human capital. The epidemic also threatens to erode the already *existing* human capital stock, as the death of many of the continent's most skilled workers reduces the average productivity of those left behind. Finally, the epidemic threatens to sap away the savings and physical capital assets of households and nations across the continent, thereby reducing the productivity of workers who rely on physical capital to make use of their skills.

Of course, the effects of the epidemic on the accumulation and productivity of human capital in Africa are likely to go beyond those explored here. For example, to the extent that states are forced to reorient their fiscal priorities to health spending, to care for those already infected and dying, education systems may find themselves starved for funding. Furthermore, the orphaning of millions of children across the continent may be expected to leave communities unable to rear children with the traditional level of care or attention. The four effects emphasized in this chapter are relevant to understanding the economics of human capital and have the potential over the long run to, if not offset, at least reduce the stock of human capital and the economic gains from that capital in countries affected by HIV/AIDS.

Our analysis is not meant to be a counsel of despair, however. Rather, it illustrates the likely need for adjustment, for example in countries' educational policies and priorities, including teacher salaries and placement, class size, spending on student transportation (given the particular difficulties in staffing small rural schools), and other changes to minimize the effects of AIDS on the availability and quality of schooling. It also illustrates the logic of ensuring that information about public efforts to contain the epidemic, and successes in those efforts, are well publicized, because this may help maintain demand for schooling in the face of short-term perceptions of declining returns. The analysis has implications for expected growth in the region, and thus for fiscal expectations and the sustainability of the large debt stock borne by many African countries. For the countries worst hit by the AIDS epidemic, it reinforces the logic of massive donor support, to reduce the probability of countries falling into the wrong, low-level, "poverty trap" equilibrium by fighting the disease itself and by helping finance the additional costs of meeting all the development challenges the region faces, including the education challenge. Finally, for the community of research economists, it illustrates the multiple links among health, education, and economic growth; the relevance of the demand as well as the supply side for sustaining and increasing education; and, more generally, the centrality of human capital to development progress.

References

Acemoglu, Daron, 1997, "Matching, Heterogeneity, and the Evolution of Income Inequality," *Journal of Economic Growth*, Vol. 2, No. 1, pp. 61–92.

———, and Jorn-Steffen Pischke, 1999, "Beyond Becker: Training in Imperfect Labor Markets," *Economic Journal Features*, Vol. 109, No. 3, pp. F112–F142.

African Development Forum, 2000, "HIV/AIDS and Economic Development in Sub-Saharan Africa," report of a conference on "AIDS: The Greatest Leadership Challenge," Addis Ababa, Ethiopia, December 3–7.

Ainsworth, Martha, and Innocent Semali, 1998, "Who Is Most Likely to Die of AIDS? Socioeconomic Correlates of Adult Deaths in Kagera Region, Tanzania," in *Confronting AIDS: Evidence from the Developing World*, ed. by Martha Ainsworth, Lieve Fransen, and Mead Over (Brussels: European Commission).

Barro, Robert J., and Jong-Wha Lee, 1996, "Barro-Lee Data Set: International Measures of Schooling Years and Schooling Quality" (Washington: World Bank).

———, 2000, "International Data on Educational Attainment Updates and Implications," Working Paper No. 7911 (Cambridge, Massachusetts: National Bureau for Economic Research).

Béchu, N., 1998, "The Impact of AIDS on the Economy of Families in Côte d'Ivoire: Changes in Consumption Among AIDS-Affected Households," in *Confronting AIDS: Evidence from the Developing World*, ed. by M. Ainsworth and others (Brussels: European Commission).

Becker, Gary S., K.M. Murphy, and R. Tamura, 1990, "Human Capital, Fertility, and Economic Growth," *Journal of Political Economy*, Vol. 98, No. 5, pp. S12–S37.

Behrman, Jere R., and Nancy Birdsall, 1983, "Quality of Schooling: Quantity Alone is Misleading," *American Economic Review*, Vol. 73, No. 5, pp. 928–46.

Behrman, Jere R., Nancy Birdsall, and M. Székely, 2001, "Economic Policy and Wage Differentials in Latin America," Penn Institute for Economic Research Working Paper No. 01–048 (Philadelphia: University of Pennsylvania).

Behrman, Jere R., S. Duryea, and M. Székely, 1999, "Schooling Investments and Macroeconomic Conditions: A Micro-Macro Investigation for Latin America and the Caribbean," Working Paper No. 407 (Washington: Inter-American Development Bank).

Bigsten, Anne, and Steve Kayizzi-Mugerwa, 1999, *Crisis, Adjustment, and Growth in Uganda: A Study of Adaptation in an African Economy* (London: Macmillan).

Birdsall, Nancy, 1996, "Public Spending on Higher Education in Developing Countries: Too Much or Too Little?" *Economics of Education Review,* Vol. 15, No. 4, pp. 407–19.

———, 1999, "Education: The People's Asset," CSED Working Paper No. 5 (Washington: Brookings Institution).

———, and Juan-Luis Londoño, 1997, "Asset Inequality Matters: An Assessment of the World Bank's Approach to Poverty Reduction," *American Economic Review, Papers and Proceedings,* Vol. 87, No. 2, pp. 32–37.

Birdsall, Nancy, and L. O'Connell, 1999, "Putting Education to Work in Egypt," paper presented at a conference on "Growth Beyond Stabilization: The Prospects for Egypt," Cairo, February 3–4.

Birdsall, Nancy, Richard H. Sabot, and Thomas C. Pinckney, 1997, "Equity, Savings, and Growth," CSED Working Paper No. 8 (Washington: Brookings Institution).

Birdsall, Nancy, David Ross, and Richard H. Sabot, 1995, "Inequality and Growth Reconsidered: Lessons from East Asia," *World Bank Economic Review,* Vol. 9, No. 3, pp. 477–508.

Bishai, David, and others, 2003, "Does Biological Relatedness Affect Child Survival?" *Demographic Research,* Vol. 8, Art. 9.

Bloom, David E., and David Canning, 2000, "Public Health: The Health and Wealth of Nations," *Science,* Vol. 287, pp. 1207–08.

———, and P.N. Malaney, 1999, "Demographic Change and Economic Growth in Asia," CAER II Discussion Paper No. 58 (Cambridge, Massachusetts: Harvard University).

Case, Anne, Christina Paxson, and Joseph Ableidinger, 2004, "Orphans in Africa: Parental Death, Poverty, and School Enrollment," *Demography,* Vol. 41, No. 3, pp. 483–508.

Deheneffe, Jean-Claude, Michael Caraël, and Amadou Noumbissi, 1998, "Socioeconomic Determinants of Sexual Behaviour and Condom Use," in *Confronting AIDS: Evidence from the Developing World,* ed. by M. Ainsworth and others (Brussels: European Commission).

Deininger, Klaus, Marito Garcia, and K. Subbarao, 2003, "AIDS-Induced Orphanhood as a Systemic Shock: Magnitude, Impact, and Program Interventions in Africa," *World Development,* Vol. 31, No. 7, pp. 1201–20.

Filmer, Deon, 1998, "The Socioeconomic Correlates of Sexual Behaviour: A Summary of Results from an Analysis of DHS Data," in *Confronting AIDS: Evidence from the Developing World,* ed. by M. Ainsworth and others (Brussels: European Commission).

Hamoudi, Amar, and Nancy Birdsall, 2002, "HIV/AIDS and the Accumulation and Utilization of Human Capital in Africa," Working Paper No. 2 (Washington: Center for Global Development).

Joint United Nations Programme on HIV/AIDS (UNAIDS), 2004, *2004 Report on the Global AIDS Epidemic* (Geneva).

————, United Nations Children's Fund (UNICEF), and U.S. Agency for International Development (USAID), 2004, "Children on the Brink 2004: A Joint Report of New Orphan Estimates and a Framework for Action" (Geneva).

Kalemli-Ozcan, Sebnem, Harl E. Ryder, and David N. Weil, 2000, "Mortality Decline, Human Capital Investment, and Economic Growth," *Journal of Development Economics*, Vol. 62, No. 1, pp. 1–23.

Kelley, Allen C., and Robert M. Schmidt, 1996, "Saving, Dependency, and Development," *Journal of Population Economics*, Vol. 9, No. 4, pp. 365–86.

————, 1999, "Economic and Demographic Change: A Synthesis of Models, Findings, and Perspectives" (unpublished; Durham, North Carolina: Duke University).

Lau, Lawrence J., and others, 1996, "Education and Economic Growth: Some Cross-Sectional Evidence," in *Opportunity Foregone: Education in Brazil,* ed. by Nancy Birdsall and Richard H. Sabot (Baltimore, Maryland: The Johns Hopkins University Press for the Inter-American Development Bank).

Malaney, P., 2000, "The Impact of HIV/AIDS on the Education Sector in Southern Africa," CAER Discussion Paper No. 81 (Cambridge, Massachusetts: Harvard University).

Menon, R., and others, 1998, "The Economic Impact of Adult Mortality in Households in Rakai District, Uganda," in *Confronting AIDS: Evidence from the Developing World,* ed. by Martha Ainsworth, Lieve Fransen, and Mead Over (Brussels: European Commission).

Mincer, Jacob, 1974, *Schooling, Experience, and Earnings* (New York: National Bureau of Economic Research and Columbia University Press).

Morgan, Dilys, and others, 2002, "HIV-1 Infection in Rural Africa: Is There a Difference in Median Time to AIDS and Survival Compared with That in Industrialized Countries? *AIDS*, Vol. 16, No. 4, pp. 597–604.

Mutangadura, Gladys B., 2000, "Household Welfare Impacts of Mortality of Adult Females in Zimbabwe: Implications for Policy and Program Development" (unpublished; Washington: International AIDS Economics Network).

Pritchett, Lant, 1999, "Where Has All the Education Gone?" (unpublished; Washington: World Bank).

Psacharopoulos, George, 1994, "Returns to Investment in Education: A Global Update," *World Development,* Vol. 22, No. 9, pp. 1325–43.

Schultz, Theodore W., 1961, "Investment in Human Capital," *American Economic Review*, Vol. 51, No. 1, pp. 1–17.

————, 1989, "Education Investments and Returns," in *Handbook of Development Economics*, Vol. I, ed. by Hollis B. Chenery and T.N. Srinivasan (Amsterdam: North Holland Press).

Sen, Amartya, 1999, *Development as Freedom* (New York: Alfred A. Knopf).

United Nations Children's Fund (UNICEF), 2000, *The Progress of Nations 2000* (New York). Available via the Internet: www.unicef.org/pon00/contents.htm.

United Nations Development Programme, 2000, *Botswana Human Development Report 2000*. (New York). Available via the Internet: www.undp.org/hiv/hdr2000.

Williamson, Jeffrey G., 1998, "Growth, Distribution, and Demography: Some Lessons from History," *Explorations in Economic History*, Vol. 35, No. 3, pp. 241–71.

World Bank, 2000, *Can Africa Claim the 21st Century?* (Washington: World Bank).

———, 2001, *World Development Indicators* (CD-ROM and print) (Washington).

———, 2004, *World Development Indicators* (CD-ROM and print) (Washington).

5

The Impact of HIV/AIDS on Poverty and Inequality

ROBERT GREENER

M ost studies on the economic impact of HIV/AIDS focus on such variables as GDP growth or income per capita. Early studies, incorporating the impact of HIV/AIDS in a one-sector neoclassical growth model,
found that although the impact of HIV/AIDS on GDP growth is substantial, the impact on GDP per capita may well be small. Later studies refined
this approach, for example by considering a larger number of sectors,
including some demand-side effects, or allowing for an impact of changes
in life expectancy on individuals' decisions.[1]

However, these studies provide little information about how changes in
income are distributed among the population. Empirical studies and more
casual evidence show that HIV/AIDS does have a serious adverse effect on
the households it strikes, through the costs of care (both financial costs
and the opportunity cost of otherwise productive time reallocated to care)
and loss of income. Other households may provide support to households
affected directly or may take care of children whose parents have fallen ill
or died. More generally, HIV/AIDS affects all households through its
macroeconomic repercussions, for example through changes in wages, and
these macroeconomic effects may also differ among households.

In light of these facts, the average change in income per capita contains very little information that is relevant from a policy perspective.

---

[1]For a broader discussion of studies of the impact of HIV/AIDS on economic growth, see
Haacker (Chapter 2, this volume).

More generally, studies of the impact of HIV/AIDS on economic growth, imputing aggregate changes in saving or focusing on the behavior of some representative agent, can yield misleading results. For example, HIV/AIDS can affect the accumulation of human capital at the level of individual households, in particular if children have to take time off from school to care for sick dependents, or if households can no longer afford to send children to school. A macroeconomic analysis focusing on a representative individual would not capture many of these effects.

These concerns have motivated new research on the impact of HIV/AIDS on economic growth, focusing on the effects on households. Most notably, Bell, Devarajan, and Gersbach (Chapter 3, this volume) use an overlapping-generations framework in which the death of a parent affects the children's education through a loss in household income, through a breakdown in the direct transfer of human capital from parent to child, and as the decline in returns to human capital associated with higher expected mortality makes investment in children's education less attractive. In this framework HIV/AIDS has the potential to increase poverty, as children of parents who died of AIDS are endowed with less human capital and will receive lower salaries in their working years. With less human capital and less family income, their children, in turn, will end up with less human capital, and so on. In this framework, then, HIV/AIDS can have adverse effects that persist over generations.

This chapter pursues a different and in some ways complementary approach. Rather than discussing the repercussions of the impact of HIV/AIDS on households for the economy and economic growth, it describes a method of analyzing the impact of HIV/AIDS on households that draws on an aggregate macroeconomic framework and uses existing household income and expenditure surveys.[2] Thus it is possible to draw inferences about the impact of HIV/AIDS for different types of households. In particular, the chapter will assess how HIV/AIDS may alter poverty levels (as affected households are pushed below some poverty line) or the extent of inequality (if more poor households than rich households are affected, or if the income shock to the poor is relatively greater than for the rich households).

---

[2]Although the chapter's emphasis is more general, the analytical part draws on and uses numerical examples from an earlier study focusing on Botswana (Greener, Jefferis, and Siphambe, 2000).

The chapter is organized as follows. The first section provides some context, in particular on the links among poverty, inequality, and welfare. The second discusses the impact of HIV/AIDS on households, as well as some methodological issues and additional data requirements pertaining to the analysis of poverty and inequality. The third section reports estimates of the impact of increased HIV/AIDS-related mortality on inequality and poverty in Botswana, and the final section concludes.

Poverty, Inequality, and Welfare

Before outlining the chapter's approach to assessing changes in poverty and inequality due to HIV/AIDS, it is worth taking a step back to discuss how these measures of the impact of HIV/AIDS relate to welfare more generally. First, the analysis focuses on household income and, because of data limitations, does not take into account household wealth. This is an important limitation: the ownership of assets enables households to mitigate the impact of income shocks on consumption, because it enables them to smooth consumption over time, and because the volatility of income from assets is presumably less volatile than income from labor in the present context.

A second and somewhat related point is that a household's welfare depends not just on its consumption but also on the risks to living standards that the household faces. These risks are related to, but go well beyond, the risk to household income. For example, Crafts and Haacker (Chapter 6, this volume) focus on the link between increased mortality risk and welfare. Also, HIV/AIDS can erode existing support instruments, for example from the extended family or the community (see also Whiteside, 2002). Certain public services—for example, free health services—can also mitigate the economic burden of the disease. There is evidence that, in countries with escalating HIV epidemics, health services at first cannot fully cope with the greatly increased demand and have to resort to rationing. However, very substantial efforts are under way to rapidly increase access to antiretroviral treatment in developing countries. Since poor households would not be able to afford the costs of such treatment, these efforts also have implications for the impact of HIV/AIDS on poverty. HIV/AIDS also results in a substantial increase in the number of orphans. Children living in families affected by HIV/AIDS see their living standards fall as household income declines and expenditure is reallocated to the care of the infected family member. Orphaned children tend to live in poorer households and may have limited access to education.[3] For various reasons, the impact of HIV/AIDS on children is likely to be more severe in low-income households. A government policy of universal access to education, together with other measures to support children affected by HIV/AIDS, can mitigate this adverse impact. For example, the decline in school attendance for orphans is lower in countries with higher overall enrollment rates, suggesting that impediments to education for the poor are low in those countries.

Third, the emphasis of this chapter's analysis is on the short run, treating HIV/AIDS as a mortality shock that affects wage rates and the distribution of income across households. In the longer run it is necessary to address how the distribution of income among households evolves over time, as households dissolve and new ones are formed, and as income shocks not related to HIV/AIDS change the distribution of income. This is discussed in more general terms in Haacker (Chapter 2, this volume), using an approach similar to that of Booysen (2003); Bell, Devarajan, and Gersbach (Chapter 3, this volume) offer an analysis of the long-term effects of HIV/AIDS as income shocks, the loss of parents, and a decline in returns to human capital affect the accumulation of human capital.

Measurement Issues

The study of the impact of HIV/AIDS on poverty and income inequality draws on many different types of data. Numerous studies analyze the impact of HIV/AIDS at the household level. These studies, however, are typically based on relatively small samples and not representative of the overall population; also, the data are presented in a way that yields few insights in terms of changes in poverty and inequality.

To arrive at estimates of the impact of HIV/AIDS on poverty and inequality, this chapter therefore uses additional data on households' composition, income, and expenditure; estimates of the macroeconomic effects of HIV/AIDS; and demographic estimates of the impact of HIV/AIDS. Appropriate definitions of poverty and inequality are also required.

---

[3]The United Nations Children's Fund (UNICEF, 2003) reports that school attendance rates for orphans were 13 percent lower than for nonorphans in sub-Saharan Africa. The median dependency ratio for households with orphans (1.8) was 20 percent higher than that for nonorphan households (1.5).

Households

HIV/AIDS typically begins to affect a household's income during the illness of an HIV-positive household member. If the infected person's income depends on his or her productivity (as it often does, for example, in smallholder agriculture), the income loss sets in during the illness. If the individual works in the formal private sector or the public sector, however, provisions for sick leave or disability benefits, or both, may mitigate the loss. In addition, to the extent that the working time of household members is diverted from productive activities to the care of the ill family members, the household's income will decline further. Eventually, if an HIV-positive member dies, his or her income is lost to the household. However, for employees in the formal private or the public sector, life insurance or a pension scheme (possibly including pensions for surviving dependents) can mitigate the loss.

HIV/AIDS also affects households' incomes indirectly through its macroeconomic effects, whether any household member is affected by HIV/AIDS or not. If, for example, increased mortality makes certain categories of labor more scarce while demand is largely unaffected, wages for that labor will rise, and with them the incomes of the households that receive those wages. More generally, HIV can affect the level of wages across all skill categories. For example, the neoclassical growth model predicts that a decline in the rate of growth of the working-age population will result in an increase in the capital-labor ratio; as the marginal product of labor then rises, so will wages. Some studies suggest that when large numbers of workers in the formal sector with relatively high incomes die, they are replaced by "surplus labor" from the informal sector, thus raising average income. On the other hand, the deteriorating economic outlook and higher production costs can result in a decline in investment and thus in employment opportunities.

Households affected by HIV/AIDS face additional costs of two major kinds. The first is the increased cost of medical treatment for HIV-positive members who are beginning to develop symptoms of AIDS and are experiencing more frequent illnesses. The total expenditure of a household will depend on its income and circumstances. Wealthy households may opt for very expensive private treatment, using the results of the latest medical research, which can keep infected people asymptomatic for extended periods. The poorest households will be forced to rely on public medical provision but will still face additional costs for transport and food. The second additional cost is the cost of a funeral when the ill household member dies. Funerals can be very expensive, often requiring a large number of people to be fed for many days, in addition to the costs of the casket and cere-mony. The total expenditure will again depend upon the household's income.

Impact on Poverty and Inequality

The household studies referred to above yield limited insights into the impact of HIV/AIDS on poverty and inequality, mainly because of the lim-ited sample size. One important study from a methodological point of view is Booysen (2003), which is based on a panel of 355 South African households, with three observations for each. Booysen shows that the inci-dence of poverty is higher for households affected by HIV/AIDS (35 per-cent of which were classified as poor) than for those not affected (21 percent were classified as poor). Dividing the sample into five income quintiles, Booysen then shows that the income ranking of households affected by HIV/AIDS is more likely to deteriorate and less likely to improve than that of other households. These results are reinforced by sev-eral regressions suggesting that HIV/AIDS did indeed contribute to the observed differences in poverty levels and income mobility.

The data on the distribution of income across households that form the basis of this chapter's assessment of the extent of and changes in income inequality come from a national household income and expenditure sur-vey in Botswana. This survey provides data on household composition (the number, age, and sex of household members), household income and its sources, and detailed household expenditure.

The extent of inequality in the analysis below makes use of the Gini coefficient, which measures the difference between the observed dis-tribution of income (across households or individuals) and perfect income equality. The Gini coefficient lies between zero and one. A value of zero corresponds to the situation in which every person in a group has exactly the same income, and a value of one corresponds to the opposite extreme where one person receives all the group's income and everyone else has none. Thus a higher Gini coefficient indicates greater income inequality.

Poverty can be defined in absolute or relative terms. As an example of the former, one can define a critical income level, based on household composition, a basket of basic needs, and the cost of that basket in the household's location. Households are classified as poor if their income is less than this *poverty datum line* (PDL). The *household poverty rate* then refers to the percentage of households with income below the PDL, and the *individual poverty rate* (or the poverty head count) is defined as the percentage of all individuals who live in households with income below the PDL.

However, in assessing the impact of HIV/AIDS on poverty, it is necessary to determine how additional, HIV/AIDS-related expenses interact with the PDL by adding to the cost of the basic basket the required cost of medical treatment or, in the case of death, a funeral. Later on, once a household member dies from HIV/AIDS-related causes, the household no longer has to meet the deceased person's expenditure requirements (medical and cost of living), and the PDL for the household needs to be adjusted accordingly. Such a household is less likely to be classified as poor. Whether the expenditure effects described here increase or decrease total poverty depends on the magnitude of the expenditures considered.

Another useful statistic is the *income dependency ratio*. This is the average number of people within a household who are supported by a household member who is employed and earning an income. This is usually considered to be a sensitive indicator of household poverty and of the vulnerability of a household to the loss of an income earner. The situation of the poorest households is represented by the lowest income quartile: the 25 percent of households with the lowest incomes per capita. The two statistics chosen below to measure the situation of the poorest households are lowest-quartile household income and the lowest-quartile income dependency ratio.

Data on HIV prevalence are usually obtained from sentinel surveys, most commonly from blood tests at antenatal clinics. These data are available only for subgroups of the population such as pregnant women, sex workers, or hospital patients. To draw inferences from these data on HIV prevalence for the whole population by age and sex, a model of the spread of HIV infection and of AIDS in a population is required; estimates of HIV prevalence by population group are then obtained by fitting the parameters of the model to the available observations (see Epstein, Chapter 1 of this volume, for a more detailed discussion of this approach).

For the analysis performed here, it is necessary to draw inferences on HIV prevalence at the household level from the available estimates by age cohort and sex. The principal challenge here is that the likelihood that a household member is infected depends on the other household members' HIV status. For example, regular sexual partners are likely to infect each other, and infants are often infected at birth or during breastfeeding if the mother is HIV-positive. In the absence of sufficient data to estimate the correlation of HIV status among household members, researchers often use aggregate estimates of HIV prevalence for individual household members; this approach, however, overestimates the share of HIV-affected households and underestimates the share of households with multiple HIV infections.

An Application to Botswana

The analysis presented here makes use of household income and expenditure data from the Botswana Household Income and Expenditure Survey (HIES) conducted in 1993/94.[4] The survey recorded household characteristics, such as the age and sex of all household members and the location of the household, and measured all sources of income and items of expenditure. Because these data on household characteristics are static, they are not suitable for a dynamic analysis. In particular, they cannot be used to trace how households' income changes over time, as does Booysen (2003), or to model how households dissolve over time and new households are formed.

The definition of poverty (the PDL) used here comes from a major study of poverty and poverty alleviation carried out by the Botswana Institute for Development Policy Analysis (BIDPA) in 1996 on behalf of the Botswana Ministry of Finance and Development Planning (1996). The study made use of data from the HIES conducted in 1985/86 and 1993/94 and added a definition of poverty based on the cost of a basket of basic goods and the structure and location of individual households.

Macroeconomic Effects

Estimates of the macroeconomic impacts of HIV/AIDS also come from a Botswana Ministry Finance and Development Planning study (Botswana Ministry of Finance and Development Planning, 2000). An equilibrium model comprising two sectors and three factors was constructed for the Botswana economy, following the approach used for Tanzania by Cuddington (1993). The model distinguished between skilled and unskilled labor and between the formal and informal sectors. The impacts of HIV/AIDS operated through the supply of labor and through investment growth.

The study considered a number of different scenarios in order to deal with uncertainties in the assumptions. Under the most likely scenario,

---

[4]The analysis in this section is based on earlier work by Greener, Jefferis, and Siphambe (2000).

HIV/AIDS reduced the growth rate of GDP by 1.5 percentage points, so that after 25 years the economy would be 31 percent smaller than it would otherwise have been. GDP per capita for the survivors was virtually unaffected by HIV/AIDS because of the projected population impact. However, GDP in Botswana has a significant rent component arising from mining revenue, which accrues almost entirely to the government rather than to households. In this situation, where HIV/AIDS leaves the rent component unchanged but GDP per capita remains the same, household income per capita nevertheless falls by 5 to 10 percent.

The same scenario predicted that unemployment among unskilled workers would be 8 percent lower as a result of HIV/AIDS. The existing shortage of skilled workers would be exacerbated, causing skilled wages to rise by 12 to 17 percent. The model also predicted an 18 percent rise in the capital-output ratio, confirming the expected factor substitution away from labor.

Demographic Effects

To assess the impact of HIV/AIDS at the household level, AIDS was assigned in a random fashion to individuals in the population. Given the structure of households in Botswana, this leads to the outcome that 49 percent of households are affected by HIV/AIDS (that is, have at least one infected member). To the extent that HIV occurs in "clusters," such that individuals are more likely to be infected if other family members are, the total share of households with an infected member would be less than 49 percent, but more households would be affected with multiple infections. The analysis then assumed that all infected household members die within 10 years, and the income and expenditure of each household were recalculated based on the resulting, depleted household structure.

As a result of the employment structure in Botswana, 26 percent of households in the analysis lose income as a result of the death of an income earner. This is less than the total percentage affected by HIV/AIDS because of the country's high rate of unemployment. A key assumption in this analysis is that susceptibility to HIV is not related to employment status or skill level. If otherwise,[5] the percentage of households losing income

---

[5]Evidence from the 2000 and 2001 sentinel surveys suggests a weak relationship between HIV status and employment status for pregnant women, with HIV prevalence slightly higher among employed women.

would be lower or higher than 26 percent: lower if the unemployed are more susceptible, and higher if they are less susceptible to HIV.

The analysis predicts that many small households will be wiped out by AIDS. Approximately 6.9 percent of households disappear altogether over the 10-year period, because all of the household members are infected. This represents about 1.9 percent of the total population. These percentages would be even higher if HIV clusters within households.

Impact on Inequality and Poverty

As a first step, to separate the direct impact of increased mortality on households from the macroeconomic repercussions, the impact of HIV/AIDS on inequality associated with the deaths of HIV-positive household members is analyzed on the assumption of no changes in the macroeconomic environment (wage rates) or HIV/AIDS-related expenditure. In this simplified analysis, households face a loss of income but also experience a corresponding fall in their long-run basic needs (since there are fewer people in the household) and hence have a lower PDL. The top panel of Table 5.1 shows the results for this base case.

The analysis indicates that the income per capita of households will fall by 10 percent as a result of HIV/AIDS and the loss of income earners, in the absence of any effects on unemployment or wages. The analysis predicts no overall change in the level of inequality as measured by the Gini coefficient. This means that, despite an overall downward shift in income per capita and a change in the ordering of households by income (those affected by AIDS see their income fall, but unaffected households do not), the resulting pattern of inequality appears to be not measurably different from the starting point.

However, the analysis also predicts rising poverty as a result of HIV/AIDS. The share of households below the PDL (the household poverty count) rises by 6 percentage points, and the share of individuals in poor households rises by 4 percentage points. The difference between these two figures reflects a difference in impact among households of different sizes: large households are more likely than small households to become poor as a result of AIDS. The income dependency ratio increases from 5.4 to 6.4, or by about 20 percent. This means that every income earner can, on average, expect to acquire one extra dependent as a result of HIV/AIDS over the next 10 years.

The situation is considerably worse for households in the lowest quartile of the income distribution. The income dependency ratio for this group is expected to rise from 16 to 24, or by 50 percent. In other words,

Table 5.1. Estimated Impact of HIV/AIDS on Income, Inequality, and Poverty in Botswana

	All Households					Poorest Quartile	
	Income per capita (pula a month)[1]	Gini coefficient	Household poverty count (percent)	Individual poverty count (percent)	Income dependency ratio	Income per capita (pula a month)[1]	Income dependency ratio
Base case							
Without HIV/AIDS	215	0.51	37.7	47.8	5.4	43	15.8
With HIV/AIDS	193	0.51	43.7	51.9	6.4	36	23.7
Difference							
Absolute	−22	0.00	6.0	4.0	1.1	−8	7.9
In percent	−10	0	16	8	20	−18	50
Including macro-economic effects							
Without HIV/AIDS	215	0.51	37.7	47.8	5.4	43.3	15.8
With HIV/AIDS	199	0.51	42.7	50.9	5.9	37.6	19.7
Difference							
Absolute	−16	0.00	5.0	3.1	0.5	−5.6	3.9
Percent	−8	0	13	6	10	−13	25

Source: Greener, Jefferis, and Siphambe (2000).
[1]In 2000, one dollar was worth about 5.12 pula (year average).

every income earner in this category can, on average, expect to support an extra eight dependents as a result of HIV/AIDS. There is a corresponding fall of 18 percent in the average income of households in the lowest quartile—nearly double the income loss among the population as a whole. This analysis implies that the poor are particularly vulnerable to the impacts of HIV/AIDS.

The results with respect to poverty rates also suggest that the finding, based on the Gini coefficient, of little change in inequality needs to be qualified. In fact, the impact of HIV/AIDS on poor households (whether measured by income loss or by a higher income dependency ratio) is worse than for the rest of the population. Taken by itself, the differential effect on poor households' incomes alone indicates that the Gini coefficient should rise. The fact that it does not means that a second effect must be at work: although the bottom of the income distribution drops further, HIV/AIDS appears to reduce inequality for the higher-income quartiles.

At the very bottom of the income distribution, the analysis also predicts a dramatic increase in the number of destitute households, defined for this purpose as households with no income earners. The proportion of households with zero income rises by 1.5 percentage points, the proportion with income per capita of less than 10 pula a month rises by 2.1 percentage points, and the proportion with income per capita of less than 25 pula a month rises by 2.5 percentage points. Thus, however destitution is defined, it is likely to rise by 1.5 to 2.5 percent of all households over the next 10 years. Applied to the population of Botswana, this implies an increase in the number of destitute households by 4,000 to 7,000 over the decade.

Adding the Macroeconomic Effects

The macroeconomic scenario described above (Botswana Ministry of Finance and Development Planning, 2000) projects that unemployment falls by 5.7 percent with HIV/AIDS and the incomes of skilled workers rise by 12.2 percent. Thus some households experience an income gain as a household member finds new employment, and households with skilled wage earners benefit from an increase in the overall wage level.

The addition of the macroeconomic effects reduces the impact on overall income per capita from 10 percent to 8 percent (bottom panel of Table 5.1). This analysis therefore predicts a fall of at least 8 percent in household income per capita, despite the earlier finding that aggregate GDP per capita is unlikely to fall as a result of HIV/AIDS. The Gini coefficient is not sensitive to the addition of income effects and does not change significantly from the base value. The addition of the income effects also mitigates the impact on poverty to a small extent. The impact on the household poverty rate falls from 6 percentage points to 5, and the impact on the individual poverty rate from 4 percentage points to 3. However, owing to the decline in the unemployment rate, the rise in the income dependency ratio is mitigated considerably, increasing by 10 percent rather than 20 percent in the base case. This means that each wage earner can, on average, expect to bear "only" half an extra dependent.

The income dependency ratio for the lowest quartile of households is projected to rise from 16 to 20, or by 25 percent. The income effects thus halve this expected impact as well. Nevertheless, every income earner in this category can, on average, expect to support an extra four dependents as a result of HIV/AIDS. There is a fall of 13 percent in the average income of households in the lowest quartile when the income effects are included, compared with 18 percent in the base case. This supports the conjectures about the vulnerability of the poorest households.

Expenditure Effects

This analysis of the demographic effects of HIV/AIDS is limited to the effect of increased mortality on the structure of households. Thus it does not lend itself easily to an analysis of HIV/AIDS-related expenditures, because these (with the exception of funeral expenses) are mostly linked to the treatment of and care for HIV/AIDS-related health conditions. However, it is possible to draw some more general inferences regarding the role of expenditure effects.

High-income households are likely to be covered by medical aid schemes and to fall within their rules and restrictions. This option is clearly not available for households in the lowest income quartile, whose income per capita is around 75 pula a month (at current prices), and who are not in any case covered by medical aid schemes. These poorer households will be forced to make use of the state health system, which will bear any costs of treatment. However, these households will still face a variety of additional costs—for example, for transportation to and from clinics and hospitals and for additional nutrition requirements. Those households that consult traditional healers will have to meet those costs directly.

The middle two income quartiles in Botswana spent about 3 percent of their income for medical purposes in the 1993/94 HIES. If this were quadrupled, to 12 percent, their total monthly expenditure at current prices would be about 32 pula, which is about one-tenth the amount available to high-income households—and nowhere near the amount needed for effective treatment. Many households, even those above their PDL, will be forced to choose between AIDS treatment and other, basic needs such as food and shelter. This will inevitably lead to both an increase in and a deepening of poverty.

Eventually, all households with HIV-positive members will also be required to meet their funeral costs. For the purpose of this analysis, these costs can be annualized over a 10-year period. They will also be related to household income but might be expected to lie in the range of 1,500 to 10,000 pula. A funeral costing 4,000 pula, annualized over 10 years, would cost the average household about 35 pula a month, or about 12 percent of household income per capita.

Discussion and Conclusions

This chapter's analysis of the impact of HIV/AIDS in Botswana suggests that HIV/AIDS does have a substantial effect on inequality and poverty. Although the Gini coefficient, an aggregate measure of the inequality of the income distribution, does not change significantly, it appears that this result masks two different effects working in opposite directions. Whereas poor households appear to be more vulnerable to income losses owing to increased HIV/AIDS-related mortality (an effect that by itself would increase inequality as measured by the Gini coefficient), income inequality among higher-income households appears to decline. Almost all the changes in poverty derive from the direct income shocks to households that lose the income of a member who dies from HIV/AIDS; the broad macroeconomic effects play a minor role in this regard. This reinforces the point made at the outset that estimates of the impact of HIV/AIDS on aggregate economic variables such as GDP provide little information regarding the impact on poverty.

There are, however, several limitations to this analysis. First, it focuses on the effects of HIV/AIDS on households' earned income—investment income is not affected by the death of a household member. However, to the extent that households invest their wealth in the domestic economy, the macroeconomic effects of AIDS could lead to changes in their investment income. Because the share of investment income in a household's income is typically higher at the top of the income distribution, taking into account the role of this income would presumably result in some reassessment of the impact of HIV/AIDS on inequality.

Second, a more complete assessment of the impact of HIV/AIDS on poverty and inequality would require a more elaborate demographic model than is used here. The example presented in this chapter essentially treats HIV/AIDS as a one-time mortality shock. Although this approach yields indicative estimates of the impact of HIV/AIDS in the longer run, it does not address income losses that result from the illness of a household member or from the diversion of the productive time of other household members to the ill person's care. Nor does it address the changes in household structure that result from the aging of all household members by 10 years, such as gains and losses in potential working members, the dissolution of households as some household members die, and the formation of new households.

References

Booysen, Frederick le Roux, 2003, "Poverty Dynamics and HIV/AIDS Related Morbidity and Mortality in South Africa," paper presented at an international conference on "Empirical Evidence for the Demographic and Socio-Economic Impact of AIDS," Health Economics and HIV/AIDS Research Division, University of KwaZulu-Natal, South Africa, March 26–28.

Botswana Ministry of Finance and Development Planning, 1996, "Study of Poverty and Poverty Alleviation" (Gaborone, Botswana).

———, 2000, "Macroeconomic Impacts of the HIV/AIDS Epidemic in Botswana" (Gaborone, Botswana).

Cuddington, John T., 1993, "Further Results on the Macroeconomic Effects of AIDS: The Dualistic, Labor-Surplus Economy," *World Bank Economic Review,* Vol. 7, No. 3, pp. 403–17.

Greener, Robert, Keith Jefferis, and Happy Siphambe, 2000, "The Impact of HIV/AIDS on Poverty and Inequality in Botswana," *South African Journal of Economics,* Vol. 68, No. 5, pp. 888–915.

Greener, Robert, P. Ward, J. Pitso, and L. Hunter, 2000, "Review and Evaluation of HIV/AIDS Related Data for an Expanded National Response to the HIV/AIDS Epidemic in Botswana" (Gaborone, Botswana: Ministry of Finance and Development Planning).

United Nations Children's Fund, 2003, *Africa's Orphaned Generations* (New York).

Whiteside, Alan, 2002, "Poverty and HIV/AIDS in Africa," *Third World Quarterly,* Vol. 23, No. 2, pp. 313–32.

6

Welfare Implications of HIV/AIDS

Nicholas Crafts and Markus Haacker

The HIV/AIDS epidemic has resulted in significant increases in mortality rates in the affected countries, and it is now the leading cause of death in southern Africa. In Botswana, one of the worst-affected countries, with an adult HIV prevalence rate of 37.3 percent, mortality among the working-age population had increased to 3.8 percent a year (of which 3.7 percentage points, or 96 percent, is HIV/AIDS related) by 2004. Correspondingly, life expectancy has decreased substantially, frequently wiping out gains achieved over several decades. For example, life expectancy at birth is now estimated at less than 40 years for Botswana and Zambia (declines of 41 and 17 years, respectively, compared with a no-AIDS scenario).[1]

A considerable number of studies have addressed the impact of HIV/AIDS on GDP per capita.[2] Some have used a neoclassical growth framework to estimate the impact on aggregate output or income, whereas others have used a general equilibrium model with a larger number of sectors. Studies also differ according to the types of labor or human capital captured, the extent of labor mobility between sectors, the extent of international or domestic capital mobility, and the assumptions regarding the impact of HIV/AIDS on productivity. Although most studies project a

---

[1]Unless stated otherwise, all estimates of HIV prevalence rates quoted in this paper are from Joint United Nations Programme on HIV/AIDS (UNAIDS, 2004), and estimates of the impact of HIV/AIDS on mortality and life expectancy were provided by the International Programs Center at the U.S. Census Bureau (see Epstein, Chapter 1, this volume).

[2]See Haacker (Chapter 2, this volume) for a discussion of the literature.

small negative impact of HIV/AIDS on output per capita, the estimates are very sensitive to the underlying economic assumptions. For example, a study on South Africa (with an adult HIV prevalence rate of about 20 percent) commissioned by ING Barings (2000) projects that GDP per capita will *increase* by about 9 percent by 2010 compared with a no-AIDS scenario. Arndt and Lewis (2001), using similar demographic assumptions, estimate that GDP per capita will be 8 percent lower in 2010, again compared with a no-AIDS scenario.[3]

Estimates of the impact of HIV/AIDS on GDP are useful, even essential, in many contexts, for example as a key indicator of living standards and as a summary measure of the broad economic repercussions of the epidemic. Because the various components of the government's tax base (such as corporate profits, individual incomes, or imports) are closely linked to the level of economic activity, changes in economic growth also have direct fiscal implications.

However, changes in GDP or in income per capita give a very crude picture of the economic impact of HIV/AIDS, in several ways. First, the impact differs across individuals and households, mainly depending on whether or not a given household has a member who becomes infected. Changes in the distribution of income result, which aggregate economic indicators, such as GDP, fail to capture (see Greener, Chapter 5, this volume). Second, poor households, which account for a small share of GDP, are less able to accommodate adverse shocks to income or expenditure (such as health expenditure) and are therefore more vulnerable to HIV/AIDS. More broadly, changes in income do not capture the substantial increase in risk associated with increased mortality and reduced life expectancy, the risk of losing relatives, and a decline in living standards for those infected, their relatives, and—eventually—their surviving dependents.

Some of these shortcomings of aggregate indicators have been recognized in the literature and practice of economic development (see, for example, Sen, 1999). Most prominently, the United Nations' Millennium Development Goals not only constitute a political and economic agenda, but also define a comprehensive set of economic development indicators. The United Nations Development Programme assigns equal weights to measures of income per capita, educational attainment, and life

---

[3]The differences between the two studies arise mainly because ING Barings (2000) puts much emphasis on demand-side effects, whereas Arndt and Lewis (2001) assume that HIV/AIDS has an impact on productivity growth (rather than the level of productivity), and that this impact accumulates over time.

expectancy in calculating its Human Development Index (HDI; UNDP, 2001; see also Crafts, 2002). Most of the gains in the HDI over the past century resulted from gains in life expectancy, which in many countries will be largely lost as a consequence of HIV/AIDS. As noted by Haacker in Chapter 2 of this volume, although countries like Botswana, South Africa, and Swaziland would have attained living standards comparable to those in Brazil or Russia by 2001 (which have HDIs around 0.77) had the HIV/AIDS epidemic never occurred, their HDIs instead compare with countries like Bolivia (for South Africa) or India and Cambodia (for Botswana and Swaziland).

To sum up, the most direct welfare effects of HIV/AIDS are associated with increased mortality. For example, the losses in life expectancy in the worst-affected countries are reversing all the health gains achieved over the past century (Stanecki, 2000); HIV/AIDS is the biggest factor contributing to decreases in healthy life expectancy in Africa overall (Mathers and others, 2000), and in Zimbabwe about 15 percent of the population younger than 15 years were orphans in 2001.

Against this background, the purpose of this chapter is twofold. The first is to develop and present new quantitative indicators of the welfare effects of HIV/AIDS by evaluating the welfare cost of increased mortality. The second, given that this approach yields estimates of the welfare cost of HIV/AIDS as a percentage of GDP, is to provide some perspective on the earlier impact studies that focused on output and income.

The approach uses a technique originally developed to assess the impact of health, environmental, or work safety interventions, focusing on the value of statistical life (VSL). Estimates of the VSL are generally obtained from microeconometric studies relating differences in wages between employment categories to differences in mortality risks (see Miller, 2000, and Viscusi and Aldy, 2003). Provided that these observed wage differentials accurately reflect willingness to pay for a decrease in mortality, these estimates of the VSL can then be used to assess the costs and benefits of certain policy interventions.

More recently, this approach has been used in macroeconomic studies assessing the impact of improved health standards on economic welfare. For example, Nordhaus (1998, 2002) finds that, for the United States over 1900–95, the contribution of health improvements to living standards was similar in magnitude to the contribution of increased consumption. Crafts (2001), drawing on Nordhaus (1998), reports similar findings for the United Kingdom over the period 1870–1998.

This chapter adapts this method to the study of the economic impact of HIV/AIDS. Although the key concept translates very easily, certain limitations are important to bear in mind. One is that few empirical studies on the VSL are available for lower-income countries, and none are available for sub-Saharan Africa. Hence the usual shortcomings associated with out-of-sample predictions apply (see Bowland and Beghin, 2001, for a discussion of this point). In particular, income in sub-Saharan Africa is lower than in those countries for which studies are available; life expectancy is lower; the informal sector is larger; the structure of (formal sector) labor markets, including the coverage of social insurance systems, is different; average educational attainment is lower than in those countries for which empirical studies are available; and, in most countries, the changes in mortality associated with HIV/AIDS are generally larger than those in the available studies. Also, the estimates presented here reflect the impact of increased mortality only, not of the deterioration in overall health.[4] Thus our point estimates are subject to considerable uncertainty; nevertheless, they do show that HIV/AIDS has a catastrophic welfare impact that dwarfs the economic assessments based on income per capita.[5]

The first section of the chapter outlines the methodology used. The second section then discusses the demographic data and projections used, and the third presents estimates of the impact of HIV/AIDS on welfare for selected countries. The final section concludes.

A Method of Accounting for Increased Mortality

The approach followed in this chapter is built on two simple premises. Individuals like higher income, and they like to live longer. The (somewhat simplified) outlook on life of these individuals can be illustrated by means of a utility function, which relates expected lifetime utility U to annual income Y and life expectancy LE:

$$U = F(Y, LE). \tag{1}$$

Consider a situation with $Y = Y_0$ and $LE = LE_0$, and hence $U_0 = F(Y_0, LE_0)$, where subscripts index time periods or different states of nature. Assume

---

[4]A more refined measure of the impact of HIV/AIDS on life expectancy is the "disability-adjusted life expectancy" (DALE), used, for example, by the World Health Organization (see Mathers and others, 2000). This chapter does not follow this approach because sufficiently detailed demographic projections are not available, and because extending our method of accounting for the VSL to changes in DALE is not straightforward.

[5]Using a similar method, Jamison, Sachs, and Wang (2001) study the impact of HIV/AIDS on economic growth and "real income."

Figure 6.1. Impact of HIV/AIDS on Welfare Accounting for Changes in Life Expectancy

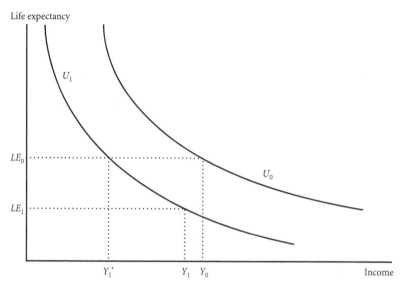

that, because of an HIV/AIDS epidemic, income falls to $Y = Y_1$, life expectancy declines to $LE = LE_1$, and utility becomes $U_1 = F(Y_1, LE_1)$, as illustrated in Figure 6.1. An economist focusing on the impact of HIV/AIDS on income per capita might find a very small effect ($Y_1 - Y_0$), but this does not take into account the possibility that most of the welfare loss comes from the decline in life expectancy, not the decline in income. Instead, therefore, we measure the welfare loss associated with HIV/AIDS as the decline in income, $Y_1^* - Y_0$, that, for a given life expectancy, would yield the same level of welfare as the actual changes in income *and* life expectancy associated with HIV/AIDS. Formally, Y_1^* can be calculated as

$$F(Y_1^*, LE_0) = F(Y_1, LE_1). \tag{2}$$

More specifically, we assume that an individual values consumption and life expectancy according to the following lifetime utility function:

$$U[\{c_t\}, \{\mu_{s,t}\}, \rho, s] = \int_s^\infty u(c_t) e^{-\int_s^t (\rho + \mu_{s,v}) dv} dt, \tag{3}$$

where $\{c_t\}$ denotes the individual's consumption stream over time, s stands for the individual's initial age, $\{\mu_{s,t}\}$ is the set of time-varying mortality rates of an individual with initial age s at time t, with t ($\in (s, \infty)$), and ρ gives the discount rate. The individual's budget constraint is

$$\int_s^\infty c_t e^{-\int_s^t r_v dv} dt = \int_s^\infty y_t e^{-\int_s^t r_v dv} dt, \tag{4}$$

where y_t stands for the individual's income at time t. For simplicity, we assume that income is constant over an individual's life span (that is, $y_t = y^*$) and that the real interest rate equals the discount rate. In this case the optimal level of consumption is $c_t = c^* = y^*$, and the optimized level of lifetime utility is equal to

$$V(\{\mu_{s,t}\}, y^*, \rho, s) = u(y^*) \int_s^\infty e^{-\int_s^t (\rho + \mu_{s,v}) dv} dt, \tag{5}$$

or $V(\{\mu_{s,t}\}, y^*, \rho, s) = u(y^*) LE(\{\mu_{s,t}\}, \rho, s)$,

with $LE(\{\mu_{s,t}\}, \rho, s) = \int_s^\infty e^{-\int_s^t (\rho + \mu_{s,v}) dv} dt.$ \hfill (6)

In other words, lifetime utility is the product of an individual's flow utility from the consumption stream y^* and the discounted life expectancy LE.

Empirical studies of the VSL generally link observed differences in income, for example across professional categories, to differences in mortality risk. For a constant mortality rate $\mu_{s,t} = \mu$, using equation (5), lifetime utility becomes $V = u(y^*)/\delta + \mu$, and the change in income y^* that would compensate for an increase in mortality, leaving V unchanged, is equal to

$$\left.\frac{dy^*}{d\mu}\right|_{V=\bar{V}} = -\frac{dV/d\mu}{dV/dy^*} = \frac{u(y^*)}{u'(y^*)(\delta + \mu)} = \frac{u(y^*)}{u'(y^*)} LE, \tag{7}$$

or, equivalently,

$$\frac{dy^*}{y^*} = \frac{u(y^*)}{u'(y^*)y^*(\delta + \mu)} d\mu = \frac{u(y^*)LE}{u'(y^*)y^*} = d\mu, \tag{8}$$

which is the specification on which most empirical studies are based. Once the coefficient of $d\mu$ is estimated based on equation (8), the VSL can be obtained as

$$VSL = \frac{u(y^*)}{u'(y^*)y^*(\delta + \mu)} y^* = \frac{u(y^*)LE}{u'(y^*)y^*} y^*, \tag{9}$$

which is the implied compensation for one statistical death. As an illustration, suppose that an empirical study finds that a professional mortality risk of 0.1 percent annually is associated with a salary that is 10 percent higher than for a comparator group. This would mean that the VSL is 100 times the applicable income level.

Because, in the context of the HIV/AIDS epidemic, we deal with mortality rates that differ across age groups and over time, it is more appropriate to focus on the induced change in (discounted) life expectancy rather than the changes in mortality rates. Using equation (6), the change in utility can be described as the sum of the change in income (weighted by marginal utility) and the change in the discounted life expectancy:

$$\frac{d(V)}{V} = \frac{u'(y^*)dy^*}{u(y^*)} + \frac{dLE}{LE}. \tag{10}$$

What we are interested in is the change in income that is as bad (or good) as some change in life expectancy. This can be obtained, using equation (10), as −1 times the change in income that would leave welfare V unchanged, following a change in life expectancy. Thus the incremental change in income that is "equivalent" to an incremental change in life expectancy is given by

$$\frac{dy^*}{y^*} = \frac{u(y^*)}{y^*u'(y^*)} \frac{dLE}{LE}. \tag{11}$$

Equation (11) directly relates to the empirical estimates of the VSL from equation (9), as

$$\frac{dy^*}{y^*} = \frac{VSL}{y^*LE} \frac{dLE}{LE}. \tag{12}$$

Although most studies, which focus on small changes in mortality rates, use a linear framework, this approach seems inappropriate in the present context of comparatively large changes in mortality rates or life expectancy. Although equation (11) or equation (12) can be used for any utility function of the general form used above to calculate the welfare losses associated with declining life expectancy in a piecemeal fashion, assuming a constant-elasticity utility function allows us to integrate equations (11) and (12), which yields

$$y^* = constant \cdot LE^{u(y^*)/y^*u'(y^*)} = constant \cdot LE^{VSL/y^*LE}, \tag{13}$$

where the coefficients $u(y^*)/y^*u'(y^*)$ and VSL/y^*LE are constant by assumption. The discrete percentage change in income that would restore the previous level of utility following a change in life expectancy is

$$\frac{\Delta y}{y^*} = \left[\frac{LE + \Delta LE}{LE} \right]^{VSL/y^*LE} - 1. \tag{14}$$

Table 6.1. Impact of HIV/AIDS on Mortality and Life Expectancy in Selected Countries
(Percent except where stated otherwise)

Country	HIV Prevalence Rate, Ages 15–49, End of 2003[1]	Mortality, All Ages, 2004		Mortality, Ages 15–49, 2004		Mortality, Ages 15–49, Projected 2010		Life Expectancy at Birth, 2004 (years)	
		Total	From AIDS	Total	From AIDS	Total	From AIDS	Actual	Without AIDS
Botswana	37.3	2.9	2.5	3.8	3.7	3.6	3.5	34.2	75.7
Côte d'Ivoire	7.0	1.5	0.4	1.1	0.6	1.1	0.7	48.4	55.7
Ethiopia	4.4	1.5	0.2	1.0	0.4	1.0	0.4	48.7	53.1
Haiti	5.6	1.3	0.3	0.9	0.5	0.9	0.5	52.6	60.2
South Africa	21.5	2.9	2.5	2.3	2.0	2.1	1.9	44.1	66.7
Vietnam	0.4	0.6	0.02	0.2	0.03	0.2	0.04	70.4	70.9
Zambia	16.5	2.1	1.0	1.9	1.4	1.9	1.4	39.4	56.2

Source: UNAIDS (2004); U.S. Census Bureau, International Programs Center, International Data Base and unpublished tables.

[1]Data refer to the population aged 15–49.

Data

All demographic estimates and projections used in this chapter were provided by the International Programs Center (IPC) of the U.S. Census Bureau (see Epstein, Chapter 1 of this volume for a more extensive discussion). These include annual data on population size and mortality, by age group (five-year cohorts) and sex, from the (estimated) onset of the epidemic in each country through 2050. Importantly for the purpose of this chapter, they also include a counterfactual scenario excluding the impact of HIV/AIDS. Whereas the IPC provides mortality rates by five-year cohort, we have derived mortality rates for each year of age through linear intrapolation.

Table 6.1 provides some demographic indicators for the impact of the HIV/AIDS epidemic. The countries have been chosen to include not only some of the worst-affected countries in southern Africa (such as Botswana, South Africa, and Zambia), but also some countries with relatively high HIV prevalence rates in other parts of Africa and elsewhere (Côte d'Ivoire, Ethiopia, Vietnam, and Haiti). The impact of HIV/AIDS on mortality rates and life expectancy is catastrophic in the worst-affected countries. In Botswana, the worst-affected country covered in Table 6.1, for example, life expectancy has dropped to 34 years, compared with 76 years in a no-AIDS scenario; overall mortality has risen about almost eightfold, to 2.9 percent; mortality in the working-age population (ages 15–49) has risen 27-fold, to 3.8 percent. Even in countries where the HIV/AIDS epidemic has not (or

Figure 6.2. Mortality Rates by Age and Sex in South Africa, 2004
(Percent)

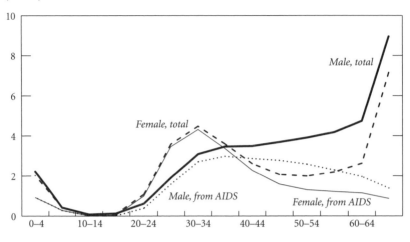

Source: International Programs Center, U.S. Census Bureau.

not yet) escalated to such dimensions, the impact is severe. In Haiti, with an adult HIV prevalence rate of about 6 percent, overall mortality increases by one-third, and life expectancy decreases by about 8 years. In Vietnam, with an adult HIV prevalence rate of only 0.4 percent, life expectancy decreases by half a year, and mortality increases by 15 percent (not percentage points) among the working-age population and 4 percent among the total population.[6]

Complementing the aggregate data, Figure 6.2 shows the impact of HIV/AIDS on mortality by age and sex, using South Africa as an example. Because of HIV/AIDS, male mortality rates increase very substantially between ages 20 and 39 and reach 3.5 percent for the group aged 40–44, of which 86 percent is HIV-related; for older ages mortality increases more slowly, as HIV/AIDS-related mortality declines while mortality for other reasons increases with age. Female mortality rates rise even higher and peak somewhat earlier (because of higher rates of male-to-female viral transmission and because sexual activity tends to begin at an

---

[6]It is important to note that the adult HIV prevalence rate for Vietnam, in turn, is actually lower than for many countries for which comparable demographic estimates and projections of the impact of HIV/AIDS are not available, such as Brazil (0.7 percent), India (about 0.7 percent), Russia (1.1 percent), Spain (0.7 percent), and the United States (0.6 percent).

earlier age among females) at 4.5 percent for the group aged 30–34, of which 96 percent is HIV-related. In the present context, one lesson from Figure 6.2 is that mortality rates and thus remaining life expectancy vary quite substantially by age. This implies that average mortality rates, for different age distributions of the population or age profiles of mortality, can have different implications for life expectancy and thus for welfare. Below we therefore evaluate the impact of HIV/AIDS on welfare by age group.

Impact of HIV/AIDS on Welfare

The focus of our analysis is on the countries worst affected by HIV/AIDS. Very few empirical studies on the VSL for these countries, or countries with similar levels of income per capita, are available. We therefore proceed by discussing the available literature, particularly cross-country "meta" studies that include low- or medium-income countries in the sample; we then apply the most suitable specifications to the analysis of the impact of the HIV/AIDS epidemic.

Miller (2000) draws on 68 studies from 13 different countries, finding income elasticities of the VSL between 0.95 and 1.00. Projecting beyond the range of his sample, he estimates the VSL at about $40,000 for Nigeria in 1997, when GDP per capita was about $250 (both numbers are in 1995 dollars).

Bowland and Beghin (2001) attempt to address the problem of out-of-sample prediction by focusing on specifications that, according to several criteria, perform well for the lower-income countries in their sample. For their preferred specification, they find an income elasticity of 1.52. The willingness to pay for a reduction in mortality is positively related to education; the availability of insurance has a strong negative effect.

Viscusi and Aldy (2003), the most comprehensive study available at present, discusses, among other issues, data problems, the role of unionization, and the effects of age. Using estimates of the VSL from 46 studies (about two-thirds of which are from the United States), they find income elasticities of 0.51 to 0.53.

A recent study by Mrozek and Taylor (2002) finds an elasticity of the VSL with respect to earnings of 0.46 to 0.49 when observations from outside the United States are included in the sample. Importantly, they also find evidence that the VSL declines with risk. However, their sample features mortality rates much lower than those considered here, and they use a complex specification that includes variables for which data are not available for the countries of interest here. Thus it is not possible to adapt their findings to the present context.

The most useful starting point for our investigation is the study by Miller (2000), which conditions the VSL on GDP per capita rather than wages. Thus the specification for the VSL that we adopt is

$$VSL_1 = 136.7 * \frac{GDP}{capita}. \tag{15}$$

which is based on regression (4) in Miller (2000). This specification implies that the elasticity of the VSL with respect to income is equal to 1. For example, for a country with GDP per capita of $28,800 (the mean of Miller's sample), the VSL is equal to $3.9 million.[7]

In the studies discussed above, the estimated income elasticities of the VSL range from about 0.5 to 1.5. Using the sample average of Miller (2000) as a starting point, it is possible to accommodate different elasticities ε using the following equation:

$$VSL_1 = 136.7 \left(\frac{GDP/capita}{US\$28,800} \right)^{\varepsilon} \frac{GDP}{capita}, \tag{16}$$

In light of the substantial differences in GDP per capita among the countries considered here, the choice of the income elasticity in the VSL function obviously has a large impact on the estimates of the VSL. In a country with income per capita of $1,000, for instance, the VSL would be equal to $137,000 for an income elasticity of 1, but it could range from $25,500 to $733,600 for income elasticities between 0.5 and 1.5. Alternatively, this would imply that, with an income elasticity of 1.5, the VSL (in terms of GDP per capita) in a country with GDP per capita of $1,000 is only about 19 percent what it would be in a country with income per capita of $28,800, but over 500 percent of the latter's income per capita if the income elasticity is 0.5. Although one would expect to observe an income elasticity somewhat larger than 1, since we do not explicitly account for variations in human capital,[8] these large variations in the relative valuation of life seem implausible when considering countries with large differences in income per capita. Overall, an income elasticity of around 1, as proposed by Miller (2000), appears to be a good approximation. Our estimates below

---

[7]Whereas Miller uses GDP data in 1995 dollars, we use data at 2001 prices, which are 16 percent higher.

[8]The accumulation of human capital implies a postponement of earnings. In countries with more human capital, an increase in mortality would thus have a stronger impact on lifetime earnings, and hence on the VSL.

Table 6.2. Estimated Welfare Effect of Increased Mortality in Selected Countries
(Percent except where stated otherwise)

Country	Change in:				
				Welfare	
	Mortality (in percentage points)	Life expectancy	Discounted life expectancy	Based on decline in life expectancy	Based on decline in discounted life expectancy
2004, evaluated at age 0					
Botswana	1.6	−55.1	−39.5	−76.7	−83.9
Côte d'Ivoire	0.3	−13.1	−8.8	−29.5	−34.5
Ethiopia	0.2	−8.4	−5.6	−20.5	−24.2
Haiti	0.2	−12.6	−8.4	−26.4	−31.4
South Africa	0.8	−34.0	−23.8	−57.6	−66.0
Vietnam	0.01	−0.8	−0.5	−1.6	−2.0
Zambia	0.8	−30.1	−20.5	−58.4	−64.8
2004, evaluated at age 15					
Botswana	2.6	−62.5	−50.0	−88.6	−93.6
Côte d'Ivoire	0.4	−14.8	−11.2	−35.8	−41.9
Ethiopia	0.2	−9.6	−7.2	−24.7	−29.5
Haiti	0.3	−14.2	−10.7	−33.0	−39.3
South Africa	1.1	−38.1	−29.8	−69.0	−77.4
Vietnam	0.02	−1.0	−0.7	−2.2	−2.9
Zambia	1.0	−34.5	−26.3	−67.9	−74.8
2004, aggregate[1]					
Botswana	3.1	−59.1	−49.2	−88.9	−92.9
Côte d'Ivoire	0.4	−13.3	−10.5	−37.3	−43.5
Ethiopia	0.2	−8.5	−6.6	−25.3	−30.0
Haiti	0.3	−12.7	−10.0	−33.9	−40.1
South Africa	1.1	−32.3	−26.6	−69.6	−76.9
Vietnam	0.02	−0.8	−0.6	−2.3	−2.9
Zambia	1.1	−32.3	−25.5	−68.8	−75.1
Projected 2010, aggregate[1]					
Botswana	3.3	−61.1	−51.1	−89.5	−93.4
Côte d'Ivoire	0.4	−14.9	−11.8	−40.2	−46.9
Ethiopia	0.3	−10.3	−8.1	−29.7	−35.1
Haiti	0.3	−12.9	−10.2	−33.7	−40.2
South Africa	1.4	−37.8	−30.5	−75.5	−82.0
Vietnam	0.03	−1.1	−0.9	−3.4	−4.3
Zambia	1.1	−31.8	−25.2	−67.3	−74.1

Sources: Authors' calculations based on the model described in the text and data from the International Programs Center, U.S. Census Bureau (see Epstein, Chapter 1 of this volume).

[1] Average of welfare losses by age group, with age groups weighted by survival rates.

are therefore based on the link between life expectancy and equivalent change in income as specified in equation (14), using the VSL estimate from equation (15).

Because the impact of HIV/AIDS on mortality and life expectancy depends on an individual's age, Table 6.2 provides estimates of welfare losses evaluated at age 0 (top panel) and age 15 (second panel), as well as estimates of the average welfare loss, obtained as a weighted average of welfare losses by age group, with age groups weighted by their survival rates (third panel).[9] As a robustness check regarding the discount rate applied to life expectancy—see equations (3) and (6)—we provide estimates of the impact of HIV/AIDS on welfare based on the change in life expectancy or the change in the discounted life expectancy, using a discount rate of 2 percent. The average mortality rates reported in the first column are derived from estimated mortality rates by age group for 2004, weighted by the survival rates implied by these mortality rates. This means that, unlike the population averages reported in Table 6.1, they do not depend on other demographic trends, such as changes in birthrates.

Table 6.2 shows that the welfare losses caused by the HIV/AIDS epidemic are significant even for countries with relatively low prevalence rates, and horrific for the worst-affected countries. For Vietnam, with an adult HIV prevalence rate of 0.4 percent, welfare losses already exceed 2 percent of GDP (third panel of Table 6.2). In Zambia, with an adult HIV prevalence rate of 16.5 percent, they exceed two-thirds of GDP, and in Botswana, with an adult HIV prevalence rate of 37.3 percent, they are around 90 percent of GDP.[10]

Reflecting the age pattern of HIV/AIDS-related mortality (Figure 6.1), which (apart from an increase in infant mortality) rises from about age 15 and peaks at about ages 30–35, the decline in welfare for those at age 15 (second panel of Table 6.2) actually exceeds the change in welfare evaluated at age 0 (first panel of Table 6.2). For older generations the welfare loss eventually declines, as HIV/AIDS has a smaller impact on the remaining life expectancy.

The HIV/AIDS epidemic is evolving, and, for most countries, HIV/AIDS-related mortality rates are projected to increase over the next several years (see Table 6.1). The bottom panel of Table 6.2 therefore reports estimates of aggregate welfare changes for 2010. Reflecting changes

---

[9]We attach equal weight to the relative decline of lifetime utility for each individual, regardless of age. Alternatively, it is possible to assign larger weights to younger people, for example assigning a 50 percent loss in life expectancy for someone aged 15 a larger weight than for someone aged 50. Since HIV/AIDS-related mortality is concentrated among a relatively narrow, middle-aged group, the weights applied to each age group do not make a big difference.

[10]Crafts and Haacker (2002) provide estimates for a larger group of countries, based on demographic estimates and projections available at that time.

in mortality rates, welfare losses increase further for most countries. For South Africa, for example, the projected welfare losses rise by 5 percent of GDP, to about 75–82 percent of GDP.

Conclusions

This paper has attempted to quantify the welfare effects of the HIV/AIDS epidemic. Using estimates and projections of the impact of HIV/AIDS on mortality rates and life expectancy, and drawing on existing studies on the value of statistical life, we estimate the welfare loss of HIV/AIDS as the loss in income per capita that would have the same effect on lifetime utility as the increase in mortality.

Although our point estimates of welfare losses are subject to a high degree of uncertainty, they are of a much higher magnitude (generally, more than 10 times larger) than the available estimates of the impact of HIV/AIDS on output and income per capita. For South Africa, for example, the available projections of the impact of HIV/AIDS on GDP per capita range from –8 percent to +9 percent by 2010. This paper, in contrast, evaluates South Africa's welfare loss associated with increased mortality at around 80 percent of GDP. Thus the estimated changes in GDP per capita, although valuable in some other regards, not only give an incomplete picture of the welfare effects of HIV/AIDS, but, as far as welfare is concerned, appear negligible compared with the direct effect of increased mortality.

It is important to bear in mind certain limitations of our analysis. Our estimates are subject to the usual problems associated with out-of-sample projections: the bulk of studies on the VSL deal with countries with higher GDP per capita than those considered here, and the available studies deal with changes in mortality that are smaller than those observed in the countries significantly affected by HIV/AIDS. Also, our measure of welfare is entirely based on changes in mortality and does not take into account the direct and indirect effects of HIV/AIDS on the health status of the population.[11] However, the magnitude of our estimates suggests that our key finding—that the direct welfare effects of HIV/AIDS through increased mortality substantially outweigh even the worst projections of the impact

---

[11]HIV/AIDS directly affects the health status of those infected, but it also has indirect health effects, for example through an increase in infections like tuberculosis or declines in the general quality of health services owing to overwhelming demand.

on GDP per capita—is robust to alternative specifications or broader definitions of welfare.

References

Arndt, Channing, and Jeffrey D. Lewis, 2001, "The HIV/AIDS Pandemic in South Africa: Sectoral Impacts and Unemployment," *Journal of International Development,* Vol. 13, No. 4, pp. 427–49.

Bowland, Bradley J., and John C. Beghin, 2001, "Robust Estimates of Value of a Statistical Life for Developing Economies," *Journal of Policy Modeling,* Vol. 23, pp. 385–96.

Crafts, Nicholas, 2001, "The Contribution of Increased Life Expectancy to Growth of Living Standards in the UK, 1870–1998" (unpublished; London School of Economics).

———, 2002, "The Human Development Index, 1870–1999: Some Revised Estimates," *European Review of Economic History,* Vol. 6, No. 3, pp. 395–405.

———, and Markus Haacker, 2002, "Welfare Implications of HIV/AIDS," IMF Working Paper 03/118 (Washington: International Monetary Fund).

ING Barings, South African Research, 2000, "Economic Impact of AIDS in South Africa. A Dark Cloud on the Horizon" (Johannesburg, South Africa).

Jamison, Dean T., Jeffrey D. Sachs, and Jia Wang, 2001, "The Effect of the AIDS Epidemic on Economic Welfare in Sub-Saharan Africa," CMH Working Paper Series No. WG1:13 (Geneva: Commission on Macroeconomics and Health, World Health Organization).

Joint United Nations Programme on HIV/AIDS (UNAIDS), 2004, *2004 Report on the Global AIDS Epidemic* (Geneva).

Mathers, Colin D., and others, 2000, "Estimates of DALE for 191 Countries – Methods and Results," Global Programme on Evidence for Health Policy Working Paper No. 16 (Geneva: World Health Organization).

Miller, Ted R., 2000, "Variations Between Countries in Values of Statistical Life," *Journal of Transport Economics and Policy,* Vol. 34, Part 2, pp. 169–88.

Mrozek, Janusz R., and Laura O. Taylor, 2002, "What Determines the Value of Life? A Meta-Analysis," *Journal of Policy Analysis and Management,* Vol. 21, No. 2, pp. 253–70.

Nordhaus, William, 1998, "The Health of Nations: Irving Fisher and the Contribution of Improved Longevity to Living Standards," Cowles Foundation Discussion Paper No. 1200 (New Haven, Connecticut: Cowles Foundation).

———, 2002, "The Health of Nations: The Contribution of Improved Health to Living Standards," NBER Working Paper No. 8818 (Cambridge, Massachusetts: National Bureau of Economic Research).

Sen, Amartya, 1999, *Development as Freedom* (New York: Alfred A. Knopf).

Stanecki, Karen A., 2000, "The AIDS Pandemic in the 21st Century. The Demographic Impact in Developing Countries," paper presented at the 13th International AIDS Conference, Durban, South Africa, July.

United Nations Development Programme (UNDP), 2001, *Human Development Report 2001: Making New Technologies Work for Human Development* (New York).

Viscusi, W. Kip, and Joseph E. Aldy, 2003, "The Value of a Statistical Life: A Critical Review of Market Estimates Throughout the World," NBER Working Paper No. 9487 (Cambridge, Massachusetts: National Bureau of Economic Research).

7

The Impact of HIV/AIDS on Government Finance and Public Services

Markus Haacker

HIV/AIDS is a serious challenge to economic development. Increasing mortality and morbidity reduce living standards directly and have repercussions that affect all areas of the economy. Individuals and households face increasing risks, both directly through the risk of infection, and indirectly as formal and informal social insurance mechanisms are eroded. Companies face productivity losses and increasing costs of medical and death-related benefits. At the macroeconomic level, economic growth declines as the population grows more slowly and as reduced national saving, rising costs, and declining economic prospects deter investment.[1]

Against this background, this chapter examines the implications of HIV/AIDS for government finance and public services. In countries afflicted by HIV/AIDS epidemics, governments' capacities are diminished by increasing mortality, and domestic revenue slows, even as the demand for certain government services, most notably in the health sector, expands.[2] Along these lines, this chapter will address three broad questions:

---

[1]For a broader discussion of the macroeconomic effects of HIV/AIDS, see Haacker (Chapter 2, this volume).

[2]Barnett and Whiteside (2002) also discuss the impact of HIV/AIDS on the public sector but take a wider perspective, covering the impact of HIV/AIDS on political processes in more detail. Braimah (2004) provides a much shorter discussion of the issues discussed here; his study also considers broadly the responses to HIV/AIDS from a public sector perspective.

- *What is the impact of HIV/AIDS on government employees, personnel costs, and the efficiency of public services?* Increased mortality, concentrated among the working-age population, results in disruptions to public services and, over time, will change the age composition of public servants. At the same time, governments frequently offer health and other benefits to public servants that are generous by national standards, and the costs of these benefits are likely to rise.
- *What are the implications of HIV/AIDS for public policy, and what are the fiscal consequences?* The most direct policy responses are efforts at prevention (for example, through the mass media, education, or workplace interventions) and the expansion of public health services. Through the adverse economic consequences of HIV/AIDS on individuals and households, the epidemic also creates challenges for social policy, in particular regarding the very substantial numbers of orphans. In light of the key role of education in economic development and also HIV/AIDS prevention, this chapter also discusses the impact of HIV/AIDS on the education sector.
- *How does HIV/AIDS affect government revenue, and what is the role of external finance?* HIV/AIDS has an adverse impact on the domestic tax base, and thus on government revenue. For most countries with high HIV prevalence, external grants account for a large proportion of general health expenditure and probably an even greater proportion of expenditure related to HIV/AIDS. Also, since external grants are frequently disbursed not through the government budget, but directly from the donor to the implementing agency, coordination of the various agencies active in this area is an important aspect of the government's agenda.

With data still scarce and our present understanding of the broad economic effects of HIV/AIDS still poor (at least in terms of a quantitative macroeconomic analysis), this chapter will not arrive at conclusive answers to these three questions. Instead, the aim of this chapter is to formulate an analytical framework and to synthesize the data that are available, to assist policymakers in developing a policy response to HIV/AIDS. At the same time, the fiscal repercussions of HIV/AIDS—its impact on the civil service, government expenditure, and government revenue—go far beyond what is generally subsumed under the costs of or the response to HIV/AIDS. For countries with severe epidemics, HIV/AIDS is therefore a general fiscal policy issue, and this chapter aims to contribute to an improved understanding of the consequences of HIV/AIDS from this angle as well.

The chapter is organized as follows. The first section analyzes how HIV/AIDS affects the government's human capacities through increased mortality. Because of medical and death-related benefits and other costs related to increased attrition, the costs of public services increase for all areas of government. The losses in efficiency of public services, however, extend beyond the disruptions associated with increased attrition. For example, the age composition of government employees changes as many more die young and many fewer reach retirement age. The next four sections highlight various areas of government services or public expenditure particularly affected by HIV/AIDS: HIV prevention, care, and treatment; education; social expenditure; and pension schemes. HIV/AIDS also has an impact on government revenue. Therefore the chapter's sixth section discusses changes in domestic government revenue and the financing of general and HIV/AIDS-specific health expenditure. In many low-income countries, external grants play a very important role in financing HIV/AIDS-related expenditure, and this is the topic of the seventh section. The penultimate section discusses some issues pertaining to the impact of HIV/AIDS in the longer run. The final section concludes.

Impact on Government Employees and Personnel Costs

The HIV/AIDS epidemic affects all levels and functions of government as an increasing number of government employees fall ill and die. Beyond the disruptions to public services associated with increased attrition rates, HIV/AIDS also affects the composition of government employees in various dimensions and the level of human capital available to the government. Also, because government employees generally enjoy some form of retirement, death-related, and medical benefits, the government's personnel costs increase.

Increased Mortality

Higher mortality and morbidity affect public services through higher attrition and absenteeism of government employees affected by HIV/AIDS, and through lower productivity owing to their deteriorating health. More broadly, HIV/AIDS also results in higher absenteeism among those not infected—for example, as these workers are obliged to care for sick family members and to attend funerals. The demographic implications of the epidemic are treated in more detail elsewhere in this volume; this section therefore only briefly highlights some of the consequences for the public sector and discusses the available evidence.

Figure 7.1. Mortality Rates by Age and Sex in Namibia, 2004
(Percent)

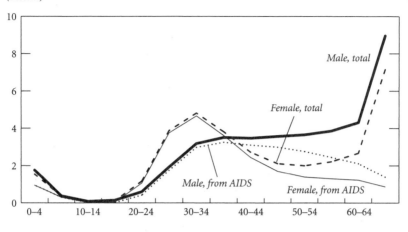

Source: International Programs Center, U.S. Census Bureau.

To illustrate the implications of the demographic impact of HIV/AIDS, Figure 7.1 shows the estimated mortality pattern by age and sex for Namibia in 2004. With an estimated prevalence rate of 21 percent, Namibia is one of the countries worst affected by HIV. Mortality peaks at 4.2 percent at ages 30–34 for females, and at 3.2 percent at ages 40–44 for males. The impact of HIV/AIDS on mortality has been discussed in more detail elsewhere (see, in particular, Epstein, Chapter 1 of this volume), and this chapter will not duplicate that discussion. Regarding the impact on the civil service, it is important to note that for ages 20–54, a range that includes most public servants, mortality averages 2.5 percent, of which AIDS accounts for 2.2 percentage points, or almost 90 percent. This means that, for this age group, mortality increases about 7½-fold for men and almost 12-fold for women. The data also show a strong sex bias, with women affected at an earlier age and suffering higher mortality overall.

One of the most thorough studies so far of the impact of HIV/AIDS on government workers covers the staff of five ministries in Malawi (Government of Malawi and United Nations Development Programme (UNDP), 2002). It shows that death-related attrition rates increased substantially between 1990 and 2000, for example, from 0.1 percent to 0.7 percent for the Ministry of Education, and from 1.1 percent to 2.7 percent for the police service. Although these data are subject to some uncertainty, the age profile of the observed mortality, peaking at ages 30–34, suggests that

Figure 7.2. Malawi: Mortality by Age and Sex in the Public Sector, 1990–2000
(Absolute numbers)

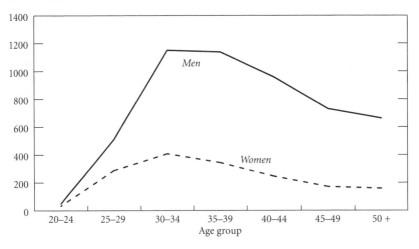

Source: Government of Malawi and UNDP, 2002.

much of it is related to HIV/AIDS (Figure 7.2).[3] Vacancy rates, meanwhile, are very high, ranging from 37 to 77 percent. This suggests that government employees cannot be replaced easily and that an increase in the attrition rate may be causing serious disruptions to the affected government units.

Increased attrition, in addition to its adverse impact on current government operations, has structural effects that accumulate over the years. Most important, the age composition will change, as fewer government employees survive until retirement or to any given age. Also, in most countries with severe HIV/AIDS epidemics, women are disproportionately affected. Table 7.1 shows the probabilities of 20-year-old men and women surviving until various ages, using estimated mortality rates from Zambia (which is among the countries with the highest HIV prevalence rates worldwide) for 2003. The overall (male and female) probability of survival from age 20 until age 30 falls to about 85 percent, from about 95 percent in the absence of HIV/AIDS. The impact of HIV/AIDS in this example is so severe that, whereas only about 3 in 10 20-year-old males would be

---

[3]Figure 7.2 reports mortality in absolute numbers of deaths rather than as percentages of the public sector workforce. The higher mortality observed for men reflects the fact that most public sector employees are men. The study does not report the absolute numbers of male or female government employees over this period.

Table 7.1. Zambia: Estimated Survival Probabilities for 20-Year-Olds, by Sex, 2004
(Percent)

| | Probability of Survival Until Indicated Age | | | |
| | Male | | Female | |
Age	Actual	In absence of AIDS	Actual	In absence of AIDS
30	87.8	94.5	82.9	96.1
40	62.8	88.4	52.2	91.0
50	41.5	80.2	37.9	84.3
60	26.7	67.7	29.3	74.3

Source: Author's calculations, based on U.S. Census Bureau estimates of mortality rates for 2004.

expected to die before age 60 in the absence of HIV/AIDS, in its presence only about three in ten are expected to *survive* until age 60. Table 7.1 also shows that women are affected more severely than men, and at an earlier age. For 20-year-old women the survival rate until age 60 declines from three-fourths to less than 30 percent, and the impact of HIV/AIDS on 20-year-old women's mortality until age 30 (an increase of 13.2 percentage points) is about twice the impact for men (6.7 percentage points).

Personnel Costs

HIV/AIDS-related personnel costs for the general civil service (as opposed to the costs of expanding certain public services, such as health, which are discussed further below) can broadly be categorized in terms of absenteeism (of the sick staff members themselves, and of other employees who will attend their funerals), sick leave, medical benefits, death-related benefits, and the additional costs of replacing staff lost due to HIV/AIDS (most notably training costs).[4]

As the health status of those infected deteriorates, and as the need to care for sick relatives increases, HIV/AIDS results in an increase in absenteeism. Because absenteeism, unlike sick leave, is characterized by informal absences, whether for extended periods or only for several hours at a time, it is very difficult to measure. For instance, the Government of Malawi and

---

[4]Much of the literature on the costs of HIV/AIDS to the private sector also applies; see Haacker (Chapter 2, this volume) for a discussion. However, the impact of HIV/AIDS on personnel costs in the public sector is generally larger, because benefits tend to be more comprehensive (partly because of a larger share of permanent employees in the public sector), and because the private sector is more likely to adjust benefits downward in response to rising costs. Barnett and Whiteside (2002) make a similar point.

UNDP (2002) estimate that absenteeism averages 65 days a year for employees with full-blown AIDS, and 15 days a year for those who are infected but have not yet developed the full symptoms. This means that if 2 percent of public servants have full-blown AIDS, and another 20 percent take health-related absences of 15 days each, then absenteeism will amount to 2.0 percent of all working hours (assuming 220 working days in a year).

Grassly and others (2003) estimate that absenteeism amounts to an average of 1.3 months annually per HIV-infected employee, with each infected worker experiencing 12 to 14 illness episodes before the terminal illness (Government of Malawi and UNDP, 2002). With an overall HIV prevalence rate of 20 percent, this would mean a rise in absenteeism of 2.2 percent.

When public servants become too sick to work, they can usually request sick leave at full or reduced pay for a specified period. In Zambia, for example, the Ministry of Agriculture, Food, and Forestry allows for a continuous absence of 90 days at full pay, and another 6 months at half pay. In Swaziland a public servant may take up to 6 months of sick leave at full pay, and another 6 months at half pay. Although these examples cannot be generalized (provision for sick leave differs substantially across countries), these two examples suggest that, for a country where 2 percent of public servants drop out of the service for HIV/AIDS-related reasons, about 1 to 1.5 percent of all public servants may be on sick leave at a given time as a consequence.

Apart from morbidity-related absenteeism and sick leave, another primary cause of absenteeism is attendance at the funerals of those who have died of AIDS. At the aggregate level, it is possible to draw some conclusions on the impact of HIV/AIDS-related mortality on funeral attendance. If, for example, mortality rises by 2 percentage points, 40 people attend each funeral, funeral attendance requires an absence of 2 days (including travel time), and total working time each year is 220 days, then HIV/AIDS will increase absenteeism by 0.7 percentage point. However, these aggregate numbers are likely to understate the disruptions caused by funeral attendance. As government employees die of AIDS and their colleagues attend the funeral, the work of the affected government agency can come to a standstill.

Altogether, these considerations suggest that the impact of HIV/AIDS on the productivity of government employees can be considerable. For a country with HIV/AIDS-related mortality of 2 percent, absenteeism and sick leave would absorb 2 to 3 percent of the total working time of public servants. At least in the case of informal absences (and in light of existing budget constraints), it is likely that this would not translate into additional hiring, but instead into reduced productivity and reduced delivery of public services. Moreover, the problem of increased absenteeism will be compounded by an increase in vacancies if positions are not filled immediately. Although these increased vacancies do not directly contribute to costs (indeed, for a given number of positions, an increase in vacancies would reduce personnel costs), they are likely to exacerbate service disruptions.[5]

In countries with weak governance and nontransparent public records, the efficiency of the public service may also suffer if deceased government employees remain on the payroll, to the benefit of corrupt government officials or the surviving dependents. In this case increased mortality would result in an increase in the number of "ghost workers."

Government employees generally enjoy some form of medical benefits, which can take the form of medical insurance, free (and possibly privileged) access to public health services, or discretionary funds (for example, at the ministerial level). HIV prevention, care, and treatment are discussed in more detail below. However, some aspects are specific to the government's role as an employer. In particular, workplace prevention measures (by reducing the incidence of new infections) and the provision of care and treatment (by improving the health status of government employees and reducing mortality rates) not only reduce other HIV/AIDS-related costs but also mitigate losses in the efficiency of government services, discussed below. The costs and financial benefits of HIV/AIDS workplace interventions have been discussed in some detail for the private sector, for example by Rosen and others (2004) and Simon and others (2000).[6] One of the lessons from these studies, which also applies here, is that the financial benefits from improvements in prevention measures and medical services are significant, and they need to be taken into account when assessing the overall fiscal effects of HIV/AIDS.

Death-related benefits comprise funeral benefits, lump-sum benefits paid to surviving dependents, and pensions to surviving dependents (typically the deceased worker's spouse and under-age children). Because public pension funds may cover the civil service only or parts of the private sector as well, this issue is treated in more detail below. Government agencies often cover the funeral expenses of their employees, whether by formal

---

[5]JTK Associates (2002), in a study of the impact of HIV/AIDS on three government ministries in Swaziland, emphasizes the high level of vacancies, which increases the workload of the remaining government employees. The study points out that, "should the central agencies continue growing at the same rate as in the past several years (i.e. at close to 2% [a year]), recruitment will need to double to accommodate the loss of personnel to AIDS."

[6]See also Haacker (Chapter 2, this volume), which draws on this earlier literature.

or informal arrangement. The cost can be substantial. For instance, in a sample of households from South Africa, the cost of a funeral averaged four monthly salaries; the average cost of a single funeral to the Ministry of Education in Zambia was $176 (in 2001 dollars), or 11 percent of an average annual salary.[7] Thus, if all government employees are eligible for funeral grants in the range of 1 to 4 monthly salaries, and if the HIV/AIDS-related mortality rate is 2 percent, the total cost will equal about 0.2 to 0.7 percent of the total wage bill. If the government also provides funeral grants for family members of its workers, the total could be substantially higher.

Because government employees who have fallen sick or died need to be replaced, HIV/AIDS also has implications for the costs of training. Depending on the employee's job category, these costs range from small amounts for basic on-the-job training to very substantial investments involving several years of training abroad. Training costs may appear in the government budget directly (for example, when line ministries conduct training events) or indirectly (through increased allocations to general or vocational educational institutions, or informal training on the job); if the public servants lost due to HIV/AIDS are not replaced by similarly qualified staff, the primary cost will be a decline in the quality of the civil service.

The increase in training costs due to HIV/AIDS can be calculated in different ways. One way is to multiply the estimated average cost of training per person by the number of new staff needed. Another is to assess, using more aggregated data on the existing capacities and budgets of educational institutions, how much these institutions will have to expand.

Following the first approach, Grassly and others (2003) estimate, for the case of Zambia, the cost of training one teacher over two years at $413 to $606 (in 2001 dollars), an amount equal to about four monthly salaries. In this case, if mortality among teachers increases by 2 percent, the additional training of teachers will cost an amount roughly equivalent to 0.7 percent of the wage bill for teachers. However, for positions requiring several years of university education, the costs can be much higher. Topouzis (2003), citing another study from Zambia, reports annual costs of university education of between $2,500 and $3,000; professional staff at the Ministry of Agriculture, for example, usually have at least five years of university training.

---

[7]See Steinberg and others (2002) for South Africa, and Grassly and others (2003) for Zambia.

The primary advantage of the second approach is that it requires fewer data: in its simplest form, all one needs is data on attrition rates with and without AIDS. For example, if staff attrition is 2 percent without HIV/AIDS, and HIV/AIDS raises it by 1 percentage point, then, for every 100 public servants, three rather than two new staff members need to be hired and trained annually, corresponding to an increase of 50 percent in required training. This method can also be applied to identifying bottlenecks in the capacities of relevant training institutes.

One very important factor in determining training costs, especially in health services, is brain drain. The emigration of trained workers can greatly increase the number of people who need to be trained to replace employees who have died, or to meet the requirements of an expanded response to HIV/AIDS. Especially in low-income countries, recent graduates may leave the country to take higher-paid positions in other countries in the region or further abroad. To some extent this is presumably included in estimated rates of attrition, but such measures do not capture brain drain among new graduates. If, for example, 20 percent of graduates immediately take jobs abroad, estimates of the required costs of training using the first method described above would need to be adjusted upward by 20 percent. The second method, which applies a multiplier to the total number of people actually trained, does account for this form of brain drain, provided that the rate of brain drain does not change in response to increased HIV prevalence.

One other consideration is often overlooked in analyses of the cost of training, namely, that at the national level the number of job candidates with suitable skills is limited. In the worst-affected countries in sub-Saharan Africa, there is considerable slack in the labor market for the lower educational categories. For higher educational or skill categories, however, the labor market is much tighter, and hiring additional staff in these categories would crowd out hiring by other employers. Thus any policy to compensate for or offset the impact of HIV/AIDS on the public sector, or to expand various categories of public services, needs to be consistent with the situation in the labor market and with the country's overall development objectives.

Efficiency of Public Services

HIV/AIDS increases the number of government employees taking early retirement for medical reasons or dying in service. Increased attrition rates and absenteeism for medical reasons or to attend funerals (discussed above) cause disruptions to work processes and thus affect the efficiency of public services.

Some of the efficiency losses—those related to sick leave, increased absenteeism for medical reasons, and funeral attendance—have already been discussed in the context of personnel costs. In a private sector context these losses would result in an increase in unit costs, which can be interpreted either as an increase in production costs to achieve a given output, or as a decline in the productivity of a given number of employees.[8]

In the public sector these losses are most likely to result in a decline in the quality of services rather than additional hiring, for two reasons. First, almost all government employees are permanent employees, and the positions of those falling ill cannot be filled before they either die or retire. Thus the responsibilities of an ill employee are typically taken on by someone else in an acting capacity (who in turn usually must pass on some of his or her normal responsibilities) or shared between colleagues in the same unit. Second, staff allocations are typically driven by a centralized annual budget process, and so there is little flexibility to hire additional staff to cover bottlenecks in particular units, especially on a temporary basis.

These efficiency losses are likely to go beyond those caused by increased absenteeism. Once a government employee dies or retires, the position cannot be filled instantaneously. Many government jobs, in particular senior positions, need to be advertised, the applications screened, and candidates interviewed. The government agency then selects one or more candidates and makes offers, which may be rejected or may have to be negotiated. Once a candidate accepts an offer, the appointment needs to be confirmed. Especially for senior positions, the entire process can take several months or more to complete.

Aggregate estimates of increased absenteeism do not reflect differences in the extent to which the workload of government employees can be reallocated temporarily during episodes of sickness. Generally, those staff members who are most difficult to replace are those holding critical positions at the nodes of the government's organization or internal communications, or whose positions are endpoints in the localized delivery of services, especially in rural areas. The first group includes primarily senior government staff, who often have advanced degrees and many years of

---

[8]Note, however, that the increase in staff required to achieve a particular output generally exceeds the percentage of working time lost to HIV/AIDS. The reason is that labor can be interpreted as a homogeneous factor of production only in very special circumstances. More commonly, each worker fulfills a certain role within an organization, which requires certain specific skills; any replacements would have to match those skills. Since labor is not easily divisible, this matching can be hard to achieve.

experience. When these public servants fall ill, the efficiency of the government units reporting to them can be undermined. Government services in rural areas are particularly vulnerable because the units providing these services are generally smaller or more decentralized. Examples include local schoolteachers and agricultural extension workers (see Topouzis, 2003). In the smallest local government units (such as a school with one or two teachers), it is simply impossible to cover for the sickness or death of a public servant by reallocating work to co-workers. Also, because of the distances involved, supervisors are likely to be less aware of an increase in health-related absenteeism.

The change in the age structure of government employees also has implications for the efficiency of public services. Again, senior government staff are typically drawn from a pool of public servants with many years, even decades, of experience. Increased mortality means that this pool is shrinking. Assume, for example, that a minister has to be appointed, and that ordinarily there would be six candidates on the short list, all of them about 50 years of age. If the example from Table 7.1 is representative of government employees at this level, the likelihood is that, of the six candidates who would have ordinarily made the short list, three will be dead by the age of 50.[9] Although this statistical probability may or may not affect any particular appointment, it does indicate a catastrophic loss of senior public servants in total, which would have a severe impact on the quality of management of government agencies and decision making at the highest levels.

More generally, the efficiency of an organization at any level may depend on the number of employees who "know the ropes" and who have developed their problem-solving skills through experience. By thinning out this stock of experience, increased mortality—in addition to disruptions caused by sickness and higher attrition—can have an accumulative effect. These longer-term effects are captured in the term "institutional memory." An institution's memory is largely embodied in its staff, and especially in those employees who have stayed with the institution for a long time. To gain a sense of the implications of HIV for institutional memory, consider its impact on the number of government employees with a tenure of 10 years. Suppose that the attrition rate, excluding HIV/AIDS-related mortality, is 2 percent and that with HIV/AIDS it rises

---

[9]This is calculated as the survival probability until age 50 divided by the survival probability in the absence of HIV/AIDS. The increase in attrition is higher among women than among men, reflecting the differing impact of HIV/AIDS by sex.

by another 2.4 percentage points (in line with the above example for Namibia). In the absence of HIV/AIDS, attrition over a 10-year period would be 18 percent, but *including* the effects of HIV/AIDS it is 36 percent. Equivalently, institutional memory (here measured by the number of employees remaining with the institution for 10 years) declines by 22 percent.[10]

Prevention, Care, and Treatment

The preceding section focused on the general impact of HIV/AIDS on the civil service and on personnel costs. This section turns to the government's activities in fighting the epidemic through the prevention of new infections, antiretroviral treatment, and other forms of care. The section begins with a discussion of the most recent estimates of global resource needs for HIV/AIDS-related activities from the Joint United Nations Programme on HIV/AIDS (UNAIDS), mapping out the various components of the global response to the epidemic. In light of the central role of prevention measures in turning back the epidemic, and their crucial role in strengthening efforts to expand access to treatment for people living with HIV/AIDS, prevention programs are discussed next. An analysis of general health expenditure and human resources in some of the worst-affected countries follows, leading into the discussion on care and treatment. That discussion takes a broad perspective, including an assessment of the macroeconomic costs and benefits of antiretroviral treatment. Finally, in most countries with severe HIV epidemics a substantial proportion of HIV/AIDS-related expenditure is financed through external grants and concessional lending, and therefore the section ends by focusing on issues related to and trends in external financing.

Estimates of Global Resource Needs

UNAIDS's latest estimates of global resource needs for an expanded response to AIDS in low- and middle-income countries, issued in June 2004 (UNAIDS, 2004b, shown in Table 7.2) provide some information on priority interventions from a global perspective. The prioritization dif-

---

[10]Let attrition without HIV/AIDS be denoted as α, and attrition owing to HIV/AIDS as β. Ten-year attrition rates are then computed as $1 - (1 - \alpha)^{10}$ and $1 - (1 - \alpha - \beta)^{10}$, respectively. (For convenience, it is assumed that attrition rates are not correlated with tenure.) The decline in institutional memory is then defined as $1 - [(1 - \alpha - \beta)]/[(1 - \alpha)]^{10}$.

Table 7.2. Estimated Costs of Scaling up HIV/AIDS Activities in Low- and Middle-Income Countries, 2005

Item	Millions of Dollars	Percent of Total Costs
Prevention-related activities		
General population interventions		
Mass media	96	0.8
Voluntary counseling and testing	1,101	9.5
Total for general population interventions	1,197	10.3
Programs for key populations at high risk		
AIDS education in schools	95	0.8
Outreach for out-of-school youth	633	5.5
Interventions focused on sex workers and their clients	384	3.3
Interventions focused on men who have sex with men	342	3.0
Harm reduction programs	124	1.1
Workplace prevention	505	4.4
Prevention programs for people living with HIV	34	0.3
Prevention for special populations[1]	115	1.0
Total for programs for key populations at high risk	2,232	19.3
Service delivery	2,569	22.2
Condom social marketing	147	1.3
Public and commercial sector condom provision	865	7.5
Improving management of sexually transmitted infections	660	5.7
Prevention of mother-to-child transmission	167	1.4
Blood safety	224	1.9
Postexposure prophylaxis	1	0.0
Safe medical injections	93	0.8
Universal precautions	394	3.4
Other prevention	18	0.2
Total for service delivery	2,569	22.2
Total for prevention-related activities	5,998	51.7
Orphan support		
Orphanage support	509	4.4
Community support	364	3.1
School fees	204	1.8
Total for orphan support	1,077	9.3
Treatment and care	3,815	32.9
Palliative care	271	2.3
Diagnostic testing	24	0.2
Treatment for opportunistic infections	349	3.0
Prophylaxis for opportunistic infections	114	1.0
Antiretroviral therapy	2,875	24.8
Laboratory monitoring for antiretroviral therapy	182	1.6
Total for treatment and care	3,815	32.9
Policy, advocacy, administration, and research	545	4.7
Program costs	155	1.3
Total, all items	11,592	100.0

Sources: UNAIDS (2004b), and author's calculations.
[1]Prisoners, migrants, truck drivers, and others.

fers, however, from country to country. For example, countries with low HIV prevalence at present would be advised to place more emphasis on general prevention; in countries where the epidemic is concentrated in particular subgroups, targeted prevention programs would carry a larger weight. Estimates of resource needs for treatment also reflect an assessment of how quickly access to treatment can be expanded in a given country.[11] Total resource needs for low- and middle-income countries in 2005 are estimated at $11.6 billion, just over half of which (52 percent) goes toward prevention-related activities, 9 percent for social expenditure, 33 percent for treatment, and 6 percent largely for overhead expense and research.

Within the category of preventive activities, some measures aim at specific population groups, largely those at high risk of infection (such as sex workers, men who have sex with men, prisoners, migrants, and truck drivers). In order to reach young people before HIV prevalence in their cohort rises, prevention strategies for this group should include education in the classroom (at relatively low additional cost, since it is delivered through an existing service), and outreach programs for out-of school youth (who are at greater risk of contracting the virus). Workplace programs, at 4.4 percent of total costs, are an important channel for reaching prime-age adults. These measures are complemented by interventions targeting the general population, such as mass media campaigns and voluntary counseling and testing. The latter is one of the more expensive components of the total response, accounting for 9.5 percent of total costs. Whereas these measures aim primarily at education and modification of risky behavior, other prevention measures (those under the heading "service delivery") focus on specific efforts to reduce infection risk through sexual contact (condom provision), during pregnancy or at birth, or through exposure to infected blood (blood safety protocols and safe injections).

Because of the vulnerability of children in households affected by HIV/AIDS,[12] the global response to HIV/AIDS, as envisaged in the estimates of resource needs, includes provisions targeted at orphans and the households and communities who care for them; these resource needs amount to 9.3 percent of the total. Some of these measures aim at

---

[11]Because some of these estimates are politically sensitive, UNAIDS does not release estimates at the country level.

[12]See also Haacker (Chapter 2, this volume), Birdsall and Hamoudi (Chapter 4, this volume), and Bell, Devarajan, and Gersbach (Chapter 3, this volume), and the section titled "Focus—AIDS and Orphans: A Tragedy Unfolding," in UNAIDS (2004a).

improving orphans' material living standards (for example, through orphanage and community support), whereas others are directed to improving access to education (for example, through subsidies to cover school fees).

About one-third (32.9 percent) of the total estimated resource needs go toward expanded treatment and care. Within this category, antiretroviral therapy (24.8 percent) and associated laboratory costs (1.6 percent) together account for the largest share. The remainder (6.5 percent) covers the estimated costs of palliative care and treatment and prophylaxis for opportunistic infections.

Although the line items in Table 7.2 also describe the major components of an HIV/AIDS program at the country level, the mix of interventions also depends on the state of the epidemic and on the government's policy objectives: many of the interventions, especially in the areas of care, treatment, and social expenditure, are very strongly linked to the rate of HIV or AIDS prevalence in the country. The mix can also vary according to the main transmission modes of the virus, which can differ between and within countries. In designing a broad HIV/AIDS program, it is also important to acknowledge the close interrelationships between some interventions. For example, achieving and maintaining high rates of coverage of antiretroviral treatment will often be possible only if prevention measures succeed at keeping the number of new infections low.[13] At the same time, the option of receiving treatment is a major incentive for AIDS victims to seek counseling and testing. Some sense of the range of national responses can be gleaned from countries' announced plans for their general response to HIV/AIDS. For example, Botswana's National Strategic Framework for HIV/AIDS 2003–09 is at once a national plan and a means of engaging government ministries and regional entities in the national response, requiring each to formulate its own response to HIV/AIDS (see Botswana National AIDS Coordinating Agency, 2003; see also Masha, Chapter 9 of this volume). An important feature of South Africa's Operational Plan for Comprehensive HIV and AIDS Care, Management, and Treatment (Government of the Republic of South Africa, 2003) is the strong emphasis on embedding the response to HIV/AIDS within the government's objective of broadening and improving access to health care.

---

[13]UNAIDS (2004a, p. 69) points out that "without sharply reducing HIV incidence, expanded access to treatment becomes unsustainable. Antiretroviral therapy providers will be swamped by demand."

From a broad fiscal perspective, three points about Table 7.2 are worth making. First, it is unclear how the analysis on which the table is based has incorporated the fixed costs of rapidly expanding HIV/AIDS-related services, especially in the area of treatment, other than through assumptions regarding feasible rates at which HIV/AIDS-related services can be expanded. Second, the strategy to improve access to treatment for HIV patients is normally part of a broader strategy for the health sector, and it is often difficult or infeasible to distinguish investments in HIV/AIDS-related services from those in health services generally. Third, in most cases the table shows only the direct fiscal costs of HIV/AIDS-related interventions. The total fiscal costs, however, also include the indirect effects (for example, higher personnel costs and reduced domestic revenue, both of which are treated elsewhere in this chapter), but these are usually not included in studies focusing on the response to HIV/AIDS.

Prevention-Related Activities

Prevention programs are the centerpiece of the public response to HIV/AIDS. The epidemic has a devastating effect not only on the individuals affected, but also on their households and, in countries with high prevalence rates, on societies (see Haacker, Chapter 2 of this volume). Improved access to treatment can mitigate these effects, but they can be avoided only if successful prevention measures bring down the number of infections. However, the broader microeconomic, macroeconomic, and social costs of HIV/AIDS are not included in standard estimates of the cost-effectiveness of prevention and treatment programs, either because they cannot easily be quantified, or because the studies focus on the financial costs of HIV/AIDS-related programs only. Nevertheless, even from this narrow perspective, some prevention measures are known to be highly cost-effective (as discussed further below), and institutions such as UNAIDS emphasize the role of effective prevention programs as a prerequisite to successfully expanding access to treatment. Against this background, the discussion here will focus on a few issues that are particularly relevant from a fiscal and general policy perspective. A comprehensive discussion of the various types of prevention measures is beyond the scope of the chapter; UNAIDS (2004a, 2004b), Global HIV Prevention Group (2003), and World Bank AIDS Campaign Team for Africa (2001) are useful starting points.

Although innovations in the market for antiretroviral drugs and enhanced political commitment have vastly increased the potential to provide, through the public sector, treatment to large numbers of people living with HIV/AIDS, the disease remains, by a large margin, the leading cause of death in sub-Saharan Africa, and no cure yet exists. Moreover, in light of the limited capacities of providers of antiretroviral treatment, the only way to provide sustainable expanded access to treatment is by sharply reducing the incidence of HIV through expanded prevention programs (UNAIDS, 2004a). The link also runs in the opposite direction: improved access to treatment enhances prevention efforts, such as voluntary counseling and testing, by adding an incentive to get tested for HIV.

The most common "recipes" for enhanced prevention programs distinguish between low-prevalence and high-prevalence settings. In the former, prevention measures are targeted at key populations at risk (such as sex workers, injecting drug users, and men who have sex with men), to keep the epidemic from spreading through the general population. In the latter, these measures are complemented by strategies aiming at broader segments of society (UNAIDS, 2004a; see also Table 7.2). Programs targeting high-risk groups are also among the most efficient preventive interventions. For example, World Bank (2003), on the basis of assessments of alternative measures in Guatemala, Honduras, and Panama, suggests that the most cost-effective measures include free condom distribution to high-risk groups; information, education, and communication targeting these groups; as well as some measures aimed at the more general population, such as social marketing of condoms and voluntary counseling and testing. The Global HIV Prevention Group (2003) also stresses the control of sexually transmitted diseases, safe injections for drug users, and the prevention of mother-to-child transmission.

The most comprehensive studies of the costs of prevention programs, as well as of the costs of care and treatment, are World Bank AIDS Campaign Team for Africa (2001) and Creese and others (2002). The World Bank study aims at costing an expanded global response to HIV/AIDS and presents estimates in a format similar to that in Table 7.2. It also reports estimates of the underlying unit costs. Creese and others (2002) synthesize the available cost estimates at the country level; in addition to unit costs, they provide estimated costs per HIV infection averted and per disability-adjusted life year saved (Table 7.3).

Table 7.3 reinforces the points made about the interrelationships among prevention, care, and treatment in the context of a national response to HIV/AIDS. The estimated costs of preventive measures per HIV infection prevented are lower (in most cases, much lower) than the costs of care and treatment (which are discussed in more detail below) per infection. This shows clearly that prevention measures are the key compo-

Table 7.3. Cost of Selected Prevention Measures in Various Countries in Sub-Saharan Africa
(Dollars, of 2000)

Measure[1]	Cost per HIV Infection Averted	Cost per DALY[2] Saved
Blood safety	18–950	1–43
Condom distribution	11–2188	1–99
Diagnosis and treatment of sexually transmitted diseases	271	12
Prevention of mother-to-child transmission[3]	20–308	1–12
Peer education for sex workers	79–160	4–7
Voluntary counseling and testing	393–482	18–22

Source: Creese and others (2002).

[1]The source study also covers the costs of various forms of care and of antiretroviral treatment, which are omitted here.

[2]Disability-adjusted life year.

[3]The table shows the costs of single-dose nevirapine only.

nent of an effective national HIV/AIDS program: as UNAIDS (2004a) puts it, they are the "mainstay of the response to AIDS."[14]

Table 7.3 also points toward some weaknesses in the available literature on the costs of prevention programs. The unit costs reported range widely, reflecting, to some extent, the fact that several measures were subsumed under one heading. (For example, in the case of condom distribution, different measures targeted people of different risk categories.) However, much of the discrepancy related to cost differences across countries. Thus it is very difficult to make inferences regarding global resource needs from country-level studies or, vice versa, to draw conclusions regarding costs at a national level from global estimates.

Finally, the cost estimates in Table 7.3 should be interpreted as average costs in specific situations. The marginal effectiveness of spending on any specific prevention program would eventually decline, and the cost of an additional HIV infection averted would increase. Determining the optimal mix of prevention measures therefore requires a more sophisticated model, such as the GOALS model developed by the Futures Group (see Stover, Bollinger, and Cooper-Arnold, 2003).

---

[14]This conclusion is valid even from a purely financial perspective, looking at only the direct costs of prevention and treatment, but it is even more compelling when the broad economic and social impacts of HIV/AIDS are taken into account. As a practical matter, expanding access to treatment is subject to constraints, even when financing can be secured, the most notable of which are limited human resource and implementation capacities. However, these constraints themselves can be relaxed if successful prevention programs reduce the number of new infections.

Most of the literature dealing with the financial aspects of the response to HIV/AIDS (including this chapter) focuses on the costs of care and treatment, especially (over the past several years) the cost of antiretroviral treatment. This emphasis may seem to contrast with the very important role attributed to preventive measures in the global response to HIV/AIDS, as evident, for example, from UNAIDS's (2004b) estimates of total resource needs (of which preventive measures account for half), but it does not necessarily signify a contradiction. The resource requirements for prevention are estimated roughly according to the number of people at risk of contracting HIV/AIDS. Except in countries with very low HIV prevalence, the share of people at risk (and thus the resource requirements for prevention) is similar across countries, and so are the fiscal and human resource implications of expanded prevention measures. In contrast, the level of required health expenditure mirrors the number of people living with HIV/AIDS in a country, which differs very substantially across countries, so that estimates of the costs of treatment can result in very substantial shifts in health spending or in overall public expenditure. As a consequence, spending on prevention does not raise the same type of fundamental issues regarding the management of public sector financial and human resources that expanded care and treatment do. In particular, because expanded treatment draws not only on the government's financial resources (which, for most developing countries with severe epidemics, are substantially enhanced by foreign grants), but also on certain scarce human resources, such as physicians, the obstacles to achieving desired coverage rates can be complex and have therefore attracted a "disproportionate" share of research compared with the respective roles of treatment and prevention in national HIV/AIDS programs.

In some regards, however, the situation and policy challenges regarding expanded prevention measures are similar to the obstacles to increased access to treatment. This applies, in particular, to the limited coverage rates of prevention measures. In sub-Saharan Africa in 2001, only 6 percent of people had access to voluntary counseling and treatment, and only 1 percent of pregnant women had access to treatment to prevent mother-to-child transmission (Global HIV Prevention Group, 2003). Within countries, coverage of prevention is also correlated with social status (as is access to treatment); for example, fewer out-of-school youth have access to prevention programs than do youth attending school.

One important aspect of government's prevention efforts is measures targeted at public servants. The cost of increased HIV/AIDS-related mortality to the government, both in financial terms and through its adverse effect on the delivery and productivity of public services, has already been discussed. Enhanced prevention measures help to contain these costs.[15] However, because the government is instrumental in formulating and implementing the national response to HIV/AIDS, introducing awareness programs at government agencies also helps to reinforce the government's policies and thus the national response in this area.[16]

Health Sector Resources

The ability of the domestic health sector to cope with the HIV/AIDS epidemic and the extent of the challenge to improve treatment for HIV/AIDS—within the context of the government's development objectives for the health sector in general—are determined by the quality and coverage of existing health services, and these in turn depend on the available financial resources and health personnel.[17] As a starting point, Table 7.4 provides data on the strength of the health sector—health expenditure, human resources, and access to various forms of heath services—in a selection of countries affected by HIV/AIDS worldwide. The countries covered (in the table and below) include those with the highest prevalence rates overall, as well as a few countries with lower prevalence rates, to illustrate the still-significant effects of HIV/AIDS in these countries. (The United Kingdom and the United States are also included as comparators.) Total health expenditure per capita ranges from $3 a year in Ethiopia to more than $200 a year in Botswana, Brazil, and South Africa; these figures correspond to roughly 0.1 percent and 4.0 percent, respectively, of U.S. spending per capita on medical care.

These differences in spending on health services across countries mainly reflect differences in GDP per capita. As a percentage of GDP, the range in health expenditure is much narrower, from 3.3 percent for Swaziland to 8.6 percent for South Africa. To put it another way, whereas absolute expenditure varies across the developing countries in the table by a factor of 75, expenditure as a share of GDP differs by a factor of only 2.6.

If the purchasing power of the dollar differs across countries, because prices for services and nontraded goods are lower in lower-income countries, health spending in dollar terms is a poor indicator of the quality of

---

[15]This is discussed in more detail in Haacker (Chapter 2, this volume) in the context of the private sector.

[16]For example, Botswana's National Strategic Framework on HIV/AIDS includes HIV prevention policies for each ministry.

[17]This point is also discussed by Over (Chapter 10, this volume).

Table 7.4. Selected Indicators of the Quality of Health Services in HIV/AIDS-Affected Countries

Country	Health Expenditure per Capita, 2001			Physicians per 100,000 Population	Nurses per 100,000 Population	Hospital Beds per 1,000 Population	Access to Essential Drugs 1997, (percent of population)[2]
	Dollars	Dollars at PPP[1]	Percent of GDP				
Botswana	202	516	6.6	23.8 (1994)	219.1 (1994)	1.2 (2001)[3]	90
Brazil	222	559	7.6	127.2 (1996)	41.3 (1996)	3.1	40
Côte d'Ivoire	39	92	6.2	9.0 (1996)	31.2 (1996)	. . .	80
Ethiopia	3	29	3.4	2.9 (1995)[3]	. . .	. . .	. . .
Haiti	23	93	5.0	16.0 (1995)	10.7 (1997)	0.7	30
Lesotho	21	133	5.5	5.4 (1995)	60.1 (1995)	. . .	80
Malawi	13	45	7.8	2.8 (1995)	. . .	1.34 (1998)	. . .
Mozambique	12	67	5.9	. . .	. . .	0.9	50
Namibia	121	499	7.0	29.5 (1997)	168.0 (1997)	0.3	80
South Africa	225	971	8.6	56.3 (1996)	471.8 (1996)	0.8[3]	80
Swaziland	39	143	3.3	15.1 (1996)	. . .	0.7	. . .
Tanzania	12	23	4.4	4.1 (1995)	85.2 (1995)	0.9	. . .
Thailand	69	237	3.7	24 (1995)	87 (1995)	2.0 (1995)	95
Uganda	15	88	5.9	. . .	18.7 (1996)	0.9	70
Zambia	20	44	5.7	6.9 (1995)	113.1 (1995)	. . .	. . .
Zimbabwe	44	142	6.2	13.9 (1995)	128.7 (1995)	0.5	70
Memorandum:							
United Kingdom	1,398	1,384	7.6	180 (2000)	. . .	4.1 (2000)	. . .
United States	4,956	4,956	13.9	279.0 (1995)	972.0 (1996)	3.6 (2000)	. . .

Sources: WHO (2004b); WHO, *Estimates of Health Personnel,* various years; World Bank (2004b); Ministry of Health, South Africa; Ministry of Health, Botswana; country sources; and authors' calculations.

[1]PPP is purchasing power parity (nominal dollars are adjusted for differences in the purchasing power of the dollar in different countries).

[2]Share of the population for which a certain minimum of essential drugs is available within one hour's walk.

[3]Public hospitals only.

services. At exchange rates adjusted for purchasing power differences (called purchasing-power-parity, or PPP, exchange rates), total health expenditure per capita ranges from $23 a year in Tanzania to $971 a year in South Africa, corresponding to between 0.5 and 19.6 percent of U.S. health expenditure per capita (Table 7.4).[18] Although these differences are substantial, the data are likely to understate somewhat the availability of health services to the typical residents of low-income countries compared with those in industrialized countries, for three reasons. First, older people

---

[18]PPP exchange rates also have the advantage that they respond less to short-term fluctuations in the nominal exchange rate. On the other hand, PPP exchange rates are estimated from the prices of a comprehensive bundle of goods and services, which in many cases differ from the goods and services used by the health sector.

generally account for a disproportionate share of health expenditure, and the age distribution of southern African countries is tilted toward the young. Second, the official data are likely to exclude the informal sector (including moonlighting physicians; see Over, Chapter 10 of this volume), which presumably is larger in low-income countries. Third, in the lowest-income countries, those individuals who can afford it may seek treatment abroad; national data would not capture these outlays.

Another difficulty in interpreting the available national data on general access to health services is that health spending may be skewed toward spending in expensive hospital facilities, available only in few major cities and towns, rather than toward basic health services with universal coverage; the aggregate data do not show which of these is the case. However, Gupta, Verhoeven, and Tiongson (2001) find that higher aggregate public health expenditure is associated with better health status for the poor, especially in low-income countries, and Castro-Leal and others (2000) report that although public spending on health care does favor the better-off, it is nevertheless "reasonably progressive," in that inequality in the distribution of benefits is less than that in the distribution of income. However, authors such as Filmer, Hammer, and Pritchett (2000, 2002) highlight the role of provider incentives in the delivery of health services,[19] and they note the possibility of a crowding out of private markets for health care—both issues that are also relevant in the context of HIV/AIDS.

More generally, public health expenditure, in the absence of general access to private health insurance (the case in many low-income countries), provides implicit insurance, and thus mitigates the economic risks associated with sickness.

An alternative indicator of the quality of health services is the availability of skilled staff. The best-trained health workers—physicians—are extremely scarce in the poorest countries in the region. Among the countries covered in Table 7.4 Ethiopia and Malawi are at the bottom of this measure, with about 3 formally trained physicians per 100,000 people, about 1 percent of the level in the United States. However, in the poorer countries a larger range of health services is provided by staff who are not formally qualified as physicians. For example, the ratio of nurses to doctors ranges from 10 to 1 to 20 to 1 in southern African countries, whereas a ratio of 3 or 4 to 1 is more common in industrialized countries.

---

[19]World Bank (2004a) and Over (Chapter 10, this volume) provide a more thorough discussion of some of these issues.

In addition to data on financial and human health resources, Table 7.4 includes two indicators of access to health services. The availability of hospital beds serves as a measure of the availability of health services at the high end. It is also relevant because one of the frequently reported consequences of HIV/AIDS is rising occupancy rates of hospital beds by HIV patients. Although differences between countries on this measure are less pronounced, the *quality* of hospital beds, in terms of the available facilities and services, and in light of the data on health expenditure, is likely to differ substantially across countries. Access to essential medicines (defined as the share of the population for which a minimum of essential drugs are available within one hour's walk; World Bank, 2001) ranges from 30 to 95 percent and is more indicative of the geographical coverage of basic health services. However, limited geographical coverage also translates into higher costs of accessing health care, which creates a barrier to access, especially for the poor.

Impact of HIV/AIDS on the Health Sector

The impact of HIV/AIDS on the health sector and the challenges countries face in implementing their response to the epidemic depend on the scale of the epidemic, but also on the available health resources relative to the scale of the epidemic (Table 7.5).[20] Some inferences can be drawn from the estimated increases in mortality. Although HIV/AIDS reduces the prevalence of certain diseases, since many individuals do not live long enough to be afflicted by those diseases related to old age,[21] the overall health status of the population declines, and the demand for health services expands. Moreover, that demand is likely to increase more than proportionally with the spread of HIV, because it affects primarily individuals of working age, who account for a disproportionate share of health expenditure (see Over, Chapter 10 of this volume). Also, the treatment of AIDS and the opportunistic infections that accompany it tends to be more costly than that of many other common diseases (see, for example, Hansen and others, 2000).

In 5 of the 15 countries covered in Table 7.5, HIV/AIDS accounted for more than half of all deaths in 2000. Following the increase in HIV preva-

---

[20]Also relevant are the available financial resources in the health sector and how these relate to the estimated costs of treatment. This financial dimension is discussed in some detail later in the chapter.

[21]This is a reason why the difference between deaths from all causes and AIDS-related deaths narrows in countries with high HIV prevalence.

Table 7.5. Selected Indicators of the Impact of HIV/AIDS on the Health Sector in Sub-Saharan Africa
(Percent except where stated otherwise)

Country	Mortality, All Ages, 2004		Mortality, All Ages, Projected 2010		Share of Hospital Beds Occupied by HIV Patients, Various Years[1]	Number of AIDS Patients per Physician[2]
	Total	From AIDS	Total	From AIDS		
Botswana	2.9	2.5	2.9	2.6	60–70	156.7
Côte d'Ivoire	1.5	0.4	1.4	0.5	. . .	77.8
Ethiopia	1.5	0.2	1.4	0.3	. . .	151.7
Haiti	1.3	0.3	1.1	0.3	. . .	38.1
Lesotho[3]	1.5	0.6	2.5	1.7	. . .	535.2
Malawi[3]	2.2	1.0	2.4	1.4	30–80	507.1
Mozambique	2.1	0.7	2.2	1.0	30	. . .
Namibia	1.8	1.3	1.9	1.5	. . .	72.2
South Africa	2.0	1.3	2.3	1.6	26–70	38.2
Swaziland[3]	2.0	1.0	3.2	2.4	50–90	257.0
Tanzania	1.7	0.6	1.5	0.5	40–70	214.6
Uganda	1.3	0.3	1.1	0.2	50	. . .
Zambia	2.1	1.0	1.9	0.9	60–80	239.1
Zimbabwe[3]	2.2	1.7	3.2	2.7	50–80	177.0

Sources: U.S. Census Bureau and as noted below.
[1]Estimates obtained from various websites and news agencies.
[2]See text for an explanation of how this indicator has been calculated.
[3]For countries indicated, estimated mortality refers to 2002 rather than 2004, and projections are based on data available in 2002.

lence in many countries over the last several years, mortality rates are expected to rise further: by 2010, HIV/AIDS will account for more than half of all deaths in 11 of the 15 countries covered in Table 7.5.[22]

Table 7.5 also reports two indicators relating the demand for HIV/AIDS-related health services to the available resources. One of these is a frequently reported measure of the impact of HIV/AIDS, namely, the share of hospital beds occupied by patients with HIV/AIDS-related diseases. Especially in the worst-affected countries, hospital occupancy rates may understate the impact on health facilities, because hospitals may operate above capacity yet reported rates do not exceed 100 percent, and because reported rates may mask a deterioration in the overall quality of health services, if hospitals respond to increased demand by rationing. On

---

[22]Since the issue of expanding treatment to HIV patients is discussed just below, it should be noted that, in terms of the health sector response, mortality rates are endogenous. Countries that succeed in rolling out access to antiretroviral treatment—a possibility not included in the above projections—would see a slowdown in the increase in mortality.

the other hand, the numbers reported generally refer to clinical beds; in surgical and pediatric wards the share of HIV patients is lower.

Table 7.5 relates HIV prevalence to the available human resources of the health sector. The indicative estimates of the numbers of AIDS patients per physician are based on the assumption that 10 percent of HIV-positive individuals seek the services of a trained physician. Although this figure is admittedly arbitrary, it is more meaningful than the simple ratio of the number of HIV-positive individuals to physicians, because many infected persons are asymptomatic and do not know they are infected. The estimates illustrate that, in order to expand health services and treatment for HIV patients, it is crucial to overcome the existing shortages in human resources. In only two of the countries with prevalence rates over 20 percent (Namibia and South Africa) is the ratio of HIV patients to doctors lower than 100 to 1. At the other extreme, it exceeds 500 to 1 for Lesotho and Malawi.[23] Looking forward, the number of health personnel required will also depend on (or, if the targets for training and hiring additional staff are missed, constrain) the response to HIV/AIDS. Although successful prevention programs contribute to keeping down the number of people requiring treatment, ongoing efforts to substantially expand access to treatment will also, all else equal, increase the number of patients, mostly because successful antiretroviral treatment extends life expectancy.

By highlighting the existing human resource constraints, Table 7.5 illustrates the potentially severe consequences of increased attrition of health personnel themselves, whether due to higher mortality rates among them or to brain drain. It was shown above, in a more general public sector context, that the implications of increased mortality for the required number of newly trained staff can be substantial. The consequences of increased mortality for the functioning of the health sector are presumably even more severe than for the public service in general, because the demand for health services is increasing sharply at the same time that supply is shrinking.

Especially in countries with very low income per capita (and thus low salary levels), brain drain is another source of losses of qualified personnel. Some of these highly skilled workers may move from one to another of the countries covered in Table 7.5, but others will leave the region altogether. For Zimbabwe, a country ravaged both by HIV/AIDS and by a severe economic crisis, Noguera and others (2003) report that only 18 per-

---

[23]As indicated in Table 7.2, some of the available data on health personnel are almost 10 years old. The lack of timely data obviously introduces a substantial margin of error.

cent of available pharmacist posts at Harare Central Hospital were filled, and that vacancies for nurses ranged from 27 percent (at Harare Central) to 50 percent (at Bulawayo city health clinics). To the extent that the HIV/AIDS epidemic worsens a country's economic prospects and creates poorer working conditions for health personnel, competing demands for health personnel in other, more affluent markets will likely result in further losses of skilled personnel.

Fiscal Effects of an Expanded Effort at Treating HIV/AIDS

The discussion now turns to an assessment of the financial costs of expanding treatment. Most of the earlier literature distinguished between the treatment of opportunistic infections, on the one hand, and antiretroviral treatment, which attacks the virus causing AIDS directly, on the other. The main reason for this dichotomy was that antiretroviral treatment was very expensive: a year's treatment frequently cost several times GDP per capita in countries with severe epidemics, and many times average health spending per capita. Antiretroviral treatment was therefore not considered a viable option for public health services in many low- and middle-income countries. However, prices of antiretroviral treatment have come down markedly in recent years (partly as a result of efforts to broaden access to treatment), and this approach to treatment has therefore become a central component of national and international strategies to fight the epidemic and mitigate its impact. Many countries have started to offer antiretroviral treatment through their public health services. Access remains limited in low- and middle-income countries, however: WHO (2004c) estimates that only 440,000 people in these countries were receiving this form of treatment as of mid-2004.

Opportunistic infections occur as HIV suppresses the immune system and people living with the virus become more susceptible to infections. Some of these diseases, such as tuberculosis, are relatively common even in the absence of HIV/AIDS, but HIV has resulted in a substantial increase in their incidence, both directly, because people living with HIV/AIDS are more likely to become infected, and indirectly, as the resulting higher prevalence of tuberculosis means that more people who are not HIV-positive also get infected.

Various studies have estimated the costs of expanding treatment for opportunistic infections on the basis of case histories of HIV-positive patients and the unit costs of different treatments. One of the more comprehensive studies, that by the World Bank AIDS Campaign Team for Africa (2001), estimates the cost of care for an opportunistic infection and its related symptoms at between $247 and $359 for a low-income country, and between $471 and $698 for the higher-income countries in sub-Saharan Africa. Creese and others (2002) synthesize the studies available at the time of their writing and provide indicators of the cost-effectiveness of various forms of treatment. Hansen and others (2000) assess the costs of treatment of HIV-positive and HIV-negative patients in hospitals and find that the costs per stay were about twice as high for the former. Although the cost per inpatient day did not differ substantially between the two groups, HIV-positive patients stayed longer in the hospital. The most common conditions presented by HIV-positive patients were tuberculosis, pneumonia, and meningitis. Since these are known to be three of the most common opportunistic infections among patients with AIDS, it is likely that most of these infections were for HIV/AIDS-related conditions.

If indeed the costs per inpatient day are similar for HIV-positive and HIV-negative patients, it is possible to draw certain inferences regarding the costs of HIV/AIDS-related treatment from the reported data on hospital occupancy rates by HIV patients, most of whom are presumably being treated for opportunistic infections (see Table 7.5). This would allow one to attribute a certain percentage of the total costs of hospital care to HIV/AIDS. Observed hospital occupancy rates, however, indicate in the first place the impact of HIV/AIDS on limited health sector resources. If a very high proportion of hospital beds are occupied by HIV patients, in the absence of a very substantial increase in the number of beds, this means that hospitals are dealing with the increased demand for their services by rationing, admitting patients only at a later stage of HIV infection than before. Thus the quality of health services declines as existing resources are overwhelmed by increased demand.

Substantial reductions in the price of antiretroviral drugs have opened the door to greatly increased access to highly active antiretroviral therapies (HAARTs): for example, the 3 by 5 initiative of the World Health Organization (WHO) aims to provide HAARTs to 3 million patients by 2005. However, given the limited health resources in many countries and the heavy toll the HIV epidemic is taking on the health sector, increasing access to antiretroviral drugs on this scale poses substantial challenges, in terms of the required financial resources, the available health facilities and distribution channels for medical supplies, and the training of health personnel.

This chapter is concerned with health policy primarily from a fiscal perspective and in the context of the government's overall development objectives. In light of the broad macroeconomic repercussions of rolling out

Table 7.6. Economic Costs and Benefits of Highly Active Antiretroviral Treatment

Costs	Benefits
Drugs	Delay in costs of treatment of opportunistic
Human resources	infections
Health facilities and other infrastructure	Gain in productive capacity of economy
	Increased fiscal revenue
	Favorable indirect and long-term
	macroeconomic effects
	Increased individual welfare

access to antiretroviral treatment (discussed, for example, in Haacker, Chapter 2 of this volume), it is therefore necessary to take a more comprehensive perspective, taking into account the indirect fiscal and macroeconomic consequences. Table 7.6 illustrates the costs and benefits of antiretroviral treatment from a public policy perspective. The costs of treatment are discussed in more detail below; here the focus is on the costs of the drugs themselves, the required health personnel, and the costs of the required infrastructure—for example, distribution systems and medical laboratories. The most direct fiscal effects stem from delays in the need to treat opportunistic infections. However, the fiscal gains go well beyond this. As mortality declines and the loss of skills is mitigated, the productive capacity of the economy is strengthened. Looking further ahead, much of the delayed impact of HIV/AIDS on the economy (for example, through accumulated losses of human capital) is also mitigated. As a consequence, the domestic tax base improves, and so therefore does government revenue. Masha (Chapter 9, this volume), looking at Botswana, suggests that these indirect fiscal gains can offset a significant proportion of the costs of a program to improve access to antiretroviral treatment.

At the most general level, the government has a broad mandate to enhance welfare, and public expenditure is ultimately a means to this end. In the context of HIV/AIDS, some authors (for example, Crafts and Haacker, Chapter 6 of this volume) suggest that the primary effects of HIV/AIDS on welfare derive from increasing mortality rather than changes in income. From a somewhat different angle, the International Crisis Group (2001) emphasizes the impacts of HIV/AIDS on economic risk and security in general.

As the government, possibly with substantial external support (as discussed below), sets out to expand access to antiretroviral treatment, it needs to take into account not only the financial cost of purchasing the drugs, but also the cost of delivering the services: these include the financial costs, the health personnel required, and the necessary infrastructure (laboratories, distribution channels, and so forth). In the wake of substantial reductions in the costs of antiretroviral drugs and the required laboratory tests, widespread access has become a real possibility. In 2001 the Harvard Consensus Statement (Harvard University, Individual Members of the Faculty of, 2001) estimated the total cost per patient of antiretroviral treatment in low-income countries at $1,123, of which $650 was for the drugs themselves (at the average price). WHO estimates the average drug cost of first-line treatment in low-income countries (the average cost of four commonly used combination therapies as of April 2004) at $488 a year. That cost is likely to come down further; for example, WHO (2004a) reports that one form of treatment is now available at a cost of $168 a year, and the Clinton Foundation has developed a program that makes two forms of antiretroviral treatment available at only $140 a year.[24] These first-line treatments are frequently complemented by more expensive second-line treatments, to be used if the first-line treatment fails. As a consequence, the average drug cost for the whole program, including second-line treatments, will be higher.

In estimating the total cost of antiretroviral treatment, it is necessary also to include the cost of monitoring tests, as well as personnel and overhead costs. In addition to the Harvard Consensus Statement, which includes a comprehensive estimate of the cost of treatment, several studies have estimated the total cost of treatment for individual countries.

A study from Zambia (Kombe and Smith, 2003) puts the annual cost per patient at $488 in 2003 (including $277 for drugs and $178 for monitoring tests) and $1,752 for second-line treatment; these numbers exclude most personnel costs, which the study treats in the context of overall human resource constraints. A subsequent study (Kombe and Smith, 2004), reports similar costs of first-line treatment for Uganda of $483 a year. Kombe, Galaty, and Nwagbara (2004) estimate the total annual cost per patient in Nigeria at $742; this estimate includes somewhat higher drug costs than in the Zambia and Uganda studies, as well as $161 in labor costs, which the other two studies excluded.

A study of the cost of antiretroviral treatment in Mexico (Bautista and others, 2003) takes a broader perspective. Focusing on the total utilization of health facilities by patients receiving treatment, both before and after initiation of antiretroviral therapy, this study also captures such indirect effects as declines in the cost of care for opportunistic infections. After ini-

---

[24]This price, however, applies only in the context of a comprehensive program to expand access to treatment. The arrangement is also discussed in more detail below, in the context of changes in the international market for antiretroviral drugs.

tiation of antiretroviral therapy, the cost per patient increased from about $1,000 a year to between $3,000 and $4,000 a year, with drugs accounting for three-fourths. Other cost components, such as the costs of hospitalization and of outpatient visits, did not decline, suggesting that any indirect financial effects associated with improvement in patients' health are small and, even within these line items, offset by the additional requirements of antiretroviral treatment.[25]

Among country policy documents, South Africa's Operational Plan is noteworthy for including very detailed budget estimates. It envisages increasing the number of patients receiving antiretroviral treatment to about 1 million in fiscal year 2007/08, at a cost of 4.5 billion rand, the largest components being the costs of drugs (about one-third), personnel costs (somewhat less than one-fourth), and monitoring tests (close to one-fifth). For fiscal year 2004/05, projected costs per patient are 1,955 rand for drugs, and 806 rand for laboratory tests (about $300 and $125, respectively).

In addition to the costs of drugs and laboratory tests, antiretroviral treatment will place heavy demands on available health personnel. Kombe and Smith (2003) estimate that treating 10,000 patients will require 13 trained physicians, 13 nurses, 32 laboratory technicians, and 15 pharmacists. In this example, achieving full coverage of antiretroviral drugs, with 100,000 patients in the first year and 330,000 patients in the fifth year, would require 130 physicians and 316 technicians in year one, rising to 429 physicians (about 50 percent of Zambia's current physician workforce) and 1,043 technicians (more than twice the number of technicians in Zambia) by year five.

These examples show that a strategy to expand antiretroviral treatment, in addition to securing the financial requirements, needs to be carefully planned in terms of the human resource requirements, identifying potential bottlenecks well in advance and addressing them through training.[26] WHO's 3 by 5 initiative, for example, acknowledges this need and includes a very substantial training component (WHO, 2003b, 2004a). Looking ahead, the number of patients receiving antiretrovirals, for any given cri-

---

[25]This study differentiates between highly active antiretroviral treatment (triple therapy) and simpler forms of antiretroviral treatment (monotherapy and double therapy), which were available earlier. In this chapter, "antiretroviral treatment" refers to highly active antiretroviral treatment.

[26]However, for the poorest of the countries facing severe epidemics, this task is complicated by the potential for brain drain, as trained health personnel are attracted by higher salaries abroad.

Table 7.7. Indicative Estimates of the Costs of HIV/AIDS-Related Health Services
(Percent of GDP except where stated otherwise)

Country	Costs of HIV-Related Health Services, 2010 Total	For antiretroviral treatment	Total Health Expenditure, 2001	Total Health Expenditure, 2001 (dollars per capita)	Public Health Expenditure, 2001	Total Government Expenditure, 2001	Domestic Government Revenue, 2001
Botswana	0.8	0.6	6.6	202	4.4	40.8	41.9
Côte d'Ivoire	1.4	1.0	6.2	39	1.0	16.6	17.0
Ethiopia	9.7	7.0	3.6	3	1.5	29.1	18.8
Haiti	0.8	0.6	5.0	23	2.7	10.0	...
Lesotho	3.8	2.8	5.5	21	4.3	43.0	40.8
Malawi	7.8	5.7	7.8	13	2.7	33.1	18.4
Mozambique	6.6	4.8	5.9	12	4.0	34.6	13.3
Namibia	1.4	1.0	7.0	121	4.7	30.1	31.9
South Africa	0.6	0.4	8.6	225	3.6	26.8	24.3
Swaziland	1.3	1.0	3.3	39	2.3	30.7	26.9
Tanzania	2.5	1.8	4.4	12	2.1	16.1	11.4
Uganda	2.2	1.6	5.9	15	3.4	19.8	10.9
Zambia	3.9	2.8	5.7	20	3.0	32.1	19.1
Zimbabwe	3.3	2.4	6.2	44	2.8	37.6	27.1

Sources: WHO (2004a); IMF World Economic Outlook/Economic Trends in Africa database; and author's estimates.

teria for starting antiretroviral therapy, will increase sharply over the first years of the program.

At the onset of antiretroviral therapy, the health status of the patient typically improves markedly, making him or her less susceptible to opportunistic infections such as tuberculosis and cryptococcal meningitis. This will result in some savings in treatment costs, both directly and indirectly through reduced spread of these infections. These financial gains, however, are likely to taper off, because antiretroviral treatment only delays rather than halts the progression of the disease.

Table 7.7 provides some indicative estimates of the financial resource requirements for expanding the treatment of opportunistic infections and improving access to antiretroviral treatment. Actual coverage rates for the different forms of treatment presumably differ among these countries, as does the ability of each country's health services to expand medical care. The purpose of the table, however, is to compare the financial implications of attaining a given standard of health care. The estimated costs are therefore based on a coverage rate for the care for opportunistic infections of 10 percent in 2003, rising to 50 percent by 2010. For antiretroviral treatment it is assumed that the number of patients receiving the treatment through public health services is negligible in 2003 and that coverage rises to 50 percent by 2010. (These assumptions regarding coverage rates are similar to those made by the Commission on Macroeconomics and Health (2001), which assumes that, by 2015, coverage rates will rise to 70 percent for treatment of opportunistic infections, from an initial 10 percent, and to 65 percent for antiretroviral treatment, from less than 1 percent.) Patients are assumed to receive treatment for opportunistic infections for the two years before death. Antiretroviral treatment starts at the same time but extends life (and thus delays the period through which patients need treatment for opportunistic infections) by an additional three years. The assumed cost of treatment of opportunistic infections is $400; the cost of antiretroviral treatment is assumed to fall to $450 by 2010; this is consistent with drug costs of around $150 and personnel and other costs of $300. This approach may understate the costs for some countries with higher income per capita (such as Botswana and South Africa) covered in the table, relative to the lower-income countries, for two reasons.

First, about one-fourth to one-third of the costs of expanded access to treatment are commonly attributed to personnel costs. These can be expected to be higher in countries where average income is higher. In the absence of wage data, one way of accommodating this in the estimates is to assume that personnel costs are proportional to income per capita. However, income per capita also depends on many other factors, including the size of the formal sector; therefore, simply scaling up wage rates for health personnel in line with income per capita does not necessarily yield more reliable results. It is also worth noting that the estimated cost of treatment in the Operational Plan for South Africa (the country with the highest income per capita in Table 7.7), discussed above, is not much higher than for the other countries for which detailed estimates were available. Although this could also reflect differences in methodologies, it suggests that the bias introduced may not be large.

Second, to obtain consistent indicators for the challenges countries are facing as they expand access to treatment, the estimates presented here are based on coverage rates that are equal across countries. Because lower-income countries generally find it more difficult to achieve these targets, the result may be lower coverage rates in these countries. (Over, in Chapter 10 of this volume, discusses the challenges to expanding antiretroviral treatment in more detail.) As a result, the gap in actual health expenditure as a percentage of GDP (rather than expenditure required to achieve uniform coverage rates) may turn out to be lower.

Table 7.7 summarizes estimates of the costs of attaining the specified targets in coverage rates of treatment of opportunistic infections and antiretroviral treatment. The latter accounts for the bulk of expenditure (around three-fourths in most countries), because increased life expectancy owing to antiretroviral treatment means that a larger number of patients will receive this form of treatment.[27] Overall, the costs are substantial for all the countries covered in the table, ranging from 0.6 percent to 9.7 percent of GDP. These differences in cost stated as a percentage of GDP partly reflect differences in income per capita. Therefore, two of the countries with very high HIV prevalence, Botswana and South Africa, are among those that could conceivably finance substantially expanded access to treatment. However, even for these countries the financial burden is daunting, corresponding in South Africa to 17 percent of the health budget and over 2 percent of total government expenditure in 2001. On the other hand, the required expenditure exceeds 5 percent of GDP for three countries (Ethiopia, Malawi, and Mozambique) and exceeds total public health expenditure (as a percentage of GDP in 2001) for these and four other countries (Côte d'Ivoire, Tanzania, Zambia, and Zimbabwe).

A key obstacle to an enhanced response to HIV/AIDS is existing capacity constraints, the most serious of which relate to the shortage of human resources.[28] Even if sufficient financing were available, a shortage of trained personnel could mean that the available funds would not be spent, or that they would not be spent effectively because the quality of the program is compromised. UNAIDS (2003b), in its Progress Report on the Global Response to the HIV/AIDS Epidemic, reports that in one-third of the countries covered a lack of human resources hampered the response to HIV/AIDS. For Botswana and South Africa, which are among the wealthiest countries in sub-Saharan Africa and have relatively well-developed health sectors (see Table 7.4), the report notes that "[in Botswana] the shortfall in human resources has become a major concern" and that the "main challenge [in South Africa] to implementation relates to capacity, especially with respect to health workers' clinical skills." For the same reasons, WHO's strategic framework for the 3 by 5 initiative, which aims at substantially improving access to antiretroviral treatment, stresses the

---

[27]For example, if 0.5 percent of the population start antiretroviral treatment each year (at our target coverage rate of 50 percent, consistent with an overall prevalence rate of around 10 percent, or a prevalence rate for the working-age population of about 20 percent, as for example in Namibia or South Africa), our assumptions mean that about 2.5 percent of the population will eventually receive treatment. Treatment for opportunistic infections, which may or may not be concurrent with antiretroviral treatment, last two years, and, at coverage rates of 50 percent, only 1 percent of the population would receive it.

[28]A point also made by the Commission on Macroeconomics and Health (2001, p. 50).

need for additional financial resources for health systems in general, improvements in the physical infrastructure, programs to address the increased mortality and morbidity of health workers, improved procurement and distribution systems, and measures to stimulate demand through community mobilization (WHO, 2003a).

Education

The public education sector is one of the focal points of a broad policy response to HIV/AIDS, primarily reflecting the role of education in prevention. More generally, "education is a major engine of economic and social development" (World Bank, 2002), and it relates directly or indirectly to several of the Millennium Development Goals. From a macroeconomic perspective, education and the accumulation of human capital are a key ingredient to achieving sustainable growth (as discussed in more detail in Birdsall and Hamoudi, Chapter 4 of this volume). In countries afflicted by HIV/AIDS, however, the capacity of the education sector is weakened through increased teacher mortality. On the other hand, HIV/AIDS also results in lower birthrates and increased child mortality, so that the number of children (and thus the demand for education) grows more slowly. Finally, orphans and children living in households affected by HIV can find their access to education impaired; public policy has a role in mitigating the adverse consequences of HIV/AIDS for these children.

Education contributes to HIV/AIDS prevention in two major ways. First, education in general facilitates access to information, thus contributing to HIV prevention while also raising health standards and improving living conditions. By reducing girls' economic dependency, education can also reduce their vulnerability to HIV/AIDS. Second, public education is an important channel for delivering HIV prevention efforts to young people, promoting lower-risk sexual behavior, and thus avoiding HIV infections as young people become sexually active. Using an existing infrastructure (the public education system) also lowers the cost of these efforts.[29] However, the role of public education in HIV prevention also reinforces the need to ensure access to education for children affected by HIV/AIDS.

---

[29]World Bank (2002) provides a thorough discussion of the role of public education in HIV prevention.

Table 7.8. Zimbabwe: New Teachers Required to Maintain Given Pupil-Teacher Ratios

Year	Total	Number of New Teachers Required			Increase in New Teachers Required (percent)	Number of New Teachers Required as Percent of Graduates		Increase in Share of Graduates Becoming Teachers (percent)
		In presence of AIDS		In absence of AIDS		In presence of AIDS	In absence of AIDS	
		As replacements for AIDS deaths	For other causes					
2005	6,655	3,452	3,204	5,478	21.5	2.1	1.6	29.0
2010	6,695	3,610	3,085	6,227	7.5	2.3	1.8	23.2
2015	6,507	3,401	3,105	6,837	−4.8	2.6	2.1	22.3

Source: Author's calculations using U.S. Census Bureau estimates of mortality rates for 2003.

Maintaining a Sufficient Number of Teachers

While the increased mortality of teachers means that more teachers need to be trained to replace those lost to HIV/AIDS, HIV/AIDS also affects birth rates and infant mortality, thereby reducing the size of the school-age population. To estimate this impact, numerous studies have assessed the change due to HIV/AIDS in the number of new teachers who need to be trained in order to maintain some given pupil-teacher ratio (see, for example, Malaney, 2000; and Birdsall and Hamoudi, Chapter 4 of this volume). Table 7.8 shows the results of such an exercise for Zimbabwe.[30] By 2005 the number of new teachers required rises from 5,478 to 6,655, or 21.5 percent. More than half of these teachers (3,452) would replace teachers who have died for HIV/AIDS-related reasons. However, the number of new teachers who do not replace those who have died of AIDS, reflecting the slowdown in the young population, declines very substantially (to 3,204, a decline of about 40 percent). By 2015, as the school-age population stagnates, the number of new teachers required actually declines by 5 percent, despite much higher teacher mortality, compared with projections excluding the impact of HIV/AIDS.

---

[30]The calculations are based on demographic projections from the International Programs Center at the U.S. Census Bureau and on data on the numbers of pupils and teachers in primary and secondary education from UNESCO's *World Education Report 2000* (UNESCO, 2001; see also Haacker, 2002). In the absence of HIV/AIDS, teacher attrition rates are assumed to be 5 percent. Although these are lower than the attrition rates frequently reported, the latter are gross rates (excluding teachers who are rehired), whereas the analysis here is interested in net attrition.

These results match estimates from other studies, indicating that the impact of HIV/AIDS on the number of new teachers required is small and may actually decline. This is no source of comfort, however. Fewer students also means that the pool from which new teachers are drawn shrinks. Although, in the example above, the absolute number of teachers who need to be trained in 2015 declines by 4.8 percent, their share of the population at age 19 (roughly the population from which new teachers are drawn) increases from 2.1 percent to 2.6 percent (by no means all of whom would have the required educational background), or by 22.3 percent. Thus, in order to meet the need for teachers, an increasing share of educated individuals would have to become teachers, leaving fewer skilled people to work in other sectors of the economy. Moreover, the earlier discussion of the disruptions to public services caused by increased mortality and morbidity applies to teachers as well. Increased absenteeism among teachers and a larger number of vacancies in teacher positions would imply that a constant pupil-teacher ratio would actually signify a decline in the quality of education. This problem is probably most relevant for rural and small local schools, where, as noted previously, the loss or sickness of a teacher cannot be temporarily covered by colleagues.

Securing Access to Education

HIV/AIDS can impede access to education for children living in affected households and for orphans. Households with sick members are likely to suffer income losses, either directly, if household members are too sick to work, or indirectly, if other household members divert time from other productive activities to the care of sick relatives. If these households can no longer afford to send children to school, or if children have to contribute to household income or help care for sick relatives, their access to education is compromised. Orphans are likely to be even worse off, because they tend to live in poorer households and may suffer discrimination in favor of the head of household's biological children.[31]

Table 7.9 sheds some light on the impact of HIV/AIDS on children in seven African countries. HIV/AIDS has increased the number of orphans substantially in all of these countries: in several, about one-sixth of the

---

[31]For an in-depth study focusing on South Africa, see Case, Pakson, and Ableidinger (2002).

Table 7.9. Orphans in Selected Sub-Saharan African Countries

Country	Orphans as Share of Young Population, 2003 (in Percent)[1]		Average Dependency Ratio[2]		Ratio of Orphans to Nonorphan Children Attending School
	All orphans	AIDS orphans	Households with orphans	Households with children but no orphans	
Botswana	15.1	10.6	1.4	1.7	0.99
Côte d'Ivoire	13.3	6.2	1.4	1.5	0.83
Ethiopia	13.2	3.4	1.5	1.6	0.60
Malawi	17.5	8.7	1.5	2.0	0.93
South Africa	10.3	4.5	1.4	1.7	0.95
Uganda	14.6	7.5	1.7	2.3	0.95
Zimbabwe	17.6	13.5	1.4	2.2	0.85

Sources: UNAIDS/UNICEF/USAID (2004); and UNICEF (2003).
[1]Children are defined as persons aged 0–17.
[2]Number of dependents of all ages divided by the number of working-age adults in the household.

child population were orphans in 2001, more than half of whom were AIDS orphans. Reflecting increasing mortality among adults, the share of orphans is expected to rise further in some of the worst-affected countries, to more than 20 percent by 2005 in Botswana and Zimbabwe. Estimated increases in dependency ratios suggest that orphans frequently live in lower-income households. For example, the dependency ratios for Zimbabwe (1.4 for nonorphan households with children, 2.2 for orphan households) suggest that income per capita among households with orphans may be 20 percent lower than among other households with children.[32] Among the countries covered, the difference in school enrollment rates between orphans and nonorphans ranges from a rather low 1 percentage point in Botswana to 40 percentage points in Ethiopia. In general, countries with high enrollment rates overall (which tend to be those countries whose education systems cover a substantial proportion of the poor) show small declines in enrollment rates for orphans.

Although the impact of orphanhood on school enrollment seems to be smallest in countries with universal or near-universal education, some microeconomic evidence suggests that income and wealth have an important role in mitigating the adverse effects on orphans, and that financial assistance can have a highly favorable impact on orphans' enrollment rates. For example, data reported by Ainsworth, Beegle, and Koda (2002)

---

[32]This assumes that the share of income earners among working-age household members, and their incomes, do not differ systematically between the two groups of households.

suggest that enrollment rates among orphans living in households receiving financial assistance were much higher than among orphans outside of such households. For single-parent orphans, enrollment rates were 20 percentage points higher with financial assistance, whereas for orphans who had lost both parents the difference was close to 50 percentage points.[33]

Thus, to protect access to education in general and to mitigate the impact of HIV/AIDS on the life prospects of orphans, governments face three challenges. First, they need to minimize the disruptions to education caused by increased absenteeism and mortality, especially in rural areas. Second, they need to ensure that a sufficient number of teachers are trained to compensate for increased attrition. Third, they need to set up support mechanisms (such as subsidies to school fees) to offset orphans' disadvantages in access to education. As the preceding section showed, this generally means that although the *absolute* number of teachers trained may not have to increase (because the number of pupils declines at the same time), an increasing *share* of graduates will have to become teachers. Casual observation might suggest that failure to meet the third objective would facilitate meeting the other two. This apparent trade-off, however, is shortsighted: even though a declining enrollment rate might make it easier to meet a given targeted pupil-teacher ratio, it also means that the number of children receiving an adequate education—the key output of the education sector—would decline. The number of educated people (and thus the pool from which teachers are drawn) would shrink, and the share of graduates who would have to become teachers to achieve target enrollment rates would increase.

In several countries with severe epidemics, the orphan population is projected to increase to more than 15 or even 20 percent of the young population (ages 0 to 17) by 2010. Securing unimpeded access to education for orphans can therefore represent a significant logistical and fiscal challenge. Consequently, national governments (see, for example, Botswana's National Strategic Framework on HIV/AIDS), international agencies like UNAIDS, and bilateral donors (as evident, for example, from the first round of grants under the U.S. President's Emergency Plan for AIDS Relief, or PEPFAR) have made programs to improve the situation of orphans a key component of their policy frameworks on HIV/AIDS.

---

[33]The numbers for nonorphans, paternal orphans, maternal orphans, and two-parent (full) orphans are 57.3, 49.0, 47.1, and 25.6 percent enrolled without financial assistance, and 62.0, 68.3, 70.8, and 73.2 percent enrolled with financial assistance, respectively (Ainsworth, Beegle, and Koda, 2002).

Social Expenditure

The categories of social expenditure most directly affected by HIV/AIDS are public health expenditure (interpreted as a form of social insurance), spending targeted at orphans (including income support and subsidies for school fees), and various forms of income support for other affected persons. This paper will touch on only the most important issues (Chapter 8 of this volume, by Plamondon, Cichon, and Annycke, provides a more comprehensive discussion, including coverage rates of social insurance schemes in the worst-affected countries and a quantitative assessment). Especially in countries where health insurance coverage is low, public health expenditure, discussed above, plays an important role in mitigating the economic burden of disease on the affected households. However, as HIV/AIDS weakens and eventually kills a household's income earners, or as other household members have to reallocate time to their care, household income declines and some of the remainder must be diverted to cover the costs of care and treatment. The loss of family members dying for HIV/AIDS-related reasons has further implications for poverty, as assessed by Greener (Chapter 5, this volume). Thus outlays related to social assistance schemes for poor households are likely to rise. Because it primarily strikes young adults, HIV/AIDS is associated with an increase in the number of orphans, as already discussed; they are particularly vulnerable because even a temporary episode of poverty can compromise their access to education. The government may also operate social insurance schemes providing pensions or lump-sum benefits for the elderly, surviving dependents, or disabled persons. Because most of these schemes are contributory, so that HIV/AIDS affects revenue as well as expenditure, pension schemes are covered separately below.

Coverage of formal, contributory social security schemes in most countries facing severe epidemics is limited, but some provide various forms of income support from the general budget. For example, in Botswana residents over age 65 are entitled to a monthly pension of 151 pula (about $30), and in South Africa male residents over age 65 and female residents over 60 are entitled to a means-tested pension of up to 640 rand (about $100) a month (for details see U.S. Social Security Administration Office of Policy, 2003). With fewer residents reaching old age, the cost of public income support to the elderly declines, but the fiscal cost of disability benefits rises: for example, South Africa's pension is also extended to the permanently disabled. More-comprehensive social security programs are generally contributory, which implies that often they are accessible to permanent employees in the public and formal private sectors only. However,

HIV/AIDS affects the number of poor households, so that social expenditure targeted at the poor, such as destitution allowances or any form of means-tested grants, is likely to rise.

Orphans are likely to experience at least temporary hardship during the sickness of their parents or other household members, and their access to education can be impaired if they have to care for sick relatives or are discriminated against in their foster families.[34] For these reasons UNAIDS and major donors have included orphan support as one of the focal points of their comprehensive HIV/AIDS programs (see Table 7.2). Having already discussed the impact of HIV/AIDS on orphans in some detail, in the context of access to education, this discussion will merely add some notes from a social policy perspective. First, universal access to education is a powerful weapon for fighting poverty in general. Since the decline in orphans' enrollment rates tends to be lowest in countries with high overall enrollment (indicative of an education system that is accessible to the disadvantaged segments of the population), such systems are also likely to be more effective at keeping orphans in school. However, orphans are also likely to experience a decline in their material living standards. Case, Paxson, and Ableidinger (2002), for example, provide evidence on this score from South Africa, which is also supported by the available data on dependency ratios in orphan versus nonorphan households (Table 7.9). Given the large numbers of children being orphaned by HIV/AIDS, mitigating the impact on their living standards and securing their access to education will become the key challenge for social policy in countries with severe epidemics, if it is not already.

Pension Schemes

Pension schemes encompass many different institutional arrangements, some operated directly by the government, and others operating independently but with some government oversight and a government guarantee, explicit or implicit, of the pension fund's obligations.[35] Coverage may

---

[34]Case, Paxson, and Ableidinger (2002, abstract) "find that orphans in Africa on average live in poorer households than non-orphans, and are significantly less likely than non-orphans to be enrolled in school. However, orphans' lower school enrollment is not explained by their poverty: orphans are equally less likely to be enrolled in school relative both to non-orphans as a group and to the non-orphans with whom they live."

[35]For a survey of social security issues in sub-Saharan Africa, see Barbone and Sanchez (1999). The most comprehensive and up-to-date survey of existing pension arrangements is U.S. Social Security Administration, Office of Policy (2003).

extend to government employees only, or to the private sector, or to the general public. Although increased mortality results in a decline in the number of recipients of old-age pensions, outlays on pensions for surviving dependents (the spouse and any under-age children) may increase. Quantitatively, the impact of HIV/AIDS on pensions can amount to a very substantial proportion of the cost of the epidemic.[36] JTK Associates (2002) finds that, to accommodate the impact of HIV/AIDS, contributions to the Swazi public employee pension fund would have to increase by between 2 and 4 percent of the government's payroll. Since the pension fund is contributory, the costs of HIV/AIDS may accrue either to the government, through increased contributions to the pension fund from general revenue, or to government employees, through increased contributions or reduced benefits.

A distinction is commonly made between defined-benefit pension schemes and defined-contribution schemes (the latter including provident funds). Pension benefits under a defined-benefit scheme are typically calculated using a formula based on the duration of contributions and on the contributor's salary or contribution level during his or her last years of work. Because benefits are not tightly linked to accumulated contributions, such schemes are more vulnerable to the demographic shifts associated with HIV/AIDS. In addition to old-age pensions and survivor benefits, defined-benefit schemes typically provide disability benefits, funeral grants, or other death-related lump-sum benefits. Outlays on these benefits are strongly affected by HIV/AIDS, because they rise essentially proportionally with HIV prevalence or mortality.

Under a defined-contribution scheme, participants' contributions are credited, after certain deductions, to their individual accounts within the scheme. At retirement, participants are entitled to receive back their accumulated contributions plus accrued interest, either as a lump sum or as an annuity. If the participant dies before retirement, the accumulated amount is paid out to the heirs. Most defined-contribution schemes also include some elements of defined-benefit schemes, for example to cover the risks of death in service and of disability. The costs of these risk benefits, as well as a share of administrative costs, are subtracted from the contributions. As a consequence, either the accumulated amount available at retirement is smaller than it would be without these benefits (see, for example, Sanlam, 2004), or contribution rates must be adjusted upward to pay for the

---

[36]This is discussed in some detail in Haacker (Chapter 2, this volume), in the context of the private sector.

benefits. Increased HIV/AIDS-related mortality has little impact on participants' balances under a defined-contribution scheme, because all contributions (net of administrative costs and any risk benefits) credited to any individual account are eventually paid out.[37] However, with increased mortality the total funds administered by the scheme are likely to decline, as contributors (or their surviving dependents) tend to withdraw their accumulated balances earlier than they would have otherwise.

Assessing the net financial impact of HIV/AIDS on the costs of pensions is a complex undertaking. Although fewer contributors reach retirement age and draw retirement pensions, those dying of HIV/AIDS often leave behind young spouses (who may be infected as well) and dependent children, who may be eligible for survivors' pensions. A full quantitative analysis would require complex demographic modeling and therefore is beyond the scope of this chapter. Among the more detailed studies extant, Plamondon, Cichon, and Annycke (Chapter 8, this volume), using a hypothetical example of a country in sub-Saharan Africa, find that HIV/AIDS raises pension outlays by 0.5 percent of GDP by 2015 (from 1.7 percent of GDP without AIDS to 2.2 percent, or by 29 percent). This reflects a 16 percent decline in the number of old-age pensioners, offset by increases in the numbers of disability pensioners (by 64 percent), widows (also by 54 percent), and orphans (which almost treble). The net impact on the fiscal balance or required social security contributions would depend on whether the contributor base remains unchanged (because workers dying of AIDS are replaced) or shrinks. The study examines scenarios along both lines.

Government Revenue and the Financing of Health Expenditure

HIV/AIDS affects domestic government revenue through its adverse effects on the macroeconomy and thus the tax base. Fiscal policy needs to take these changes into account, both in terms of the medium-term fiscal framework and in the context of resource mobilization in the fight against HIV/AIDS. The first part of this section therefore discusses some of the implications of HIV/AIDS for domestic government revenue. In light of the key role of the health sector in mitigating the impact of the epidemic,

---

[37]However, if the quality of the pension fund's portfolio is low, increased mortality would drain the funds available for such investments and could accelerate the pension fund's eventual insolvency. If the government, explicitly or implicitly, guarantees the obligations of the pension fund, it may have to bail the fund out, at a considerable cost.

and the substantial role of private and external financing, the second part provides a more detailed discussion of the financing of health expenditure. External grants, an important source of health financing in low-income countries, are considered in the context of the international response in the next section of the chapter.

Domestic Government Revenue

Essentially all macroeconomic studies of countries with severe HIV epidemics agree that GDP growth will slow, leaving GDP substantially lower than what might have been expected before the epidemic escalated.[38] As a consequence, growth in the domestic tax base, and thus in domestic government revenue, also slows, complicating the government's efforts to cope with the increased demand that the epidemic places on its services. As the present discounted value of tax revenue declines, it also becomes more difficult to service a given level of public debt.[39]

The components of domestic revenue most likely to be adversely affected by HIV/AIDS are income taxes and import duties. Corporate income tax revenue declines as increased expenses for training, medical and death-related benefits, and lower employee productivity raise personnel costs for a given level of output. To the extent that companies can pass on these costs to their employees (by cutting benefits or salaries), this will result, all else equal, in a decline in personal income tax revenue. Import duties decline to the extent that the increased demand for health services causes imported medical products, which tend to have reduced or even zero tariff rates, to crowd out other imports on which full duties are paid. Privately financed health expenditure is particularly likely to have such an effect. The government could respond by mobilizing additional resources, for example by raising taxes. Zimbabwe, for example, financed increasing HIV/AIDS-related expenditure through a 3 percent surcharge on payroll taxes, earmarked toward an HIV/AIDS fund. However, in light of the substantial burden of HIV/AIDS on the private sector, the scope for raising additional revenue from this source is limited.

For many countries in sub-Saharan Africa, royalties from various forms of resource extraction (such as oil, minerals, and timber) account for a large share of domestic revenue. There are reasons to believe that these

---

[38]The macroeconomic impact of HIV/AIDS is discussed in much more detail in Haacker (Chapter 2, this volume).

[39]In a different context, Easterly (2001) suggests that failure to respond to the growth slowdown after 1975 was an important cause of the debt crises of the 1980s and 1990s.

activities may be less vulnerable to the HIV epidemic. One reason is simply that a large share of the sector's value added derives from economic rents on the extracted resources rather than from labor. Second, large-scale resource extraction is often conducted by multinational firms, who bring in expatriates to staff key positions and are thus less vulnerable to HIV/AIDS-related shortages in the supply of certain skills; their high value added per employee may also make it profitable for these firms to provide expensive medical treatment to key employees. Third, if these companies pay comparatively high wages to employees with lower skills, they will be able to replace employees lost to HIV/AIDS relatively easily. However, these companies, too, face disruptions to production associated with increased attrition, and, for permanent employees, higher coverage rates of various forms of benefits (medical, pension, and other) mean that the impact on personnel costs is relatively high.

With respect to health expenditure, patient contributions provide another potential source of domestic financing. However, the still-substantial cost of antiretroviral treatment relative to most households' incomes means that high co-payments will effectively exclude poor households from treatment. To achieve equitable access to treatment, co-payments would have to be means-tested, adding to the administrative costs of the program. More broadly, in countries without a well-functioning private insurance sector, public health services are an essential element of social insurance, and substantial user fees would add to the economic costs of HIV/AIDS for the affected households.

Financing of Health Expenditure

Table 7.10 summarizes available information on the financing of health expenditure in some countries affected by HIV/AIDS. In principle, health expenditure can be financed from government general revenue, public social insurance, external grants, or private insurance, or directly by the individuals or households affected.

The share of public expenditure in total health expenditure varies considerably across African countries, from 16 percent in Côte d'Ivoire to 79 percent in Lesotho. Virtually all public health expenditure is financed by either taxation or external resources; with the exception of Thailand, public health insurance does not play a significant role in any of the countries covered. Especially for countries with relatively low income per capita, external assistance is an important source of financing; in Malawi it accounts for fully 87 percent of public health expenditure, and 41 percent of total health expenditure.

Table 7.10. Financing of Health Services in Selected HIV/AIDS-Affected Countries, 2001

Country	Total Financing		Public Financing as Percent of Total	Public Excluding External Resources as Percent of Public Expenditure	All private as percent of total financing	Private Financing			
						Out of pocket			Prepaid as percent of private expenditure
	Per capita (dollars)	Percent of GDP				Percent of total financing	Percent of private expenditure		
Botswana	202	6.6	66.2	0.6	33.8	11.9	35.3		64.7
Brazil	222	7.6	41.6	1.2	58.4	37.4	64.1		35.9
Côte d'Ivoire	39	6.2	16.0	20.0	84.0	75.3	89.7		10.3
Ethiopia	3	3.6	40.5	84.7	59.5	50.4	84.7		15.3
Haiti	23	5.0	53.4	80.3	46.6	21.1	45.3		54.7
Lesotho	21	5.5	78.9	7.6	21.1	21.1	100.0		0.0
Malawi	13	7.8	35.0	75.7	65.0	28.4	43.7		56.3
Mozambique	12	5.9	67.4	54.7	32.6	12.8	39.3		60.7
Namibia	121	7.0	67.8	5.6	32.2	5.8	17.9		82.1
South Africa	225	8.6	41.4	1.0	58.6	13.0	22.1		77.9
Swaziland	39	3.3	68.5	11.5	31.5	31.5	100.0		0.0
Tanzania	12	4.4	46.7	63.2	53.3	44.3	83.1		16.9
Thailand	69	3.7	57.1[1]	0.2	42.9	36.5	85.0		15.0
Uganda	15	5.9	57.5	43.1	42.5	22.7	53.4		46.6
Zambia	20	5.7	53.1	91.7	46.9	33.7	71.8		28.2
Zimbabwe	44	6.2	45.3	17.2	54.7	28.6	52.2		47.8

Source: WHO (2004b).

[1]Includes 26.8 percent of total public health expenditure financed by the social security system.

Although some African countries with large shares of private health expenditure feature some form of private health insurance, in many the share of private out-of-pocket health expenditure is high by international standards, especially as a proportion of total private health expenditure. This likely reflects the relatively minor role of private health insurance in many low-income countries. Correspondingly, for Botswana, Namibia, South Africa, and Zimbabwe—countries with a relatively well-developed insurance sector—private out-of-pocket health expenditure is less of a factor. In some countries the lack of private health insurance appears to be compensated by public health expenditure.

Detailed data like those presented in Table 7.10 are not available for the financing of HIV/AIDS-related health expenditure specifically. However, Martin (2003) analyzes the financing of HIV/AIDS-related public expenditure in Botswana, Lesotho, Mozambique, South Africa, and Swaziland.[40] Her findings show that the role of external finance for HIV/AIDS-related expenditure is even more pronounced than that for general health expenditure. With the exception of South Africa, which receives very little external aid, external financing accounted for between 79 and 85 percent of HIV/AIDS-related public expenditures in these countries.

External Finance and the International Response

External finance plays a very important role in the financing of HIV/AIDS-related expenditure, but the fiscal implications of the international response to HIV/AIDS are much broader. Most important, changes in the international market for drugs have facilitated the import of cheaper generic versions of patented drugs for countries facing a health emergency. Partly as a response to these developments, a regulated market for generic versions of antiretroviral drugs is emerging, with the aim of making these drugs available to low-income countries at the lowest possible cost. As a consequence, the emphasis of the international response has broadened from an early focus on prevention to a strategy that includes substantially expanded access to antiretroviral treatment.

At the same time, international donors—governments, multilateral organizations, and nongovernmental organizations (NGOs)—have substantially increased their funding of HIV/AIDS-related projects. Complementing the above discussion of the financing of health expenditure at

---

[40]The study also covers Zimbabwe, but data on HIV/AIDS-related expenditure were not available for this country.

the country level, this section will therefore look at global trends in the financing of HIV/AIDS-related expenditure. The management of substantial aid flows, whether they go through the budget or are directly disbursed to NGOs working in the affected countries, poses challenges to the host government and the donor agencies. For example, the activities of the various government agencies and NGOs need to be coordinated, or else the country's limited human resources may be overwhelmed. (The macroeconomic impact of large aid flows on the current account is discussed in Chapter 2 of this volume.) Looking ahead, there is the potential for a "maturity" mismatch between expenditure and its funding: whereas grants are typically short-term (although often with the expectation that they will be renewed) and may be subject to delays in disbursement, HIV/AIDS-related spending—especially investments in treatment—involves longer-term financial commitments.

Changes in the International Market for Antiretroviral Drugs

In 2001 the TRIPs (Trade-Related Aspects of Intellectual Property Rights) agreement of the Doha round of World Trade Organization negotiations formalized trade rules governing patented goods. This is highly relevant for the international market in pharmaceutical products: because research and development costs in the pharmaceutical industry are high, companies can only recover these costs by charging sizable markups over production costs while the products are under patent. Importantly in the context of HIV/AIDS, the TRIPs agreement formalized rules whereby a country facing a public health emergency could grant a "compulsory license," requiring a foreign pharmaceutical firm to license a domestic producer to produce generic versions of its patented medicines for domestic consumption. However, many African countries do not have any domestic pharmaceutical industry to speak of. Partly reflecting growing international concern over the escalating HIV/AIDS crisis, the agreement was therefore subsequently extended to allow countries without domestic production capabilities to import generic versions of patented drugs.

Besides opening the door to the import of generic drugs to combat AIDS, this option also improves the bargaining power of countries facing HIV epidemics when negotiating with the original producers of the drugs. Major reductions in the prices of antiretroviral drugs have already been achieved by individual agreements between pharmaceutical companies—the patent holders or producers of generic versions—and governments of affected countries.

However, changes in the international market for antiretroviral drugs, together with the associated fall in the prices of these drugs for developing countries, have resulted in and are being reinforced by the emergence of a more regulated market, in which NGOs or government agencies act as intermediaries. For example, the Clinton Foundation has established a program that aims to reach 2 million people in four African and several Caribbean countries by 2008. It was able to secure low prices for some types of antiretroviral treatment (about $140 a year) by securing the commitment of the participating countries to substantially roll out antiretroviral drug treatment programs, and by helping to raise funds to cover the costs of the program. The companies involved were able to reduce the price of the drugs because the program guarantees the drug makers a high and predictable volume of sales, and because the arrangement allows companies to save on marketing and distribution costs.[41] Other major initiatives, including PEPFAR, which have a broader HIV/AIDS agenda, also involve bulk purchases of antiretroviral drugs.

Global Financing of HIV/AIDS-Related Expenditure

HIV/AIDS-related spending and funding have increased sharply over the last several years. Estimates of household spending on HIV/AIDS are available for only a few countries (and, where available, are frequently based on small samples). Therefore most of the available data relate to spending by national governments or to sources of financing. Such institutional spending has risen considerably over the last several years for low- and middle-income countries, from about $300 million in 1996 to $4.2 billion in 2003 (see Summers and Kates, 2003). Accounting for most of these increases are increases in national spending (from $20 million in 1996 to $1.0 billion in 2003) and in bilateral grants (from $160 million to $2.0 billion over the same period). The largest contributor at present is the United States, which today accounts for about 20 percent of global funding.

The patterns of financing differ very substantially across regions and countries. According to the HIV/AIDS national accounts published by the Regional AIDS Initiative for Latin America and the Caribbean (SIDALAC), external finance plays a relatively minor role in the Latin America and Caribbean region, accounting for only 1.7 percent of total funding,

---

[41]WHO (2004a, p. 25) suggests, however, that the guarantees that participating countries or programs need to provide to benefit from this low price are "difficult to provide given the relatively small size of their antiretroviral treatment programmes and uncertainty about long-term funding."

Table 7.11. Estimated Funding for HIV/AIDS Spending in Low-Income Countries by Source, 2003

Source	Millions of Dollars
Total	4,232
U.S. government bilateral	852
Other government bilateral	1,163
Global Fund[1]	547
U.N. agencies	350
World Bank[2]	120
Foundations and other NGOs	200
Governments of affected countries	1,000

Source: Summers and Kates (2003).
[1]HIV/AIDS spending only.
[2]Grant component of concessional loans.

whereas the domestic public sector accounts for 84.6 percent of HIV/AIDS spending.[42] In sub-Saharan Africa, although data are available for only a few countries, it seems clear that external finance is the most important source of funding.[43] For example, Martin (2003) estimates that external finance accounted for between 79 and 85 percent of all HIV/AIDS spending in Botswana, Lesotho, Mozambique, South Africa, and Swaziland in 2002. UNAIDS (2004b) reports that external financing in Ghana accounted for 74 and 59 percent of all HIV/AIDS-related expenditure in that country in 2002 and 2003, respectively.

Summers and Kates (2003) estimate that total HIV/AIDS-related funding in low-income countries, excluding private health expenditure, amounted to $4.2 billion in 2003 (Table 7.11). This estimate was based on budget allocations for HIV/AIDS-related grants. Actual disbursements on HIV/AIDS-related activities were somewhat lower, because not all the budgeted grants were disbursed in 2003. As a consequence, Summers and Kates's estimates are about $600 million higher than those provided by UNAIDS (2004b).[44] The largest discrepancies between funding and spending relate to the activities of the Global Fund to Fight AIDS, Tuberculosis, and Malaria, contributions to which are counted as funding, whereas grant

---

[42]Data from UNAIDS (2004b). More detailed data are available on SIDALAC's website, www.sidalac.org.mx.

[43]The most notable exception is South Africa, which does not receive substantial amounts in external grants, because of its relatively high income per capita.

[44]UNAIDS (2004b) estimates total expenditure of $4.7 billion, including $2.1 billion from within-country sources (unlike the Summers and Kates data, these include private expenditure). Excluding within-country sources from both sets of estimates yields expenditures of $3.2 billion and $2.6 billion, respectively.

disbursements are counted as spending. Since the Global Fund disbursed only about 17 percent of what it received in that year, there is a discrepancy of about $400 million.[45] Similar discrepancies can and commonly do arise as bilateral grants that are pledged are not disbursed, either because the recipient does not meet some formal condition attached to the grant, or because capacity constraints prevent the recipient from implementing the funded project.

UNAIDS (2004b) estimates, on the basis of existing funding commitments, the emergence of major new multilateral and bilateral donors (such as the Global Fund and PEPFAR, respectively), and current trends, that HIV/AIDS funding in low- and middle-income countries will increase to just over $8 billion in 2005 and about $10 billion in 2007. Reflecting the important and growing role of the Global Fund (which received $1.4 billion in contributions in 2003) and PEPFAR (which may provide up to $15 billion over five years), multilateral and bilateral sources account for most of this increase.[46] The largest share of these resources (43 percent) will be needed in sub-Saharan Africa. However, even this lion's share is much lower than the region's share of people living with HIV/AIDS worldwide: sub-Saharan Africa is home to 66 percent of all HIV-positive individuals worldwide. This discrepancy may reflect the fact that expenditure on prevention is spread more evenly across countries than expenditure on care and treatment, that unit costs for some interventions are lower in Africa than in other regions (in line with its lower income per capita), or that the expansion of services in Africa is impeded by capacity constraints in the short run.

These estimates can be compared against projections of global resource needs (UNAIDS, 2004b) of $11.6 billion in 2005 (as discussed in some detail above; see Table 7.2), and $19.9 billion in 2007. The WHO's 3 by 5 initiative, which is more narrowly geared toward medical interventions (palliative care, treatment of opportunistic infections, and antiretroviral treatment account for about 70 percent of total costs), is estimated to cost between $3.1 billion and $3.8 billion, depending primarily on what prices are assumed for the various forms of antiretroviral treatment used (see Gutierrez and others, 2004). Now somewhat outdated in terms of its finan-

---

[45]The low ratio of disbursements to receipts largely reflects the fact that the Global Fund typically commits its funds over several years and is only starting operations. Grants committed accounted for 80 percent of contributions received in 2003, according to the Global Fund's financial statements (Global Fund to Fight AIDS, Tuberculosis, and Malaria, 2004).

[46]For a more comprehensive profile of PEPFAR and the Global Fund, see UNAIDS (2004b).

cial projections, but still very valuable for its broad assessment of the link-ages between macroeconomics and health and its articulation of a broader strategy for investment in health for human development, is the study by the Commission on Macroeconomics and Health (2001). That study esti-mated that an additional $14 billion would be needed by 2007, and around $22 billion by 2015, to scale up the response to HIV/AIDS in 83 low- and middle-income countries.

By all these accounts, the amounts available to fund the response to HIV/AIDS fall well short of the projected resource needs. According to the estimates by UNAIDS, the projected gap between resource needs and avail-able resources amounts to $3.3 billion in 2005—a shortfall of about 30 percent. On the basis of current commitments and funding trends, UNAIDS projects that this gap will grow, both in absolute and in relative terms, to $9.7 billion by 2007.

In the absence of increased funding, this emerging (and, according to current projections, growing) resource gap will raise serious political and ethical questions. The most immediate is one of rationing: what will be the appropriate mix of interventions if the required levels of funding are not attained? It may turn out that some countries are successful in planning and implementing a comprehensive response to HIV/AIDS, and attract sufficient funding, while others fail to overcome obstacles to an expanded response. Since countries with a well-functioning health infrastructure in place and a broader human resource base are in a better position to imple-ment such a program, allocating HIV/AIDS funds primarily according to medical criteria could intensify existing inequities between countries, in terms of access to health care and key development indicators such as life expectancy. Rationing can also affect inequities within countries, if, for example, treatment for HIV patients is offered only at a limited number of health facilities located primarily in urban areas. On the other hand, avail-ability of funding may prove not to be the binding constraint to expand-ing access to treatment, if only a limited share of the population seeks HIV/AIDS-related services, such as voluntary counseling and testing, and the uptake of treatment remains low.

Managing HIV/AIDS-Related Aid Flows

As the global response to HIV/AIDS unfolds, many countries will expe-rience substantial increases in health and other HIV/AIDS-related expen-ditures, largely financed by external grants. For some countries, especially those with very low income per capita, the additional requirements for an adequate response to HIV/AIDS exceed current health expenditure. This means that health services need to be expanded very rapidly in order to achieve significant coverage rates for treatment and other HIV/AIDS-related interventions. Challenges to the government include formulating a comprehensive strategy that optimizes the allocation of HIV/AIDS-related funds and is consistent with overall health and development objectives, and coordinating the activities and programs of various donors and implementing agencies—public sector, private sector, and NGOs.[47]

Managing this substantial and rapid increase in health services and coordinating among the various government agencies, donors, and implementing agencies and NGOs poses a difficult challenge. However, many countries affected by HIV/AIDS already start from a situation in which public health services and health facilities operated by various NGOs coexist, and external grants play a key role in enhancing the quality and expanding the geographical coverage of their health services. As external grants are used to strengthen existing health services eroded by increased HIV/AIDS-related demand, to make treatment available to more patients (often using existing health facilities), or to increase the availability of health services, this will strengthen these countries' mixed system of health facilities operated by the government, NGOs, and private providers. Depending on the national strategy on HIV/AIDS or donor objectives, however, the mix of public and private providers may change. (Bennett and Fairbank, 2003, also stress the impact on procurement and distribution of drugs and related commodities.)

There is a need for coordination at the national level—among the government, donors, implementing agencies and NGOs, and civil society—to ensure that the national response to HIV/AIDS is consistent with overall health and development objectives, and to avoid duplication of activities. By developing a strategic framework, the various participants can ensure that the response to HIV/AIDS is adequate at all levels and that the available funds are allocated optimally. Close coordination between the various agencies and civil society would also enhance accountability and complement the oversight and financial control mechanisms of the government and donors.

One area where potential trade-offs exist is the often-limited availability of trained personnel.[48] As the international response has evolved to include

---

[47]Bennett and Fairbank (2003) provide a thorough assessment of the health "system-wide effects of the Global Fund to Fight AIDS, Tuberculosis, and Malaria." Although their discussion goes beyond HIV/AIDS-related activities, the issues they raise apply directly to the discussion here.

[48]On the issues raised in this paragraph, see also Over (Chapter 10, this volume).

substantially enhanced access to antiretroviral treatment, and as this has increasingly become financially possible, major initiatives to expand access to treatment have addressed the lack of human resources in two ways. The first is by developing forms of treatment that minimize the demands on highly trained health personnel. The second is by focusing on training and retaining a sufficient number of health personnel to achieve targets for increased access to treatment (see, for example, WHO, 2003a, 2003b).[49] Especially for countries with relatively low income per capita, this may also involve increasing salaries for health personnel, to reduce brain drain and absenteeism. Nevertheless, the expected increase in the demand for qualified health personnel is substantial, and the government, in cooperation with the various donors and implementing agencies, needs to ensure that increases in HIV/AIDS-related health services do not create bottlenecks elsewhere. Although trade-offs in the allocation of a given number of health personnel exist in the very short run, they can be resolved in the longer run. Major initiatives like the WHO's 3 by 5 initiative, as well as many country proposals submitted to the Global Fund, include provisions for the training of additional health personnel. To the extent that this training is synchronized with the expansion of HIV/AIDS-related services, there will be no adverse effect on other areas of health service provision.

For health services that are largely financed by grants, the sustainability of financing—and thus, in many cases, of the funded services—is an issue. Establishing new health services often implies a political commitment on the part of the government, which cannot easily be reversed should funding dry up. (For example, the closure of hospitals is often a hotly contested political issue.) Outside the HIV/AIDS context, many grants finance investments in infrastructure, with government bearing some of the investment costs and all the operating costs. For these grants (provided that the government decides that it can sustain the operating costs), sustainability is less of an issue, since the time frame of the grant is similar to that of the project, and delays in disbursements can frequently be accommodated simply by delaying the project. HIV/AIDS-related grants, however, are primarily applied to the current costs of programs, and increased access to treatment—treatment that is cost intensive in terms of medical supplies and human resources—will reinforce this trend. Once these health services are established, scaling them down in response to shortfalls in aid flows would be very difficult, not to mention undesirable from a

---

[49]Over (Chapter 10, this volume) provides a thorough discussion of the changes in the demand for and supply of health services.

public health perspective, and would leave the government financially and politically vulnerable.

Impact of HIV/AIDS in the Longer Run

There are three key areas in which an assessment of the impact of and the response to HIV/AIDS highlights fundamentally different challenges in the longer run. One is that coping and prevention strategies are less affected in the longer run by preexisting capacity constraints. Whereas the emphasis in the short run is on optimizing the response given institutional, physical, and social constraints, in the longer run these constraints are endogenous. Another is that most of the analysis of the adverse impact of HIV/AIDS focuses on the disruptions caused by HIV/AIDS-related morbidity and mortality. However, some of the impact of HIV/AIDS may accumulate over time. Examples include the effects of HIV/AIDS on institutional memory, discussed above, and the implications for investments in physical and human capital. The third is the indirect effect on the fiscal balance of the government's response to HIV/AIDS, if it succeeds in bringing down HIV prevalence and mitigating the macroeconomic impact.

The government's response to HIV/AIDS is subject to financial constraints and existing capacity constraints, both in terms of human resources and in terms of physical infrastructure. For example, with trained health personnel in short supply, a given increase in health spending may fail to achieve a commensurate increase in health services coverage. Strategies to improve access to treatment for HIV patients, in addition to the financing of drugs, therefore emphasize investments in health personnel and facilities. The WHO's 3 by 5 initiative, for example, includes a strong training component.

Most of the literature on the economic and developmental impact of HIV/AIDS, whether on the macroeconomy, on the public service, on the private sector, or on households, focuses on current disruptions caused by increased mortality and morbidity. However, much of the adverse impact of HIV/AIDS may become evident only in the longer run. One example, discussed above, is institutional memory. An institution may be able to accommodate the loss of an additional 2 or 3 percent of its staff in a given year, replacing them through internal reassignments or newly recruited staff with similar skills. Replacing an additional 25 percent of its staff over 10 years, however, may prove much more difficult and damaging to the organization's efficiency, as institutional memory is weakened and the range and depth of the staff's experience deteriorate.

To the extent that the government succeeds in reducing HIV prevalence rates and mitigating the macroeconomic effects, the fiscal balance will improve. For example, reduced HIV prevalence results in lower personnel costs, reduced health expenditure, and reduced social outlays. It will also mitigate the slowdown in GDP growth, and thus in the growth of the domestic tax base. Masha (Chapter 9, this volume) shows that a sound HIV/AIDS policy framework can yield both savings on some types of HIV/AIDS-related expenditure and improvements in domestic revenue, which can offset a significant proportion of the costs of implementing the framework. These gains, however, derive largely from reduced mortality and morbidity. Thus, given the long time it takes for preventive measures to reduce the incidence of HIV infection, these financial gains have little impact in the short run. Yet even though the macroeconomic effects do not appear immediately, including a macroeconomic assessment in a policy framework on HIV/AIDS can help in informing the choice of policy targets.

Conclusions

HIV/AIDS poses a huge challenge to governments facing severe epidemics. Even as the demand for certain categories of public services (most importantly, health services) increases substantially, the capacities of governments to cope with the epidemic are eroded, in part because of increased mortality and morbidity among government employees. The analysis in this chapter shows that the impact of HIV/AIDS on government employees goes far beyond the disruptions and increased costs associated with increased attrition owing to HIV/AIDS. As mortality among young adults increases, the age composition of the civil service changes. Fewer public servants survive to an age when they might normally be candidates for higher managerial positions; as a result, some of these positions must be filled with less qualified or less experienced people, and the quality of decision making is likely to deteriorate.

The most visible impact of HIV/AIDS on governments' operations has been on health services and expenditures. With antiretroviral treatment initially out of reach for all but a few AIDS victims, the emphasis in the health sector was on palliative care and the treatment of opportunistic infections. The existing health services had insufficient capacity to cope with the increased demand, and health facilities responded by reducing access to care for less urgent medical conditions. Following the dramatic decline in the prices of antiretroviral treatment, and with financial support from the international community, much of the emphasis has shifted toward improving access to that treatment. Given the still-limited availability of health personnel and the toll that HIV/AIDS is taking on government employees, providing antiretroviral treatment in a way that makes the most efficient use of trained staff is an integral part of the approach.

Grants from international and bilateral donors play a critical role in the financing of HIV/AIDS-related expenditure. UNAIDS estimates that, in 2003, more than three-fourths of public expenditure on HIV/AIDS in developing countries worldwide (including the activities of NGOs) was financed by external grants. Thus a government that presents to potential international donors a sound policy framework for fighting the epidemic and mitigating its impact may be able to cover most of its costs through grants. However, such grants typically finance only those expenditures that directly relate to HIV/AIDS. Most of the more indirect costs of HIV/AIDS—increasing personnel costs, rising social expenditure, and a decline in domestic revenue as the tax base is eroded—would still be covered by the government from its own resources, and the analysis in this chapter has shown that these costs can be substantial.

The analysis presented here grew out of the experience of providing economic policy advice in countries facing severe HIV/AIDS epidemics. Considering the impact of and the response to HIV/AIDS from a fiscal policy perspective is important for a variety of reasons. First, in countries with severe epidemics, HIV/AIDS affects all areas of public services and the domestic tax base, and it forces substantial increases in spending in some services. In these circumstances, one simply cannot conduct responsible fiscal policy without taking into account the broad impact of HIV/AIDS on government employees and the budget. Second, efforts to fight the epidemic and mitigate its impact have important consequences for the budget and the management of public services, in the form of increased expenditure, increases in required personnel, and the need to coordinate the activities of international donors. Finally, a successful HIV/AIDS policy, by reducing the number of new infections and improving the health status of people living with HIV, can mitigate the impact of HIV/AIDS on the economy as a whole, and thus soften the impact on public services and the government budget.

References

Ainsworth, Martha, Kathleen Beegle, and Godlike Koda, 2002, "The Impact of Adult Mortality on Primary School Enrolment in Northwestern Tanzania," Africa Region Human Development Working Paper (Washington: World Bank).

Barbone, Luca, and Luis-Alvaro Sanchez B., 1999, "Pensions and Social Security in Sub-Saharan Africa: Issues and Options," World Bank Africa Region Working Paper No. 4 (Washington: World Bank).

Barnett, Tony, and Alan Whiteside, 2002, *AIDS in the Twenty-First Century—Disease and Globalization* (Basingstoke, United Kingdom, and New York: Palgrave Macmillan).

Bautista, Sergio Antonio, and others, 2003, "Costing of HIV/AIDS Treatment in Mexico" (Bethesda, Maryland: Abt Associates).

Bennett, Sara, and Alan Fairbank, 2003, "The System-Wide Effects of the Global Fund to Fight AIDS, Tuberculosis, and Malaria: A Conceptual Framework" (Bethesda, Maryland: Abt Associates).

Botswana National AIDS Coordinating Agency, 2003, *Botswana National Strategic Framework for HIV /AIDS 2003–09* (Gaborone, Botswana).

Braimah, Samuel D., 2004, "HIV/AIDS and the Public Sector" (unpublished; Durban, South Africa: Health Economics and HIV/AIDS Research Unit, University of KwaZulu Natal).

Case, Anne, Christina Paxson, and Joseph Ableidinger, 2002, "Orphans in Africa," NBER Working Paper No. 9213 (Cambridge, Massachusetts: National Bureau of Economic Research).

Castro-Leal, Florencia, and others, 2000, "Public Spending on Health Care in Africa: Do the Poor Benefit?" *Bulletin of the World Health Organization,* Vol. 78, No. 1, pp. 66–74.

Commission on Macroeconomics and Health, 2001, "Macroeconomics and Health: Investing in Health for Economic Development" (Geneva: World Health Organization).

Creese, Andrew, Katherine Floyd, Anita Alban, and Lorna Guinness, 2002, "Cost-Effectiveness of HIV/AIDS Interventions in Africa: A Systematic Review of the Evidence," *The Lancet,* Vol. 359, pp. 1635–42.

Easterly, William R., 2001, "Growth Implosions and Debt Explosions: Do Growth Slowdowns Cause Public Debt Crises?" *Contributions to Macroeconomics,* Vol. 1, No. 1.

Filmer, Deon, Jeffrey Hammer, and Lant Pritchett, 2000, "Health Policy in Poor Countries: Weak Links in the Chain," Policy Research Working Paper No. 1874 (Washington: World Bank).

———, 2002, "Weak Links in the Chain II—A Prescription for Health Policy in Poor Countries," *World Bank Research Observer,* Vol. 17, No. 1, pp. 47–66.

Global Fund to Fight AIDS, Tuberculosis, and Malaria, 2004, *Annual Report 2003* (Geneva).

Global HIV Prevention Group, 2003, "Access to HIV Prevention—Closing the Gap" (Seattle, Washington, and Washington, D.C.: Bill and Melinda Gates Foundation and Kaiser Family Foundation).

Government of Malawi and United Nations Development Programme (UNDP), 2002, "The Impact of HIV/AIDS on Human Resource in the Malawi Public Sector" (Lilongwe, Malawi).

Government of the Republic of South Africa, 2003, "Operational Plan for Comprehensive HIV and AIDS Care, Management and Treatment for South Africa" (Pretoria).

Grassly, Nicolas C., and others, 2003, "The Economic Impact of HIV/AIDS on the Education Sector in Zambia," *AIDS*, Vol. 17, No. 7, pp. 1039–44.

Gupta, Sanjeev, Marijn Verhoeven, and Erwin Tiongson, 2001, "Public Spending on Health Care and the Poor," IMF Working Paper No. 01/127 (Washington: International Monetary Fund).

Gutierrez, Juan Pablo, and others, 2004, "Achieving the WHO/UNAIDS Antiretroviral Treatment 3 by 5 Goal: What Will It Cost?" *The Lancet*, Vol. 364, pp. 63–64.

Haacker, Markus, 2002, "The Economic Consequences of HIV/AIDS in Southern Africa," IMF Working Paper 02/38 (Washington: International Monetary Fund).

Hansen, Kristian, and others, 2000, "The Costs of HIV/AIDS Care at Government Hospitals in Zimbabwe," *Health Policy and Planning*, Vol. 15, No. 4, pp. 432–40.

Harvard University, Individual Members of the Faculty of, 2001, "Consensus Statement on Antiretroviral Treatment for AIDS in Poor Countries" (Cambridge, Massachusetts: Harvard University).

International Crisis Group, 2001, "HIV/AIDS as a Security Issue" (Washington and Brussels).

Joint United Nations Programme on HIV/AIDS (UNAIDS), 2002, *Report on the Global HIV/AIDS Epidemic* (Geneva).

———, 2003a, "Report on the State of HIV/AIDS Financing (Revised/Updated June 2003)" (Geneva).

———, 2003b, "Progress Report on the Global Response to the HIV/AIDS Epidemic" (Geneva).

———, 2004a, *2004 Report on the Global HIV/AIDS Epidemic* (Geneva).

———, 2004b, "Financing the Expanded Response to AIDS—July 2004" (Geneva).

Joint United Nations Programme on HIV/AIDS (UNAIDS), United Nations Children's Fund (UNICEF), and U.S. Agency for International Development (USAID), 2004, "Children on the Brink 2004" (Geneva, New York, and Washington).

JTK Associates, 2002, "The Impact of HIV/AIDS on the Central Agencies of the Government of Swaziland" (Mbabane, Swaziland).

Kombe, Gilbert, David Galaty, and Chizoba Nwagbara, 2004, "Scaling Up Antiretroviral Treatment in the Public Sector in Nigeria: A Comprehensive Analysis of Resource Requirements" (Bethesda, Maryland: Abt Associates).

Kombe, Gilbert, and Owen Smith, 2003, "The Costs of Anti-Retroviral Treatment in Zambia" (Bethesda, Maryland: Abt Associates).

———, 2004, "Emerging Issues in Implementing Antiretroviral Treatment in Sub-Saharan Africa: Evidence from Zambia and Uganda," paper presented at the conference of the International AIDS Economics Network, Bangkok.

Malaney, Pia, 2000, "The Impact of HIV/AIDS on the Education Sector in Southern Africa," CAER II Discussion Paper No. 81 (Cambridge, Massachusetts: Harvard Institute for International Development).

Martin, H. Gayle, 2003, "A Comparative Analysis of the Financing of HIV/AIDS Programmes in Botswana, Lesotho, Mozambique, South Africa, Swaziland, and Zimbabwe" (Pretoria, South Africa: Human Sciences Research Council).

Noguera, Marilyn, and others, 2003, "Zimbabwe: Antiretroviral Therapy Program: Issues and Opportunities for Initiation and Expansion" (Arlington, Virginia: DELIVER, John Snow Inc.).

Opuni, Marjorie, and Stefano Bertozzi, 2003, "Financing HIV/AIDS Prevention and Care in Low- and Middle- Income Countries (September 2003)." Available via the Internet: hivinsite.ucsf.edu/InSite.

Rosen, Sydney, and others, 2004, The Cost of HIV/AIDS to Businesses in Southern Africa," AIDS, Vol. 18, pp. 317–24.

Sanlam, 2004, "The 2004 Sanlam Survey on Retirement Benefits" (Bellville, South Africa).

Simon, John, and others, 2000, "The Response of African Businesses to HIV/AIDS," in Commonwealth Secretariat, HIV/AIDS in the Commonwealth 2000/01 (London: Kensington Publications).

Steinberg, Malcolm, and others, 2002, "Hitting Home: How Households Cope with the Impact of the HIV/AIDS Epidemic" (Washington: Kaiser Family Foundation).

Stover, John, Lori Bollinger, and Katharine Cooper-Arnold, 2003, "Goals Model for Estimating the Effects of Resource Allocation Decisions on the Achievement of the Goals of the HIV/AIDS Strategic plan (Version 3.0)" (Glastonbury, Connecticut and Washington: The Futures Group International).

Summers, Todd, and Jennifer Kates, 2003, "Global Funding for HIV/AIDS in Resource Poor Settings" (Washington: Kaiser Family Foundation).

Topouzis, Daphne, 2003, "Addressing the Impact of HIV/AIDS on Ministries of Agriculture: Focus on Eastern and Southern Africa" (Geneva and Rome: UNAIDS and FAO).

United Nations Children's Fund (UNICEF), 2003, "Africa's Orphaned Generation" (New York).

United Nations Educational, Scientific, and Cultural Organization (UNESCO), 2001, World Education Report 2000 (Paris).

United States Social Security Administration, Office of Policy, 2003, "Social Security Programs Throughout the World: Africa, 2003" (Washington).

World Bank, 2001, World Development Indicators 2001 (Washington).

———, 2002, "Education and AIDS—A Window of Hope" (Washington).

———, 2003, "HIV/AIDS in Central America: An Overview of the Epidemic and Priorities for Intervention" (Washington).

———, 2004a, World Development Report 2004: Making Services Work for Poor People (Washington).

———, 2004b, World Development Indicators 2004 (Washington).

World Bank AIDS Campaign Team for Africa, 2001, "Costs of Scaling HIV Program Activities to a National Level in Sub-Saharan Africa: Methods and Estimates" (Washington).

World Health Organization (WHO), 2003a, "Treating 3 Million by 2005—Making It Happen: The WHO Strategy" (Geneva).

———, 2003b, "Scaling up Antiretroviral Treatment in Resource-Limited Settings: Making It Happen" (Geneva).

———, 2004a, "Investing in a Comprehensive Health Sector Response to HIV/AIDS—Scaling up Treatment and Accelerating Prevention" (Geneva).

———, 2004b, *World Health Report 2004* (Geneva).

———, 2004c, "3 by 5 Progress Report—December 2003 Through June 2004" (Geneva).

8

Financial Effects of HIV/AIDS on National Social Protection Schemes

PIERRE PLAMONDON, MICHAEL CICHON, AND PASCAL ANNYCKE

Through its demographic and economic effects, the HIV/AIDS pandemic poses a huge challenge to the financial management of national social protection systems. For example, increased mortality owing to HIV/AIDS may reduce the number of contributors to pension schemes. And although the share of contributors reaching retirement age declines, the number of surviving dependents entitled to benefits increases. At the same time, the demand for health services increases. Using a simplified social budget model, this chapter tries to assess the potential financial effects of HIV/AIDS on national social protection schemes.

The institutional arrangements and coverage of social insurance schemes differ substantially across developing countries, and often only a small proportion of the population is covered by formal schemes. The chapter therefore begins with an overview of social protection arrangements and coverage in low-income developing countries. The next section discusses the demographic and economic impact of HIV/AIDS, using the hypothetical case of a country ("Demoland") hard hit by HIV/AIDS. The concluding section assesses the impacts of HIV/AIDS on different elements of social protection schemes, on the social budget, and on the fiscal balance.

Social Protection Arrangements and Coverage in Developing Countries

Formal public social protection systems cover only a minority of the population in developing countries, particularly in Africa. Typically, such

Table 8.1. Total Public Social Expenditure by Major Function in Six World Regions, 1990–93
(Percent of GDP)

Region	Total Expenditure	Pensions	Health Care	Other
All countries	14.5	6.6	4.9	3.0
Africa	4.3	1.4	1.7	1.2
Asia	6.4	3.0	2.7	0.7
Europe	24.8	12.1	6.3	6.4
Latin America and Caribbean	8.8	2.1	2.8	3.9
North America	16.6	7.1	7.5	2.0
Oceania	16.1	4.9	5.6	5.6

Sources: International Labour Organization (1999 and forthcoming).

protection in developing countries (that is, transfers organized by the state or by social partners) consists of pension schemes for formal sector workers, public health care systems, and a variety of other benefits of lesser financial importance.

Health care systems in developing countries are built around state delivery systems, which are often co-financed by out-of-pocket co-payments by patients at the point of delivery. As regards pensions, the majority of countries follow the social insurance approach, but four countries in Africa—Botswana, Mauritius, Namibia, and South Africa—have noncontributory pension schemes. Means-tested antipoverty benefits are rather rare and mostly of an ad hoc nature.

The availability of data is notoriously bad. Table 8.1 describes in highly aggregated fashion the composition of overall national social protection expenditure in the major regions of the world. In the early 1990s pension and health expenditure accounted for more than 70 percent of total social expenditure in most regions. Africa spends considerably less on social protection than the other regions. In Africa, where ratios of total public expenditure to GDP have been substantially lower, and fiscal deficits higher, than in other regions, the percentage of public expenditure going into the social protection sector also appears to be lower than elsewhere.[1] There is little reason to believe that the situation has changed markedly over the last decade, but no recent comprehensive data exist.[2]

---

[1] See World Bank (2000, Table 14).

[2] The data situation on social expenditure will improve when the International Labour Organization resumes its inquiry into the cost of social security in 2004 or 2005.

Data on coverage are even scantier than data on expenditure. The following subsections describe what little is known about the level of coverage in the two main expenditure items in national social budgets.

Health Care Coverage

In principle, most developing countries provide health services to their citizens through a network of public sector delivery units, such as health centers, dispensaries, and government hospitals. The existence of such facilities, however, does not necessarily mean that people enjoy meaningful access to basic health services. Access may be compromised by
- lack of facilities or services in a given region,
- large distances separating people from the nearest health care delivery facility,
- poor quality of care in the nearest facility or facilities, or
- high user charges that constitute a barrier to access for the poor.

Again, internationally comparable indicators on access to care are few. Access to and quality of care can generally be estimated only indirectly. Table 8.2 provides some basic statistics on ratios of health care staff to population in Africa and compares them with ratios in the United Kingdom, the United States, and Germany. The United Kingdom can be regarded as providing a "lean" health service by industrial country standards, and Germany's as an amply staffed service, with that of the United States somewhere in between.

Table 8.2 shows that, with a few notable exceptions, the staffing ratio (the number of health care staff per 100,000 people) in Africa is typically less than 10 percent of the U.K. ratio. This can be interpreted in one of two ways: either access to care is dramatically worse for virtually all of the population in most African countries than in Europe, or access meets or approaches European levels for some in these countries but a large proportion of the population have no access at all. Most likely the figures reflect a combination of the two. However, there are indications that a substantial proportion of the population in many African countries do not seek help from health professionals in the event of illness (Table 8.3). This fact indicates the existence of either physical or monetary barriers to access.

It is hard to predict how the understaffed and underfunded health systems of developing countries will be affected by increasing HIV infection rates.[3] If capacity utilization is already at its limit, and cannot be expanded

---

[3]See Over (Chapter 10, this volume) for a more detailed discussion of the impact of HIV/AIDS on health systems.

Table 8.2. Staffing Ratios in National Health Care Systems in Selected African and Comparator Countries in the Mid-1990s
(Personnel per 100,000 population except where otherwise stated)[1]

Country	Year	Physicians	Nurses	Midwives	Dentists	Pharma-cists	Total	Total (percent of U.K. level)
Benin	1995	5.7	20.4	7.9	0.3	...	34.3	4.3
Burkina Faso	1995	3.4	19.6	3.4	0.3	...	26.7	3.3
Cameroon	1996	7.4	36.7	0.5	0.4	...	45.0	5.6
Cape Verde	1996	17.1	55.6	...	1.5	...	74.2	9.2
Central African Rep.	1995	3.5	8.8	4.9	0.2	...	17.4	2.2
Chad	1994	3.3	14.7	2.3	0.2	...	20.5	2.6
Côte d'Ivoire	1996	9.0	31.2	15.0	...	...	55.2	6.9
Eritrea	1996	3.0	16.0	2.2	0.1	...	21.3	2.7
Ghana	1996	6.2	72	53.2	0.2	...	131.6	16.4
Guinea	1995	13	55.7	5.2	...	...	73.9	9.2
Kenya	1995	13.2	90.1	...	2.2	...	105.5	13.1
Lesotho	1995	5.4	60.1	47	0.5	...	113	14.1
Liberia	1997	2.3	5.9	4.3	0.1	...	12.6	1.6
Mali	1994	4.7	13.1	3	0.1	...	20.9	2.6
Namibia	1997	29.5	168	116.5	4	...	318	39.6
Niger	1997	3.5	22.9	5.5	0.2	...	32.1	4.0
Nigeria	1992	18.5	66.1	52.4	2.6	...	139.6	17.4
Senegal	1995	7.5	22.1	6.6	1.2	...	37.4	4.7
Somalia	1997	4	20	...	0.2	0.1	24.3	3.0
South Africa	1996	56.3	471.8	...	17.8	...	545.9	68.0
Togo	1995	7.6	29.7	10.4	0.7	...	48.4	6.0
Zimbabwe	1995	13.9	128.7	28.1	1.3		172	21.4
Memorandum:								
United Kingdom	1993	164	497	43.3	39.8	58.2	802.3	100.0
Germany	1998	350	957	11.3	75.9	57.7	1,451.9	181.0
United States	1995	279	972	...	59.8	...	1,310.8	163.4

Source: World Health Organization Statistical Information System (WHOSIS).
[1]Numbers may not sum to totals because of rounding.

quickly, the new demand due to increased morbidity cannot be accommodated. In this case, there will be no impact on the cost of delivery systems—people will simply go uncared for. However, in light of the increased demand for HIV/AIDS-related health services and a crowding out of other health services, the system will most likely try to adjust, by requiring fresh public resources, seeking external funding, or diverting resources from other purposes.

Pension Coverage

Social insurance schemes in developing countries, where they exist, typically provide pensions and short-term cash benefits. Pensions are generally of much greater financial importance in the long run. The share of the

Table 8.3. Indicators of the Utilization of Care in Selected Sub-Saharan African Countries in the Mid-1990s
(Percent)

Country and Income Quintile	Share of Persons Reporting Illness During Past 4 Weeks	Care Sought by Persons Reporting Illness			
		None	Modern (public)	Modern (private)	Other, including traditional
Côte d' Ivoire					
Poorest	30	73	26	1	0
Richest	50	35	55	10	0
Ghana					
Poorest	33	59	23	14	4
Richest	58	43	28	24	5
Guinea					
Poorest	24	60	15	0	25
Richest	32	31	52	6	11
Madagascar					
Poorest	20	72	20	3	5
Richest	34	52	29	16	3
South Africa					
Poorest	12	25	46	23	6
Richest	26	14	9	74	3
Tanzania					
Poorest	12	42	37	17	4
Richest	22	27	32	39	2

Source: Castro-Leal and others (2000).

labor force that contributes to social insurance schemes is typically very low, because the informal sector is large and most social security institutions have difficulty enforcing the legally required contributions. Moreover, coverage of the formal labor force is high only in countries where the public sector dominates formal employment.

Figures for the early 1990s (Barbone and Sanchez, 1999) show that, in many African countries, fewer than 10 percent of the labor force are covered by national pension systems (Table 8.4). More recent data (for 1998) reveal that the coverage of social security schemes was only 19.4 percent in Kenya, 12.5 percent in Zambia, and 9.6 percent in Ghana (Baruti, 2003), levels that are very low when one considers that these three countries have some of the best organized social security systems in sub-Saharan Africa.

Public pension arrangements vary greatly in Africa, ranging from social insurance schemes to provident funds to social assistance schemes. In some countries the only existing pension scheme applies to state employees, and sometimes only a subset of those. As Table 8.5 shows, the majority of old-age pension arrangements are based on the social insurance

Table 8.4. Coverage of Formal Pension Systems in Selected Sub-Saharan African Countries
(Percent)

Country	Year	Covered Wage Bill as Fraction of GDP	Contributors as Share of Labor Force
Burundi	1993	5	3.3
Cameroon	1993	5.5	13.7
Côte d'Ivoire	1989	11	9.3
Ghana	1993	5.7	7.2
Kenya	1993	6.8	25
Madagascar	1993	...	5.4
Mali	1990	...	2.5
Niger	1992	5	1.3
Senegal	1992	...	6.9
Tanzania	1992	...	4.3
Togo	1993	...	6.6
Zambia	1994	...	10.2

Source: Barbone and Sanchez (1999).

principle, which links retirement pensions to contributions paid during the years spent at work. The majority of the population are excluded from old-age pension arrangements altogether, and typically the elderly continue to work regardless of age. When workers become disabled or exhausted by old age, traditional African family solidarity dictates that they be supported by their children.

Demographic and Economic Impact of HIV/AIDS

For our analysis we have built a model based on a hypothetical country called Demoland, which we will use to simulate the impact of the HIV/AIDS pandemic on social security. The demographic and economic characteristics of Demoland are similar to those that prevail in some countries in sub-Saharan Africa, the world region worst affected by HIV/AIDS. We assume that Demoland has a population of 14.8 million people in 2000, the starting year of the simulation. The population is young: 43 percent are under age 15, and only 5 percent are 60 and over. The total fertility rate is 5.1 children per woman. GDP per capita in 2000 is $720 at the current exchange rate, corresponding to $1,400 at purchasing power parity, and real GDP is growing at a rate of 5 percent a year. Productivity per worker is increasing at 1.2 percent a year. Labor force participation rates are 76 percent for males and 63 percent for females, and the unemployment rate is 13 percent. It is estimated that 20 percent of the labor force is in the informal sector.

Table 8.5. Pension Arrangements in Sub-Saharan African Countries

Country	Type of Arrangement	Special System for Public Employees?
Benin	Social insurance	Yes
Botswana	Universal program	Yes
Burkina Faso	Social insurance	Yes
Burundi	Social insurance	Yes
Cameroon	Social insurance	Yes
Cape Verde	Social insurance	Yes
Central African Republic	Social insurance	No
Chad	Social insurance	No
Congo, Dem. Rep. of	Social insurance	Yes
Congo, Rep. of	Social insurance	No
Côte d'Ivoire	Social insurance	Yes
Equatorial Guinea	Social insurance	No
Ethiopia	Social insurance	Yes
Gabon	Social insurance	Yes
Gambia	Pension scheme and provident fund	Yes
Ghana	Social insurance	For army only
Guinea	Social insurance	No
Kenya	Provident fund	Yes
Liberia	Social insurance and social assistance	No
Madagascar	Social insurance	Yes
Malawi	No countrywide arrangement	Only
Mali	Social insurance	Yes
Mauritania	Social insurance	Yes
Mauritius	Noncontributory program and social insurance	Yes
Niger	Social insurance	Yes
Nigeria	Social insurance	Yes
Rwanda	Social insurance	No
São Tomé and Príncipe	Social insurance	No
Senegal	Social insurance	Yes
Seychelles	Social security fund	No
South Africa	Social assistance	Yes
Sudan	Social insurance	Yes
Swaziland	Provident fund	Yes
Tanzania	Provident fund and social insurance	No
Togo	Social insurance	Yes
Uganda	Provident fund	Yes
Zambia	Provident fund	Yes
Zimbabwe	Social insurance	No

Source: U.S. Social Security Administration, Office of Policy (2003).

Demographic Impact

It is assumed that 700,000 Demolanders are infected with HIV. Ten percent of the adult population (those aged 15–49) are estimated to be HIV-positive. AIDS caused 72,000 deaths in 2000. In the absence of HIV/AIDS, life expectancy at birth would be 56 years for males and 59 years for females. With HIV/AIDS, however, life expectancy at birth has dropped to

Figure 8.1. Demoland: Mortality Rates by Sex, With and Without AIDS, 2010
(Percent)

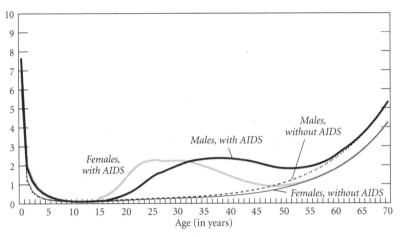

Source: Authors' model described in the text.

49 and 54 years, respectively. It is assumed that HIV/AIDS prevalence will reach its peak in 2010 and that preventive measures will make AIDS gradually disappear by 2050.

Demoland introduced its pension scheme 30 years before, in 1970. The country's social security law calls for coverage of the entire labor force, but because of compliance problems and the size of the informal sector, only 34 percent of the workforce (for both males and females) actually contribute to the scheme. The present legal contribution rate is 8.0 percent of insured earnings. Pension expenditure represented 1.1 percent of GDP in 2000.

Public health expenditure in Demoland amounts to 2.5 percent of GDP, and private health expenditure for 1 percent of GDP. Other social programs, with total annual spending of 1.2 percent of GDP, include unemployment insurance, sickness and maternity benefits, a basic disability program, tax-financed family benefits, and a limited social assistance program.

HIV/AIDS will cause a dramatic increase in mortality for two critical age groups: the very young (0–4 years) and young adults (15–49 years). Figure 8.1 shows projected mortality rates for the peak year 2010. The additional deaths due to AIDS are concentrated in the population between ages 15 and 50. The additional mortality for men is likely to appear at slightly higher ages than for women. The additional mortality among the very young results from transmission of HIV from mother to child.

Figure 8.2. Demoland: Projected Life Expectancy for Men, Without and With Impact of AIDS
(Years)

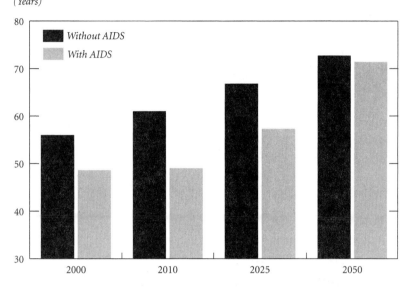

Source: Authors' calculations using model described in the text.

These changes in mortality will have a major impact on life expectancy. In the scenario without AIDS, life expectancy at birth is assumed to increase gradually and continuously from its present level of 56 years for males and 59 years for females in 2000 to 72 years for males and 77 years for females in 2050. In the scenario with AIDS, in contrast, life expectancy does not improve until 2010, after which it starts to increase so as to eventually approach the without-AIDS values only in 2050 (Figure 8.2).

HIV/AIDS may also affect fertility, in part because more women will become widows and stop bearing children, but also because women infected by HIV will be in too poor health to bear children or will decide to have no more. In the base scenario (that is, without the impact of HIV/AIDS), it is supposed that the total fertility rate decreases from 5.1 children per woman in 2000 to 2.1 in 2025 and remains at that level thereafter. Taking into account the impact of HIV/AIDS, it is supposed that the ultimate rate of 2.1 will be reached more rapidly, in 2010 instead of 2025.

The combined effects of HIV/AIDS on mortality and fertility in the projected population can be very important. Figure 8.3 illustrates the pop-

Figure 8.3. Demoland: Population Pyramids by Sex, Without and With Impact of AIDS

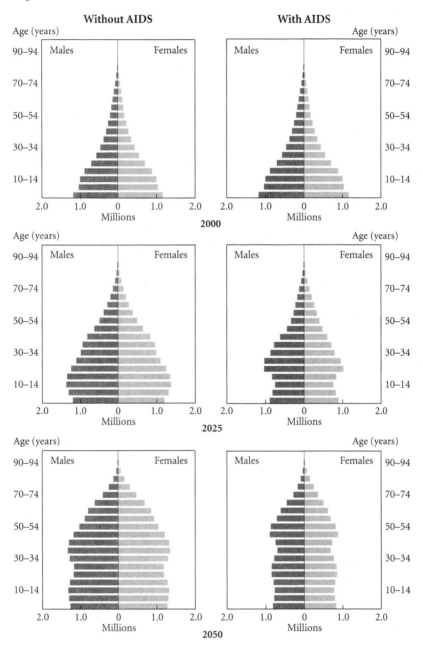

Source: Authors' calculations using model described in the text.

ulation structure with and without HIV/AIDS, using population pyra-mids. Under the no-AIDS scenario, the total population of Demoland increases from 14.8 million in 2000 to 34.1 million in 2050, for an average annual growth rate of 1.7 percent. With AIDS, however, the population reaches only 22.6 million in 2050, because of fewer births and higher mor-tality. The figure shows the combined effect of lower fertility and higher infant mortality on the population below age ·20, which represents the future workforce and social security contributors. Figure 8.3 also shows that mortality due to AIDS will prevent a large proportion of the popula-tion from reaching retirement age.

Economic Impact

HIV/AIDS affects the economy in many different ways. For example, increased mortality and morbidity adversely affect productivity, increased expenditure on health is likely to affect public and private saving, and increased production costs and a deteriorating economic outlook affect investment behavior. In analyzing the financing of social security, the most important economic variables are GDP (or, more specifically, the tax base for domestic government revenue), labor force participation rates, and the number of contributors to the social security scheme.

A detailed analysis of the impact of HIV/AIDS on GDP is beyond the scope of this chapter.[4] For Demoland it is assumed that HIV/AIDS causes a reduction in GDP growth of 2 percentage points (from 5 percent to 3 percent) initially (2000–04) and that the impact of HIV/AIDS on GDP growth then gradually diminishes to 1.5 percentage points in 2005–09, 1 percentage point in 2010–19, and 0.5 percentage point thereafter.

Labor productivity increases by 1.2 percent a year in the scenario with-out AIDS. With HIV/AIDS, productivity is assumed to increase at a rate of only 1.0 percent a year until 2039 and to return to its earlier growth rate thereafter. For simplicity, we assume that salary increases go hand in hand with increases in productivity.

As regards the impact of AIDS on labor supply, it is assumed that the participation rates of men will be lower at all ages except 15–24 (Table 8.6). For women, the need for children and widows to seek employment will cause their participation rates to rise at all ages below 44. Reflecting slower GDP growth, the unemployment rate in the with-AIDS scenario is

---

[4]See Haacker (Chapter 2, this volume) for a discussion of the macroeconomic effects of HIV/AIDS.

Table 8.6. Demoland: Assumptions on Labor Force Participation Rates by Age and Sex
(Percent of working-age population)

Age (years)	Scenario 1 (No AIDS)		Scenarios 2–4 (With AIDS)	
	Males	Females	Males	Females
15–19	58	37	65	50
20–24	89	44	90	60
25–29	97	47	90	60
30–34	98	49	90	60
35–39	99	49	90	60
40–44	98	51	90	60
45–49	97	51	90	50
50–54	97	49	90	50
55–59	90	46	60	30
60–64	88	39	20	20
65–69	72	23	20	20

Source: Authors' model described in the text.

assumed to increase from 14 percent in 2000 to 20 percent in 2015, and then decrease as total population falls as a result of AIDS mortality.[5]

For contribution-financed social security schemes, such as the pension scheme discussed below, the assumptions regarding the number of contributors are critical. In assessing the impact of HIV/AIDS on contribution rates, we distinguish four different scenarios. *Scenario 1* is the base scenario, without AIDS. In *scenario 2* the number of contributors changes in proportion to the change in the total number of workers, so that the percentage of workers covered by the scheme is held constant. For these two scenarios, the assumed coverage rates are presented in Tables 8.7 and 8.8.

In *scenario 3* the number of contributors to the social security scheme is the same as in the base scenario. This reflects the assumption that, because of the size of the uncovered population and of the informal sector, all contributors dying from AIDS are replaced by workers previously not covered by the scheme. This scenario may also be realistic in the context of a civil service pension plan, which is the principal pension arrangement in a large number of developing countries. *Scenario 4*, the most pessimistic scenario, freezes the number of contributors at its 2000 level, on the assumption that AIDS deaths and slower economic growth prevent any increase in the covered population.

---

[5]Unemployment rates in many developing countries are significantly above these levels, sometimes reaching 40 percent or more. In that context our assumptions may appear optimistic. However, as described earlier, high unemployment combined with an abundance of unskilled labor may make it easier to replace workers dying from AIDS with unemployed workers or workers from the informal sector. Consequently, keeping the unemployment rate low may generate a greater impact of AIDS on the social security system.

Individual Social Protection Schemes and the Fiscal Balance

HIV/AIDS will most likely increase expenditure on all social protection schemes and consequently affect the budgetary situation of the government. This section presents the financial implications of the epidemic on the individual schemes and shows how they affect the social budget and the fiscal balance of Demoland.

Table 8.7. Demoland: Assumptions on Social Security Coverage Rates by Age and Sex, 2000
(Percent)

Age (years)	Males	Females
15–19	20	20
20–24	25	25
25–29	30	30
30–34	40	35
35–39	40	40
40–44	50	45
45–49	50	50
50–54	60	55
55–59	60	60

Source: Authors' model described in the text.

Pensions

The impact of HIV/AIDS on pension schemes may be viewed from two perspectives. On the expenditure side, AIDS is expected to reduce the number of old-age pensions in the long term, but to increase survivors' and disability pensions in the short term. On the revenue side, AIDS will have an impact to the extent that a smaller total population will cause a reduction in the number of people employed, and to the extent that those employed persons affected by HIV/AIDS are among the contributors to the scheme. The reality in most developing countries is that the coverage of social security schemes is far from complete, and it can be assumed in some cases that new contributors will replace—at least partly—those who die from AIDS. However, the extent of this substitution is unknown. Thus we analyze two scenarios with respect to the impact of AIDS on the number of contributors to the Demoland pension scheme: a zero-substitution scenario and a full-substitution scenario.

The impact of HIV/AIDS on *old-age pensions* varies over time. Initially, the number of pensions will be almost unaffected, because the disease mainly strikes persons younger than 50 (Figure 8.4). But later, when the generations now younger than 50 reach retirement age, the scheme will experience a reduction in the number of old-age pensioners.

The number of *disability pensions* will be affected by several factors.

Table 8.8. Demoland: Assumptions on Social Security Coverage Rates by Sex and Year
(Percent)

Year	Males	Females
2000	34	34
2010	35	35
2020	36	36
2030	37	37
2040	38	38
2050	37	38

Source: Authors' model described in the text.

Figure 8.4. Demoland: Projected Number of Old-Age Pensioners Without and With Impact of AIDS
(Millions)

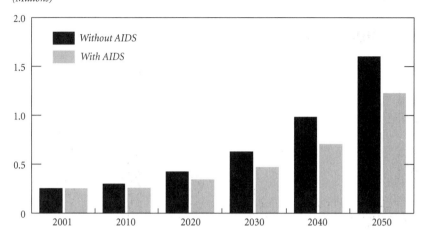

Source: Authors' calculations using model described in the text.

The incidence of new disability cases should increase as workers in the late stages of AIDS become incapacitated. However, the average duration of disability pensions should fall because of the relatively rapid and fatal course of AIDS. Moreover, if the period from incapacitation to death is relatively short—for instance, because life-prolonging drugs are unavailable—it may well happen that only a few persons will claim the disability pension and receive benefits for more than a short period.

Figure 8.5 presents one possible scenario in which the presence of AIDS multiplies the incidence of disability by a factor of 5 from 2000 to 2010, after which the multiplier gradually falls to 1 between 2010 and 2050. In choosing these values, we have assumed that those who die from AIDS will be eligible for a disability pension for at least a short period before death. In addition, it is assumed that the average duration of disability pensions is reduced for those afflicted by AIDS. Finally, it is assumed that the mortality rates of disability pensioners are five times higher than in the base scenario from 2000 to 2010 and that this factor thereafter declines gradually to unity between 2010 and 2050.

As regards *survivors' benefits*, AIDS will increase the number of widows and widowers (Figure 8.6) and the number of orphans (Figure 8.7). If the pension scheme provides for a funeral grant, expenditure on such benefits will increase sharply. On the other hand, the duration of widows' and widowers' pensions should decrease as a result of HIV/AIDS, since sur-

Figure 8.5. Demoland: Projected Number of Disability Pensioners Without and With Impact of AIDS
(Millions)

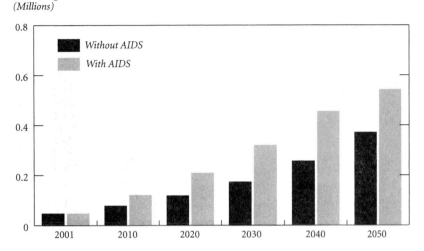

Source: Authors' calculations using model described in the text.

viving spouses have a high probability of having been infected by HIV themselves before the death of their spouse. The increase in the number of orphans' pensions will be proportionately larger than that for widows' and widowers' pensions, because the death of the insured person typically happens at an early age, when there are many dependent children under the age of 20 (as in the Demoland case) in the household.

HIV/AIDS will have an impact on *pension scheme revenue* to the extent that it affects the number of contributors, their earnings, and contribution rates. Below we assume that contribution rates are adjusted regularly so that pension outlays equal pension revenue at all times. The macroeconomic assumptions for each of four scenarios are described above.

The global impact of HIV/AIDS on the cost of a social security pension scheme will vary over time. In the short run the additional survivors' and disability pensions will increase expenditure, and HIV/AIDS may (depending on the scenario) have the effect of reducing the number of contributors through death or incapacitation. In the longer run HIV/AIDS is expected to reduce the number of persons who reach retirement age, thus reducing expenditure on old-age pensions.

In scenario 2, where HIV/AIDS affects the number of contributors in the same proportion as the entire labor force, the present contribution rate of 8 percent becomes insufficient as early as 2000. The contribution rate must be increased in increments, to 10.5 percent in 2010 (Table 8.9),

Figure 8.6. Demoland: Projected Number of Widows Without and With Impact of AIDS
(Millions)

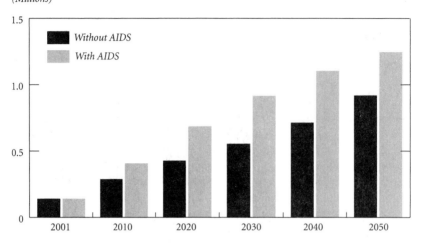

Source: Authors' calculations using model described in the text.

because of the increasing expenditure pattern and the lower salary base resulting from HIV/AIDS. Scenario 3, where HIV/AIDS does not affect the number of contributors, also requires an increase in contribution rates compared with the base scenario without HIV/AIDS, but the increase is more gradual than in scenario 2. In the worst-case scenario, scenario 4, the contribution rate has to increase rapidly, to 17.3 percent in 2020 and eventually to 23.2 percent in 2050.

It may be helpful to compare the general average premium for the pension scheme under the various scenarios. The general average premium is defined here as the minimum constant contribution rate sufficient to finance all benefits of the scheme over the period 2000–50. In the base scenario the general average premium would be 10.3 percent, whereas in scenario 2 it rises to 11.4 percent. This means that, in scenario 2, the advent of AIDS requires an immediate and sustained increase in the contribution rate of 1.1 percentage point over the next 50 years. On the other hand, if we assume that HIV/AIDS does not affect the number of contributors because of full substitution by previously uncovered workers (scenario 3), the general average premium increases only to 11.0 percent, or by 0.7 percentage point. In the least favorable scenario, scenario 4, the general average premium would be 16.5 percent.

The above discussion assumes a typical defined-benefit pension scheme. *Other types of pension arrangements* may exist in a number of

Figure 8.7. Demoland: Projected Number of Orphans Without and With Impact of AIDS
(Millions)

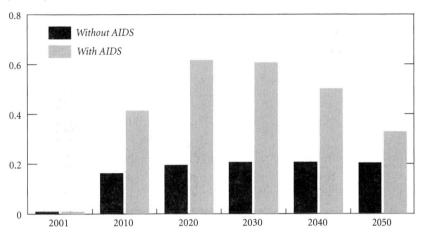

Source: Authors' calculations using model described in the text.

countries, which will thus face the AIDS threat in a different way. Box 8.1 describes the impact of AIDS in the context of a defined-contribution (or provident fund) arrangement and shows how this type of scheme is equipped to address the issue of HIV/AIDS.

Health

Health expenditure related to HIV/AIDS can be divided into curative care and prevention. In a developing country, health care may be offered by the public sector, by the private sector, or by foreign-based donors. In the case of Demoland, it is assumed that all public expenditure on health is financed from general revenue and that no national health insurance scheme exists.[6] Initially, most of the additional need for health services due to HIV/AIDS goes unmet. Through 2003, only 10 percent of opportunistic infections are treated, partly reflecting limited capacity at the local level, but also limited take-up of HIV-related health services because of stigmatization. The public sector does not provide any antiretroviral (ARV) treat-

---

[6]In fact, the private sector may provide some health treatments, and thus the economic effect of HIV/AIDS may extend beyond the fiscal effect, but given the high cost of treating HIV patients it is assumed here that the private sector provides very limited coverage and that most health expenditure is supported by the government.

Table 8.9. Demoland: Required Pension Contribution Rates
(Percent)

Year	Scenario[1]			
	1	2	3	4
2000	8.0	8.2	8.0	8.3
2001	8.0	8.5	8.2	8.9
2002	8.0	8.8	8.6	9.6
2003	8.0	9.1	9.0	10.4
2004	8.0	9.4	9.3	11.1
2005	8.1	9.6	9.5	11.7
2010	8.4	10.5	10.1	14.1
2020	9.0	11.7	10.1	17.3
2030	10.0	11.3	10.7	19.9
2040	11.8	11.7	12.0	21.6
2050	15.5	15.2	15.2	23.2

Source: Authors' calculations using model described in the text.

[1]Scenario 1 is a no-AIDS scenario; in scenario 2 the change in the number of contributors is proportional to the change in the total number of workers, so that the percentage of workers covered by the scheme is held constant; in scenario 3 contributors dying from AIDS are replaced by workers previously not covered by the scheme, so that the number of contributors is the same as in the scenario without AIDS; and in scenario 4 the number of covered workers remains constant.

ment through 2003, although a small percentage of patients (fewer than 1 percent of those requiring treatment) may receive ARV drugs through pilot projects or private providers. In 2004 the government embarks on an ambitious program to improve access to treatment, reaching coverage rates of 45 percent (for ARV treatment) and 40 percent (for opportunistic infections) by 2007, and 65 percent and 70 percent, respectively, by 2015.[7] Annual spending per patient is $400 for opportunistic infections and $500 for ARV treatment, enough to cover the costs of the drugs and of service delivery.[8] HIV patients are assumed to need treatment for opportunistic infections for the last two years of their lives, and ARV treatment is assumed to begin two years before the patient would otherwise die and to extend life by three years, so that patients receive treatment for a total of five years.[9]

In most countries afflicted by HIV/AIDS, the effects on health expenditure are very small initially, because the health sector is not well equipped to deal with the additional demand, or because fixed budget allocations

---

[7]The assumed coverage rates are inspired by targets proposed by the Commission on Macroeconomics and Health (2001).

[8]These estimates are derived from Schwartländer and others (2001) and Individual Members of the Faculty of Harvard University (2001), using updated prices for ARV drugs.

[9]See Schwartländer and others (2001). An economic side effect of ARV treatment is that it reduces or delays outlays on treatment of opportunistic diseases.

mean that, in the short run, hospitals and doctors must resort to rationing. In Demoland, public health expenditure increases by only about 2 percent (0.05 percent of GDP) by 2000. As coverage rates for ARV treatment and opportunistic infections increase, public health expenditure rises by 0.3 percent of GDP by 2005, 1.1 percent of GDP by 2010, and 1.3 percent of GDP by 2015, in which year HIV/AIDS-related expenditure amounts to 52 percent of initial public health expenditure.

Other Social Security Schemes

Unemployment insurance schemes are rather rare in developing countries. We assume that Demoland is one of the few countries with such a scheme for the formal sector. In our example, as already mentioned, the unemployment rate increases from 14 percent in 2000 to 20 percent in 2015. After 2015, because HIV/AIDS reduces the working-age population, the unemployment rate starts to decrease and eventually (after 2025) falls below the rate in scenario 1. Demoland's unemployment insurance scheme is financed by employer and worker contributions that together equal 1 percent of covered earnings initially. In line with the increase in unemployment, we assume that unemployment insurance contributions will have to increase gradually to 1.5 percent of covered earnings in 2015.

In our example, *short-term benefits* include sickness, maternity, and on-the-job injury benefits. We assume that the cost of sickness benefits increases by 50 percent as a result of HIV/AIDS, from 0.50 percent of payroll to 0.75 percent. Maternity benefits (0.5 percent of payroll in 2000) follow the decrease in the fertility rate as a result of HIV/AIDS, and the cost of on-the-job injury benefits is unaffected, remaining at 1.0 percent of payroll.

We assume that tax-financed *family benefits* are unaffected by HIV/AIDS. Any change in the country's demography is compensated by a change in benefit amounts so as to keep total expenditure constant.

A basic *social assistance* program exists in Demoland. The program's expenditure, financed from general revenue, amounts to 0.25 percent of GDP. We assume that HIV/AIDS increases poverty and that the government will have to support those in need because of loss of income or increased personal health care expenses. We further assume that the number of social assistance recipients doubles in 2000 because of AIDS and that the number of additional recipients increases over time in line with the demographic projections presented above. Under these assumptions the cost of the social assistance program doubles in 2000, to 0.50 percent of GDP, and reaches 0.90 percent of GDP in 2015.

Box 8.1. Impact of AIDS on Defined-Contribution Pension Schemes

This box addresses the financial impact of HIV/AIDS in the context of defined-benefit pension schemes, which are the most common form of public sector pension scheme. However, certain developing countries have adopted other forms of pension provision, such as provident funds or other forms of defined-contribution systems. Defined-contribution pension schemes have also become more common in the private sector, as companies seek to contain the rising costs of risk benefits associated with HIV/AIDS (see Rosen and Simon, 2003).

Under a defined-contribution scheme, contributions are accumulated in an individual account, and the accumulated amount is normally paid at retirement in the form of an annuity, a lump sum, or scheduled withdrawals. The usual death benefit under a defined-contribution scheme is a refund of the amount accumulated on behalf of the accountholder (the sum of contributions previously paid plus accumulated interest) at the time of death. If death occurs not long after the worker has started contributing to the scheme, the accumulated amount will be low. Using the same 8 percent contribution rate as in the Demoland case, the table presents the accumulated value of a defined-contribution account at different ages for a worker who started contributing to the scheme at age 20.

The regular income that can be purchased from the accumulated account is far below the current salary if death occurs before age 45. This also shows that defined-contribution schemes are poorly adapted to face the threat of AIDS, because they cannot provide regular long-term income to the survivors of par-

Impact of HIV/AIDS on the Social Budget and the Fiscal Balance

Table 8.10 presents the social budget of Demoland without and with the impact of HIV/AIDS, respectively. Without HIV/AIDS total social expenditure represents 5.0 percent of GDP in 2000, of which 2.5 percent of GDP is for public health expenditure and 1.1 percent for pensions. Under this scenario, total social expenditure grows modestly through 2015, from 5.0 percent of GDP to 5.4 percent, mainly because of increased expenditure on pensions. Since pensions are financed from payroll contributions from employers and workers, the burden on general revenue decreases slightly during the period, from 3.2 percent of GDP to 3.1 percent.

The HIV epidemic already has a significant effect on social expenditure in 2000. Compared with the scenario with no AIDS, current social expenditure rises by 0.5 percent of GDP (10 percent), mainly because of increased outlays for social assistance. In light of our assumptions based on limited historical coverage rates for HIV/AIDS-related health services, health expenditure increases only very modestly at this stage. By 2015

Accumulated Pension Contributions in a Defined-Contribution Scheme[1]

Age of Worker (years)	Current Salary (dollars)	Accumulated Value of Account (dollars)	Ratio of Accumulated Account Value to Current Salary	Value of a $1-a-Year Life Annuity to a Surviving Spouse (dollars)	Spouse's Income from Life Annuity (percent of current salary)[2]
25	5,853	3,096	0.5	19.4	2.7
30	6,851	7,122	1.0	18.6	5.6
35	8,020	13,017	1.6	17.6	9.2
40	9,388	21,502	2.3	16.5	13.9
45	10,989	33,552	3.1	15.2	20.1

Source: Authors' calculations.

[1]It is assumed that workers enroll in the pension plan at age 20, that their starting salary is $5,000 and increases by 3.2 percent (nominal) a year, that each individual account earns interest at 6.0 percent a year, and that the life annuity is indexed at 2 percent a year.

[2]Calculated as 100 × (accumulated account value / current salary) / value of $1-a-year life annuity).

ticipants in the age groups most affected by HIV/AIDS (those aged 20–45). On the other hand, some provident funds allow the prepayment of the account balance in the case of certain defined events before retirement. Such a provision may help pay medicines and hospital expenses and support the worker's family during his or her last months of life.

social expenditure reaches 8.4 percent of GDP in this scenario, an increase of 3.2 percent of GDP relative to a situation with no HIV/AIDS. Most notably, HIV/AIDS results in an increase in health expenditure of 1.3 percent of GDP by 2015 (with much improved access to HIV/AIDS-related health services, including ARV treatment), pension outlays rise by 0.5 percent of GDP, and social assistance payments rise by 0.7 percent of GDP, relative to the no-AIDS scenario.

To assess the impact of increased social expenditure on the fiscal balance, it is also important to take into account the financing of that expenditure. We have assumed that pensions, unemployment insurance, and short-term benefits are financed by contributions; the increase in expenditure on these items (1 percent of GDP) is offset by increased contributions.[10] As a conse-

---

[10]Additional sources of financing are changes in reserves and investment income of social security institutions. In our example, these items play a minor role. However, in a situation with significant reserves of the social security system, these can be used to smooth peaks in contribution rates or taxes to finance HIV/AIDS-related expenditure.

Table 8.10. Demoland: Social Budget Without and With Impact of HIV/AIDS
(Percent of GDP)[1]

Item	Without Impact of AIDS				With Impact of AIDS			
	2000	2005	2010	2015	2000	2005	2010	2015
Expenditure								
Total current social expenditure	4.7	4.9	5.1	5.4	5.2	6.1	7.5	8.4
Pensions	1.1	1.3	1.5	1.7	1.1	1.5	1.8	2.2
Health (public expenditure only)	2.5	2.5	2.5	2.5	2.6	2.8	3.6	3.8
Unemployment	0.1	0.2	0.2	0.2	0.2	0.2	0.3	0.4
Short-term benefits	0.3	0.3	0.3	0.4	0.3	0.4	0.5	0.6
Family benefits	0.5	0.4	0.4	0.4	0.5	0.5	0.5	0.5
Social assistance	0.2	0.2	0.2	0.2	0.5	0.7	0.8	0.9
Change in reserves	0.2	0.2	0.1	—	0.2	0.2	0.2	0.1
Pension insurance	0.2	0.2	0.1	—	0.2	0.2	0.2	0.1
Health insurance	—	—	—	—	—	—	—	—
Short-term benefits	—	—	—	—	—	—	—	—
Unemployment insurance	—	—	—	—	—	—	—	—
Total social expenditure	5.0	5.1	5.2	5.4	5.4	6.3	7.7	8.5
Income								
Social security contributions	1.6	1.7	2.0	2.2	1.6	2.1	2.6	3.2
Pension insurance	1.1	1.3	1.5	1.6	1.1	1.5	1.8	2.2
Health insurance	—	—	—	—	—	—	—	—
Short-term benefits	0.3	0.3	0.3	0.4	0.3	0.4	0.5	0.6
Unemployment insurance	0.1	0.2	0.2	0.2	0.2	0.2	0.3	0.4
Investment income	0.2	0.2	0.2	0.2	0.2	0.2	0.2	0.2
Pension insurance	0.2	0.2	0.2	0.2	0.2	0.2	0.2	0.2
Health insurance	—	—	—	—	—	—	—	—
Short-term benefits	—	—	—	—	—	—	—	—
Unemployment insurance	—	—	—	—	—	—	—	—
Income from general revenue	3.2	3.2	3.0	3.1	3.6	4.0	4.9	5.1
Total income	5.0	5.1	5.2	5.4	5.4	6.3	7.7	8.5

Source: Authors' calculations.

[1]Numbers may not sum to totals because of rounding.

quence, the balance of the social budget (financed from general revenue) increases by 2.0 percent of GDP by 2015. This could be financed from an increase in external grants or from domestic revenue. As detailed by Haacker (Chapter 7, this volume), a substantial proportion of health expenditure in most countries severely affected by HIV/AIDS currently is financed in this way.[11] However, other components of the additional costs (such as most forms of social assistance) are usually financed from domes-

---

[11]Summers and Kates (2003), updating estimates by the Joint United Nations Programme on HIV/AIDS (UNAIDS), project that over three-fourths of institutional spending on HIV/AIDS in developing countries in 2003 was financed through external assistance. Martin (2003), in a study of several countries in southern Africa, reports similar findings.

tic revenue. Thus, financing these expenditures, to the extent that they are not financed externally, would require an increase in tax and other revenue or cutbacks in other areas.

Improving the Coverage of Social Protection Schemes to Cope with HIV/AIDS

How can governments of developing countries meet the social challenges posed by HIV/AIDS and its expected severe budgetary consequences? The social challenges are of a twofold nature. On the one hand, health care has to be provided to those affected. On the other hand, the victims of the pandemic and their families need income support to prevent the medical disaster caused by AIDS from turning into a social disaster. Improving the coverage of social protection schemes appears to be the solution.

Because traditional social insurance transfers fail to reach the majority of the population, both in Africa and in other developing countries, and given that the AIDS pandemic will affect all population subgroups, more-universal income replacement schemes could be effective new instruments in the struggle against AIDS-triggered poverty. A universal flat-rate pension for the elderly, the disabled, and survivors, paid to all persons over a certain age (on the basis of residency, for example), is one way to provide basic income to families that have an elderly member. Such a measure combats old-age poverty while also reinforcing the intergenerational support so urgently needed among AIDS families with a missing generation. Ancillary benefits or additional conditions attached to a universal pension can be used to provide supplementary income for families to take care of AIDS-affected individuals; they may also help prevent children from having to leave school at an early age to earn an income. According to all available experience, a universal pension would cost on the order of 1 to 2 percent of the developing country's GDP.[12] The financing of such pensions may require the suppression of subsidies to social insurance schemes or the suppression of tax advantages for private pension schemes. Introducing universal pension benefits where they did not exist before will, of course, require substantial public debate. However, the total cost does not seem exorbitant, and a gradual introduction over 10 or more years may be feasible in a range of countries.[13]

---

[12]See the figures quoted by the Institute of Development and Policy Management and Help Age (United Kingdom, Department for International Development, 2003, Chapter 3.5).

[13]The Financial and Actuarial Service of the International Labour Organization has started an initiative to establish the financial affordability of this type of benefit.

Another way to reduce the pressure on the government budget would be to "bail in" the private sector, by introducing a public health insurance scheme financed by earmarked contributions. However, such a scheme would be introduced in an environment where HIV/AIDS is already raising companies' personnel costs, and where many companies are taking steps to contain the rising costs of health coverage related to a high incidence and high cost of care related to AIDS. Thus, fiscal measures to finance such a scheme would have to be mindful of the impact on personnel costs, especially for employees at the low end of the pay scale.

Although HIV/AIDS raises the costs of social insurance, these programs also have substantial benefits. For example, income support mitigates the adverse economic effects on the families affected, and Ainsworth, Beegle, and Koda (2002) suggest that such support has a positive effect on school enrollment rates for orphans. Improved health coverage results in fewer new HIV infections, fewer orphans, more people staying at work, fewer disability grants, and longer life expectancy.[14] Thus, in addition to mitigating the impact on the affected individuals and households and reducing the human toll, these measures would also help to reduce or even reverse the economic decline caused by HIV/AIDS, thereby helping to finance the increased costs of social security.[15]

Conclusions

Health and pension expenditure account for about three-fourths of all social expenditure in any country with a fairly well developed national social transfer system. But HIV/AIDS affects each of these two types of spending differently. These effects can be simulated, but not without a substantial degree of uncertainty. In particular, the effects on the pension system are probably less predictable than those on the health system.

As long as a pension scheme can find new contributors to replace those prematurely dying of AIDS, the impact of AIDS on national pension schemes appears to be financially manageable. However, the impact of HIV/AIDS on the number of contributors to these schemes is the great

---

[14]See Haacker (Chapter 2, this volume) for a discussion of the macroeconomic benefits of ARV treatment.

[15]See Masha (Chapter 9, this volume) for an assessment of the macroeconomic effects of Botswana's National Strategic Plan on HIV/AIDS.

unknown. For developing countries it may be assumed that high unemployment and a large informal sector will allow HIV/AIDS-related deaths in the workforce to be replaced to a considerable degree by workers from outside the formal sector and the unemployed. Even then, however, overall economic growth may slow, because the productivity of the replacements is likely to be less than that of the workers they are replacing. Moreover, the cost of training the new workers will increase the overall cost to the enterprise, also reducing growth. The dramatic results of our nonreplacement scenario show (although it describes an improbable, extreme case in which the number of contributors is frozen at the 2000 level) that the financial risks of pension schemes associated with a potential draining of the economy of qualified workers are substantial.

The social budget exercise presented in this chapter shows that the cost of social programs other than pension schemes might also increase substantially as a result of AIDS. The cost of health care, sickness, and unemployment benefits schemes may rise dramatically as HIV/AIDS puts people out of work and generates the need for income support and health care. In countries where the prevalence of HIV/AIDS is high, the burden on general revenue may put governments in a difficult financial position, even though the emerging deficits in the next decades may not be unmanageable, as our projections show.

Solutions appear to be available in the form of a set of policy options that could help address the medical, social, and financial consequences of the AIDS pandemic. Universal pensions, probably combined with more-targeted social assistance for AIDS-affected families, would help alleviate the social consequences. Abolishing tax breaks for private pension schemes could possibly finance most of the cost without increasing the emerging government deficit.[16] Investing a part of the social budget in awareness campaigns can also reduce the long-term cost. And the introduction of a national health insurance scheme could probably help close the emerging deficit. Even so, deficits will most likely increase over what they would have been under the status quo. Further tax increases may be necessary, although these may be less dramatic than is often assumed. The challenge will be to design these taxes in such a way that they do not further weaken countries' already fragile growth rates.

---

[16]The cost of South Africa's social pension is estimated to be on the order of 1.4 percent of GDP, compared with tax breaks for private pensions that currently amount to 1.7 percent of GDP.

Bibliography

Ainsworth, Martha, Kathleen Beegle, and Godlike Koda, 2002, "The Impact of Adult Mortality on Primary School Enrollment in Northwestern Tanzania," Africa Region Human Development Working Paper (Washington: World Bank).

Annycke, Pascal, 2003, "The Impact of HIV/AIDS on Security for the Elderly in Africa," paper presented at the African Technical Consultation "Economic Security and Decent Work," Tanzania, May.

Barbone, Luca, and Luis-Alvaro Sanchez B., 1999, "Pensions and Social Security in Sub-Saharan Africa: Issues and Options," World Bank Africa Region Working Paper No. 4 (Washington: World Bank).

Baruti, Elias, 2003, "Extension of Social Security Coverage to the Poor in the Informal Urban Sector in Tanzania Through Micro Credit," paper presented at the Inaugural Tanzanian Biennial Development Forum.

Bollinger, Lori, and John Stover, 1999, "The Economic Impact of AIDS in Angola" (Washington: The Futures Group International)

Bonnel, René, 2000, "HIV/AIDS: Does it Increase or Decrease Growth in Africa?" Working paper (Washington: World Bank).

Castro-Leal, Florencia, and others, 2000, "Public Spending on Health Care in Africa: Do the Poor Benefit?" *Bulletin of the World Health Organization,* Vol. 78, No. 1, pp. 66–74.

Cichon, Michael, 2002, "A Global Social Trust Network: Investing in the World's Social Future" (Geneva: Financial, Actuarial and Statistical Services Branch, International Labour Organization).

Commission on Macroeconomics and Health (CMH), 2001, "Macroeconomics and Health: Investing in Health for Economic Development" (Geneva: World Health Organization).

Cuddington, John T., 1993, "Modeling the Macroeconomic Effects of AIDS, with an Application to Tanzania," *World Bank Economic Review,* Vol. 7, No. 2, pp. 173–89.

———, and John D. Hancock, 1993, "Assessing the Impact of AIDS on the Growth Path of the Malawian Economy," *Journal of Development Economics,* Vol. 43, No. 2, pp. 363–68.

———, 1995, "The Macroeconomic Impact of AIDS in Malawi: A Dualistic, Labour Surplus Economy," *Journal of African Economics,* Vol. 4, No. 1, pp. 1–28.

Individual Members of the Faculty of Harvard University, 2001, "Consensus Statement on Antiretroviral Treatment for AIDS in Poor Countries" (Cambridge, Massachusetts).

International Labour Organization, 1997, "International Inquiry into the Cost of Social Security 1990–1993" (unpublished; Geneva). Available via the Internet: www.ilo.org/public/english/protection/socfas/research/css/cssindex.htm.

———, 1999, "ILO Action Against HIV/AIDS—A Draft Framework for Global and Regional Initiatives" (Geneva).

————, 2000, "HIV/AIDS: A Threat to Decent Work, Productivity and Development," document for discussion at the Special High-Level Meeting on HIV/AIDS and the World of Work, Geneva, June 8.

————, 2001, "Côte d'Ivoire—Evaluation actuarielle du régime des pensions obligatoires de la Caisse Générale de Retraite des Agents de l'Etat au 31 décembre 1998" (Geneva).

————, 2002a, "ILO Compendium of Official Statistics on Employment in the Informal Sector," Stat Working Paper 1 (Geneva).

————, 2002b, "A Global Social Trust Network: Investing in the World's Social Future" (Geneva: Financial, Actuarial and Statistical Services Branch, International Labour Organization).

————, 2002c, "Contributing to the Fight Against HIV/AIDS Within the Informal Economy: The Existing and Potential Role of Decentralized Systems of Social Protection" (Geneva).

————, forthcoming, *Social Protection Financing* (Geneva).

Joint United Nations Programme on HIV/AIDS (UNAIDS), 2000a, "AIDS Epidemic Update: December 2000" (Geneva).

————, 2000b, "Côte d'Ivoire – Epidemiological Fact Sheet on HIV/AIDS and Sexually Transmitted Infections" (Geneva).

————, 2000c, "Guidelines for Studies of the Social and Economic Impact of HIV/AIDS" (Geneva).

Kamuzora, Peter, 1999, "Extension of Formal Social Security Schemes in the United Republic of Tanzania" (Dar es Salaam, Tanzania: University of Dar es Salaam)

Martin, H. Gayle, 2003, "A Comparative Analysis of the Financing of HIV/AIDS Programmes in Botswana, Lesotho, Mozambique, South Africa, Swaziland, and Zimbabwe" (Pretoria, South Africa: Human Sciences Research Council).

Rosen, Sidney, and Jonathon Simon, 2003, "Shifting the Burden: The Private Sector's Response to the AIDS Epidemic in Africa," *Bulletin of the World Health Organization*, Vol. 81, pp. 131–37.

Schwartländer, Bernhard, and others, 2001, "Resource Needs for HIV/AIDS," *Science*, Vol. 292, No. 5526, pp. 2434–36.

Sehgal, Jag M., 1999, "The Labour Implications of HIV/AIDS: An Explanatory Note," Discussion Paper on HIV/AIDS and the World of Work (Geneva: International Labour Organization).

Summers, Todd, and Jennifer Kates, 2003, "Global Funding for HIV/AIDS in Resource Poor Settings" (Washington: Kaiser Family Foundation).

Tossa, José, forthcoming, "SPERs Benin" (Geneva: Social Protection—Financial, Actuarial, and Statistical Services Branch, ILO).

United Kingdom, Department for International Development, 2003, "Non-contributory Pensions and Poverty Prevention in Developing Countries: A Comparative Analysis between South Africa and Brazil" (London).

United Nations, 1999, *World Population Prospects: The 1998 Revision*" (New York).

U.S. Social Security Administration, Office of Policy, 2003, *Social Security Programs Throughout the World: Africa, 2003* (Washington).

World Bank, 1999, *Confronting AIDS: Public Priorities in a Global Epidemic* (New York: Oxford University Press).

———, 2000, *World Development Report 2000/01* (Washington).

9

An Economic Assessment of Botswana's National Strategic Framework for HIV/AIDS

Iyabo Masha

Botswana's economic transformation during the past 30 years is one of the most highly regarded success stories of the African continent. Real GDP grew at an average annual rate of 13.9 percent between 1965 and 1980, and 11.3 percent between 1980 and 1989, making Botswana the world's fastest-growing economy during the period. Between 1990 and 1998, however, GDP growth averaged only 4.75 percent a year. Real GDP per capita increased by an average of 5 percent a year, reaching $3,417 in 1997/98 and $3,170 in 2003. Botswana made major strides in terms of standard development indices as well. The under-5 mortality rate, which had been 151 per 1,000 live births in 1971, declined to 48 per 1,000 by 1991. By 1996 net primary enrollment was 95 percent, more than double the 1971 rate. In 1993, 47 percent of Batswana (the name for the people of Botswana) lived below the official poverty threshold, compared with 59 percent in 1985. These substantial economic gains resulted in part from the discovery of large mineral deposits in 1968, and mining value added now accounts for about a third of GDP. But in addition to the discovery of diamonds, the pursuit of prudent and consistent macroeconomic policies has resulted in a stable macroeconomic environment.

These gains, however, are gravely threatened by the scourge of HIV/AIDS. Botswana has one of the highest HIV/AIDS prevalence rates in the world: a 2002 survey estimated that about 35.4 percent of adults aged 15–49 years carried the virus. The overall prevalence rate has more than doubled since 1992, and an estimated 138,000 Batswana had died of

AIDS by 2002, out of a population of about 1½ million. The high prevalence rate has resulted in declining life expectancy, from 65 years in 1991 to 56 years in 2001, according to official census data. The infant mortality rate is estimated at 55.2 per 1,000 live births, compared with 48 per 1,000 in 1991, and in contrast to an estimated 26.3 per 1,000 in the absence of AIDS. The U.S. Census Bureau (2003) projects that population growth during 2010–20 will average –2.1 percent a year, compared with +3.6 percent a year during 1980–90. In addition to the human consequences, the macroeconomic impact of the epidemic has been researched, and many studies, drawing on demographic projections and standard economic theory, have modeled the long-term negative impact of HIV/AIDS on total factor productivity, labor, capital, and output, among other variables.[1]

The HIV/AIDS epidemic poses a serious challenge to achieving the government's objectives of poverty reduction, economic diversification, and growth. These objectives, formally articulated in Botswana's medium-term economic framework, the National Development Plan 9 (NDP-9, covering 2003–09), depend crucially on the government's ability to attract foreign investment into areas outside of mining, and to undertake the structural reforms needed to increase private sector participation in the economy. The National Strategy for Poverty recognizes that HIV/AIDS is both cause and consequence of poverty, unemployment, and inequality and aims to eliminate poverty in Botswana by 2016. The strategy seeks to direct antipoverty interventions toward the root causes affecting income, capacity, and participation, by integrating poverty reduction strategies into the medium-term economic framework. The costs of these programs are increased further by the huge outlays required to manage the HIV/AIDS epidemic. Coming at a time when diamond output is plateauing, the immediate challenge facing the government is how to finance the cost of fighting the epidemic while mitigating its adverse consequences. Effective management of the epidemic would enable Botswana to moderate the decline in human development indices and the adverse macroeconomic impact of the disease.

The government of Botswana has developed a National Strategic Framework (NSF) for HIV/AIDS covering the period 2003–09. The NSF is a comprehensive, multisector program for managing the epidemic, with the objective of having an HIV-free generation by 2016. This chapter assesses the macroeconomic impact of HIV/AIDS in Botswana under the assump-

---

[1]See Bloom and Mahal (1995), Green and others (2002), and Haacker (2002a).

tion that implementation of the NSF program succeeds in lowering the HIV prevalence rate. This assessment is undertaken by incorporating the improvements that are hoped to ensue under the NSF program scenario into existing macroeconomic models of the impact of HIV/AIDS.

The plan of the chapter is as follows. The first section discusses the management of HIV/AIDS in Botswana, with particular focus on the new NSF. The second section discusses the broad macroeconomic repercussions of the NSF. To the extent the demographic impact of HIV/AIDS is mitigated, the economic effects, for example on GDP growth, will also be less pronounced. To assess the impact of HIV/AIDS on government finance, it is therefore important to take into account these indirect effects of government efforts to combat the epidemic. The final section concludes.

Response to HIV/AIDS in Botswana

The approach taken by the government of Botswana to managing the HIV epidemic has evolved as the infection has spread through the population. Whereas the focus in the early phase was mainly on preventive health care, by 1993, with prevalence rates already as high as 23 percent, comprehensive medical and social care was included in the overall HIV/AIDS management scheme. Although the government of Botswana does not disaggregate expenditure on HIV/AIDS ex ante, budgetary allocations to the health sector have increased substantially, from 2.2 percent of GDP in 2000/01 to 4.0 percent in 2003/04, and both the public and the private sectors in Botswana have put in place extensive awareness programs and integrated health care arrangements for HIV-positive employees.[2]

The Medium-Term Program II for HIV/AIDS (1996–2002) was the first framework to take a multisectoral approach, consolidating program activities over a dispersed number of agencies. The NSF, the successor to the Medium-Term Program II, represents the most ambitious attempt so far to grapple with the epidemic. The framework offers a systematic, multi-

---

[2]According to Botswana's National AIDS Coordinating Agency (NACA, 2003), the private sector, state enterprises, and civil society are expected to implement an agreed Minimum Internal Package for HIV/AIDS prevention. Debswana Corporation, Botswana Telecommunications, Barclays Bank of Botswana, Standard Chartered Bank, and Botswana Power Corporation are some of the firms that are implementing comprehensive workplace AIDS policies, some of which extend to their subcontractors.

Box 9.1. Objectives of the National Strategic Framework

- Increase the number of persons within the sexually active population (especially those aged 15–24) who adopt HIV prevention behaviors in Botswana by 2009.
- Decrease HIV transmission from HIV-positive mothers to their newborns by 2009.
- Decrease the prevalence of HIV in transfused blood in the country.
- Increase the level of productivity of people living with HIV/AIDS, especially those on antiretroviral therapy.
- Decrease the incidence of tuberculosis among HIV-positive patients in the country.
- Broaden the skills of health workers (doctors and nurses) to accurately diagnose and treat opportunistic infections.
- Ensure the implementation of the NSF Minimum HIV/AIDS Response Packages by all sectors, ministries, districts, and state enterprises.
- Ensure the full implementation of all planned HIV/AIDS activities at all levels.
- Minimize the impact of the epidemic on the persons infected, those otherwise affected, public services, and the economy.
- Create a supportive, ethical, legal, and human rights-based environment conforming to international standards for the implementation of the National Response.

sectoral approach to managing the epidemic and makes the National AIDS Coordinating Agency (NACA), chaired by the president of Botswana, the focal point for facilitating and coordinating the various HIV/AIDS interventions in the country. The overriding objective of the NSF is "to eliminate the incidence of HIV and reduce the impact of AIDS in Botswana" (NACA, 2003).

The NSF formulates a broad response to HIV/AIDS in the areas of prevention, care, and support; management of the national response; mitigation of the economic impact; and strengthening of the legal and ethical environment. It specifies 10 objectives (see Box 9.1) and defines time-bound quantitative targets and indicators by which to measure progress within the framework (Table 9.1). Treatment focuses on the administration of antiretroviral drugs, to prolong the life span of infected persons and increase average productivity. The mother-to-child transmission program provides treatment for pregnant women to reduce the transmission of HIV at birth. In addition, treatment of tuberculosis and opportunistic and sexually transmitted diseases as well as voluntary counseling and test-

Table 9.1. Botswana: Quantitative Targets and Outcome Indicators of the National Strategic Framework for the Population at Risk
(Percent except where stated otherwise)

Target and Outcome Indicator[1]	Baseline	2006	2009
Voluntary counseling and testing			
Increase in HIV prevention and knowledge	34	80	100
Adoption of HIV prevention behavior	. . .	50	80
Decrease in HIV prevalence among sexually active population	6	50	80
Increase in number of people who utilize services	8	70	95
Mother-to-child transmission			
Share of HIV-positive women receiving complete course of antiretroviral therapy	34	70	100
Reduction in infected infants born to HIV-positive mothers	40	20	10
Antiretroviral therapy			
Number of HIV-positive persons eligible for and receiving therapy in 12-month period	8,000	45,000	85,000
Share of people living with AIDS returning to productive life	. . .	100	100
Sexually transmitted diseases			
Decrease in prevalence among sexually active population	2	50	100

Source: NACA (2003).
[1]Table does not include all targets and outcome indicators. See source for details.

ing, which are targeted at a wider audience than the HIV infected, are intended to reduce the rate of new HIV infections.[3]

Many of the specific measures undertaken within the NSF are directed toward bringing down the number of new HIV infections through voluntary counseling and testing, the treatment of sexually transmitted diseases, and programs to reduce mother-to-child transmission. The NSF targets an increase in the adoption of preventive behavior from a baseline 34 percent of the 15–49 age group in 2001 to 80 percent in 2006 and 100 percent in 2009. The treatment of other STDs, targeted to reach 100 percent of the population at risk by 2009, is intended to reduce the risk of contracting or passing on the virus, and—combined with counseling and testing—to help modify risky behavior among the sexually active population. In the 2001 baseline period, 34.3 percent of HIV-positive pregnant women were receiving a course of antiretroviral treatment to reduce mother-to-child transmission. The NSF targets 70 percent coverage by 2006 and 100 percent by 2009.

The NSF also aims to substantially improve the treatment available to people living with HIV/AIDS, especially by expanding access to highly

---

[3]Patients with tuberculosis and other infectious diseases have a higher rate of susceptibility to HIV/AIDS because of their compromised immune system.

Table 9.2. Botswana: Projected Program Cost for the HIV/AIDS National Strategic Framework[1]
(Millions of pula except where stated otherwise)

Item	2002/03	2003/04	2004/05	2005/06	2006/07	2007/08	Average
Prevention of HIV infection	185.8	241.0	264.5	234.3	164.3	156.70	207.8
Provision of care and support	408.9	641.6	781.0	1,117.1	1,577.4	2,229.90	1,126.0
ART drugs	38.6	139.2	251.0	374.0	504.0	642.00	324.8
Other costs	354.3	299.4	455.5	617.6	868.3	1,419.40	669.1
Total program cost	949.0	1,182.0	1,501.0	1,969.0	2,610.0	3,806.00	2,002.8
Percent of GDP	2.78	3.16	4.04	4.84	5.92	8.00	4.99

Source: NACA (2003).
[1]Years are fiscal years beginning April 1.

active antiretroviral treatment. Under the program, the number of patients receiving treatment is slated to rise from 8,500 to 45,000 by 2006 and 85,000 by 2009. By 2009 the goal is to have all people living with HIV/AIDS return to productive life.

The projected cost of implementing the NSF is approximately 12 billion pula (about $2.4 billion) over the program years (Table 9.2). This translates into an average of 5 percent of GDP devoted to HIV-related spending a year, compared with an annual average of 4 percent of GDP spent on the entire health sector in the past three years. Botswana has already received extensive support from its development partners, who are also expected to support the new medium-term framework financially. Such support would be expected in the areas of financial and human resources, material supplies, and mitigation of the fiscal burden.

Apart from program support from the UN agencies, other partnerships include the African Comprehensive HIV/AIDS Partnership, a partnership between the Bill and Melinda Gates Foundation and the Merck Pharmaceutical Foundation, which is committed to disbursing $100 million over 2000–05. The Botswana Harvard AIDS Institute Laboratory in Gaborone is the largest of its kind in Africa, and the government has established partnerships with the U.S. Centers for Disease Control and a host of other governments and agencies. In December 2003 Botswana signed an agreement for an $18.5 million grant from the Global Fund for HIV/AIDS, Malaria, and Tuberculosis, funding a two-year program aimed at recruitment and training; strengthening treatment, care, and support activities; scaling up prevention programs; and reducing the stigma and discrimination associated with HIV infection.

As part of efforts to keep track of developments arising from the framework's implementation, the Botswana HIV Response Information Management System (BHIVRIMS) was developed to gather information and to monitor and evaluate trends and progress, as well as progress in international agreements and financial commitments. The BHIVRIMS is expected to become the institutional memory in the management of the HIV pandemic.

Demographic and Economic Impact of Botswana's National Strategic Framework

The measures spelled out in the NSF are expected to reduce the number of new infections and, through improvements in treatments available to people living with HIV/AIDS, reduce mortality among those infected. These efforts will also mitigate the adverse impact of HIV/AIDS on the economy. The analysis below shows that the potential demographic and economic effects of the NSF are substantial. This means that it is important to assess how the NSF, beyond its direct costs, will affect the fiscal balance. For example, government revenue is related to the level of economic activity, and reductions in HIV/AIDS-related mortality and morbidity affect various categories of government expenditure. An analysis of the demographic impact of the NSF, using a simple macroeconomic framework, is presented below, as well as an assessment of the effect on GDP. Finally, a preliminary assessment is made of the NSF's fiscal repercussions, through its demographic and economic effects.

Demographic Impact

The demographic estimates for the simulation were generated with the Spectrum AIM program,[4] using initial values from the Botswana Central Statistics Office, the population census projection for 1991, and the latest available data on labor force participation rates by five-year cohort from the 1995/96 labor force survey. The Spectrum population projection model makes use of detailed assumptions about fertility, mortality, and HIV prevalence rates. The projection parameters are based on information

---

[4]The Spectrum AIM model, developed by The Futures Group, is a Windows-based program designed to calculate the demographic consequences of HIV/AIDS; it can be downloaded from www.tfgi.com. Demographic data for 1991–2003 match the actual values, and the parameters used to generate the remaining years are from UN and U.S. Census Bureau projections. Epidemiological data from NACA were used for the AIDS-without-intervention scenario, and the NSF targets for the AIDS-with-intervention scenario.

from the 1991 census and HIV prevalence survey data. In simulating the projections for the impact of AIDS, historical data and NSF program baseline data were used for the AIDS-without-intervention scenario. For the AIDS-with-intervention scenario, pre-2002 data are the same as for the AIDS-without-intervention scenario, and the expected changes in population and in prevalence rates during 2003–16 reflect the targets set in the NSF. The key assumptions of the AIDS-with-intervention scenario are the following. First, prevention of mother-to-child transmission, which covered 34 percent of the at-risk population at baseline in 2002, will gradually expand to cover 70 percent by 2006. Second, voluntary counseling and testing, which also covered 34 percent of the at-risk population in 2002, will reach 80 percent coverage in 2006. Third, antiretroviral therapy will reach 90 percent coverage by 2006. Fourth, sexually transmitted disease prevalence rates will decline by 50 percent by 2006. Although the NSF's target for each of the programs is 100 percent coverage of all at-risk groups by 2009, in view of reservations about implementation capacity and possible program reach, the targets were relaxed for the purpose of the simulation, so that beyond 2006 all interventions remain at 90 percent coverage.

The simulations suggest that the program laid out in the NSF would result in a substantial decline in new HIV infections (Figure 9.1), reaching about 15,000 by 2015, compared with more than twice as many in the AIDS-without-intervention scenario. By 2005, as the antiretroviral therapy program expands, AIDS deaths would start falling rapidly, to fewer than 10,000 in 2015, compared with more than 30,000 in the same year under the AIDS-without-intervention scenario. As a consequence, the model predicts that the demographic impact of HIV/AIDS would be mitigated substantially (Figure 9.2). The overall population growth rate in 2015 would be 2 percent, compared with 0.9 percent in the AIDS-without-intervention scenario and 2.9 percent in a no-AIDS scenario.

The impact of the mother-to-child transmission program on infant mortality is a significant factor in increasing the growth rate of the population. In 1997 it was estimated that 18 percent of reported HIV cases were in children under the age of 4. Most of these children are born HIV-positive, whereas others become infected in infancy (usually through breast-feeding). For these children the progression to AIDS generally takes about one to two years, with death occurring in the third or the fourth year. NACA estimates that only about 34 percent of pregnancies benefited from the mother-to-child transmission program in the 2002 baseline period. Under the assumption that the targeted increase in participation, to 70 percent by 2006 and 100 percent by the end of the program, is achieved, the decline in the infant mortality rate arising from an effectively imple-

Figure 9.1. Botswana: HIV/AIDS-Related Deaths and New Infections Under Alternative Scenarios
(Thousands)

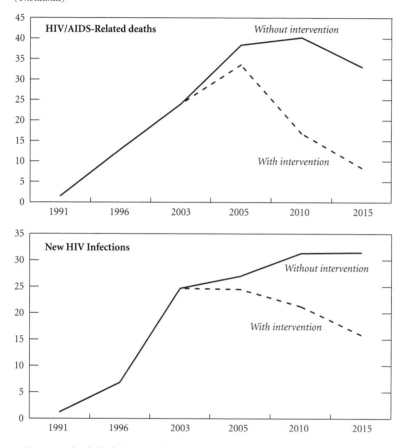

Source: Authors' calculations using data from Botswana national authorities and the Spectrum model.

mented mother-to-child transmission program results in a higher rate of population growth.

The NSF results in higher population growth rates than in the AIDS-without-intervention scenario for several reasons. First, the life span of those receiving antiretroviral treatment is extended, and mortality rates decline initially. Later on, although a number of patients on antiretroviral treatment eventually die (raising mortality in later years, other things equal), increasing coverage rates of antiretroviral treatment and a decline in new infections mean that mortality stays lower throughout the time

Figure 9.2. Botswana: Population Growth, Crude Death Rate, and Infant Mortality Under Alternative Scenarios

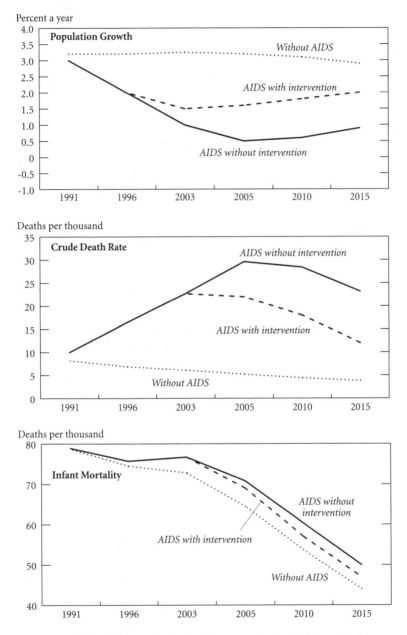

Percent a year

Population Growth

Without AIDS

AIDS with intervention

AIDS without intervention

Deaths per thousand

Crude Death Rate

AIDS without intervention

AIDS with intervention

Without AIDS

Deaths per thousand

Infant Mortality

AIDS without intervention

AIDS with intervention

Without AIDS

Source: Authors' calculations using data from Botswana national authorities and the Spectrum model.

horizon of the NSF. Second, lower mortality and morbidity among the sexually active population also mean that the decline in birthrates associated with HIV/AIDS is mitigated.

A Macroeconomic Framework

One of the earliest attempts to model the impact of the HIV/AIDS epidemic in Africa was that by Over (1992), which was based on an econometric estimation of growth in a cross section of 30 countries, looking in particular at differences in impacts by skill level and at the financing of private health expenditure. Cuddington (1993a, 1993b) and Cuddington and Hancock (1995) explored the impact of HIV/AIDS in a neoclassical growth model with one or two sectors, including a link between the age structure of the workforce and productivity, through experience or on-the-job learning.

A major study of the impact of HIV/AIDS on Botswana's economy (and still one of the most comprehensive studies available internationally) was prepared by the Botswana Institute for Development and Policy Analysis (BIDPA, 2000). Using a Solow-type production function, the study analyzed the impact in a two-sector model, using calibrated estimates. Using population projections based on the expected future path of HIV, the study derived projections of the size of the labor force and the subsequent effect of HIV/AIDS on aggregate output and output per capita through 2021, the distribution of income among different groups, and the long-term fiscal outlook. The study showed that HIV/AIDS would reduce the annual growth rate of the economy by an average of 1.5 percentage points, so that after 25 years the economy would be 31 percent smaller than it would otherwise have been.

Drawing on the BIDPA model, MacFarlan and Sgherri (2001) focused on the effect of HIV/AIDS on the long-term productive capacity of the economy. The channels through which the impacts are transmitted are labor supply and productivity, which in turn affect saving and investment, financial intermediation, and the prospects for economic diversification. The results of high HIV prevalence rates are declining productivity and increased mortality among the most economically active members of the population, leading to a reduction in capital and human resources available for production and investment, and reductions in the saving rate and real income. Assuming higher prevalence rates than used in the BIDPA study, MacFarlan and Sgherri predicted that annual GDP growth outside the mining sector would fall by 3 to 4 percentage points on average over the decade.

The principal objective of this chapter is to assess the macroeconomic effects of a comprehensive program of enhanced prevention measures and increased access to health care. Because the demographic projections do not allow for a differentiation of the impact of HIV/AIDS by sector, the model adopted is a relatively simple growth model that follows Cuddington (1993a) but extends the framework by allowing for changes in the size and productivity of the labor force arising from the implementation of a package of HIV-related interventions. The model presented is highly generalized, but it does capture the moderating effect of changing demographic patterns on the evolution of HIV/AIDS and, subsequently, its macroeconomic effect through the labor force and the capital stock.

Production in the economy, Y, is characterized by a Cobb-Douglas-type technology with constant returns to scale. Equation (1) specifies that output is a function of labor, capital, and total factor productivity:

$$Y_t = \alpha \gamma^t L_t^\beta K_t^{(1-\beta)}, \tag{1}$$

where Y_t is aggregate output, L_t represents the labor input measured in efficiency units, and K_t is the capital input. The variable γ is the rate of technological change over time, β is the share of labor in aggregate output, and capital's share is derived residually. Finally, α is a scale factor adjusted to fit the actual data in the base year.

In studies of countries in which resource extraction (such as minerals, oil, or timber) makes up a large share of GDP, it is often useful to account for this sector separately, because it is vulnerable to changes in the world prices of the extracted goods, or because the large share of economic rents in resource extraction may account for a significant share of its value added. The latter consideration also means that this sector is less sensitive to changes in domestic factor markets; this is reinforced if companies in the sector (for example, multinational mining corporations) bring in key personnel from abroad. Thus mining companies may have some scope for absorbing additional HIV/AIDS-related expenditures, and the impact of HIV/AIDS on output could be minimal.[5]

This consideration is particularly relevant for Botswana, where mining output constitutes more than a third of value added in output, as noted previously, and more than half of domestic government revenue. The analysis

---

[5]On the other hand, if profit margins are low, an increase in production costs by several percentage points (not an unusual number in the context of HIV/AIDS) could turn an operation unprofitable and even result in its closure. This consideration is particularly relevant in the longer run, when start-up and investment costs need to be considered and do not constitute sunk costs as they do in the short run.

in this chapter assumes that mining output and the number of people working in the mining sector are not affected by HIV/AIDS. This implies that mining workers who die or retire are replaced by workers from other sectors, thus exacerbating the impact of HIV/AIDS on nonmining GDP.

HIV/AIDS has an impact on labor in two ways, through the productivity of the labor force and through its size. The efficiency unit of labor is a function of the number of HIV-infected workers, as well as of the proportion of the work period lost to absence or reduced productivity:

$$L_t = \sum_{i=15}^{64} (1-z_t a_{it})\rho_{it} E_{it}. \tag{2}$$

In equation (2) the effective labor supply, L, is a function of the fraction z of the work year lost per infected worker because of HIV-related absences and reduced productivity, and the proportion a of the population that is infected with HIV. E_{it} is the employed workforce of age i at time t, and ρ measures the productivity gain that comes with experience on the job.[6] The efficiency of labor depends not only on the labor force participation rate but also on the workers' experience, which is increasing in the number of years spent working. As prevalence rates rise, progression to AIDS means that the labor force becomes younger as older and more experienced workers drop out of the labor force and are replaced by younger, less experienced workers. Denoting the population growth rate as gn,

$$gn_t = gn_t(a_t). \tag{3}$$

By equation (3) the population growth rate is a function of a, the proportion of persons infected with HIV. Higher rates of infection would result in future declines in the population, depending on how rapidly HIV infection progresses to AIDS. Capital accumulation is financed by domestic saving and foreign capital inflows, as expressed by

$$\Delta K = f(S, S_f), \tag{4}$$

where S is domestic saving and S_f net capital inflows.

The increasing cost of managing the epidemic imposes certain constraints on public and private saving, directly or indirectly. In Botswana some health care expenditure is categorized as "development" or capital expenditure. As morbidity and mortality rise, health care expenditure by

---

[6]Following Cuddington (1993a), the productivity gain is defined as a worker's experience, proxied by taking the worker's age and subtracting 15, the assumed age of entry into the labor force. BIDPA's estimate of the earnings function for Botswana assumes a starting age of 20 years in the formal sector, as follows: $\rho = \delta_1 + \delta_2(i-20) + \delta_3(i-20)$, where the δs are estimated from the earnings function of the labor force.

the government, households, and firms will be increasing in the number of HIV patients, as prevalence rates rise. Public expenditure will consist of direct health expenditure on treatment or prevention as well as some spending for training to replace absent or dead HIV-infected workers. Private sector saving is also affected, as firms increase the share of expenditure allocated to HIV prevention and care. Households will also spend more of their income on medications, funerals, visits to hospitals, and so forth. It is likely that some of these expenditures will come from income that would otherwise have been saved, thereby adversely affecting the saving rate, or from reduction of other current expenditure. Therefore the evolution of total domestic saving S_t in the presence of HIV is

$$S_t = s_t Y_t - x p a_t L_t, \tag{5}$$

where s_t is the domestic saving rate. In the AIDS-without-intervention scenario, in other words, domestic saving S_t will equal the national saving rate times income, less x, the proportion of annual AIDS expenditure financed out of savings; p, the cost per patient in pula; and $a_t L_t$, the number of HIV-infected workers in the labor force.

For simplicity, assume that net inflows of foreign direct investment are constant as a proportion of GDP. (For countries exporting capital, this investment may well be negative, in which case domestic saving exceeds domestic investment.) To the extent that HIV/AIDS results in capital flight and reduces this ratio, the impact of HIV/AIDS on GDP (and thus the macroeconomic benefits from its mitigation) will be stronger than in the model discussed here.[7]

If capital is expressed in terms of the labor force, $K/L = k$, then the period-to-period change in the capital-labor ratio is

$$\Delta k = [s(a) + s_f] f(ka) - gn(a)k - \theta k, \tag{6}$$

where θ is the depreciation rate and s_f the ratio of net capital inflows to GDP. The equation specifies the capital-labor ratio as a function of the total saving rate, production per worker, the HIV prevalence rate a, the population growth rate gn, and the depreciation rate θ.

Macroeconomic Impact of Botswana's National Strategic Framework

In the model under consideration, the macroeconomic impact of HIV/AIDS could be moderated through effective intervention programs.

---

[7]See Haacker (2002b) for a more detailed discussion of this point.

The negative effect on the labor force would be ameliorated as the rate of new infections slows and the useful life span of the infected is extended, and this will raise productivity as less working time is lost and the decline in workers' experience is mitigated. In the short run, the effect on capital accumulation will be negative, especially if a substantial proportion of the cost is financed from saving, possibly with the addition of donor-supported capital inflows. These effects could therefore result in a less pessimistic outlook for output growth than in a without-intervention scenario.

The specified model is simulated over the period 1991–2016, based on the actual values of the variables in 1991, and under three alternative scenarios: no AIDS, AIDS without intervention, and AIDS with intervention. Data for 1991 are used for the initial values of real GDP, the capital stock, and gross domestic investment. Following closely on previous work on Botswana, the labor-output and capital-output ratios are assumed to be 0.3 and 0.7, respectively, and the exogenous technological trend is set at 0.004. The depreciation rate is set at 7 percent, in line with CSO practice. In the preprogram years, separate data did not exist for the cost of HIV/AIDS treatment, but a range of 400 to 954 pula per patient was estimated based on expenditure data from the Ministry of Health. In the program years, the average cost per patient was 7,383 pula a year. In the past Botswana was able to run a surplus on the recurrent budget, which includes health care costs. In the medium-term program, however, it is assumed that Botswana finances 50 percent of the program cost from savings.

Labor force and human capital

The positive effect of the NSF program on the labor force (Figure 9.3) arises from the expanded labor force, the higher participation rate, and the impact on skill accumulation in the economy. The labor force becomes larger than in the AIDS-without-intervention scenario because various treatment options prolong the life of AIDS patients, enabling them to participate in the labor force. Furthermore, the slowdown in new infections means that newer entrants to the labor force are virtually HIV-free and not likely to drop out because of HIV-related illnesses.

In addition to the positive effect on labor force size, productivity and the efficiency of labor improve relative to the AIDS-without-intervention scenario. Although the lost human capital can only be replaced in the long run as new entrants to the labor force acquire more experience, the use of antiretroviral therapy results in a more productive life than would otherwise be the case. Although the impact of productivity may be difficult to

Figure 9.3. Botswana: Labor Force Size
(Thousands)

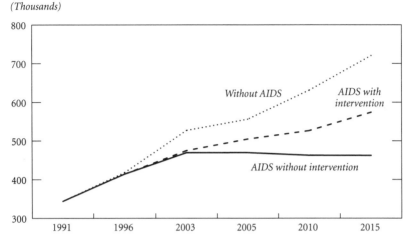

Source: Authors' calculations using data from Botswana national authorities and The Spectrum model.

measure, an analysis of the contribution to economic growth in the three scenarios (Table 9.3) shows that, in the AIDS-with-intervention scenario, the contribution of labor to changes in the growth rate improves remarkably in the medium term.

Saving and capital accumulation

The NSF program involves the commitment of substantial resources to financing the HIV/AIDS program. Therefore the effect on public and private saving in the initial program years is remarkable. Even though the model assumes that only half of the cost is financed from savings, by 2008 the contribution of capital to the change in real output is lower than in either the AIDS-without-intervention or the no-AIDS scenario. This comes about mainly because, in the AIDS-without-intervention scenario, there is no programmatic spending on HIV outside of the allocation in the health ministry's budget. Apart from public saving, private saving would also fall as firms' health care costs increase and households assume some of those costs. However, because these are one-time effects, by 2013 the capital contribution to GDP resumes its upward trend.

The implication of declining saving is a slower rate of capital accumulation in the program years. A crucial determinant of the overall outcome is the extent to which Botswana can attract the financial support of devel-

Table 9.3. Botswana: Contributions to Projected Changes in GDP Under Alternative Scenarios
(Percentage points)

		Contribution of Change in:		
Scenario and Year	Change in Real Output Growth	Total factor productivity	Capital	Labor
No AIDS				
2005	5.5	0.4	4.3	0.8
2008	5.2	0.4	4.0	0.8
2011	5.1	0.4	3.9	0.8
2012	5.0	0.4	3.8	0.8
2013	5.0	0.4	3.8	0.8
2014	4.9	0.4	3.7	0.8
2015	4.9	0.4	3.7	0.8
AIDS without intervention				
2005	4.0	0.3	3.8	−0.2
2008	3.5	0.3	3.3	−0.2
2011	3.2	0.2	2.9	−0.1
2012	3.1	0.2	2.8	−0.1
2013	3.0	0.2	2.7	−0.1
2014	3.0	0.2	2.6	0.0
2015	2.9	0.2	2.5	0.0
AIDS with intervention				
2005	4.8	0.3	3.9	0.2
2008	4.1	0.3	2.5	0.2
2011	4.0	0.3	2.5	0.4
2012	4.1	0.4	2.7	0.5
2013	4.1	0.4	2.7	0.5
2014	4.1	0.4	2.8	0.6
2015	4.1	0.4	3.1	0.6

Sources: Spectrum model software and author's calculations.

opment partners in managing the epidemic. Again, the current results are based on the assumption that 50 percent of the cost is financed from savings. Should donor support fail to materialize, requiring a greater reliance on domestic saving than projected, the outlook may be much worse than expected, because the negative effect on capital accumulation would be greater.

Overall economic growth

The most significant macroeconomic impact is the increase in the growth rate of the economy under the AIDS-with-intervention scenario compared with the AIDS-without-intervention scenario. Under the with-intervention scenario, GDP is projected to grow at an annual rate of 4.1 percent by the end of the program in 2008, compared with 3.5 percent in the absence of intervention. By 2015 GDP is growing at a rate of 4.1 percent a year under the AIDS-with-intervention scenario, compared with 2.9 percent under the without-intervention scenario; however, even the higher rate is still less than the 4.9 percent rate projected in the absence of AIDS.

A growth accounting exercise (Table 9.3) illuminates some of the dynamics of the growth simulation, in particular how the relative sizes of the mining and nonmining sectors in Botswana condition the outcome. In the AIDS-without-intervention scenario, the contribution of labor to growth is negative until 2013, since in the absence of intervention the size and productivity of the labor force contract over time. Following from the initial assumption that the effect of HIV/AIDS on the mining sector is negligible, this outcome is mainly driven by the contraction in labor force participation in the highly labor-intensive nonmining sector. The decline in capital's contribution, however, is not as remarkable because of the assumed negligible effect in the mining sector and lower capital accumulation in the nonmining sector.

Direct and Indirect Effects on Government Finances

The most thorough assessment of the fiscal effects of HIV/AIDS in Botswana is that in BIDPA (2000). The demographic projections used here correspond most closely to BIDPA's "high" scenario, to which all citations below refer.[8]

According to BIDPA, in the high scenario direct and indirect expenditure on HIV/AIDS exceeds 5 percent of GDP by 2010. Direct costs, such as the clinical cost of AIDS treatment and care, as well as the cost of awareness campaigns and other HIV/AIDS prevention measures, are projected to reach about 3.5 percent of GDP. Indirect costs (a term that is used in this chapter for all expenditures not included in specific HIV/AIDS budget line items) for social expenditure are approximately 1.5 percent of GDP. Social expenditure—mainly poverty alleviation programs aimed at redistributing income—are projected to increase by 10 percent, roughly in line with the decrease in income among those falling below the poverty line as a result of HIV/AIDS-related morbidity and mortality. The increase in allowances for the destitute and for orphans would also be commensurate with the increase in those groups, as HIV infection spreads and more income earners die from AIDS-related illnesses.

---

[8]The presentation differs, however, in that it presents estimates as percentages of GDP, whereas BIDPA presents expenditure as a percentage of recurrent expenditure, and revenue as a percentage of total revenue.

Table 9.4. Botswana: Comparison of Changes in Expenditure Categories in 2010 Projected by BIDPA (2000) and NACA (2003)
(Percent of GDP)

Item	Source of Projection		Indirect Fiscal Gains
	BIDPA	NSF	
Health and prevention	3.5	5.0	—
Social expenditure	1.5	0.7	0.8
Public service	0.8	0.3	0.5
Education	0.3	0.1	−0.2
Other	0.2	3.0	—
Indirect fiscal gains (sum)			1.1

Sources: BIDPA (2000), NACA (2003), and author's calculations.

These, however, are not the only indirect costs. BIDPA's projection envisages increased staff costs in the public service arising from an increase in the government's wage bill by about 6 percent, as a shortage of skilled labor causes their wages to be bid up. It is also expected that the increase in deaths will raise death-related benefits, funeral expenses, and disability benefits. To some extent, however, these costs could be offset by the reduction in the government's pension obligations from the higher mortality rate. Although staff costs could also arise from training and recruitment expenditure, as recruitment rises and newly recruited staff require training, declining expenditure on education would dampen some of these adverse impacts.

Table 9.4 presents BIDPA's estimates of the impact of HIV/AIDS on government expenditure in 2010; these estimates do not include a feedback effect from prevention and treatment efforts. The estimates for the indirect fiscal effects of the NSF are then obtained by, first, replacing the BIDPA estimates for health expenditure with the latest projections specified under the NACA (2003). Second, BIDPA (2000) does not include most of the overhead and other expenses related to the NSF, which are summarized under "other costs." Fiscal savings arise in the various areas of social expenditure and the costs of the public service (for example, owing to reduced costs of benefits). These are largely associated with lower mortality due to HIV/AIDS owing to measures implemented within the NSF. To obtain estimates of the savings in these expenditure categories, most of which are not budgeted for in the NSF, the projected costs of HIV/AIDS from BIDPA are then scaled down in line with lower mortality under the NSF.

Table 9.4 shows that the savings owing to feedback effects from HIV/AIDS programs can contribute to the financing of a comprehensive HIV/AIDS framework. The NSF envisages higher expenditure on health services, reflecting, to a large extent, increased access to antiretroviral treatment. "Other costs" include investment costs and smaller items that, owing to different coverage, are not comparable between BIDPA and the NSF. The savings in the areas of social expenditure, public service, and education, amount to 1.1 percent of GDP, or about 14 percent of the costs of the NSF. However, these numbers most likely understate the fiscal savings associated with the NSF, because they do not include savings within the line items of our highly aggregate presentation. Such savings arise, for example, if prevention efforts contribute to a decline in treatment costs.

Worldwide, a substantial proportion of HIV/AIDS-related expenditure is financed by external grants; the Joint United Nations Programme on HIV/AIDS (UNAIDS, 2003) estimates that, in 2003, more than three-fourths of institutional HIV/AIDS spending worldwide came from international sources, including bilateral sources, the U.N. system, the grant component of World Bank loans, and international nongovernmental organizations. For Botswana, Martin (2003) estimates that HIV/AIDS-related expenditure in 2001/02 amounted to $113 million, of which donors financed $96 million. Although Botswana's NSF does not provide any estimates of expected donor assistance, it makes repeated reference to the important role of Botswana's development partners. More generally, a broad national strategy on HIV/AIDS, developed with inputs from all layers of government, civil society, and development partners, can be used to mobilize additional funding from international donors and facilitate coordination among them.

Regarding the impact of HIV/AIDS on domestic revenue, many components of tax and other revenue can be expected to change at about the same rate as GDP. According to estimates in Kibuka and others (2004), for example, government revenue amounted to 41.9 percent of GDP in 2002/03. Excluding items such as mineral revenue (21.9 percent of GDP), interest, asset sales, and grants, revenue that would grow at a similar rate as overall economic activity accounts for 19 percent of GDP. Given that GDP increases by 25 percent by 2010 in this chapter's AIDS-with-intervention scenario, relative to the scenario without intervention, this would mean that government revenue grows by 3.8 percent of GDP. However, not all of this additional revenue can be mobilized for the financing of the NSF, because an increase in GDP and, in particular, in the size of the population also implies an increase in the demand for general government services.

Although simplistic, this analysis of the fiscal repercussions of the NSF suggests that the indirect fiscal effects of a comprehensive prevention and treatment program can contribute significantly to the program's own financing. (Of course, the indirect fiscal benefits are only part of the broader social and economic benefits arising from a successful HIV/AIDS program.) These indirect gains, in turn, are interrelated with the macroeconomic effects, which this chapter's analysis of the fiscal effects does not include explicitly. Given the size of the indirect fiscal gains (whether they can be mobilized for a program like the NSF or not), a fuller analysis is warranted, including a more disaggregated analysis of government expenditure and taking into account the linkages between the broad macroeconomic effects and the fiscal effects.

Conclusions

Botswana's NSF formulates a broad response to the HIV/AIDS epidemic around the "central goal of the National Response to HIV/AIDS," namely, "to eliminate the incidence of HIV and reduce the impact of AIDS in Botswana" (NACA, 2003), and it defines HIV/AIDS-related actions for all functional and regional divisions of government. The NSF does not spell out its potential impact in terms of human development and macroeconomic performance. However, it envisages that HIV-related death rates will be lower, that patients will have longer and more productive lives, that the number of orphans will be fewer, and that mother-to-child transmission rates can be considerably reduced.

Using a simple macroeconomic model, this chapter has sketched how to expand this strategic framework, focusing in particular on the impact on government finance. The NSF envisages a substantial allocation of resources to fighting the epidemic. However, through its demographic and macroeconomic effects, which in themselves are highly desirable, it also helps contain certain categories of expenditure, and, by mitigating the adverse effects of HIV/AIDS on the tax base, it mobilizes domestic revenue to offset some of the fiscal costs of the program.

This analysis demonstrates the benefits of integrating a strategic framework on HIV/AIDS, such as Botswana's NSF, into a broader economic and fiscal framework and, vice versa, incorporating an assessment of the indirect economic and fiscal benefits of reduced HIV incidence and improved access to treatment into a strategic framework for dealing with HIV/AIDS. From this analysis, looking narrowly at the financial costs and benefits of HIV/AIDS interventions, it appears that the indirect macroeconomic and fiscal effects are an important part of the picture. Taking a wider perspective, an analysis of the broad development impact of HIV/AIDS, and thus also of a strategic framework on HIV/AIDS, can help in defining the operational targets of such a strategy.

Appendix: Assumptions Used in the Demographic Projections

The demographic projection was generated using Spectrum, a Windows-based program developed by The Futures Group with funding from the U.S. Agency for International Development. The program uses current information on population, fertility, mortality, and migration to project the future demographic trend of a population group. There are six modules in the program, the most relevant to this exercise being the DemProj, which was used to generate the population trend, and the AIDS Impact Module (AIM), which was used to project the consequences of the AIDS epidemic.

The following information was used to generate the demographic projection for Botswana:

- Population by age and sex in the base year 1991 is presented in Table 9.A1 and is from the 2001 Botswana Central Statistics Office (CSO) *Statistical Bulletin*.
- Total fertility rates are defined as the average number of births that a female in the 15–49 age group would be expected to have in her lifetime, based on existing fertility patterns. According to the latest census data from the CSO *Statistical Bulletin*, 2001, p. 15, the total fertility rate was 6.5 for 1971, 6.6 for 1981, and 5.2 for 1991.
- Age-specific fertility rates, defined as the number of live births per 1,000 women in each age group, are averages for all of sub-Saharan Africa and are from the United Nations; they are incorporated into the Spectrum model as the default.
- Sex ratio at birth in 1991 is 92 males per 100 females and is from the CSO *Statistical Bulletin*, 2001, p. 14.
- Life expectancy at birth in the absence of AIDS is 63.3 years for males and 67.1 for females; data are from the CSO *Statistical Bulletin*, 2001, p. 15, for 1991 and United Nations population projections for subsequent years.
- Infant mortality is 87.5 per 1,000 births in 1991 and is from the *Statistical Bulletin*, 1991; for other years the Spectrum model uses the United Nations General Life Table, which translates to an assumed infant mortality rate of 54 per 1,000 births.
- Crude death rates are 13.9 per 1,000 population for 1981 and 11.5 per 1,000 for 1991, from CSO *Statistical Bulletin*, 2001, p. 15; for other years the Spectrum model uses the United Nations General Life Table, which translates to an assumed crude death rate of 8.2 per 1,000.
- International migration (net) is the model default, taken from United Nations data.

Table 9.A1. Botswana: Population by Age and Sex, 1991

Age (years)	Males	Females	Total
0–4	96,676	96,989	193,665
5–9	97,563	99,051	196,614
10–14	89,887	93,596	183,483
15–19	73,112	79,413	152,525
20–24	54,261	62,622	116,883
25–29	45,408	54,440	99,848
30–34	36,620	44,013	80,633
35–39	30,487	35,741	66,228
40–44	23,197	25,001	48,198
45–49	18,553	20,496	39,049
50–54	16,192	17,519	33,711
55–59	12,746	15,003	27,749
60–64	10,485	12,271	22,756
65–69	8,688	11,155	19,843
70–74	6,857	7,872	14,729
75+	13,668	17,214	30,882
Total	634,400	692,396	1,326,796

Source: Botswana Central Statistical Office (2001), p. 13.

References

Bloom, David E., and Ajay S. Mahal, 1995, "Does the Aids Epidemic Really Threaten Economic Growth?" NBER Working Paper No. 5148 (Cambridge, Massachusetts: National Bureau of Economic Research).

Botswana Institute for Development Policy Analysis (BIDPA), 2000, *Macroeconomic Impacts of the HIV/AIDS Epidemic in Botswana* (Gaborone, Botswana).

Botswana Central Statistical Office, 2001, *Statistical Bulletin* (Gaborone, Botswana).

Cuddington, John T., 1993a, "Modeling the Macroeconomic Effects of AIDS, with an Application to Tanzania," *World Bank Economic Review,* Vol. 7, No. 2, pp.173–89.

———, 1993b, "Further Results on the Macroeconomic Effects of AIDS: The Dualistic, Labour-Surplus Economy," *World Bank Economic Review,* Vol. 7, No. 3, pp. 403–17.

———, and John D. Hancock, 1995, "The Macroeconomic Impact of AIDS in Malawi: A Dualistic, Labour Surplus Economy," *Journal of African Economics,* Vol. 4, No. 1, pp. 1–28.

Green, John H., and others, 2002, "Botswana: Selected Issues and Statistical Appendix," IMF Staff Country Report No. 02/243 (Washington: International Monetary Fund).

Haacker, Markus, 2002a, "The Economic Consequences of HIV/AIDS in Southern Africa," IMF Working Paper 02/38 (Washington: International Monetary Fund).

———, 2002b, "Modeling the Macroeconomic Impact of HIV/AIDS," IMF Working Paper 02/195 (Washington: International Monetary Fund).

Joint United Nations Programme on HIV/AIDS (UNAIDS), 2003, "Report on the State of HIV/AIDS Financing (Revised/Updated June 2003)" (Geneva).

Kibuka, Robin, and others, 2004, "Botswana: Selected Issues and Statistical Appendix," IMF Country Report No. 02/212 (Washington: International Monetary Fund).

MacFarlan, Maitland, and Silvia Sgherri, 2001, "The Macroeconomic Impact of HIV/AIDS in Botswana" IMF Working Paper No. 01/80 (Washington: International Monetary Fund).

Martin, H. Gayle, 2003, "A Comparative Analysis of the Financing of HIV/AIDS Programmes in Botswana, Lesotho, Mozambique, South Africa, Swaziland, and Zimbabwe" (Pretoria, South Africa: Human Sciences Research Council).

National AIDS Coordinating Agency (NACA), 2003, *Botswana National Strategic Framework for HIV /AIDS* 2003–09 (Gaborone, Botswana).

Over, Mead, 1992, "The Macroeconomic Effect of AIDS in Sub-Saharan Africa," AFTN Technical Working Paper No. 3 (Washington: Population, Health and Nutrition Division, Africa Technical Department, World Bank).

U.S. Census Bureau, 2003, "International Data Base" (Washington: U.S. Census Bureau).

10

Impact of the HIV/AIDS Epidemic on the Health Sectors of Developing Countries

Mead Over

Any discussion of the impact of acquired immune deficiency syndrome (AIDS) on health care systems must distinguish between treatment of the opportunistic illnesses associated with AIDS and treatment directed at the underlying cause, namely, the human immunodeficiency virus (HIV). Treatment of opportunistic illnesses can alleviate suffering but typically extends life by only months. Treatment that controls the HIV in the patient's body, called antiretroviral therapy or ART, can be much more successful, adding years to life expectancy.

Before 2001 the annual cost of a three-drug combination ART regimen for a patient in a poor country was approximately $10,000 to $25,000. Only a few of the richest developing countries, such as Brazil and Thailand, could attempt to finance ART for their AIDS patients. In most developing countries the only patients receiving ART were the very rich or those who had access to rationed, low-price supplies through a variety of pilot or research projects. Most other patients had little access to ART, and thus the impact of AIDS on these countries' health systems could be understood simply by considering the demand for and supply of the treatment of opportunistic illnesses.

Since 2001, however, generic versions of ART medications have become available in poor countries at a cost of as little as $150 a year. In 2001, at the Doha round of World Trade Organization (WTO) discussions, both industrial and developing countries negotiated and signed a Declaration on Trade-Related Aspects of Intellectual Property Rights (TRIPs) and Public Health, which confirmed provisions already implicit in earlier WTO agreements: a country would have the right to grant "compulsory licenses" to a domestic pharmaceutical manufacturer to produce medications for domestic consumption when the national government decides there is a public health emergency. In 2003 further negotiation led to an extension of the declaration to permit countries without domestic pharmaceutical industries to import generic versions of patented drugs. Permission was made subject to the WTO's endorsement of the absence of domestic production capability, and generic manufacturers and exporters were required to ensure that the generic versions be easily distinguishable visually from the patented version.

Simultaneous with the dramatic fall in the prices of ART medication, poor countries are finding that new external sources for AIDS medication have appeared. Created in 2002, the Global Fund for AIDS, Tuberculosis, and Malaria has been funding proposals to finance the expansion of AIDS treatment in poor countries. The World Bank, which had previously financed the treatment of opportunistic illnesses and palliative care for AIDS, is allowing existing grants and credits to be reallocated to help strengthen national capacities for ART delivery. The U.S. government is dramatically increasing funding for ART in selected countries. And the World Health Organization (WHO) has joined with national governments and private foundations to announce the "3 by 5 Initiative," an ambitious plan to provide ART to 3 million AIDS patients by 2005.

Governments are struggling to understand the consequences of these rapid changes for their health care systems and to define their own policies for guiding the inflow of resources and complementing them with domestically financed initiatives. Questions they are asking include the following. How many AIDS patients do we have in our country? How many of them will come forward for ART? How many health workers do we have who can manage an AIDS patient on ART? Can our health care system achieve health benefits to AIDS patients as good as those achieved in pilot studies? Will AIDS patients crowd out other important health care programs, such as mother and child health programs, vaccination programs, and care for tuberculosis, malaria, diabetes, respiratory illness, and trauma? Will the current sources of funding for ART at some point dry up, forcing us to finance these drugs ourselves or let patients die? How can we ensure that our government and our health care system will be able to manage the inflow of resources for AIDS treatment without corruption or waste? What will be the impact of newly available, highly effective ART on the rate of new HIV infections? How should we alter our AIDS prevention programs as ART becomes widely available? How will current commitments to care for AIDS patients affect national expenditure and national priorities in the future?

The answers to these questions are complex and will necessarily differ from country to country. This chapter attempts to provide some guidance by, first, presenting a conceptual framework for analyzing the impact of AIDS on the health care system in the absence of ART, and then by adding ART to that picture.

Adjusting the Health Sector to the Treatment of Opportunistic Illnesses

AIDS affects the output of the health sector in two ways: by increasing demand and by reducing the supply of a given quality of care at a given price.[1] As a result, some HIV-negative people who would have obtained treatment for other illnesses had there been no epidemic are unable to do so, and total national expenditure on health care rises, both in absolute terms and as a proportion of national product.

Effect of AIDS on Demand for Care Before ART Was Available

Most people who develop AIDS are prime-age adults, defined as those aged 15 to 49. In the absence of AIDS, this age group typically accounts for only 10 to 20 percent of all deaths in a developing country in a given year, but the illnesses leading to these deaths typically generate a disproportionate share of total health care demand (Over and others, 1992; Sauerborn, Berman, and Nougtara, 1996). Moreover, several studies suggest that prime-age adults with AIDS tend to use more health care before death than those who die of other causes, or even than those with other prolonged illnesses. Thus the percentage increase in the demand for care by prime-age adults due to AIDS is likely to exceed the percentage increase in their mortality due to AIDS. As a result of these two factors, in a country where prime-age adults utilized one-fourth of all health care before AIDS, a given percentage increase in their demand for health care will increase total demand by at least one-fourth of that percentage. For example, a 40 percent increase in the mortality rate of prime-age adults will increase total demand for care by at least 10 percent, even though total mortality has increased by only 4 to 8 percent. If AIDS patients use ART, which prolongs their lives but does not cure them, the increase in demand will be much greater.

---

[1] This section draws on previously published material in World Bank (1997, 1999).

How much the demand for care increases in the aggregate depends on the increase in the prime-age adult death rate, which in turn depends on HIV prevalence in this group and the median time from infection to death. A stable prevalence rate of 5 percent among prime-age adults eventually increases their annual mortality by about 5 deaths per 1,000 persons if the median time from infection to death is 10 years. A prevalence rate of 30 percent, as observed in parts of southern Africa, will increase the number of deaths per 1,000 prime-age adults by 30 to 60, depending on the median time to death. In sub-Saharan Africa, where mortality rates in this age group were as high as 5 per 1,000 before the epidemic, even a 5 percent infection rate will double or triple the adult death rate. In a middle-income developing country with pre-epidemic adult mortality of 1 per 1,000, the same endemic level of HIV infection will increase prime-age adult mortality 5- or 10-fold.

Given these parameters, how much will the epidemic increase the demand for care? Consider a country where prime-age adults consumed one-fourth of all health care before the AIDS epidemic, where HIV prevalence is constant at 5 percent of prime-age adults, where the median time to death is 10 years, and where the baseline mortality rate among prime-age adults is 5 per 1,000. In this case mortality among prime-age adults will approximately double as a consequence of HIV/AIDS. If the demand for treatment is proportional to mortality for the respective causes (this depends on the costs of treatment, as well as the duration of the illness), then the demand for health services, at any given price, would increase by 25 percent. If the prevalence rate is higher, if mortality rates among those infected are higher (for given prevalence rates), or if the baseline adult mortality rate is lower, the percentage increase in demand will be correspondingly greater.

A final important factor that may increase demand is third-party payment for health care. This may take the form of private insurance, a government-run insurance program, or, more typically, health care partly financed through general taxation and offered at reduced cost to the patient. Because one or more of these types of third-party payment often cover a portion of health care costs, the price paid by the patient is usually a fraction of the cost of providing the care. Since third-party payment thus enables patients to purchase more care than they would otherwise, it increases the demand for care arising from any given level of illness, thus magnifying the price shock of an AIDS epidemic. For example, if patients themselves pay 25 percent of the cost of their care, they will reduce their utilization in response to any increase in cost by only one-fourth as much as they would if they had to pay the full increase.

Effect of AIDS on the Supply of Care Before Antiretroviral Therapy Was Available

Even as it increases the demand for care, the AIDS epidemic will reduce the supply of care available at a given price, in three ways. The magnitude of these effects will generally be larger, the poorer the country and the more widespread and severe the epidemic.

The first and largest effect is the increased cost of maintaining a given level of safety for medical procedures. Even without HIV, hospitals and clinics in poor countries may themselves pose a risk to health. Needles and other instruments are not always sterilized, rooms are often overcrowded and poorly ventilated, and care providers may lack rubber gloves and sometimes even soap. Without modern blood banks, a transfusion might infect the recipient with hepatitis B. In such situations infections of all types spread rapidly; some, including such common illnesses as pneumonia, may kill. Before HIV, however, infections picked up in a clinic or hospital were rarely fatal to persons not already in a seriously weakened state.

Because the AIDS epidemic has greatly increased the risk to patients of existing medical procedures, simply maintaining the level of safety that existed before HIV requires additional hygiene and blood screening, both of which increase the cost of care. In middle- to high-income countries, where blood screening and sterilization of injecting equipment are already the norm, the impact of AIDS is confined to the incremental cost of adding an HIV test to existing tests and using rubber gloves and face masks in situations where they were not used previously. In poor countries, where blood screening and needle sterilization were lacking before the epidemic, the resources needed to maintain the quality of care in the face of the AIDS epidemic can be substantial. For example, the annual budget of the Ugandan Blood Transfusion Service, which was established in response to the epidemic and meets the demands of the entire Ugandan national health care system for clean blood, is estimated to be about $1.2 million, including capital and recurrent costs. This amounts to about 2 percent of national public health expenditure, or about 1 percent of total national health expenditure (European Commission, 1995).

Despite the potentially high costs of blood screening, HIV has greatly increased the justification for a government role in ensuring a safe blood supply. However, there is no convincing rationale for government to subsidize the entire cost of running such a service indefinitely. Blood screening and improved collection procedures will protect blood donors and recipients. However, since the average donor and recipient do not engage in unprotected sex with a large number of partners, a person infected while giving or receiving blood is not likely to pass the infection to many others. Thus, in developing countries where the cost of establishing a safe blood supply is high, blood screening will not be among the more cost-effective approaches to preventing an epidemic based on sexual transmission.

To be sure, blood screening and better hygiene will help to prevent the spread of other infectious diseases besides AIDS. Such measures will also reduce the occupational risk of contracting AIDS and other diseases that health care workers face, and therefore reduce the amount of additional compensation needed to offset their occupational risk—an issue that will be discussed below. A careful accounting of the net cost of protecting patients from HIV by screening blood would need to take into consideration these additional benefits, for which data are lacking. However, it seems likely that, even if these benefits are taken into account, the remaining cost of screening blood and improving hygiene to protect patients from HIV/AIDS would substantially increase the unit cost of medical care.

The second factor reducing the supply of medical care at a given price is the increased attrition and absenteeism of health care workers who become infected with HIV. Like all prime-age adults, health care workers may become infected with HIV as a result of sexual contact or the use of unsterile injecting equipment outside of their work. Unlike other adults, they face an additional risk of becoming infected in the course of their work; however, this risk is generally much smaller than the risk from sexual contact. Thus whether the AIDS mortality rate among health care workers is higher or lower than among the general population depends mostly on the effects of income, education, and social status on sexual behavior. Two studies of HIV prevalence among health care workers from Africa suggest that doctors and nurses are at least as likely to become infected as other people (Mann and others, 1986; Buvé and others, 1994). If this is true elsewhere, a country with stable 5 percent HIV prevalence can expect that each year between 0.5 and 1 percent of its health care providers will die from AIDS; a country with 30 percent prevalence would lose 3 to 7 percent a year. This attrition from AIDS deaths may substantially increase the cost of health care. For example, if labor costs are half of total health care costs, and if training or recruiting a replacement worker requires a one-time expenditure equal to the worker's annual salary, then a 7 percent increase in attrition will increase total costs in the health sector by 3.5 percent.

The third way in which AIDS reduces the supply of health care is through the additional risk it imposes on health care workers. Even though most HIV-infected health care workers acquire their infection through sexual contact, in a society with a large proportion of HIV-positive patients, health care work will be more dangerous than if there were no HIV. Some students who would have become doctors and nurses will therefore choose alternative occupations, unless they are compensated with higher pay for the increased risk. A recent survey of medical and nursing students in the United States found that AIDS had indeed reduced the attractiveness of specialties in which contact with HIV-positive patients was more likely (Bernstein, Rabkin, and Wolland, 1990; Mazzullo and others, 1990). This problem is likely to be most severe in hard-hit developing countries, where HIV prevalence is much higher and rubber gloves and other protective equipment are often in short supply. In Zambia, for example, some nurses have demanded special payments to compensate for the increased occupational risk due to HIV (Buvé and others, 1994). A recent qualitative study in Ethiopia quotes health workers as saying, for example, "HIV/AIDS has increased our exposure to the virus and we fear contracting it," and "I have a son who used to be interested in joining the medical profession . . . but decided to join another profession. His reason was that he has observed the risk his parents are exposed to . . ." (Lindelöw, Serneels, and Lemma, 2003).

The magnitude of these increased costs due to higher required compensation of medical staff has not been estimated. As noted above, improved precautions in hospitals and clinics may reduce these costs. But because people respond to perceived risk rather than actual risk, such improvements may have little impact on the demand for increased compensation. Thus it seems clear that health care workers' perception of risk will either increase the cost or lower the quality of care. In either case the effect is an unambiguous increase in the cost of a quality-adjusted unit of care.

The total impact of these three effects—increased cost of preventing infections in medical facilities, attrition of health care workers due to HIV, and the additional pay that health care workers demand to compensate them for the increased risk of becoming infected—will depend most importantly on the prevalence of HIV and whether modern blood banks and hygienic practices are already in place. In a country that has 5 percent HIV prevalence among prime-age adults and lacked blood banks and blood screening before the epidemic, a conservative guess is that the cost of providing care of a given quantity and quality will rise by about 10 percent.

Now that relatively inexpensive ART is available, health care systems can use it to mitigate the effects of the attrition of workers due to HIV/AIDS and the fear of becoming infected from a patient. Workers with AIDS who adhere to ART will remain healthy and productive, and uninfected workers who know that prophylactic ART is available in case of an accidental needle stick will be less fearful of treating their patients. However, these uses of ART have costs that might be of the same order of magnitude as the original impact.

Partial Equilibrium Analysis

Taken together, increased demand and reduced supply have two related impacts: first, health care becomes scarcer and thus more expensive, and second, national health care expenditure rises. The size of these impacts depends partly on the elasticities of the demand for and the supply of care. The elasticity of demand for adult health care is usually small, since there are no close substitutes, and people who are sick and have the ability to pay will often pay whatever is necessary to get well. For simulation purposes, assume that a price increase of 10 percent would decrease utilization by only about 8 percent, for an elasticity of 0.8.

Higher prices also generally increase supply. Here, too, however, the nature of the health sector affects the response. In the very short run, perhaps a month, the supply of care is unlikely to respond much to greater demand and higher prices, whereas over the long run, the supply of physicians and inputs to health care can expand as much as necessary. Over the medium run, five years or so, one would expect the supply of care to respond somewhat to increased demand and the resulting higher price. One response observed in Canada, Egypt, India, Indonesia, and the Philippines is that physicians who work in the public sector rearrange their schedules to offer more health care privately, after their obligations to the government have been met. The elasticity of this response has been estimated at about 0.5 (Chawla, 1993, 1997; Bolduc, Fortin, and Fournier, 1996).

Under these assumptions, it is possible to estimate the impact of HIV/AIDS on the quantity and the price of health services (illustrated in Figure 10.1). It was argued above that a constant 5 percent HIV prevalence rate would increase the demand for care over the pre-epidemic level by about one-fourth and the cost of care of a given quality by 10 percent. Drawing on the assumptions in this subsection about the elasticities of demand and supply, and assuming that patients pay half the cost of their health care, the price of care would rise by about 30 percent. Total national health expenditure and the government's share of expenditure would both increase by about 43 percent ($1.3 \times 1.1 = 1.43$). With the same supply and demand elasticities, the increase would be less in a country like India,

Figure 10.1. Impact of HIV/AIDS on the Price and Quantity of Health Care

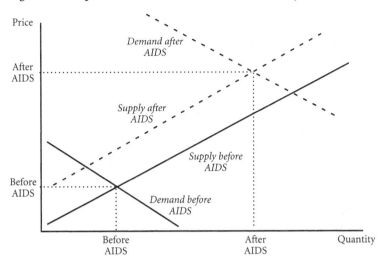

where only about one-fifth of the cost of care is paid by the government, and substantially more in many countries of Latin America and Eastern Europe, where three-fourths or more of the cost is typically subsidized.

Does the available empirical evidence support these conclusions? Measuring the scarcity of medical care through changes in the price of care of a given quality is problematic because of the difficulties in measuring quality. This is especially true in developing countries, where a general lack of data is compounded in the health sector by government subsidies and nonprice forms of rationing. In such cases the effective price of care may rise even though nominal prices remain constant. Furthermore, because of the lag between infection and death, the time between the attainment of a given HIV prevalence rate and the full impact of that rate on the demand and supply of health care can be 10 years or more. For these reasons one cannot accurately assess changes in the scarcity of health care in developing countries by observing changes in nominal prices. Nonetheless, one can get some sense of the extent to which HIV/AIDS increases the effective price of health care by considering whether the epidemic makes it more difficult to obtain care. Studies of hospital admissions data suggest that this is the case.

Table 10.1 shows the percentage of beds occupied by HIV-positive patients in six referral hospitals in developing countries that had large epidemics in the mid-1990s. The hospitals in question are the top health care institutions in each country, providing the best care available outside of a

Table 10.1. Hospital Beds Occupied by HIV-Positive Patients in Selected Cities, Circa 1996
(Percent)

City	Hospital	Share of Beds
Chiang Mai, Thailand	Provincial	50
Kinshasa, Democratic Republic of Congo	Mama Yemo	50
Kigali, Rwanda	Central	60
Bujumbura, Burundi	Prince Regent	70
Nairobi, Kenya	Kenyatta National	39
Kampala, Uganda	Rubaga	56

Source: World Bank (1999).

few expensive private clinics. Because these hospitals are at the apex of their health care pyramids, it is likely that AIDS patients make up a significant proportion of their patients. Even so, the percentage of beds occupied by HIV-positive patients is striking, ranging from 39 percent in Nairobi, Kenya, to 70 percent in Bujumbura, Burundi.

If these hospitals were operating well below capacity before the epidemic, they might have accommodated the HIV-positive patients without reducing care for the HIV-negative ones. Although no data on occupancy prior to the epidemic are available for these specific hospitals, bed occupancy rates in such hospitals typically were well above 50 percent even before AIDS appeared on the scene.

The best evidence that AIDS sometimes makes it more difficult for people not infected with the virus to get medical treatment comes from an in-depth study of Kenyatta National Hospital, the premier teaching hospital in Nairobi, Kenya. The study compared all patients admitted during a 22-day period in 1988 and 1989 with those admitted during a 15-day period in 1992 (Floyd and Gilks, 1996). The researchers found that the number of HIV-positive patients more than doubled, whereas the number of HIV-negative admissions shrank by 18 percent. Since it is very unlikely that the number of HIV-negative people in the hospital's catchment area shrank by this much, this evidence suggests that the AIDS epidemic did in fact result in some HIV-negative patients being dissuaded or barred from admission to the hospital.

Of course, no data exist on what happened to the HIV-negative patients who were not admitted. But hospital records show that the mortality rates for those who were admitted increased between the two periods, from 14 percent to 23 percent. The mortality rate for the HIV-positive patients did not increase, and other indicators of the quality of care remained constant. Thus the most likely explanation for the increased mortality rate among the HIV-negative patients is that the rationing scheme used to allocate increasingly scarce beds had the effect of changing the mix of HIV-negative patients toward those with more severe illnesses. Whether the rationing was imposed by hospital staff or was a response by prospective patients to their perception of a higher effective price of care, it is likely to have excluded some patients whose lives the hospital could have saved.[2]

Characteristics of the Market for AIDS Treatment

The substantial resource flows necessary to expand the availability of ART in poor countries will shift the demand curve for health care services upward and to the right, as depicted in Figure 10.1. In each country the size of the epidemic, together with the amount of new funding available, will determine the extent of the shift in demand. The amount of funding also affects the elasticity of the demand curve, with more funding associated with less elasticity. When the demand curve is less elastic, any increase in the cost of care is translated directly into increases in both prices and expenditure, rather than into reductions in utilization. Thus the outcome of new ART funding will depend largely on the nature of the public and private supply responses.

The model of supply implicit in Figure 10.1 is a simple one, derived from models of perfectly competitive firms. In reality only a portion of the market for health care services is served by private, for-profit health care facilities. Figure 10.2 shows that, even in the poorest countries, where health expenditure is a small proportion of domestic product, at least one-fifth of all health expenditure occurs in the public sector. Another substantial proportion of health care services is delivered by nonprofit, nongovernmental organizations, many of which are faith-based.

Agency Problems in Health Care

Patients seek the care of trained health care providers partly because these providers have specialized knowledge, and partly because the provider gives them access to pharmaceutical products and medical proce-

---

[2]In a follow-up study of the same hospital, the authors found that HIV-negative admissions were back up. However, hospital utilization had surged to over 100 percent, implying that some patients were sleeping on the floor and in hallways. Thus the quality of care was lower, and the "effective price" of care was driven upward by the epidemic (Floyd and Gilks, 1996).

Figure 10.2. Relationship of Health Expenditure Share of GDP to Public Share of Health Expenditure by World Region and by Income
(Percent)

Public share of health expenditure, 2001

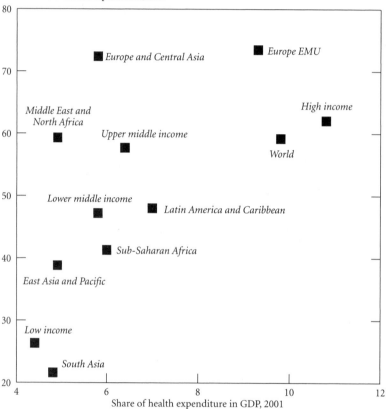

Source: World Bank (2004, Table 2.14).

dures that patients have difficulty obtaining directly. The provider serves as the agent of his or her patients, but is also, like all agents, subject to conflicting interests. Professional ethics and concern for his or her reputation both motivate the provider to be a "good" agent, making choices that the patient would make with the same information. However, the provider is also tempted to make choices against the best interests of patients. For example, the provider has an incentive to spend more on medical care of doubtful efficacy, when wasteful expenditures would benefit the provider and cannot easily be distinguished from useful expenditures by the patient.

Furthermore, the provider has some monopoly power, due not only to his or her specialized knowledge but also to the difficulty the patient would face in switching to another provider. The equilibrium between these conflicting interests can shift when the demand for health care is dramatically increased, for example by an AIDS epidemic. In situations of excess demand, the patient is less likely to be able to choose his or her provider, and the potential financial rewards to the provider from opportunistic behavior increase. Thus with excess demand the equilibrium is likely to shift toward more opportunistic provider behavior.

The situation is more complex when the provider is employed by the public sector or accountable to a third-party payer, such as a government or private health insurance fund. In these situations the provider is an agent not only of the patient, but also of the third party. With respect to the third-party payer, perfect agency on the part of the provider means maximizing efficiency and maximizing the equity of distribution of his or her output by income class. This is not always the same as maximizing quality or patient satisfaction, and thus is not completely in accord with perfect agency on behalf of the patient. The health care provider now must advise the patient in a way that balances the requirements of both these different principals against each other and against his or her own personal needs and constraints.

The government or other third-party financer of health care can observe the performance of the provider by periodically exercising supervision or in a variety of more subtle but more expensive ways. For example, the supervisor might employ actors to impersonate an individual seeking care and report the provider's behavior and treatment decisions. However, accurate quality control requires resources, which could have otherwise been spent on higher salaries for the providers, on more drugs or other medical supplies, or on public goods outside the health sector.

Furthermore, the salaries of civil servants, including health care providers, in poor countries are often extremely low, and lower than those of providers in the private sector. These low salaries combined with traditional job protection for civil servants limit the sanctions that the government can bring to bear on the provider. Indeed, evidence and experience show that, in many poor countries, the government cannot even identify and remove nonexistent employees from the payroll, much less those who do exist but only occasionally show up for work. For example, a study of civil service rolls in Honduras in 2000 found that 8.3 percent of the health workers and 5.0 percent of employees in public education receiving salaries were "ghost workers" who had either died, left the service, or never existed (Lindelöw, 2003).

Figure 10.3. Incidence of Public Health Care Expenditure by Income Quintile in Selected Countries
(Percent)

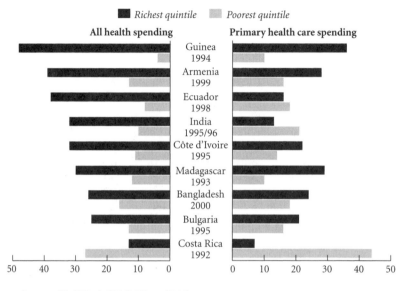

Sources: World Bank (2003); Filmer (2003).

Similarly, the patient can, in theory, learn that a given provider gives poor service or low-quality treatment and choose a different provider the next time. However, in rural areas of poor countries, alternative providers are scarce, and patients must often walk long distances to exercise this option. In that case, local providers, whether in the public or the private sector, have substantial market power and can exercise that power in their own interest, to the detriment of their patients. The result is often poor performance of the health system overall, as documented in the next section.

Poor Performance of Health Services in Poor Countries

How well do health care providers serve as agents to their two principals? Figure 10.3 casts light on whether public health care spending in poor countries is truly serving the poor—a presumed objective of the government. Note that, in most of the countries in the figure, the richest quintile benefits far more than the poorest from all health spending. Primary health care, which tends to be located in rural areas, is also biased toward the richest quintile, although less extremely so than overall health care

Figure 10.4. Unexplained Staff Absenteeism in Primary Schools and Primary Health Facilities in Selected Countries[1]
(Percent)

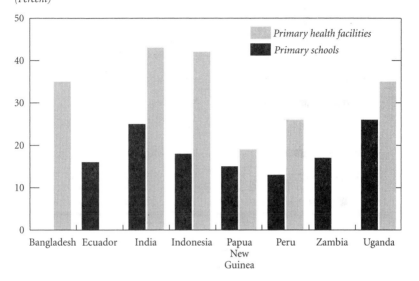

Source: World Bank (2003).
[1]Percent of all staff who were supposed to be present but were not on the day of an unannounced visit. It includes staff whose absence is excused for various reasons, such as training.

spending. As publicly financed AIDS treatment expenditure increases in poor countries, it would be surprising if this expenditure did not primarily benefit the richest AIDS patients.

Another basic indicator of the performance of health care workers is whether they show up for work. Data collected in eight countries for the World Bank's *World Development Report 2004* suggest that absenteeism is frequently a serious problem (World Bank, 2003). Figure 10.4 shows that the share of staff in peripheral health facilities with *unexplained* absences varied from 18 percent in Papua New Guinea to 43 percent in India. Variation within countries is also important. For example, in Bangladesh absenteeism among physicians is fully 75 percent, much higher than that among nonphysicians.

These data suggest that expanding ART or any other any medical program that depends on the dedicated hard work of rural public health care providers is likely to fall short of its potential unless the incentives that guide these workers' behavior are restructured. One ingredient of this restructuring will certainly be higher salaries for health care workers charged with these new responsibilities. However, a recent study from

Uganda, which compared the efficiency and quality of health care in the public sector with that in the faith-based private sector, found that, despite somewhat higher salaries, the public sector was less productive and was perceived by patients as producing lower-quality care (Reinikka and Svensson, 2003). Better performance is more likely to depend on improved supervision and a closer link between worker performance and a variety of rewards, including financial compensation and professional prestige.

Impact of Antiretroviral Medication on the Health Sector

Of the more than 40 million people worldwide believed to be infected with HIV, WHO estimates that approximately 5.9 million currently need ART to prolong their lives (WHO, 2003). Most of those in need who live in rich countries are receiving such care. But more than 3 million people living mainly in poorer countries do not currently have access to that care. Figure 10.5 shows that the gap between current coverage and need is concentrated in the poorest countries of Africa and Asia.

As mentioned previously, WHO has advanced the goal of providing ART to 3 million of the more than 5 million needing treatment by the year 2005—the 3 by 5 Initiative. The organization has focused on 34 high-priority countries (listed in Table 10.2) that, according to estimates, together have approximately that number of people currently in need of ART.

Basics of Combination Therapy for AIDS

Four classes of medications are used in ART: antiretroviral drugs, nucleoside reverse transcriptase inhibitors (NRTIs), nonnucleoside reverse transcriptase inhibitors (NNRTIs), and protease inhibitors (PIs). Each acts against HIV in a different way. The therapy recommended for patients entering ART for the first time consists of two NRTIs and one other compound, either an NNRTI or a PI. If a patient has problems with the first therapy received, he or she is moved to the second-line therapy, which is often more expensive.

Whether ART is successful in preventing HIV-related illness and prolonging the life of the patient depends most of all on how well the patient adheres to the prescribed times and doses of all of the medications. Typically the patient must take medications several times a day, at precise intervals. Some medications must be taken before eating, others after eating. The medical regime is simplified if the three drugs are packaged in the same pill,

Figure 10.5. Coverage of Adults in Need of Antiretroviral Therapy, November 2003
(Percent)

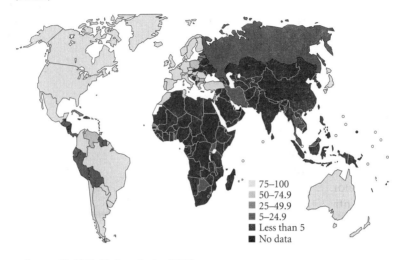

75–100
50–74.9
25–49.9
5–24.9
Less than 5
No data

Source: World Health Organization (2003).

but only a few triple-drug combinations are available in single-pill format. Imperfect adherence leads to the selection of a strain of HIV that is resistant to this drug combination. Adherence is thus important not only for the individual patient, but also to prevent the possibility that the patient will transmit a resistant strain to others, for whom the same drug combination would then not be helpful. Since, again, second- and third-line therapies tend to be more expensive, patients with resistant strains might not be able to find the right drug combination at a price they can afford.

A matter still under some dispute in the medical community is whether test results materially assist physicians attempting to manage patients on ART. So-called CD-4 tests are relatively inexpensive and track the status of the immune system. Viral load tests, which measure the quantity of virus in the bloodstream, are more expensive. The 3 by 5 program is based on the assumption that relatively few tests are needed, far fewer than have typically been funded in poor countries.

So far, the available evidence suggests that adherence to treatment regimens in developing countries has been relatively good. For example, in Uganda a pilot study reported adherence rates above 85 percent (Okero and others, 2003). However, since treatment has thus far been available only to a small fraction of the eligible populations in developing countries,

Table 10.2. High-Priority Countries for the WHO 3 by 5 Initiative

Angola	Ethiopia	Mozambique	Swaziland
Botswana	Ghana	Myanmar	Tanzania
Burkina Faso	Guinea	Namibia	Thailand
Burundi	Haiti	Nigeria	Uganda
Cameroon	India	Russian Federation	Ukraine
Central African Rep.	Indonesia	Rwanda	Vietnam
China	Kenya	South Africa	Zambia
Congo, Dem. Rep. of	Lesotho	Sudan	Zimbabwe
Côte d'Ivoire	Malawi		

Source: World Health Organization (2003).

it remains unknown how well the general population of HIV-infected people in these countries will be able to adhere.

Projected Burden if the 3 by 5 Goals Are Met

The attempt to scale up ART until 3 million patients have access will present serious challenges to most countries. WHO has projected the AIDS program expenditure for 2004/05 that would be necessary to meet the 3 by 5 goal in each of the 34 countries in Table 10.2. Figure 10.6 plots for each country this estimated expenditure against the country's population. The areas of the circles representing individual countries in the figure are proportional to their share of all AIDS patients in this group, and the straight line represents annual expenditure per capita (for the whole population, not just of AIDS patients) of $2. Countries above and to the left of the line are estimated to need to spend more than $2 per capita a year.

How does this projected expenditure compare with existing public health expenditure in the same countries? Figure 10.7 shows, for the 34 countries, the ratio of projected AIDS expenditure in 2005 to public health expenditure without AIDS in 2002. In 20 of the 34 countries, that ratio is one-third or less, so that the goal seems feasible on this measure. But in the other 14 countries, the ratio is greater than one-third, and in 3 countries it is greater than one. That is, projected total AIDS expenditure in these countries in 2005 will exceed total public health expenditure in 2002. These 14 countries, and especially the last 3, will have great difficulty absorbing the proposed AIDS expenditure.

Figure 10.8 plots the same variables in per capita terms, with each circle again proportional in size to the country's share of the 3 million AIDS patients in these countries as a group. It is somewhat reassuring to note that, of the four countries with the largest numbers of patients needing care, two lie below the line, indicating that the required increase in public

Figure 10.6. Distribution of 3 by 5 Initiative Target Countries by Projected AIDS Expenditure and Population[1]

Projected cost of AIDS in 2005 (millions of dollars)

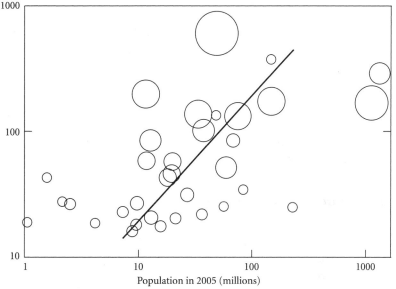

Population in 2005 (millions)

Source: Benjamin Johns, Stefano Bertozzi, and others on the WHO 3 by 5 Initiative team, personal communication with the author.

[1]Both axes scaled in logarithms. Each circle represents one country, with its area proportional to the country's share of all AIDS patients in the 34 countries (listed in Table 10.2).

expenditure will be less than one-third of current public health expenditures in these countries.

The above analyses assume that a country's ability to absorb additional AIDS expenditure depends on the magnitude of this additional expenditure relative to current public health expenditure. An alternative perspective is provided by comparing prospective expenditure with the number of physicians in the country. Several objections might be raised to this approach. First, not all physicians will be involved in AIDS care. Some will continue to specialize in other types of care, never treating an AIDS patient, whereas many general practitioners and internal medicine specialists will treat AIDS cases as an increasingly large proportion of their practices. Second, according to the guidelines developed by WHO for the 3 by 5 Initiative, certain types of paramedical personnel, including nurse practitioners and some nurses with special training, will be managing AIDS patients under the guidance of supervising physicians. Despite these draw-

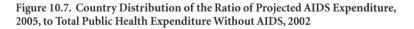

Figure 10.7. Country Distribution of the Ratio of Projected AIDS Expenditure, 2005, to Total Public Health Expenditure Without AIDS, 2002

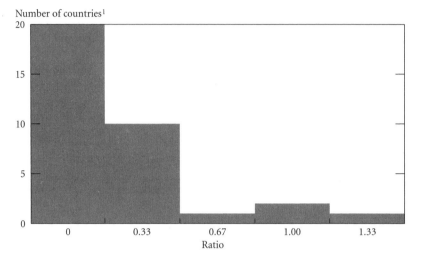

Number of countries[1]

Source: Benjamin Johns, Stefano Bertozzi, and others on the WHO 3 by 5 Initiative team, personal communication with the author.

[1]Countries are the 34 countries listed in Table 10.2.

backs, the perspective provided by this measure is potentially useful, because physicians will remain the primary decision makers in the allocation of existing and new publicly provided AIDS treatment resources.

The vertical axis in Figure 10.9 plots, for each of the 34 countries, the ratio of projected 2005 AIDS expenditure to the number of physicians in the country. The horizontal axis plots countries' GDP per capita. The circles again are proportional in size to the country's share of total AIDS patients in the 34 countries. (Both axes are scaled in logarithms for greater clarity.) The two lines divide the figure into four sections. The upward sloping line represents 10 times GDP per capita. Countries above this line will be attempting to allocate AIDS treatment resources per physician exceeding that amount. The second, vertical line separates the poorest countries (those with GDP per capita less than $500) from the less poor.

Figure 10.9 thus classifies the 34 countries into essentially three groups, summarized in Table 10.3. In the eight countries in the lower right quadrant of the figure, projected AIDS expenditure per physician in 2005 is less than 10 times GDP per capita, and GDP per capita is relatively large. These countries face a feasible challenge. The average country in this group will have to allocate about 1.8 times GDP per capita for each physi-

Figure 10.8. Distribution of 3 by 5 Initiative Target Countries by Cost of AIDS per Capita and Public Health Spending per Capita[1]

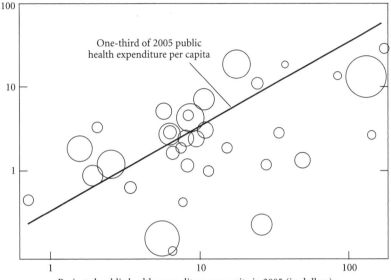

Projected cost of AIDS per capita in 2005 (in dollars)

One-third of 2005 public health expenditure per capita

Projected public health expenditure per capita in 2005 (in dollars)

Source: Benjamin Johns, Stefano Bertozzi, and others on the WHO 3 by 5 Initiative team, personal communication with the author.

[1]Both axes scaled in logarithms. Each circle represents one country, with its area proportional to the country's share of all AIDS patients in the 34 countries (listed in Table 10.2).

cian. These countries are more likely than the others in the figure to have both the economic resources and the medical resources (as proxied by the number of physicians) necessary to greatly expand ART access, should they receive the resources and direct their energy to the vigorous expansion of ART.

The 11 countries in the upper right portion of the figure face a substantial challenge. Although their economic resources are similar to those of the group of countries below them in the figure, they have more AIDS patients or fewer physicians, or both. For the average country in this group, the 3 by 5 Initiative will require that they channel new resources to AIDS care equivalent to about 113 times their 2005 GDP per capita, for each resident physician. In these countries, then, the effort to reach the 3 by 5 goal will put greater pressure on existing resources.

The remaining 14 countries in the upper left portion of Figure 10.9 (only one country lies in the lower left quadrant) face the greatest chal-

Figure 10.9. Distribution of 3 by 5 Initiative Target Countries by Cost of AIDS per Physician and GDP per Capita[1]

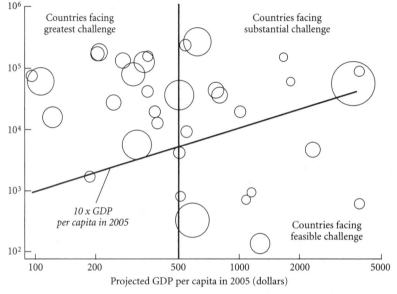

Source: Benjamin Johns, Stefano Bertozzi, and others on the WHO 3 by 5 Initiative team, personal communication with the author.

[1]Both axes scaled in logarithms. Each circle represents one country, with its area proportional to the country's share of all AIDS patients in the 34 countries (listed in Table 10.2).

lenge. Both their economic capacity and their medical capacity are small in relation to their number of AIDS cases. The average country in this group will be required to increase health spending by 368 times GDP per capita for each resident physician. In the most severely challenged country this ratio reaches 879. In all these 14 countries the attempt to spend millions of dollars on expanding ART must cope with systems that are not equipped to manage such large sums. Medical personnel are already stretching to meet current public health objectives and will have to divert time from these objectives to expand their treatment of AIDS cases. The temptations for medical personnel to divert AIDS treatment resources to other uses or to sell treatment access at black market prices will be extreme, and the resulting leakage from the system will reduce the efficiency of AIDS expenditure. As a result, in the 14 countries facing the greatest challenge, either the number of AIDS patients effectively treated will fall short of the objective, or the total expenditure required will be greater.

Table 10.3. Projected AIDS Spending in Countries Targeted by the WHO 3 by 5 Initiative

Projected Spending (as multiple of GDP per capita per physician)	Countries Facing:[1]		
	Feasible challenge	Substantial challenge	Greatest challenge
Average of countries in group	1.8	113	368
Highest country in group	8.7	441	879
Memorandum:			
Number of countries	8	11	14
Share of ART patients (percent)	21	41	38

Source: Author's calculations based on data from Gutierrez and others (2004).
[1]As identified in Figure 10.9.

Impact on Demand

The above assessment is perhaps too pessimistic in one respect: it does not take into account the reduction in the demand for treatment of opportunistic illnesses that occurs when AIDS patients are effectively treated with antiretroviral medications. In Brazil the demand for health care to treat three important types of opportunistic illness decreased during the period when that country expanded access to antiretroviral medication (Schechter, 2004). So, to the extent that the 34 high-priority countries discussed above are currently treating opportunistic illnesses in their AIDS patients, the effort to increase access to ART will be partly offset by decreased demand for treatment of these dangerous illnesses.

It is difficult to take much comfort from this possibility, however, for one reason: Brazil's level of development is much higher than that of any of the 14 countries identified in Figure 10.9 as facing the greatest challenge. Indeed, with a GDP per capita of approximately $3,000, Brazil's economic strength exceeds that of all but 2 of the 34 priority countries. Furthermore, Brazil has more physicians per capita than any other country on the list except Russia. Thus, in the classification in Figure 10.9, Brazil would have appeared in the lower right portion as one of the countries facing a feasible challenge. Lessons from Brazil may be difficult to apply to the countries facing the greatest challenge, which have on average one-sixth Brazil's GDP per capita, much higher HIV prevalence, and far less medical resources and infrastructure.

In developing countries, instead of seeing a reduction in the demand for opportunistic care, ART program managers may find themselves frustrated by insufficient uptake of the publicly financed ART care available. Reports from both Thailand and Botswana suggest that it may be difficult to recruit patients who are eligible for ART until their illness has advanced so far that they are difficult to help. In order to achieve their coverage goals, governments may find it necessary to provide incentives to patients in order to compensate them for the stigma of seeking care before they are sick, and for transportation and other costs associated with ART adherence. When such incentives are financial, they are referred to in other contexts as "conditional grants," because they are conditioned on the patient performing certain activities—in this case, seeking care and adhering to a medication regime. Such payments are not considered in the WHO estimates used above. The cost of such demand-side subsidies will inflate program costs and complicate management.

Impact on Supply

Increasing government expenditure on ART will have four effects on the supply of medical care. First, when ART is also made available to health care personnel who suffer needle-stick or other accidents that threaten to infect them with HIV, it increases their willingness to treat AIDS patients. Indeed, since health care personnel often do not know who is HIV-positive, the availability of prophylactic ART increases their willingness to supply all types of medical care.

The complexity of ART and the potential financial and professional rewards from the management of AIDS patients will increase the demand for training by medical personnel. In less poor countries some of this demand will be satisfied by the private sector. Governments may want to at least observe, if not regulate, the quality of such privately offered training in AIDS management. To the extent that countries have difficulty recruiting patients to ART regimes, they will need to reinforce and expand their voluntary counseling and testing programs and the communication campaigns that support them. Only if people trust in the confidentiality of such programs and can find a center located close to their home are they likely to seek information about their HIV status and seek care at the appropriate stage.

Physicians will benefit from greatly expanded expenditure on ART, regardless of the quality of care offered or the difficulty of accessing it. The substantial increase in the demand for their services caused by this influx of medical spending will raise both the wages and the prestige of physicians and, to some degree, of all medical personnel. Although this increase in their status is appropriate if they respond to the higher wages with increased effort and quality of care, governments may want to strengthen medical review boards and other professional systems designed to ensure that ethical considerations outweigh financial ones in the conduct of medical business.

Medium-Term Considerations

The international community has responded to WHO's appeal to treat 3 million AIDS patients by 2005. However, it has been little noticed that, in a global HIV-positive population of 40 million, 4 million or 5 million people become newly eligible for treatment each year. Thus, in the 34 priority countries, the achievement of the 3 by 5 goal will lead to a demand for "6 by 6," as 3 million additional people become eligible and in need of care before 2006. This will be followed by the need for "9 by 7," then "12 by 8," and so on.

The number of HIV-positive people receiving ART will grow rapidly, meaning that an ever-larger portion of some national populations will have to take medication every day in order to survive. The financial requirements will rise commensurately. It is not clear that the international community has given sufficient thought to this arithmetic, which cannot be avoided in the medium term. Prevention of new infections, which advocates of ART hope will be stimulated by the availability of ART, cannot affect the medium-term prospect, but it will be important over a period of 10 years or more in preventing the continued accumulation of AIDS cases needing treatment.

Another medium-term issue is equity across disease categories. In the poorest countries, neither competent expertise nor public subsidies is widely available for people needing care for cancer, end-stage renal disease, life-threatening trauma, or birth complications. Massive new public expenditure for ART will have several effects on patient access to care for these other serious medical conditions. First, since the wages of all physicians will be higher, the cost of care for these other diseases will increase even without new subsidies for AIDS care. Thus, on balance, patients with other diseases can be expected to have increasing difficulty finding affordable treatment. This tendency may be offset to some degree by the wider availability of trained personnel. However, in many poor countries the expansion of access to ART is likely to result in a hypertrophy of ART capacity without comparable development of the rest of the health care system.

Despite the complaints of patients with these underserved medical conditions, the strength of the HIV-positive lobby will grow more quickly. As the number of patients dependent on daily doses of ART increases, they will become an ever more potent interest group, influencing the formulation of health policy in all severely affected countries. A challenge to government will be to engage this group in preventing the further spread of HIV as well as in ensuring the quality and accessibility of treatment. To the extent that HIV-positive groups assist in reducing new infections, they will help ensure the affordability of continued treatment and thus serve their own long-term interests.

A Longer-Term Perspective: The AIDS Transition

The literature on the population problem in developing countries stresses the so-called demographic transition, from a growth path of high birth and death rates to one of low rates of both births and deaths. When death rates first fell in poor countries in the mid-twentieth century, there was no immediate prospect of a fall in birthrates. Instead observers were alarmed by a doubling or tripling of population growth rates. Applying the arithmetic of compound interest to these high growth rates led to use of terms like the "population explosion" and "the population bomb" (the title of a popular book in the late 1960s). In the latter half of the century, however, birthrates began to fall in one poor country after another. Sometimes they fell as a result of draconian government intervention, such as the "one child per family" policy in China or forced sterilization in India. Elsewhere countries achieved similar results through a combination of publicly financed family planning clinics, public information campaigns designed to persuade people to have fewer children, and economic development, which shifted the economic incentives of households toward having fewer but more educated children. In the early twenty-first century the story of the demographic transition from a high-birth, high-death regime to a low-birth, low-death regime is a subject of largely historical research.

Today we are arguably at the beginning of an "AIDS transition," for which aspects of the demographic transition may hold lessons. Figure 10.10 relabels the curves from the familiar depiction of the demographic transition with the analogous concepts from the AIDS transition. The role of births in the demographic transition is played by the flow of new HIV infections, and the role of overall population mortality, by AIDS mortality. As ART becomes accessible to an ever-larger proportion of those with advanced HIV-related disease, some countries are beginning to experience an increase in the growth rate of people living with HIV/AIDS, of whom an ever-larger percentage will be dependent on ART for survival.

If AIDS deaths decline while the incidence of HIV infection remains stable, there will necessarily be an "explosion" of ART patients analogous to the perceived population explosion of 40 years ago. AIDS-affected societies and the international community must hope for and should work to facilitate the transition to a new equilibrium. In this pattern the decrease in the death rate from AIDS is followed in as short a time as possible by a

Figure 10.10. The AIDS Transition

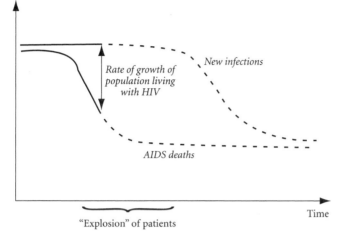

decrease in the rate of new infections, so that the growth rate of patients on ART is again reduced. Ideally the rate of AIDS deaths would fall almost to the mortality rate of the HIV-negative population, and the rate of new infections would fall even lower, so that over time the number of people dependent on ART declines. If most societies follow this path, a large cohort of patients on ART will pass through the population, but the health sector will be only temporarily (for perhaps 10 or 15 years) dominated by AIDS treatment concerns. Once both rates are again low, AIDS will become just one of many chronic illnesses, and the health sector will increasingly resemble what it would have been in the absence of the AIDS epidemic.

The AIDS transition pattern depicted in Figure 10.10 is one of victory over the AIDS epidemic, but the mechanisms for achieving that victory are not obvious. First, reducing the death rate from AIDS to a level approaching that of the rest of the population, and keeping it there, will require continued improvement in the pharmacological properties of ART, so that fewer patients fail first-line therapy and those who do can more often be helped with second- or third-line therapies. Getting the "birthrate" of new infections to fall, as the actual birthrate did in the case of the demographic transition, will require some combination of aggressive government prevention policy and autonomous individual decisions to reduce risky behavior. With respect to the former, early evidence suggests that marshalling the political will and the financial resources to offer ART to a nation's HIV-infected population will distract governments from HIV prevention programs rather than strengthen the political will to prevent new infections. For individuals the availability of ART will probably encourage voluntary counseling and testing, but it is not clear how such information will affect individual risk behavior or the consequent rate of new infections.

Figure 10.11 presents three alternative future patterns that are less optimistic than the AIDS transition pattern depicted in Figure 10.10. In all three (individually and in various combinations), the population undergoing treatment with ART will grow until, by the arithmetic of compound interest, it consumes an ever-growing portion of the total resources of the health sector and then of society as a whole.

The top panel of Figure 10.11 shows a pattern that would result if adherence rates are so low that the introduction of ART only temporarily lowers death rates, while HIV infection rates remain stable. Realization of this path would mean that the attempt to alter the course of the AIDS epidemic by expanding access to ART has not worked. There would be a "boom" in the HIV-positive population as a cohort of ART patients emerges whose lives are extended by ART, and as all HIV-infected people would experience longer life expectancy than before the ART expansion. But without a decrease in the infection rate, the gap between the growth rates of infection and AIDS mortality would be wider than before, so that the number of people dependent on ART would grow faster.

The middle panel of Figure 10.11 illustrates an ART "explosion" similar to the population explosion feared in the 1960s. The number of ART patients would grow rapidly, and compound interest would ensure that, within a decade or two, caring for people on ART would consume an impossibly high 100 percent of GDP. But the number of ART patients could grow even faster if the scenario depicted in the bottom panel of the figure should come to pass. Here the possibility of successful treatment for AIDS (as shown by the fact that the AIDS death rate falls and remains low) encourages a resumption of high-risk behavior, from which people might otherwise have abstained for fear of contracting AIDS.[3] Thus the rate of new HIV infections accelerates while that of AIDS mortality slows. The impossible outcome of 100 percent of GDP being spent for AIDS treatment arrives even sooner under this scenario.

---

[3]See Over and others (2004) for simulations, in the context of India, of the cost-effectiveness of ART with and without changes in risk behavior.

Figure 10.11. Possible Alternative Scenarios to a Successful AIDS Transition
(New infections or deaths per 1,000 population)

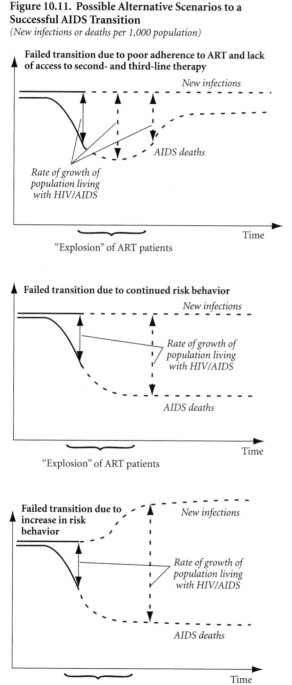

Failed transition due to poor adherence to ART and lack of access to second- and third-line therapy

New infections

AIDS deaths

Rate of growth of population living with HIV/AIDS

Time

"Explosion" of ART patients

Failed transition due to continued risk behavior

New infections

Rate of growth of population living with HIV/AIDS

AIDS deaths

Time

"Explosion" of ART patients

Failed transition due to increase in risk behavior

New infections

Rate of growth of population living with HIV/AIDS

AIDS deaths

Time

"Explosion" of ART patients

Beginning with Thomas Malthus, all who have predicted humanity's self-inflicted doom due to the arithmetic of compound interest have been proved wrong. Societies keep finding ways to avoid spending all their resources on any one sector, partly through market mechanisms (which drive up the cost of scarce resources, such as health professionals) and partly through extra-market social and political responses to scarcity (such as the apparent change in sexual mores that has reduced the rate of new HIV infections in Uganda). However, it would be irresponsible to take excessive comfort from the fact that the demographic transition has saved humankind from a modern version of the fate that Malthus predicted. To do so would be to discount, as misguided and wasted, the efforts of family planning programs and their supporters in the second half of the twentieth century. Instead governments, donors, and civil society need to work together to ensure that the second part of the demographic transition, the reduction in birthrates, finds its reflection in a reduction in new HIV infections, so that the AIDS transition does indeed resemble the previous one.

Conclusions and Policy Recommendations

The goal announced by the WHO to provide antiretroviral therapy to 3 million people by 2005 is extremely ambitious. Conservative projections of the cost of covering 3 million people in the 34 targeted countries suggest that only 8 of those countries, accounting for only 21 percent of the 3 million people, are in a situation similar to that of Brazil, with a small enough burden of AIDS patients relative to its income and its health system's capacity to put the objective of full coverage within reach. Another 11 countries, home to 41 percent of the 3 million, face a daunting challenge as they attempt to provide care for their HIV-positive populations, because they will have to expand health care spending per physician by more than 10 times their income per capita. This extra demand for health care resources will place great pressure on these countries' health care systems, driving up the price of all health care and increasing the incomes of all physicians, whether or not they deliver AIDS care. If these countries succeed, it will likely be because their economies have substantial resources, which the pressure of this new spending will bid away from alternative uses into health care generally, and into AIDS care in particular.

Facing the greatest challenge as they attempt to deliver ART are the 14 countries of the 34 that have both low incomes and weak health care systems, where 38 percent of the 3 million targeted AIDS patients envisaged under the WHO's 3 by 5 initiative are living. Their task is to channel into AIDS treatment resources per physician amounting to 20 to 500 times their income per capita, and their efforts are bound to encounter obstacles and bottlenecks. History suggests that attempts to direct such vast resources into new programs in poor countries will result in either failure to disburse or substantial leakage of resources into avenues not anticipated in the program design. Success will require a total transformation of these countries' health care systems, which international donors have already been working to transform since the 1960s. Given sufficient political commitment, however, such an unprecedented transformation may yet be possible.

Even if the 3 by 5 target is not reached, the effort to expand treatment to all 34 of these countries will in any event help large numbers of AIDS patients postpone for years the onset of opportunistic illnesses and death. This is a laudable outcome. But the opportunity cost to countries receiving these resource flows is likely to be largest in those countries where capacity is currently weakest. The health costs of diverting human resources from other parts of the health care system to AIDS care, the damage to health care institutions from the effort to prevent leakage to unintended uses (or from failure to prevent such leakage), and the fact that each person helped by the program will become dependent on the health care system for a lifetime supply of antiretrovirals—all these costs must be set against the expected health benefits. Vigorous national and international attention to the effects of these programs on the people and institutions of the recipient countries will be required to maximize these benefits and minimize the costs.

What policies can governments and donors adopt to maximize the benefits of new AIDS resource flows and minimize their cost? Although the specifics of those policies will differ in each country's program, lessons can be learned from applying the principles of improving public sector accountability detailed in *World Development Report 2004* (World Bank, 2003). As discussed earlier in this chapter, the report points out that health care providers in charge of administering an ART program are agents for two sets of principals: their patients, who are the consumers of their services, and their employers, who supervise, reward, and sanction the providers. The report argues that the effort and the quality of health care providers, like those of other public service providers, are affected not only by their professional training and ethics, but also by the quality of supervision they receive from both sets of principals, and by the strength of the incentives these principals can bring to bear.

The data presented in Figures 10.3 and 10.4 show that these providers are not currently performing even close to existing norms in many poor countries. The World Bank report argues that these deficiencies in performance are due as much to poor supervision and a lack of results-based incentives as to insufficient financing. However, success stories can be found. The increased flow of public resources that arrived at Ugandan village schools after villagers were told how much was supposed to arrive shows how powerful public disclosure can be in ensuring quality performance on the part of health care agents (Reinikka and Svensson, 2004). Contracting out health care services achieves substantial efficiency and quality improvements when the contract is properly defined and adequately funded. Over the medium run and beyond, governments can follow policies that will facilitate an AIDS transition, to a regime in which AIDS mortality begins to resemble the mortality rate of HIV-negative people and the rate of new infections drops even lower. However, alternatively, much less optimistic scenarios may also materialize and may even be likely in the absence of increased government attention to prevention programs.

The challenge in expanding access to antiretroviral treatments will be for governments and donors to monitor and evaluate the treatment programs well enough to detect signs of problems early, when they can still be corrected. Multiple experimental designs of systems to deliver ART should be allowed, to increase the chances of finding the best approach. Only through heavy investment in monitoring and evaluation will sponsors be able to track and identify failures as well as successes, and to learn how to avoid the former and ensure the latter.

References

Bernstein, C.A., J.G. Rabkin, and H. Wolland, 1990, "Medical and Dental Students' Attitudes About the AIDS Epidemic," *Academic Medicine,* Vol. 65, No. 7, pp. 458–60.

Bolduc, Denis, Bernard Fortin, and Marc-Andre Fournier, 1996, "The Impact of Incentive Policies on the Practice Location of Doctors: A Multinomial Probit Analysis," *Journal of Labor Economics,* Vol. 14 (October), pp. 703–32.

Buvé, S., and others, 1994, "Mortality Among Female Nurses in the Face of the AIDS Epidemic: A Pilot Study in Zambia," *AIDS,* Vol. 8, No. 3, p. 396.

Chawla, Mukesh, 1993, "Physician Moonlighting in Egypt" (Ph.D. dissertation; Boston, Massachusetts: Boston University, Department of Economics).

———, 1997, "Dual-Job Holdings by Public Sector Physicians in India," Department of Population and International Health Working Paper (Boston, Massachusetts: Harvard School of Public Health).

European Commission, 1995, *Safe Blood in Developing Countries: The Lessons from Uganda,* ed. by Rex Winsbury, Development Studies and Research Series (Luxembourg: Office for Official Publications of the European Communities).

Filmer, Deon, 2003, "The Incidence of Public Expenditures on Health and Development," background note for *World Development Report 2004* (Washington: World Bank).

Floyd, Katherine, and Charles F. Gilks, 1996, "Impact of, and Response to, the HIV Epidemic at Kenyatta National Hospital, Nairobi," Report 1, April (Liverpool, United Kingdom: Liverpool School of Tropical Medicine).

Gutierrez, Juan Pablo, and others, 2004, "Achieving the WHO/UNAIDS Antiretroviral Treatment 3 by 5 Goal: What Will It Cost?" *The Lancet*, Vol. 364, No. 9428, pp. 63–64.

Lindelöw, Magnus, 2003, "Public Expenditure Tracking and Service Delivery Surveys," paper presented at the 11th International Anti-Corruption Conference, May 25–28, Seoul.

———, Pieter Serneels, and Teigesti Lemma, 2003, "Synthesis of Focus Group Discussions with Health Workers In Ethiopia" (unpublished; Washington: Development Research Group, World Bank).

Mann, Jonathan, and others, 1986, "HIV Seroprevalence Among Hospital Workers in Kinshasa, Zaire: Lack of Association with Occupational Exposure," *Journal of the American Medical Association*, Vol. 256, No. 22, pp. 3099–3102.

Mazzullo, J., and others, 1990, "Influencing Choices of Medical Students to HIV-Related Careers," Abstract no. S.D.910, Sixth International AIDS Conference, San Francisco, June 20–24.

Okero, F. Amolo, and others, 2003, "Scaling up Antiretroviral Therapy: Experience in Uganda—Case Study" (Geneva: World Health Organization).

Over, Mead, and others, 1992, "The Consequences of Adult Ill-Health," in *The Health of Adults in the Developing World*, ed. by Richard A. Feachem and others (New York: Oxford University Press).

———, 2004, *HIV/AIDS Prevention and Treatment in India: Modeling the Costs and Consequences* (Washington: World Bank).

Reinikka, Ritva, and Jakob Svensson, 2003, "Working for God? Evaluating Service Delivery of Religious Not-for-Profit Health Care Providers in Uganda," Policy Research Working Paper No. 3058 (Washington: World Bank).

———, 2004, "The Power of Information: Evidence from a Newspaper Campaign to Reduce Capture," Policy Research Working Paper No. 3239 (Washington: World Bank).

Sauerborn, R., P. Berman, and A. Nougtara, 1996, "Age Bias, but No Gender Bias, in the Intra-Household Resource Allocation for Health Care in Rural Burkina Faso," *Health Transition Review*, Vol. 6, No. 2, pp. 131–45.

Schechter, Mauro, 2004, "Lessons Learned from the Scale-up of ARV Treatment in Brazil," presentation at a Workshop on Antiretroviral Drug Use in Resource-Constrained Settings, January 27–28 (Washington: Institute of Medicine).

World Bank, 1997, *Confronting AIDS: Public Priorities in a Global Epidemic.* (New York: Oxford University Press).

———, 1999, *Confronting AIDS: Public Priorities in a Global Epidemic,* (New York: Oxford University Press, rev. ed.).

———, 2003, *World Development Report 2004: Making Services Work for Poor People* (Washington: World Bank and Oxford University Press).

———, 2004, *World Development Indicators 2004* (Washington).

World Health Organization, 2003, "Treating 3 Million by 2005—Making It Happen: The WHO Strategy" (Geneva).